GOING GLOBAL

NEW OPPORTUNITIES FOR GROWING COMPANIES TO COMPETE IN WORLD MARKETS

GOING GLOBAL

NEW OPPORTUNITIES FOR GROWING
COMPANIES TO COMPETE IN WORLD
MARKETS

Lawrence W. Tuller

BUSINESS ONE IRWIN
Homewood, Illinois 60430

This publication is designed to provide accurate and
authoritative information in regard to the subject matter
covered. It is sold with the understanding that neither the
author nor the publisher is engaged in rendering legal, accounting,
or other professional service. If legal advice or other expert
assistance is required, the services of a competent
professional person should be sought.

*From a Declaration of Principles jointly adopted by a Committee
of the American Bar Association and a Committee of Publishers.*

Project editor: Paula M. Buschman
Production manager: Diane Palmer
Compositor: Precision Typographers
Typeface: 11/13 Century Schoolbook
Printer: Edwards Brothers

Library of Congress Cataloging-in-Publication Data

Tuller, Lawrence W.
    Going global : new opportunities for growing companies to compete
in world markets / by Lawrence W. Tuller.
        p.   cm.
    ISBN 1-55623-412-0
    1. Export marketing—United States—Management—Handbooks,
manuals, etc. 2. International business enterprises—United States-
-Management—Handbooks, manuals, etc. 3. Corporations, American-
-Handbooks, manuals, etc. I. Title.
HF1416.5.T85 1991
658′.049—dc20   90–46849

Printed in the United States of America
1 2 3 4 5 6 7 8 9 0 EB 8 7 6 5 4 3 2 1

To Susan,
serving her country and humanity in the South Pacific,
and
to Charles and Maggie,
sailing to the far reaches of the globe, who have learned by experience that we are
all one people inhabiting one world and that human differences are only skin deep.

PREFACE

This is not a book about the global adventures of resource-rich corporations. The purpose of this book is to provide workable tools for corporate managers, business owners, and professionals, whose companies or clients are not actively competitive in the global arena. I have written this book to meet three objectives: (1) to stimulate business leaders to seek expansion opportunities in global locations, (2) to provide comprehensive sourcing information and references for anyone to get started in global trade, and (3) to propose workable programs for companies of any size to take advantage of new marketing techniques and financing resources specifically designed for the development and penetration of worldwide markets.

Can growing companies survive and prosper in the global marketplace? The financial, marketing, resource, and management support columns are already in place for those who want to use them. This book shows you where to find them and how to use them. It opens the door to global trade for survival and prosperity in the 21st century.

All dominant factors influencing success in the global marketplace are clearly explained: global economics, applicable U.S. tax regulations, overviews of major worldwide market opportunities, country surveys, creative global financing programs, business structures, successful global marketing strategies, credit and collection tools, shipping and transport mechanics, cost saving importing techniques, guides to government and private technical, marketing and financial assistance, steps to acquire a foreign company, and methods for coping with dissimilar customs and language barriers. Detailed instructions and reference sources mark the trail through the jungle of unfamiliar global practices.

Following the recommendations set forth in this book won't assure every company of success. Global strategies and tactics only work for intelligent managements willing and able to adopt a global mentality. A company will be successful in the global arena only by reaching beyond traditional policies and practices to open the door to a new world.

Enormous populations with unfulfilled demand are ready to explode in South America, Central America, the Caribbean, Eastern Europe, the Soviet Union, South Africa, and the Pacific Basin. Japanese, Western European, Canadian, South Korean, and Taiwanese private enterprise stands poised to capture these lucrative markets. To remain competitive in the global game, American companies must reassess their role in global development. They must restructure products and policies to garner their fair share of these long-term growth markets.

Global trade is already upon us. It is here to stay. It will continue to be a predominant factor in the evolution of political and social institutions in the next century. The surest, most expedient, and probably the only way to sustain and materially increase a company's sales and profits is to join the parade of those who already understand this phenomenon. I hope that this book helps point the way.

Lawrence W. Tuller

ACKNOWLEDGMENTS

A vast number of people—friends, clients, and business associates—have knowingly and unknowingly contributed to this book and made its writing and publication possible. To single out individual contributors would be unfair to those omitted. Yet to ignore extraordinary contributions would be equally remiss.

Ernest Perreault, whose perception, insight, and breath of global knowledge taught a neophyte how small the world really is; Vernon Twombly, who had the foresight and confidence to entrust entrepreneurs with global responsibility; Frank Yanni, whose profundity in global trade and insightful understanding of worldwide cultures encouraged me to begin my global journey; Claude Bassine, who provided patient guidance and friendship in otherwise dismal foreign ports; Doreen Ashley, whose penchant to experience the sights and sounds of the world added inspiration and excitement to exploring global opportunities; and, of course, Michael Snell whose guidance and encouragement created this project in the first place.

L.W.T.

AUTHOR'S NOTE

The information contained in this book was compiled from a wide variety of sources. Opinions and interpretations differ on certain topics. Many of the tips and recommendations are based on the author's personal experiences in the global arena which may not be the same as others.

Global trade is dynamic. Sources of information, political and economic conditions in the nations and regions of the world, and the importance and priorities placed by the U.S. government on trade and support of differing countries change frequently and radically.

For all of these reasons, while every effort has been made to ensure accuracy and timeliness in the data presented herein, neither the author nor the publisher assumes responsibility for errors, omissions, or misinterpretations. Opinions identified as the author's are his alone and do not reflect the opinion or interpretation of the publisher or other organizations or persons associated with the writing or production of this book.

L.W.T.

INTRODUCTION

Speculating on the demise of smaller companies in the face of multinational, global competition, an increasing number of concerned clients and business associates have asked the crucial question: Is it possible to enter the global arena without international experience and a fat bank account?

I began asking myself the same type of question. Is it possible for growing but less endowed companies to actively participate in the boom of the 21st century or are they doomed to remain entrenched in the quagmires of bureaucratic red tape and a shrinking credit base? Is there room in this new trading sphere to compete effectively with the Mitsubishis, British Telecoms, Unilevers, SKFs, Siemens, Saint-Gobains, and General Electrics of the world or is global competition too complex for smaller companies? Will traditionally local and regional companies cast aside provincial thinking and pick up the gauntlet proffered by a new economic world, or will tightening credit and shrinking domestic markets force an ever increasing number to seek protection in the bankruptcy courts?

The Wall Street Journal, the *New York Times,* business magazines, and mainstream authors recount the global exploits of well-known multinational corporations. Noted foreign analysts and informed bureaucrats predict burgeoning investment by cash-rich corporations in China, Eastern Europe, and Southeast Asia. Media pundits tout the forward-thinking of giant construction, high-tech, food processing, and pharmaceutical corporations preparing to foist American products and services on a newly launched European Community.

Clearly, growing American companies have yet to make a mark. Only the adventuresome have dared to stand up to the global giants. Fewer than 1 percent of small and midsize companies (fewer than 500 employees or under $150 million sales) actively participate in global trade. Not surprisingly, many of those who became active players have since grown beyond this size.

Mention international trade as a viable opportunity and most business owners and managers think immediately of exporting, and perhaps importing. Suggesting that a company seriously consider taking the next step onto the global battlefield normally brings such comments as, "We already have enough business in this country." "It's hard enough competing with Mitsubishi and Toyota here, what chance would we stand in Japan?" "International is only for the big boys." "We don't have enough cash or manpower to enter that league." "We already export—that's enough." And on and on. Global trade appears too costly, difficult to manage, risky, or confusing.

Such fear of the unknown is a very natural reaction. Decades of protectionist federal policies, inappropriate public education, and unpublicized global maneuverings by giant, multinational corporations, have brainwashed a large percentage of the American public into believing that the United States remains self-sufficient. Nothing could be further from the truth.

Rapid escalation of market dominance by foreign producers proves the dependency of American consumers and industries on global trade. The continued shrinking of America's natural resource base forces us to rely on oil, timber, minerals, and agricultural products from other nations. Increasing financial irresponsibility and improprieties auction American assets to the highest foreign bidder. These factors all point to the radical transformation already under way from a self-sufficient nation to one relying on others more abundantly endowed.

Nonglobal businesses stand by helplessly watching their domestic market shares rapidly slip away to Japanese, British, West German, and Canadian competitors. Our only reaction to the increasing number of American companies being acquired by foreign investors is to plead with the federal government for ever more oppressive regulations and trade restraints. Australian, Chilean, South Korean, and now Soviet goods flood the U.S. market, taking a rapidly increasing share of Americans' disposable income.

Yet few companies retaliate by doing the same in these countries. We seem frozen in place, immobilized, apparently unable to accept the fact that global trade is already firmly entrenched as a way of life in America. The "we" versus "them" syndrome continues to paralyze business leaders from taking appropriate action to save their markets.

For years, exporting and importing have been the effortless way to explore international markets and foreign sources of materials. Other than a few farsighted visionaries, most business leaders, government officials, and self-proclaimed media experts equate exporting with international trade. Although certainly an important aspect of modern-day business, exporting and importing cannot, by themselves, make American businesses competitive on a global scale. They are only the beginning.

Japan, Great Britain, France, and the Netherlands, among others, learned long ago that to truly compete in world markets a company must go beyond exporting. If it wants to compete effectively, a company must establish its own manufacturing, distribution, and retailing facilities on foreign soil. It must source materials wherever they exist. It must utilize foreign labor to produce and sell its products. It must meet foreign competitors head-on in their home markets. And it must use global financial resources to fund these activities. In other words, to survive in the world economy, a company must view its resources and markets as global—not domestic on one hand and international on the other.

To compete worldwide, a global mentality, once prevalent in our forefathers, must return to American boardrooms and policy centers. Global interdependence of companies and countries has forced other industrialized nations to reexamine trade barriers, restrictions on foreign participation in their economic bases, and the strategic, long-term importance of global trade. Similar reexaminations must occur in the United States.

At the dawn of the 21st century, world leaders are beginning to accept the inevitable realignment of economic boundaries. They are beginning to reject nationalistic protectionism as unworkable. They are beginning to recognize economic stability and transnational interdependence as the cornerstones of social and political survival. No nation remains self-sufficient. In the next century we must all rely on the global community to survive and prosper. If our government leaders remain unable or unwilling to lead the way through intelligent federal trade policies, then the private sector must step forward and assume command. The call for interdependence cannot go unanswered.

Such analyses and arguments are not profound. Global thinking journalists, academicians, bureaucrats, media analysts, and a handful of industry leaders have recognized these phenomenon for some time. Library and bookstore shelves abound with volume after volume describing global change in the context of multinational corporations. Examples of how General Electric, Cummins Engine, Pepsi Cola, Ford, Sears, General Motors, and a handful of other well-known giants have met and conquered global challenges permeate books, magazines, TV documentaries, newspaper accounts, and even the movies. And not surprisingly. To date, the responsibility for sustaining American economic stability in the global arena has fallen to large corporations.

Perhaps I am also guilty of falling prey to the storybook appeal of giant power brokers. Accounts of multinational successes and failures are used throughout this book to illustrate what can and can't be done in the international sphere.

Can your company compete in the global arena? Without question! Can your company prosper and survive without going global? The odds are stacked against you. Will you take the necessary steps to equip your company with global skills? Only you can decide. Godspeed.

CONTENTS

SECTION V
LOOKING TO THE FUTURE

LIST OF FIGURES

SECTION I

DECIDING TO GO GLOBAL

CHAPTER 1

TIME TO GO GLOBAL

MAJOR TOPICS

KEY POINTS

1. **America Is Already a Global Economy**. The gap widens between the profitability and growth of those companies successfully engaging in global trade and those refusing to expand their horizons. The latter face increasing difficulties maintaining a domestic market share. Foreign competitors accustomed to trading in the global marketplace take a continually larger share of America's domestic markets. Smaller and midsize firms are learning that the price, quality, and service offered by foreign competitors often surpass their own capabilities. They find that domestic financing options shrink while global firms seem to have an abundance of cash. As the U.S. economy shows signs of slowing, burgeoning overseas markets offer the only viable salvation.

2. **Exporting as a Beginning**. Most nonglobal companies think first of exporting as a way to increase sales and profits. Certainly as a viable starting point, exporting has its own unique marketing, financing, shipping, and collecting procedures. Currency and political risk tend to frighten many off. A variety of options exists to assist the exporter in obtaining orders and arranging financing. Expert assistance can be obtained for handling shipping documentation. Credit insurance ensures getting paid. Insurance against currency fluctuations and political risk mitigates these problems.

3. Direct Foreign Investment. Though exporting is a start, to become globally competitive a company must expand through direct foreign investment. Determining where to invest, how to finance the project, where to obtain investment and technical assistance, and how to manage peculiar tax, legal, and administrative matters can all be achieved with relative ease.

4. International Banking. The broad scope of international banking offers the American global company a wide choice of financial assistance. Financing arrangements unheard of domestically are readily available for foreign investment.

5. Cultural Dissimilarities. Cultural barriers also tend to dissuade entrance to global markets. Strange languages, unfamiliar business practices, and the vagaries of international travel present a frightening panorama of difficulties to the beginning global trader. But once again, answers are readily available. Cultural disparities should never be an excuse for abrogating global opportunities.

Jack Roresaw had been a client for several years. We had just completed another acquisition of a small chemical filter manufacturer. Over the past four years, including this most recent addition, Jack had acquired a total of five small filter companies with a combined sales of more than $24 million. As we basked in the euphoria of another closing, I mentioned that Jack should begin investigating a foreign location for his next acquisition. "Don't be crazy, Larry. We're doing perfectly well right here in the States. Why take the risk of going overseas? I don't even have a passport!"

My response pointed out that several German and French companies were already encroaching on his domestic markets with plants in the United States. I commented that there was a burgeoning demand for both liquid and gaseous filtration systems in a number of Third World countries, especially parts of South and Central America. As a further inducement, I argued that without entering the global arena I doubted his companies would remain profitable over the long term.

"That's the dumbest advice I've ever heard," was his only response, and that ended the conversation. Now, four years later, Jack is steadily losing domestic market shares to foreign competitors. He still refuses to accept the concept of global markets.

America is already a participant in the global economy. To believe otherwise would be to close one's eyes to the food, clothing, shelters, and automobiles that we all use indiscriminately every day. An immense number of products used and consumed in our daily lives are imported from foreign countries. But the global influence is not only felt in the items we consume or use. Foreign ownership extends to American banks, stock exchanges, universities, farmland, commercial and industrial real estate, shipping lines, and utility companies. Over 50 percent of deposits in American banks are owned by foreigners. We are employed by foreign companies in virtually every industry.

Americans also support foreign countries. We export automobiles, soup, leather goods, wheat, watches, refrigerators, airplanes, pharmaceuticals, weapons, and oranges. Many of these exports contain products previously imported: meat from New Zealand in Campbell's soup. Components, assemblies, and structural parts from Japan for Boeing 757s and 767s. Steel from Germany, aluminum from Korea, and rubber from Brazil go into Fords and Chevrolets sold to Europe and Latin America.

American financial service industries are even more global. Americans make bank deposits in Hong Kong, the Netherlands, and Germany. Stock and bond issues of American companies can be placed on the London exchange. Insurance policies from Prudential, Aetna, and Equitable cover risks in India, Mexico, and Saudi Arabia.

Basic research to discover cures for AIDS, cancer, multiple sclerosis, and birth defects is being done on a global basis—not merely confined to American laboratories. Space, communications, oceanography, and computer technologies are also developed worldwide and shared among nations. Nothing that touches our lives can be claimed as purely American.

The nations of the world, including the United States, have already become truly interdependent one with the other. All facets of our business, financial, and personal lives are so intertwined with our neighbors that to believe for even one moment that Americans, or anyone else, can remain in isolation from the economics, politics, or social problems of everyone else is the epitome of naïveté.

Notwithstanding the obvious, the vast majority of American business leaders continue to deny the influence of the global economy. The predominant attitude of small, midsize, and many large retailers, manufacturers, distributors, and service companies is that America remains self-sufficient and independent of foreign influence. It's hard to believe that in the face of such obvious globalization as the acquisition of Allied and Federated Stores by the Canadian Campeau, most of the major publishers by foreign investors such as the Australian Murdoch, and major equity interests in such financial firms as Goldman Sachs and First Boston by Japanese and Swiss investors, that Americans continue to believe in protectionist and isolationist business policies. Yet they do.

The attitude of Jack Roresaw is not unique. Of the literally millions of small and midsize American businesses (under $150 million sales or 500 employees), less than 8 percent were involved in any type of international trade during 1988. Ninety-two percent of the largest business base in the world continues to ignore the global community. On the plus side, it does appear that the rate of global participation by these companies is increasing. In the first half of 1989, the percent participating rose dramatically to nearly 12 percent. That's a 50 percent increase! There seem to be four major reasons for this awakening:

1. Price and quality competition in American markets from imported products is becoming more severe.
2. Direct competition from foreign owned American companies is escalating.
3. The overextension of business debt forces companies to look offshore for additional growth funds.
4. Domestic markets for many goods and services are beginning to shrink as recessionary pressures deepen and military spending diminishes.

COMPETITION FROM IMPORTS

One of the hallmarks of the global economy is that goods, technology, and money know no national boundaries. Regardless of protectionist tariffs, trade barriers, quotas, voluntary trade agreements, and even radical currency swings, the market determines what and where products will be sold—not government or industry protectionist policies. The only exception comes about when imports of specific products are totally banned by political mandate or ideology in countries such as Albania, Cuba, or Iran. Yet, even in these highly controlled economies, protectionist walls are crumbling and American goods are beginning to find a way in.

The American government has tried hard to restrict imports of specific products at one time or another. Imports of steel, textiles, motorcycles, automobiles, polyethylene materials, certain pharmaceuticals, and many other products have been intentionally restricted in an effort to protect American producers. The argument from industrial and union leaders has been that low-cost foreign products will force the closing of plants and entire companies, thus leading thousands to the unemployment lines. Harley-Davidson, USX, the United Auto Workers, and many others have used this argument for years. In truth, however, even with severe import trade restrictions, protected companies and entire industries have inevitably continued to decline in profitability and the number of jobs. The steel and textile industries are perfect examples.

Even with the protection of stringent trade barriers, these companies continued down the path to extinction. Americans consume increasing amounts of foreign steel products, clothing, foodstuffs, motorcycles, and automobiles. Although the reasons vary, foreign firms exporting to the United States have learned to compete in a market-controlled environment.

In some cases, imports remain price competitive with domestic goods, even with added import duties. In others, the market willingly pays higher prices than competing domestic products, recognizing the higher quality of goods. In still others, design, fashion, and product utility lead American consumers to foreign imports in preference to domestic products.

"The Germans and the Swedes have always made better cars. That's why I keep buying BMWs or Volvos. They just work better and last longer." "I'll take a Panasonic stereo any day over an RCA. The Japanese have always led in state-of-the-art electronics." "Why should I buy dress shirts from Arrow when I can get the same or better product made in Taiwan or Korea for half the price?" "Chilean grapes just taste better than those from California." These comments can be heard on any street corner, office, or store in America.

The fact is, that regardless of government trade restrictions, imports of most goods are here to stay. They compete effectively with American products. In many cases they are better made, lower priced, or look better. To compete in the U.S. marketplace, American producers must learn the same cost-effective production, distribution, and marketing techniques of foreign competitors.

To this end small and midsize companies are beginning to look at their own production and marketing requirements with a global mentality. They are starting to look to low-cost offshore sources of raw materials. They are beginning to import their own subassemblies from low-labor cost countries. Markets are beginning to be defined not as domestic or export, European or Pacific Basin, Middle East or Latin American, but global.

FOREIGN OWNED AMERICAN BUSINESSES

Achieving enormous success exporting to the American market, the next logical step for foreign producers has been to establish production and distribution centers on American soil. A strong growing market, combined with political and currency stability, have led increasing numbers of British, German, French, Dutch, and, recently, Japanese companies to buy into America. Some have built their own facility—such as several automobile manufacturers. Others have conserved time and trouble and merely gobbled up existing American companies—such as those in the building products and publishing industries. Still others have taken the easy road and formed partnerships and joint ventures with American firms—such as in the pharmaceuticals and financial services industries.

The methods are unimportant. What is important is that investment by foreign companies in American businesses totaled over $380 billion through mid-1989, exceeding for the first time, American investments abroad. Small consolation can be gained by the announcement of Japan's leading financial newspaper, *Nihon Keizai Shimbun* in mid-1990, that a survey of 218 large Japanese firms indicated that direct investment in North America, excluding mergers and acquisitions, was $3.48 billion in the year ending March 31. This was down $4.29 billion from the previous year. New Japanese investment may be declining slightly, but it is becoming more diversified. Japanese investors are branching out into technology transfer and forming joint ventures with North American partners.

Foreign owned or controlled American companies have intensified the competitive domestic marketplace even more. By transporting their business acumen to American soil, these global firms no longer depend on exports to tap the American market. This infusion of expertise opens the door to even more intense price and quality competition.

Many small and midsize businesses are seeing American markets shrink. Foreign firms that look at their markets not as U.S. or non-U.S. but as truly global, are forcing others to do the same. A few smaller U.S. companies have picked up the gauntlet. A few have recognized that they must approach market demand and resources in every corner of the world in order to produce and market at the lowest cost. More U.S. firms are learning from their foreign brothers how to build quality into a product, how to raise capital for expansion, and how to treat customers as a valuable commodity.

THE BUSINESS DEBT CRISIS

Foreign competition from imports and direct entrance into domestic markets are not the only forces shaping the strategic planning of American companies. The financial markets also play a role. Overextension of short- and long-term credit resulting from an overactive attempt to access new domestic markets has left many small and midsize producers debt poor and strapped for cash. Debt service from highly leveraged business acquisitions drains funds otherwise available for research and development projects or improved distribution systems.

The concentration by commercial and investment banks and major venture capital funds on large corporate markets has stripped smaller firms of their primary sources of growth capital. Protectionist government and tax regulations, archaic accounting practices, and restrictive banking mentality further limit financial markets for small and midsize firms. The concentration of Wall Street on megabuck deals coupled with unrealistic high yields demanded by investors in new public issues exacerbates a growing shortage of expansion financing.

The smaller growth company that recognizes the need to meet foreign and domestic competition by entering global markets often finds that the closing of domestic capital markets precludes serious entry. The only solution is to tap overseas banking and financial sources. International merchant banks are normally the first stop. By utilizing the global expertise and financial savvy of international merchant banks, and financial markets in Tokyo, London, and Frankfort, American businesses frequently develop the global mentality through financing necessity rather than overt market decisions.

DOMESTIC ECONOMIC PRESSURES

Many industries are already experiencing severe recessionary pressures. Euphoric prognostications from government and financial leaders of ever-increasing economic prosperity are beginning to fall on deaf ears. Layoffs from IBM, Boeing, General Electric, and the automobile companies appear serious but actually account for small percentages of the total work forces of these industrial giants. When small and midsize producers are forced to contract, however, survival ramifications are more serious—especially for those businesses with overextended debt obligations. Market contraction for these companies frequently results in bankruptcy or even liquidation.

One way for these smaller companies to counteract domestic economic swings is to develop strategic plans for entering global markets— and many have done so. Aluminum furniture can be sold internationally as well as domestically. Bearings, screw machine products, and valves are needed in foreign markets as well as in Chicago, Cleveland, or Los Angeles. Foreign consumers use mustard, soup, and cereals as frequently as their American counterparts. Market demand for aspirin, antacids, and alcohol is as intense in foreign markets as in the United

States. Meeting global demand for a company's products when domestic markets shrink offers American producers a way to broaden their customer base and at least partially counteract domestic demand fluctuations.

Recent changes in the ideological domination of communism in Eastern Europe, and even more recently within the Soviet Union itself, have opened the door to enormous opportunities for American companies. With their economies in ruins, Poland, Czechoslovakia, East Germany, Bulgaria, Rumania, and the rest of the Eastern European nations have asked for, and desperately need, economic assistance from Western countries. The privatization of agricultural, consumer products, and capital goods industries within the Soviet Union and the concomitant failure of previous economic policies has left the country economically distressed.

As communist countries convert from state-controlled economies to market economies the demand for goods and services will far outstrip their internal production capabilities. Significant demand for consumer products has already begun. The next stage will be an overwhelming need for capital goods and infrastructure development. To support the importation of goods and technology, capital markets will begin to flourish. Western Europe is poised to enter a new era of economic competitiveness with the implementation of the European Community (EC) in 1992. American companies that have already begun their globalization will have first crack at these enormous new markets.

With the debt-poor domestic economy entering a period of higher unemployment and market contraction, the opening of these new global markets can easily take up the slack for those companies ready to act. It can easily be argued that the next great boom in consumer products, capital goods, technology transfer, and financial services will be in Eastern Europe and the Soviet Union. Developing a global mentality to manage this opportunity should be a top priority in American private enterprise, regardless of a company's size or industry.

Recognizing the opportunities in international trade and knowing how to grasp them are two different matters, however. Although many large corporations, so-called multinational firms, have had both the time and the financial resources to learn the vagaries of international trade by trial and error, most small and midsize companies can't afford such a luxury. If a company is losing domestic market share to foreign competition, financial ineptitude, or slipping demand for its products, something must be done. An executive might recognize the global marketplace as a path to survival but not be willing or able to commit substantial company resources to take advantage of the potential.

For those companies inexperienced in international trade but wishing to try it out, exporting is often the easiest, fastest, and least expensive way to go. Government assistance for developing an export program is prolific. Most industry trade associations offer information and assistance in locating markets. Financing schemes supported by Eximbank, private funding agencies, and commercial banks dot the landscape. Export management companies can handle the mechanics of moving products from the producer to the customer. Insurance plans exist to ensure collection of receivables. Overall, exporting is probably the best supported, easiest, and most lucrative way for the small or midsize company to increase its customer base and consequently its sales.

Many excellent articles and books offering instructive advice about every aspect of exporting fill trade journals and bookstores. Export support from the federal government waxes hot and cold. Contrary to popular myth, federal institutions such as Eximbank, Department of Commerce agencies, the Commodity Credit Corporation, and other federal organizations have previously concentrated mainly on assisting the multinational corporations. Recently, however, the pendulum has begun to swing slightly toward smaller firms. Nevertheless, much of the free money and government support remains dedicated to large corporations.

Though exporting has always been a viable way to increase sales, it does not, by itself, offer the small and midsize company much of an entrance to the global market. To take advantage of global opportunities a company must go beyond exporting. It must become intimately involved in sourcing materials and supplies overseas and then importing them back to the United States. A company must maximize its distribution channels by utilizing foreign warehousing centers. It must compete in the global marketplace by establishing manufacturing facilities, service centers, and sales offices in other countries. Competent technical and management personnel must be recruited from the global reservoir. A company must source the least expensive, longest term capital in the world market and learn to use the vagaries of currency fluctuations to its advantage. It must be quick to seize opportunities to expand through joint ventures and partnerships with other American companies or with foreign nationals.

In other words, small and midsize American producers can no longer define their source of supply, the availability of qualified workers and management personnel, their customer base, or sources of capital as domestic or international. They must look at business opportunities through global glasses. They must recognize that only by regarding the world as their marketplace can they survive in rapidly changing markets.

Such transnational practices require a change in the mind-set of American entrepreneurs, business owners, and managers. Being a truly global company mandates a mental attitude foreign to that normally exhibited in American business. Market strategy and financial plans must be rethought. Management training, production methods, and financing options must all reflect the global mentality. Definitions of customer base, labor pool, technical resources, and money management must be geared to the world as a fount of resources and a market for products.

This global mentality does not come easily. Raised in the American tradition of independence and freedom of action it is difficult to readjust one's thinking to the interdependence of a global economy. Being accustomed to market-controlled transactions and an elected political system makes government-controlled pricing and product selection difficult to comprehend. Oligarchic or social welfare political systems are equally mysterious. Yet, to survive in the 21st century, it is becoming increasingly clear that American executives must learn to cope with these facets of global business.

A global mentality requires changes in thinking about four areas:

- Management ability and training.
- Market strategy.
- Financing options.
- Strategic planning.

Owners and managers of small and midsize companies tend to be rather parochial in their approach to management proficiency. At the general management level emphasis is normally placed on a person's ability to get subordinates to operate as efficiently as possible in achieving the company's stated mission or goals. These goals are normally framed in a projection of increased earnings and returns for the next month, quarter, or year. Lip service, but little practical emphasis, is placed on the long-term growth, or even survival, of the company. With high-debt service to meet, the fear of being fired by the board of directors, or dealing with stockholder unrest, it is not surprising that CEOs take the short-term approach to management.

Nor is it surprising that many owners and managers think only in terms of the immediate market demand, local market share, or opportunities for servicing an existing customer base. Short-range thinking promotes short-range actions. Crisis management has become a byword in the annals of American business of any size or industry. Sociological, political, and financial pressures make it nearly impossible to structure a company for the long haul when today's needs must be met today. Company executives continue to manage by the philosophy that if they don't solve today's problems today, they won't be around to worry about tomorrow.

To compete in the world market this attitude must change. Those companies that have proven successful in the international sphere have managed for the long haul, not the short term. When Bechtel recruits management personnel for an overseas construction job lasting 2, 3, or 4 years, and with continuing operating responsibility for 10 years or more, they look for people who can manage the project for the duration. They search for people adept at dealing with diverse cultures and languages. They look for a work force dedicated to maximizing operating efficiencies over the long term, not just for next month or next year.

When Boeing begins the design effort for a new generation of commercial aircraft, the amortization of the R&D expenses will be against production planes sold in the world market 10, 15, 20 years into the future. Their strategic planning recognizes this long-term effort.

Strategic planning for the global markets must include the potential for long-term market growth in regions such as Latin America, China, or Southeast Asia. To be successful in the global economy, a company must evolve a strategic plan to maximize global opportunities through tapping foreign markets with products manufactured in overseas locations as well as exported from the United States. It must structure both domestic and foreign operations to bring in materials, manpower, and other resources from the least cost, highest quality suppliers, regardless of their location.

American executives must be as cognizant of specialized importing plans as they are of defined export programs. Market strategy must recognize competitive forces from global companies as well as local or regional businesses. The impact of government-owned businesses competing with private industry must be analyzed. Long-term demographic changes and political restructuring must be prophesized.

Unfamiliar financing options also predominate in the international sphere. Owners and managers must begin thinking in terms of financing structures designed for specific opportunities. Short-term commercial bank loans secured by receivables and inventory may be common for a business selling razors in the Midwest, but it won't do much good for an export program to customers in Kenya. Borrowing from an asset-based lender to purchase equipment for a plant starting up in Toledo might be an option to consider. It certainly is not an option for building a plant in Malaysia. Making a highly leveraged buyout with the help of an investment banker may be reasonable for an acquisition in California. It will never fly, however, when buying a going business in France.

A global mentality for financial managers must include weighing the pros and cons of various countertrade measures, Eurobond issues, and indirect assistance from the Agency for International Development. Financial managers of the future must become conversant with the techniques for managing different types of letters of credit, obtaining merchant bank assistance, and participation with International Development Banks.

Trying to enter global markets without the expertise of someone experienced in international trade is a common error made by American executives. To place a manager without international experience in charge of a foreign plant, distribution center, or sales office nearly always results in failure. To try to arrange financing, market products, or negotiate contracts with foreign customers without assistance from internationally experienced management personnel will always lead to disaster.

A management global mentality dictates acquiring expertise in managing international business either by employing people with this experience, or by contracting with expert professionals. No matter how much an owner or manager wishes to enter the global game, without concrete experience it is almost impossible.

Even with expert assistance and a global mentality, questions arise when beginning the international experience that must be dealt with right in the beginning. Some of those most commonly asked are:

1. How can I compete with foreign local suppliers when I have to add overseas shipping and customs costs to my prices?
2. How can I identify where the overseas markets are for my specific products?
3. How do I sell to customers who speak a different language?
4. How do I know that a foreign government won't expropriate my products or facilities?
5. What about exchange rates? They keep fluctuating widely. How can I avoid losing money on currency differentials?

6. Many markets are controlled by foreign governments. How do I sell to a customer like that?
7. How do I know foreign customers are creditworthy?
8. How do I know I'll get paid?
9. What recourse do I have if a foreign customer doesn't pay?
10. Shipping overseas is complicated. Where do I find out about shipping containers and documentation?
11. Aren't customs fees pretty high?
12. What if the ship sinks before it arrives at its destination?
13. I understand that in many cases the seller in an overseas market has to finance the buyer. We're not a wealthy company, how can we finance customers?
14. How do I sell to a foreign government or foreign customer who doesn't have the money to pay for my products?
15. What if he pays in his own currency which I can't convert to dollars?
16. How do I move money back and forth between countries?
17. How can I communicate with my overseas locations?
18. International travel is difficult and costly. How do I supervise my people stationed in a foreign country?
19. What about taxes? Am I taxed twice—once in the foreign country and again by the IRS?
20. If I deposit collections in a foreign bank, how do I get the money back to the United States?
21. Where do I find a lawyer that knows the foreign country's laws?
22. What about the method of doing business in a specific country? Most are not free market economies. How do I learn the local customs?
23. Where do I find personnel overseas to sell my products or manage my facility?
24. How do I train them?
25. What fringe benefits do I have to provide by law?
26. How do I get an audit done overseas?
27. What about passports, travel visas, and work permits? Where and how do I get them?
28. If I want to sell to Saudi Arabia, for instance, where do I locate other American companies doing business there?
29. What U.S. government agencies can I go to for assistance?
30. I hate to get involved in government bureaucracy. Are there any private organizations where I can get assistance?
31. How do I become familiar with a specific country's laws, tax statutes, labor codes, and other rules of doing business?

Answers to these questions and concerns fall under four broad headings:

- Learning procedures for selling to customers in developed or developing countries.
- Dealing with the international banking system.
- Coping with regulatory tax, legal, and accounting matters.
- Raising capital for international trade.

SELLING INTO FOREIGN MARKETS

Establishing a global presence is impossible unless the rules of marketing are understood. However, these rules vary country by country. What works in Europe, won't work in the Middle East. Marketing protocol in Southeast Asia won't apply in Brazil. Procedures for locating customers, checking credit, setting sell prices, negotiating contracts, assisting the customer in arranging financing, delivering the goods, and finally, collecting a receivable, must be based on the customs and laws of the host country.

There are five ways an American company can sell to overseas markets:

1. License technology.
2. Franchising.
3. Export products from U.S.-based facilities.
4. Sell from a facility located within the host country.
5. Export from a facility in a foreign country.

Technology Licensing

For some businesses and in some countries, the nature of the product, local restrictions governing foreign investments, or lack of management talent may preclude establishing either an export program or a physical presence overseas. Yet, penetration of the global market may open new opportunities or even become essential to a company's survival. Technology transfers through foreign licensing agreements can provide the key to unlock the door to future international trade. Technology licensing has been used extensively for years in developing markets, in Eastern European countries, and in the Soviet Union.

The major advantage of licensing over either exporting or foreign investment is that it provides an entry to global markets without requiring any financing. The biggest disadvantages are (1) the enforcement of audits and royalty payments, and (2) the risk of losing control over the technology, the production, and the marketing of proprietary products. For many smaller companies, however, the latter presents less of a problem as time goes on and even newer technologies are developed domestically to replace those licensed overseas. The ease of entry through technology licensing can frequently outweigh the risks entailed.

Franchising

A close cousin to licensing, franchising affords the American company the same opportunity to enter the global arena without incurring the headaches and cost of raising significant capital. Most of the larger companies who have franchised overseas for years—McDonalds, Kentucky Fried Chicken, Radio Shack, and so on—do, however, assist the franchisee finance his start-up, either through leasing arrangements or short-term working capital loans.

Global franchising brings with it severe headaches if the franchiser doesn't already have a sound franchise base in the United States. Beginning a franchise operation overseas without such experience is generally not a good idea, as Alweather Door and Window Corp. learned the hard way.

Alweather manufactured aluminum doors and windows. The company distributed these products in the upper Midwest through a series of home remodeling distribution centers. The CEO, Ralph Olsta, heard about the terrific opportunities opening up in several large residential developments underway in Norway and Sweden. Wishing to tap this apparently enormous new market, Olsta traveled to the Scandinavian countries to survey the circumstances for himself. While there he noticed several franchise operations sporting American names, although he never took the time to investigate how they were set up or if they were even profitable.

Returning to his plant in Tomah, Wisconsin, he announced that after careful study, he had decided to begin franchising Alweather distributorships in Norway—this year. Against advice from his management team, Olsta proceeded to negotiate franchise agreements with three Norwegian distributors in Bergen, Oslo, and Trondheim. He authorized the transfer of $300,000 to each distributor for start-up working capital loans and agreed to guarantee loans from local Norwegian banks for installation equipment and vehicles.

The franchising experiment lasted about two years, during which time all three distributorships folded. Alweather lost its initial investment of $900,000, and as guarantor, had to come up with another $315,000 to settle bank debts. That was the last time Olsta ever mentioned international trade or franchising to his management team.

On the other hand, if domestic franchising is already a way of life for a company, it shouldn't have any trouble overseas; assuming its products, distribution policies, franchise procedures, and contracts are all adapted to the specific market being served. Also, financing sources already established in the United States can probably be extrapolated to global financing arrangements.

Exporting from the United States

Exporting is the easiest and least expensive way for small and midsize companies to enter the global marketplace. It doesn't require much additional overhead expense, and the risks of exporting are relatively low. Peculiarities of foreign taxes, labor laws, and business licensing can normally be avoided. And the question of managing foreign employees never arises.

Exporting requires the management of six activities not common to domestic marketing. In most cases the exporter must:

1. Assist the buyer in financing the transaction.
2. Locate, communicate with, and in many cases, negotiate with customers having a different language, customs, and demands.
3. Manage ocean shipping and customs clearance for delivery of the products.
4. Collect receivables without the use of the court system as a last resort.

5. Deal with potential political upheaval and expropriation of funds or products.
6. Manage currency fluctuations and translations from soft to hard currency.

Arranging Buyer Financing

When exporting from the United States it is common practice to assist the buyer to arrange financing for the transaction. This requirement exists when exporting to either Third World or developed nations. It is not unusual for a buyer to expect an exporter to arrange the entire financing package, although in some cases partial assistance may be all that is required. A variety of financing sources can be called on. The Eximbank is generally the first stop. Private financing agencies, bank letters of credit, and other bank instruments can also be used. In addition, the federal government and several state governments have established agencies specifically designed to assist the small and midsize company arrange export financing. Many of these agencies can arrange trade credit for the foreign buyer as well as short-term working capital loans for the exporter.

Even more financing assistance can be expected in the future. With the anticipated explosion of market demand in Eastern Europe, the U.S. government, for political purposes, will probably increase both direct financing and financial guarantees to American companies willing to enter these markets. The opening of the EC, provides further impetus for both federal government and private sponsorship of financing packages for the American exporter. The availability of financing to support export marketing efforts already transcends similar assistance for domestic business, and one can only imagine the lucrative opportunities likely to exist in the years ahead.

Locating and Selling to Foreign Customers

Peculiarities in locating and closing orders with foreign customers continue to be major deterrents to establishing an export program. Domestically, identifying potential customers, negotiating sell prices, managing customer service activities, and delivering the product to a customer's location, are all relatively straightforward. Managing these activities in foreign lands, however, can become a nightmare.

Language and cultural differences exacerbate an already complex selling process. Strange shipping and customs requirements easily mystify the uninitiated exporter. Additional costs of maintaining a foreign sales force usually make this avenue unacceptable to most small or midsize exporters. How then can these difficulties be overcome to take advantage of new markets? Export Management Companies (EMCs) provide the means to make international trade feasible for many smaller American exporters.

Many of the larger and more reputable export management firms offer exporters a complete marketing service. They maintain a network of sales representatives in foreign countries to identify customers, negotiate sell prices, and supervise the receipt of the goods in the host country. EMCs charge a commission for these services similar to domestic sales reps. Some of these export firms specialize in certain regions—such as the Far East, Europe, or the Middle East. Others provide worldwide sales coverage.

Delivering the Product

A major problem for American exporters involves the transport of products from the United States to the customer's overseas destination. The paperwork involved in ocean shipping and customs clearance can be confusing to the uninitiated exporter. Ocean freight carries certain risks: the boat might sink, the products might be damaged, or piracy on the high seas might occur. Private marine insurance carriers provide insurance for these risks, although it is expensive.

Qualified EMCs can also handle all delivery matters for the exporter; such as customs clearances, containerization, shipping papers, and managing a freight forwarder. Although the use of an EMC involves additional selling expenses, it also relieves the exporter from any worries about complying with local laws and customs, language barriers, and unique negotiating techniques.

Employing export management firms is always less costly than staffing and managing an independent, international sales force. Fees for these specialists vary with the services performed, destination of the shipment, location of the exporter, and types of products or services marketed. By and large, however, the total cost of using an export management company is far less than if the exporter takes on these responsibilities himself. Also, in the export game, these costs can often be passed along in the selling price of the products with no effect on the exporter's profit.

Credit and Collections

Domestic credit checks and collection procedures are relatively straightforward. Dun & Bradstreet, and other credit agencies, can be used to verify the creditworthiness of a customer. Collection agencies can be employed to hassle the customer into paying. If he still refuses to pay, a supplier can always sue in a court of law. The international marketplace affords no such court of last resort, however. An exporter working through an export management company or a trading company might never meet his customer. If the customer is a foreign government, no threats of court action or foreclosure will hasten payment. These domestic collection tools just won't work. Other methods must be employed to collect from recalcitrant customers.

Foreign collection agencies exist in most regions of the world but, at best, seem to be inefficient, and difficult for an American exporter to deal with. There is no international court of law with jurisdiction over collection disputes, other than the International Arbitration Court. Using this approach can be very costly and complex. The answer lies with U.S. government-sponsored insurance issued by the Federal Credit Insurance Agency (FCIA). FCIA will insure the collectibility of any export sale for a relatively low premium. This government agency insures against commercial loss as well as foreign government expropriation. The use of letters of credit, banker's acceptances, and other bank instruments can also ensure payment. These instruments are backed by the customer's bank and confirmed valid by the exporter's bank.

Political Risk

Americans, by their nature, like to be in control of their own destiny. The mere thought of a foreign government expropriating an exporter's products before they get to market, or freezing bank accounts before payment can be made, are enough to turn away many small or midsize companies from exploring international trade. Certainly, without prudent but reasonable precautions, such possibilities do exist.

In the early 1980s, contractors and American machinery manufacturers exporting to Libya, learned one day that all American bank accounts were seized by the Libyan government. The Libyans then extracted additional tax and price concessions before releasing payment. Over the years, however, large corporations have learned to structure foreign deals to preclude this from being a normal occurrence. It can still happen, but by requiring the proper financing, shipping, and insurance arrangements, the frequency of foreign expropriation has diminished considerably. The FCIA also insures against political risk.

Bank letters of credit (LCs) placed on an American bank is another sure-fire method of avoiding expropriation. Shipping FOB port of embarkation ensures the exporter that title to his products will be transferred to the buyer at the time of shipping. If a foreign government seizes the goods, or the customer is otherwise unable to receive them, the exporter is off the hook.

Inconvertibility of Foreign Currency

Of the thousands of world currencies, only a handful are convertible to U.S. dollars in the open market. Hard currency, such as English pounds, German deutsche marks, Japanese yen, and French francs, can all be converted to dollars by any bank in the free world. But Russian rubles, Venezuelan bolivars, Saudi riyals, and Czechoslovakian korunas, along with most of the other world currencies, cannot. How then can an American exporter sell to these countries holding soft currency, when customers have no way of paying him in dollars? One answer is through the use of countertrade agreements.

As the name implies, countertrade promotes the sale of goods and services in exchange for other goods and services (other than currency). These exchanged goods or services can then be used by the initial seller himself, or they can be sold to a third party in exchange for hard currency. There is nothing mystical about countertrade procedures. They are merely another combination of marketing and financing techniques, used primarily by large corporations, to sell both goods and services in international markets.

Offset, barter, coproduction, and buy-back countertrade methods have been used for years in the aerospace and military equipment industries when selling to foreign governments of developing countries, as well as Western nations. Selling to a Third World government can often be easier, and safer, through a barter or offset arrangement, than by insisting on monetary payment.

Although complex to administer, and requiring a modicum of sophistication to negotiate, countertrade techniques are available to small and midsize companies, as well as the big boys. Countertrade can very often make the difference between closing an order and losing one.

AN ALTERNATIVE TO EXPORTING

Exporting only scratches the surface of global markets. To compete effectively in the global economy the American producer must supplement an export policy with head-to-head competition on foreign soil. This requires investing in an overseas facility for manufacturing, distribution, or marketing. Multinationals have done it for years. Foreign competitors have also been doing it in the United States for years. Now it's time for small and midsize companies to recognize this enormous opportunity to compete in the global marketplace without being disadvantaged by ocean shipping costs, time lapses in moving goods to market, reliance on noncompetitive U.S. business practices, and heavy domestic competition for overseas markets, all characteristic of the exporting model.

There are two ways to establish a foreign presence: buy, build, or lease real estate in a foreign country and start a business from scratch, or acquire a going business. Once established overseas the American company can now compete in local markets as well as export its locally made products to other foreign markets or back to the United States.

Before investing in a foreign country three steps should be undertaken to become familiar with doing business in that country:

1. Perform a survey of the economic, legal, and labor requirements of the host country.
2. Learn the specific marketing techniques peculiar to the host country.
3. Evaluate alternative means of financing the foreign operation.

The Country Survey

Once a preliminary determination of local economic factors has been made, additional information about the host country must be gathered. This is called a *country survey*. During the survey, as much detailed information as possible should be accumulated. The survey should pay particular attention to the host country's legal restrictions on foreign businesses, tax requirements, labor law peculiarities, licensing prerequisites, visa and work permit rules, business ownership restrictions, organization alternatives, and other trade regulations. Special attention should also be directed to unique or restrictive local banking regulations, especially as they relate to repatriation of a company's earnings to the United States.

Arrangements must be made with local legal and accounting professionals to represent the company in the host country. Banking affiliations must be established consistent with correspondent banking contacts in the United States. Discussions should be held with local labor representatives to assure a smooth opening, or transition. Contacts should be established with local trading companies, marketing representatives, and relevant government officials. A comprehensive country survey alleviates a great many logistical difficulties and guarantees that all relevant information has been gathered.

The best way for a business owner, or international manager, to ensure a comprehensive survey is to make one or more personal trips to the host country, and stay there long enough to get a good grasp of local business customs. Learning international norms should not be a delegated task. The step is too critical to entrust to a subordinate or an outsider. Whether striving to acquire a going business, or anticipating a business start-up, a thorough knowledge of business practices in the host country becomes essential.

Evaluating the Host Country's Marketing Customs

As part of the country survey, an evaluation should be performed to determine specifically, what marketing customs are practiced in the host country, and how these practices will influence the company's ability to do business there. Must a business maintain its own sales force, or can it use sales representatives? Can specific customer groups be targeted? How? Can an American head up the sales organization, or should a national lead the way? Are all prices negotiated, or can price sheets be used? How are customer complaints, quality failures, and product deliveries handled? These are the types of questions that must be answered before going further.

Financing an Overseas Presence

Establishing an overseas operation requires at least a rudimentary understanding of local and international financing options. Seldom, if ever, can an American company utilize funds from traditional U.S. banking sources to finance either the acquisition of a foreign business or the costs involved in a business start-up. Host country banking systems, investment peculiarities, and government subsidy options will probably be desirable at one time or another. Even for those cash-rich businesses, able and willing to finance their own foreign start-up and operation, ignoring free or low-cost money from local sources would be foolhardy.

Additionally, each country has its own legal requirements for the capitalization of companies. Some insist on minimum levels of equity. In other nations, partial ownership by the local government is mandated. In a few countries, majority ownership by a foreigner—such as an American company—is disallowed, and local partners must act as figureheads. Foreign bank financial assistance, U.S. government guarantees, joint ventures, public issues of securities on foreign exchanges, and other financing methods must be prudently considered before making the decision to invest in an overseas facility.

A careful analysis of what financial assistance the U.S. government might provide should be the starting point. For example, current federal financing programs, available to U.S. companies establishing operations under the Caribbean Basin Initiative Program, are extremely lucrative.

Other federally sponsored financial assistance is available in several African and Pacific Basin countries, in Southeast Asia, and more recently, in Poland and other Eastern European countries.

INTERNATIONAL BANKING SYSTEMS

Any American company doing business overseas eventually turns headlong into banking systems that are significantly different from the United States. For example, banks in England, Germany, Israel, Japan, France, and Italy have used off-balance-sheet financing for years as income-producing activities. American commercial banks, on the other hand, are restricted from this activity by federal and state banking regulations that specify minimum capital ratios, and by accounting principles requiring compliance with archaic reporting procedures.

Many times a foreign bank is the best source for financing a deal. At other times it is the only means of raising outside capital. Foreign banks can be used for the local deposits of collections, transferring funds worldwide, issuing letters of credit, and a myriad of other functions. Small and midsize companies generally find that foreign banks are easier to deal with, cheaper, and less inclined to hassle the customer, than their American counterparts.

Foreign banks are either clearing banks or merchant banks. The same bank might have two divisions, each performing separate activities. In other cases, clearing and merchant banks are distinctly separate entities. Clearing banks perform functions analogous to commercial banks in the United States.

Merchant banks are similar to, but not the same as, U.S. investment banks. The largest merchant banks are located in the United Kingdom and Japan. Their activities range from assisting in the financing of international trade, to acting as underwriters for securities issues and to investing in operating companies for their own account. They form the backbone of international finance. The first stop an executive should make when initiating an international trade program is at a merchant bank. Many have offices in the United States, and are easy to approach.

TAX AND ADMINISTRATIVE REQUIREMENTS

American and foreign tax regulations and foreign legal, accounting, and reporting requirements are necessary adjuncts to any international business activity. From the tax perspective, there are three concerns: (1) how to minimize U.S. taxes on foreign income, (2) how to avoid double taxation, and (3) how to minimize taxes on foreign acquisitions. American tax laws specify that a U.S. citizen or corporation must report all income received from anywhere in the world, regardless of where it was earned. Most countries have their own tax laws that require income taxes to be paid on income earned in their country, regardless of the nationality of the taxpayer. Combining the U.S. and foreign taxes can easily result in being taxed twice on the same income.

The U.S. government has enacted tax treaties or bilateral tax information exchange agreements (TIEAs) with most of its major trading partners to eliminate double taxation. Broadly speaking, those countries included in TIEAs agree to reciprocate with the IRS in exchanging pertinent income and expense information about companies doing business in their country. This clearly means that all transactions must be reported to both governments.

Normally, countries who have signed tax treaties, grant tax deductions, or tax credits, for income taxes paid to other governments. This avoids the double taxation of earned income but does nothing for the disparity on repatriated earnings. In addition, there are smaller countries, especially developing nations in Africa, Latin America, Southeast Asia, and the Middle East, that have not signed tax treaties with the United States. Without careful tax planning, income earned in these countries can easily be taxed twice.

For exporters, the Foreign Sales Corporation (FSC) rules allow an exemption of up to 15 percent of income earned through export sales. The provisions of the Internal Revenue Code are relatively clear, and many smaller exporters have found this a viable way to minimize taxes. Using an FSC does require establishing an office in a qualified, offshore country, however.

COPING WITH CULTURAL DISSIMILARITIES

The United Kingdom has always been a popular country for Americans to use as a foreign base for selling into Europe, Africa, and the Middle East. The British have easily recognizable similarities to our own culture and way of doing business, and of course, the same language. England won't suffice for Latin America and the Pacific Basin, however, and a company going global can't afford to ignore these two important growth regions. Therefore, more and more companies already engaged in international trade are coming to grips with language, cultural, and value differences, and learning to live with them.

Even though most Americans still follow their British cousins by refusing to learn a second language, an increasing number of business people are finding that, although not a prerequisite for doing business overseas, a beginner's knowledge of Spanish, French, German, Italian, or Japanese, certainly helps. Large corporations have learned that it is much easier to negotiate beneficial contracts overseas if their representatives have at least a smattering of the host country's language; which is why language schools such as Berlitz are so popular.

Gaining a familiarity with a host country's cultural idiosyncrasies also helps smooth over the rough spots when entering its markets. Little things, such as taking the time to learn how to greet people, how to dress for business meetings, how to negotiate, when to give gifts, and when to graciously receive favors, along with many other acceptable customs can smooth a company's entrance into foreign markets. The entire subject of payoffs, bribes, and kickbacks must be understood in the context of foreign business practices.

With passage of the Foreign Corrupt Practices Act in the 1970s, American businesses were put at a substantial disadvantage when competing with foreign companies. With such favors remaining common practice everywhere throughout the world, except in the United States, and especially in developing countries, American global companies must learn the techniques of dealing with this discrepancy in cultural values and laws, if they hope to remain competitive.

International travel is another subject unfamiliar to domestic business managers. Flying around the globe is as different from making the New York to Chicago run, as night is to day. Eight to 15 hours in the air, frequent hassles with immigration and customs officials, hotel and restaurant aberrations, unreliable ground transportation in the host country, passport and visa difficulties, and unfamiliar (and many times unsanitary) food and water, combine to make traveling overseas at best difficult, and at worst, a nightmare.

In addition, the cost of international travel is significantly more than domestic business trips. Hotel rooms in parts of Europe and Japan can easily reach double, or triple, the cost of similar accommodations in New York or San Francisco. Air fares from New York to Buenos Aires can frequently be two or three times domestic coast-to-coast fares. And those mysteriously unexplainable expenditures called *miscellaneous expenses* that every business traveler is familiar with, suddenly seem to quadruple when traveling overseas.

Probably the most difficult adjustment for an American to make when entering the world of global business is the realization that such tactics as hard-nosed negotiations, blunt remarks, discourteous actions, sloppy demeanor, and rapid business decisions, so common in the United States, just won't fly in international circles. Regardless of the peculiar habits and customs of the host country, an American doing business in a foreign land will be miles ahead by changing tactics.

Courtesy, understanding, and patience should become bywords. The global American should always remember that he is a guest of the host country and, as guest, is expected to display exemplary standards and performance. They represent America, not just their companies. Most foreign nationals are loyal to their own country, regardless of what they might say, and expect an American businessperson to be the same.

CONCLUSION

Any company expecting to survive in the intensely competitive environment of the 21st century must become global. The starting point is to cast off protectionist attitudes and develop a global mentality. Those small and midsize companies willing to learn the basics of international trade will be the ones that survive. Those who don't will undoubtedly falter. As in any other business activity, the company with the best product, most advanced management techniques, and willing to risk being first in the marketplace, always gains a competitive advantage. The same principle holds true in the global company.

If going global sounds complex, that's because it is. If becoming successful in the global marketplace seems to present a myriad of difficult problems, that's because it does. But if doing business in a world of unrestricted boundaries and unlimited potential seems opportunistic, going global definitely is that also. The balance of this book provides recommendations, information, guidelines and tips to assist any company of any size in any industry to open the door to global opportunities and conquer the demon of protectionist isolationism.

The next two chapters in Section I examine the complexities of international economics, the impact of U.S. tax laws on international trade, and cultural aberrations facing global American traders. Section II, "Getting Ready to Go Global," introduces criteria to be used in choosing the country or regional markets to enter, where to obtain assistance, and what steps to take to get started in global trade. Section III, "Financing Global Trade," reviews the available options for financing global trade. Section IV, "Marketing in the Global Economy," describes how to sell products or services overseas, peculiarities in ocean shipping and insurance, and methods for ensuring payment.

CHAPTER 2

A PRIMER ON
INTERNATIONAL ECONOMICS

MAJOR TOPICS

KEY POINTS

1. The Economics of Trade Policies. Protectionist trade restraints, either tariff or nontariff barriers, restrict imports from, and exports to, a given country. Strategic trade policies, such as Japan's decision to restrict importing, create further barriers to free market trade. The influence on international markets of OPEC's oil strategies, though waning now, will probably resurface in the future, as OPEC nations move downward in the oil industry. Each of these factors enters the risk/reward equation for companies entering the international trade arena.

2. Internal Economics. Policy decisions affecting the internal economics of a country, or region, can have decisive results for global traders. Major changes in European markets are expected with the implementation of EC trade regulations in 1992. There are too many unanswered questions at this time, however, for small and midsize companies to take definitive action, other than to get a foot in the door. Some indications of future changes do allow certain prognostications. Massive trading companies and a government-sponsored savings policy keep Japan's internal trade noncompetitive, and currently unattractive to the beginning investor. Multinational corporations will continue to exert major influences on world economics. Trade conflicts in developing nations afford the greatest opportunity for the investment of American production capabilities.

3. The Economics of the International Monetary System. The collapse of Bretton Woods created chaos and increased risk in the international currency exchange markets. Exchange risks must be evaluated, together with other macroeconomic factors, to judge how to manage future fluctuations. Global banking has become a major force in stabilizing the money markets, and in providing capital for foreign investments. The Latin-American debt crisis, while remaining unresolved, presents some unique opportunities to reap significant rewards with minimal risk. The International Monetary Fund provides a good measure of the risk of doing business in a specific country. The Eurodollar market offers some interesting possibilities to smaller companies for raising foreign capital thus reducing the risk of foreign investment.

All businesses face the universal commercial risks of managing the production and sale of goods and services and collecting customer receivables. Other than political expropriation, which will be dealt with in later chapters, the biggest risk a company faces in the international marketplace is a misunderstanding, or lack of understanding, of the influence of international economics on business transactions.

The economics of international trade fall into three categories: (1) government-imposed restrictions on foreign trade, (2) economic aberrations internal to the host country or region, and (3) influences from the international monetary system. By grasping the fundamentals of international economics, management should be armed with the basic tools necessary to assess the risk of engaging in global transactions. Favorable and unfavorable economic characteristics of a given market can then be evaluated in determining the benefits of entrance.

THE ECONOMICS OF TRADE POLICIES

Every government maintains trade policies perceived to be beneficial to that country. Policies of the United States, Western European countries, and Japan are complex, and replete with hundreds, if not thousands, of side agreements, formal and informal understandings, and shifting emphasis, as elected governments change. They all purport to support the notion of free trade between countries. Yet, all support a degree a protectionism, and have erected barriers to completely free trade.

Other countries, designated by some as the Third World, are developing, or emerging new nations. Their trade policies frequently reflect a dichotomy of purpose. On one hand, they fear being swallowed up by one of the world's trade giants. On the other, they encourage imports and foreign investment attempting to benefit from the industrialized Western cultures.

Communist bloc countries exhibit extremely restrictive trade policies encouraging trade between the bloc nations, but minimizing trade with free countries. Trade policies of these countries, however, are changing rapidly. For example, during the past several years, China has begun actively soliciting investments from Western private industry. At the same time, it has enforced stringent barriers to most imports and exports. The political steam of Eastern European countries is running low, and new, emerging trade policies, with less restrictive barriers, are bound to be forthcoming.

The trade policies of many Latin-American countries that are buried in debt and political turmoil remain unclear. They continue to be subject to rapid changes as the winds of fiscal and political expediency shift. The common element in all national trade policies, however, is that they have a major influence on the ability of foreign companies to transact profitable business within host country borders.

Protectionist Trade Restraints

What is meant by protectionist trade restraints? Although they take various forms and exhibit varying degrees of effectiveness, protectionist trade restraints are real, or artificial, barriers to free trade. They are consciously or unconsciously erected by government policy to protect the internal economic, social, or political systems of a country.

For over 40 years, the majority of world trade has been conducted under a set of rules between member nations known as the General Agreement on Tariffs and Trade, or GATT, for short. GATT was an attempt to promote free trade between countries by lowering trade barriers. Unfortunately for the believers in free trade, there are many loopholes within the GATT agreement. Few, if any, countries abide by it, even though most publicly proclaim strict adherence. The most widely publicized violator is Japan.

Since the end of World War II, Japan has become a major force in the global marketplace largely because it enforces highly restrictive protectionist trade restraints. During the 1950s and 1960s, the Japanese government subsidized its businesses with a variety of cleverly constructed benefits and financing arrangements. The emphasis was put on developing a sound manufacturing base, predominantly in consumer products, requiring very little R&D expenditure. Trading companies, which have been the mainstay of the Japanese economy for generations, provided the marketing, procurement, and financial support to manufacturing companies. Savings were encouraged to be funneled into productive investments.

Japanese bureaucrats, business leaders, and the population as a whole, realized quickly that to survive, this island country must develop a global export program to attract hard currency. Export became the name of the game in Japan. Hard currency went to build more factories, acquire more foreign raw materials, and develop additional exportable manufactured products.

At the same time, imports of consumer goods and other manufactured products, deemed unnecessary for the increase of Japan's manufacturing capability, were restrained. The Japanese government wanted its hard won export currency to be used for savings. Forced investment in bigger and better manufacturing facilities produced ever more export products.

Japan continues to prosper in the international marketplace because of severe protectionist trade policies prohibiting the importation of what the government defines as unnecessary products. Gradually, the wall is cracking, however, as foreign goods increasingly find their way to Japanese consumers. Though continuing to decline, a trade surplus built up over 40 years of protectionist policies will not soon disappear.

The United States has also employed protectionist trade policies almost indiscriminately throughout the past 40 years. From Japanese automobiles, to steel, to motorcycles, import restrictions have protected American companies from competing in the world market. Unfortunately, with the high cost and low productivity of American labor, the consumer has seen protectionist trade policies force prices beyond reasonable levels. Many Americans continue to be willing to pay the price for perceived higher quality foreign goods, however. All of the protectionist policies enacted by Washington over the years have not stemmed the tide of foreign imports, nor lessened the U.S. trade deficit.

The smart exporter, be it an American or a foreign company, realizes that when a country imposes restrictive import tariffs on specific goods, and the goods continue to be consumed, the only reasonable end result will be substantially increased profits to the exporter. This is precisely what happened to the Japanese automobile manufacturers. It is estimated that these Japanese producers received an extra $2.75 billion in income transfer from America during the 1981 to 1984 period, specifically attributed to U.S. tariff restrictions.

In the case of Japanese automobiles, and to a lesser extent for many electronic and capital equipment products, restrictive tariffs have not helped the American economy very much. This condition also exists for most industrialized countries, which, since the early 1970s, have experienced relatively slow rates of economic growth and a rise in surplus manufacturing capacity. Consequently, tariffs used as trade barriers to aid local businesses are increasingly being replaced by nontariff barriers. One of the most common forms of such a nontariff trade barrier is the Voluntary Export Restraint, commonly referred to as a VER.

VERs are now used to restrict trade in textiles, clothing, steel, automobiles, electronic products, agriculture, and machine tools, to mention but a few of the products affected. They represent a convenient loophole to GATT, since they are essentially informal agreements between two specific countries.

A VER is an agreement whereby the government, or an industry, in the importing country, arranges with the government or competing industry, in an exporting country, to restrict the volume (not the price) of the latter's export of one or more products. Since the agreement is voluntary on the part of the exporter, he has the right to rescind or modify it at any time. On the other hand, since it originates from the importing country, it is really voluntary only in the sense that the exporter might prefer it to more stringent barriers from the importing country.

Theoretically, VERs serve as restrictive trade measures to protect or improve a country's balance-of-payments condition, or to provide relief for industries adversely affected by foreign competition. As in any protectionist trade barrier, to the extent that it diminishes legitimate economic competition, the result is normally a higher price to consumers in the importing country. With worldwide elasticity of demand, such increased prices in one country can often drive prices up in another country. The exporter ends up winning even though volume is restricted.

When evaluating the desirability of exporting to a given country, wise managements clearly identify what VERs or other protectionist

trade barriers are currently in effect, and how competitive exporters ar
doing. Effects of VERs on both volume and margins measure the advisability of any specific global expansion.

Strategic Trade Policies

Strategic trade policies implemented by specific countries (e.g., Japan's
decision to close its doors to many imports) or by groups of countries, such
as the European subsidies for the design and manufacture of the Airbus,
exert a major influence on the desirability of doing business in one country versus another, regardless of protectionist barriers.

For generations, government economists have advocated the comparative advantages realized between countries engaged in free trade, as
being the justification cornerstone for continually striving to reduce
trade barriers. They have theorized that free markets should be allowed
to determine price, quality, and availability of products in the global
community.

Currently, however, as a result of the enormous economic gains of
countries such as Japan, and to a lesser extent Germany, both retaining
significant and far-reaching barriers to free trade, a strong case can be
made for government intervention in the free markets. Apparently such
policies yield greater national benefits to these nations than free trade.
The argument for this new approach holds that the strategic trade policy
of a government can tilt the terms of oliogopolistic competition by increasing the economic returns to domestic businesses at the expense of
foreign competitors. This seems to have been the prevalent feeling in
Washington for the past two decades.

With protectionist measures the federal government has attempted
to shift volume and profits from more efficiently competitive foreign automobile, steel, textile, and machine tool manufacturers, to U.S. companies. Such a strategy appears to work in the short term. Long-term
results, however, have not yet been counted. The continued loss of Detroit's market share and the massive contraction of the steel industry
probably indicate that free trade might have been the best policy after
all.

Obviously, the small or midsize business can't do much about changing either U.S. trade policies or those of other nations. This should not
deter the management of these companies from thoroughly investigating and understanding the current and potential future changes in strategic trade policies, however, both for domestic and for foreign investment potential.

No one knows what the future holds for such potentially opportunistic markets as Latin America, China, Eastern Europe, and South Africa.
Current events indicate developing markets for diverse products in all of
these regions. The strategic trade policies adopted by each of the governments will, to a large extent, determine their respective country's rate of
economic growth.

The exporter, or investor, who gets in on the ground floor in any of
these markets, will certainly reap benefits others miss. During the next
decade the risk/reward ratio might very well be as favorable in these re-

gions as anywhere in the world, assuming strategic trade policies are enacted to encourage foreign economic participation.

ıuence

Contrary to popular belief, it makes little business sense to base strategic economic decisions on the assumption that the Organization of Petroleum Exporting Countries (OPEC) has run out of steam. Even though the average price of crude oil on the world market has ranged between $10 and $20 per barrel since 1985, the industrialized world, and developing nations, will probably require increasing amounts of oil-based energy as populations and industries grow. This will inevitably drive future prices back up.

The long-term effect of recently spiraling prices attributed to the Iraqi muscle-flexing exercise remains unclear. A permanent standoff or a reversal of Saddam Hussein's position could result in prices steadily decreasing from an extortionable $30 to $40 per barrel to a free market level. On the other hand, a full-scale shooting war could drive prices through the roof. Regardless of such aberrations, OPEC continues to bear watching as the prime determinant of world oil supplies and, hence, prices.

In spite of extensive research and billions of dollars being spent worldwide to develop alternate sources of energy, the *World Energy Outlook through 2000* (Wilmington, Delaware: September 1986), put out by Conoco, estimates that oil's share of worldwide energy demand totaled 35 percent in 1985. This share will decrease a mere 3 percent by the year 2000. At best, there appears to be only a modest increase in nonoil fuel.

A second factor increasing OPEC's power over the ensuing 10 years will most likely be its ever increasing expansion into downstream oil industry operations. Refining, transporting, and eventually retailing, puts OPEC in the driver's seat for many years to come. What does the projected increase in OPEC power and control mean to the business manager contemplating the world market? A great deal.

In the first place, with the inevitable rise in the price of crude oil, further exploration of new, secondary, and tertiary wells will be enhanced. Any manufacturer, transporter, or service company, serving any segment of the oil industry, should find increased demand for its products. This demand will occur in the United States as well as in any country with proven or potential oil reserves.

Second, as oil prices escalate worldwide inflation will inevitably return. Those industries benefiting from a high-inflationary spiral can plan to take advantage of this cycle from the beginning. And third, oil-related products such as soap, plastic, and many chemicals, will also realize significant price increases. Establishing a firm foundation in global markets before this happens will permit a company to realize significant profit margins before competition again makes these materials superfluous in the world economy.

INTERNAL ECONOMICS

Trade policies have in the past and will probably continue to exert a dominant influence over international trade activities of American as well as foreign businesses. In addition to restrictive trade policies regulating imports and exports, internal policies have a profound effect on the economics of participating in foreign development.

European Community

One such internal economic policy already being felt around the world is the announced European Community trade agreements planned to be implemented in 1992. The precise impact such implementation will have on the economic integration with other industrialized nations remains open to debate. So far, there are more questions than answers. Once again, however, there can be little doubt, that however the details shake out, major reverberations will be felt throughout the global economy.

A few of the key, but unanswered, questions affecting U.S. businesses engaged in, or about to be engaged in, international trade are:

1. What impact will the EC have on current trade with the United States and Japan?
2. Will there be a common currency for use outside the EC?
3. If so, what will be the conversion rates with existing currency, and what mechanics will be available to make the conversion?
4. Will all trade barriers between member countries really be eliminated?
5. If so, how will this affect the monetary and fiscal policies of each country?
6. What product standardization will be necessary, such as pollution control devices for automobiles, and electric sockets?
7. Who will set these standards?
8. What is the portent for European, non-EC members, such as Switzerland, Sweden, and Austria?
9. Will there be an unfriendly protectionist movement against America?
10. How will current national customs and laws be integrated (e.g., patent laws, corporate structures, labeling laws, personnel training, and broadcast standards)?
11. What effect will a unified Germany have on the EC?
12. Will other countries be admitted to the EC at a later date?
13. What impact will escalating trade with Eastern European nations have on the EC?
14. Will there be reciprocal trade agreements reached with the current Eastern Bloc?
15. What happens to excise taxes on cigarettes, gasoline, and liquor currently imposed nationally?
16. How will variations in value-added taxes be integrated?
17. Will there be a common income tax code?
18. If so, how will it interfere with the current tax treaties with the United States?
19. When will there be a common measurement system?
20. Will it be metric, British, or other?

The number of unanswered questions whose resolution will have major economic impacts on international trade are staggering. So staggering, in fact, that many experts believe that it is impossible for the EC to begin transformation as early as 1992. Many forecast a decade of uncertainty and confusion. Some say even longer. The effect of a decision to go forward with the EC, relative to an American company's success in European markets, will probably be as big, or bigger, than the effect the "Big Bang" of 1986 had on the global banking community.

There are some clear morals to be learned from prior major economic changes in the global community, however:

1. Specific industries will certainly lose, at least initially: with the cost of transport across Europe decreasing, trucking companies, airlines, railroads, and all of their periphery industries will suffer price reductions.
2. Specific industries will profit, at least initially: with transport increasing, its infrastructure will have to be rebuilt, and road building, airport construction, rail bed improvements, and many other construction projects will flower.
3. Mounting competitive pressure will cause a concentration of manufacturing in fewer plants, albeit more highly automated than today's versions, to meet the variable consumer tastes in different European cultures.
4. Less protectionist trade policies mean requirements for more industrial standardization. The big European computer companies, along with IBM, are already lobbying for common standards to allow computers to talk to each other through telecommunication interconnects.
5. As industry becomes more privatized, government procurement of goods and services will diminish. Businesses traditionally selling to government procurement offices will have to learn how to trade with private purchasing agents.
6. Competition for the European market will encourage American, Japanese, Soviet, Israeli, and other non-EC member countries to become more aggressive and smarter. The relaxation of nontariff trade barriers within the EC, will enhance the importation of outside products and services. This means that there will no longer be a need for a foreign company to have facilities in two or more European locations. A single plant will do.
7. Multinational professional organizations (e.g., legal practices, accounting and auditing firms, consultants) will find it necessary to establish substantial offices within the EC to service both American interests and American-European joint ventures.
8. The financial community can no longer isolate itself from the needs of manufacturing and other trade companies. Investment banks must learn the ways of merchant banks and establish offices within the EC. This will make it easier for American companies to deal with friendly faces.

A number of other major changes will inevitably take place in the global marketplace as a result of the EC implementation. It's too early yet to forecast with any certainty what European markets will look like by the year 2000. It appears certain, however, that doing business in and with the EC can be a boon to the small or midsize company. But it must be willing to spend the time and make the effort to familiarize itself with developments in Europe as they unfold. An early entry into this exploding market, even if for internal economic reasons it must be minimal, should provide a company significant advantages over competitors once the EC settles down.

Latin America and the Caribbean

Future internal economic policies of Latin-American countries are even more uncertain than the EC. They are probably more crucial to the long-range growth and profitability of American companies, however. Major changes in western hemisphere trade practices during the 1990s, and beyond, will inevitably occur as a result of the internal economic and political policies in Latin America. These internal policies affect the willingness of the American government and private industry to support economic development with financing and investment assistance.

Efforts by the governments in Jamaica, Barbados, Grenada, and Dominica to stabilize their internal economic issues, increase employment, and control inflationary factors, have resulted in the implementation of the Caribbean Basin Initiative. This U.S. government-sponsored financial assistance and investment development effort has already had a major impact on the entrance of American investment in several island nations. Assistance granted American firms for the development of manufacturing and distribution facilities throughout the Caribbean has, in turn, furthered the stabilization of the region.

Current efforts by the governments of Brazil, Guatemala, Panama, and Colombia to resolve internal economic aberrations will probably result in further industrial and commercial development by foreign companies in these countries. Whenever the U.S. government initiates meaningful, long-range financial assistance to promote economic development, the rewards to American companies taking advantage of these programs are significant. Improvements come both through increased market penetration and higher profit margins. With U.S. government guarantees and financing, the risk to investors has been minimal. The proximity and cultural similarities of Latin America and the Caribbean make these regions viable options for small or midsize companies.

Japanese Noncompetitive Internal Practices

Since Japan is, and will probably continue to be, a major player in the global marketplace, it behooves Westerners to grasp the significance of the internal economic policies underlying the structure of Japanese industry that make this competitor so formidable throughout the world. Two major internal policies that conflict with Western free market philosophies are: the role of trading companies in the overall scheme of Japanese business, and emphasis on the socially desirable aspects of savings.

Since 1945, large Japanese trading companies, such as Mitsui and Hitachi, have provided the international marketing, R&D, and distribution networks for Japanese industry. Large Japanese banks, such as Sumitomo, sharing cross-ownership with the trading companies, have provided the financing. With these support activities from mutually owned trading and financial organizations, Japanese manufacturers have been free to concentrate on improving their manufacturing process, product quality, and labor productivity. The results have been startling. Quality Japanese goods have flooded the world market at prices equal to, or below, many of their competitors.

The underlying internal economic policy of the Japanese government has been that as many goods as possible should be exported to bring in foreign capital. This in turn fuels the financial fires of industrial production. Conversely, importing the least amount of product, consistent with public demand, aids in the maximization of the trade surplus.

Americans and Western Europeans, caught in the grip of ever-increasing consumption, find it difficult to understand why the Japanese people do not want more and more Western products. The answer becomes clear with the realization that for many years, the Japanese have been taught that saving is virtuous. Saving as much as possible is moral, chaste, pure, and good for society. Conversely, excess spending on consumption and personal pleasure is immoral, wicked, evil, and contrary to society's values. With this philosophy promulgated by the Japanese government, and followed religiously by the population, continuing high levels of exports and trade surpluses are inevitable.

The smaller foreign company that tries to break into this system of values faces a difficult market. The risk of competing head-on with Japanese manufacturers, on Japanese territory, probably outweighs the rewards from such a venture, at least for the foreseeable future.

Multinational Corporations

The contribution of multinational corporations to the development of world trade, and conflicts that arise with small and midsize competitors, will probably increase in many regions of the world. Anyone reading daily newspapers must realize that multinational corporations exert a tremendous amount of influence in world markets. They export worldwide and maintain facilities in every region of the world economy. They also are responsible for the transfer of technology, capital, and even labor, across national boundaries.

Though multinationals originate in countries from the Netherlands to Singapore, the most relevant to small and midsize American competitors are those located within the borders of the United States, such as General Electric, General Motors, IBM, and Dow Chemical. Those headquartered elsewhere but owning major facilities in the United States, such as Toyota, Philips Electric, ICI, and Mitsubishi, also compete directly with U.S. firms.

Through 1984, U.S. multinationals had invested more than $233 billion in foreign countries while foreign firms had invested nearly $160 billion in U.S. facilities. The U.S. Department of Commerce estimates that current foreign investment in the U.S. is just about equal to U.S. investment abroad. Clearly, the pace of cross-fertilization of industrial and commercial investments by multinationals has increased substantially. This impacts materially on the small or midsize company attempting to compete even in its own backyard. Since the best defense is often a good offense, this condition provides yet another reason for domestic companies to look to international trade for new markets, even if only for survival.

This does not mean that by entering the global marketplace a company will be free of multinational competition. On the contrary, multinational corporations have the resources, knowledge, and political clout to overshadow the impact of smaller companies. On the other hand, the enormous size of their organizations, their slowness in the decision-making process, and the fear many developing nations have of being overrun by the IBMs, Hitachis, and Exxons of the world, contribute significantly to the ability of smaller companies to compete in niche markets, regardless of multinational involvement.

Trade Conflicts in Developing Countries

Of the world's population, more than 70 percent lives in developing countries. Yet most multinationals focus on developed nations. This leaves an enormous market potential in the Third World for smaller companies. Very often, the internal trade policies of these countries offer conflicting goals that can provide stepping-stones for foreign entry. The greatest conflict arises when a nation attempts to switch from an export-dominated economy to an import substitution policy.

Most developing countries sustain their economy with exports of primary products, such as fruit, rubber, timber, raw metals, oil, and other indigenous products. Recognizing the need to become self-sufficient, Third World governments encourage the internal development of manufacturing and processing industries as substitutes for the exporting economy. With limited financial, technical, managerial, and labor resources, however, these nations must rely on foreign investment to get them started. And that's where small and midsize companies can jump in.

Even without U.S. government assistance, countertrade measures can often be used to establish production facilities in exchange for imported products and services from the United States. Companies willing to cope with the complexities of countertrade can often secure a foreign foothold with a minimum cash investment.

THE ECONOMICS OF THE INTERNATIONAL MONETARY SYSTEM

Since the collapse of Bretton Woods in 1971, the world's major currencies—the U.S. dollar, the English pound, the Japanese yen, the German mark—have been allowed to float against one another in a relatively free market. For the remainder of the 1970s, the free floating system seemed to work fairly well. No radical fluctuations marred the landscape, and the system's architects were pleased with the results from abandoning the gold standard.

The 1980s changed all that, however. During the past decade, exchange rates have become extremely unstable, experiencing free-falls and skyrocketing ascents. The U.S. dollar, for example, rose dramatically during the early part of the decade, even in the face of a mounting trade deficit. It then lost nearly 40 percent of its value between 1985 and 1988.

These wild fluctuations create an extremely unstable arena for national budgetary policies. They also prohibit an intelligent assessment of international investment strategies, product pricing, national monetary and fiscal policy, and in general, the entire global marketplace. The unexpected results of floating currency rates have caused debates between economists, government policymakers, and the financial community, about whether or not the world monetary system requires reform, and if so, what type of reform should be implemented.

International Monetary Reform and Exchange Rate Policies

Currently, there exist three schools of thought about monetary reform. The first argues that floating rates are good, and encourages speculation on future trends (which is the way a free market system should work). Therefore, floating exchange rates should be left alone.

A second approach expounds the theory that a fixed rate system should be reinstated, based on either a gold standard, or some other universally acceptable medium. The third argument supports a compromise between a floating rate and a fixed rate system, which would allow rates to fluctuate within a narrow band. Those moving beyond this range would be supported by appropriate government intervention.

All these theories are fine for the intellectuals and certainly stimulate debate within economic circles. The fact remains, however, that floating rates are currently in effect, and as such, businesses, financial institutions, and governments, must learn to cope with the vagaries of the system.

This turbulent environment has made the management of exchange rate risk an important issue for any firm involved in international trade. Articles enjoining business leaders to take this action or that action to minimize exchange rate risk have flowered in business and financial journals. The accounting fraternity regularly issues proclamations extolling the virtues of one type of accounting or another to measure the impact from exchange rate fluctuations on corporate financial statements. Government economists continue to explore alternate methods to manage, measure, and reduce the impact from exchange rate fluctuations on national monetary and fiscal policies. Academicians espouse complex formulas to evaluate the role exchange rate variations play in theoretical risk management.

The fact remains, however, that no one has been able to come up with a meaningful management technique to control currency exchange risk. A logical reason seems to be that currency fluctuations do not operate in a vacuum. They are a result of a whole conglomerate of economic forces experienced on a worldwide level; that is, inflation rates, interest rates, political unrest, financial market aberrations, and commodity prices. In addition, currency rates respond wildly to major economic shocks; for example, local wars, oil cartel maneuvers, natural disasters, and anticipated political and economic actions of the world powers. These macroeconomic factors are the real determinants of currency fluctuations.

An example of how this works was succinctly demonstrated by the international reaction to the enormous U.S. budget deficits in the early 1980s. American fiscal policy, reacting to the internal pressure for relief from the escalating deficit and fears of runaway inflation, pushed real interest rates 6 points higher than normal levels from the previous 20 years. Because of the interaction of worldwide financial markets, interest rates escalated in all OECD (Organization for Economic Cooperation and Development) countries, but not to the same extent as in the United States.

High-interest rates, coupled with continued government borrowing, brought foreign capital into U.S. markets at an alarming clip. The dollar exchange rate was pushed to new heights. This caused prices for American products to become noncompetitive in the world market, and exports dried up, further exacerbating the trade deficit. The real question was not how to manage the risk of a floating exchange rate, but rather how to reduce the government borrowings that created the astronomical inflation rise.

The risks of further isolationist (and uniformed) federal policies that drive domestic economic conditions to untenable limits impact significantly on an American company entering the international marketplace. The probability of changes in inflation and interest rates, political unrest, and major economic shocks occurring in other countries also reflect on the advisability and timing of global trade decisions by business owners and managers. Only by careful evaluation of the trading effects wrought by these economic factors can management intelligently judge the impact of currency exchange rates on global market transactions. Managing exchange rate risk with macroeconomic analyses and intelligent prognostications remains the only feasible way to cope with the impact of rate fluctuations on a company's international trade policies.

Global Banking

The role of international merchant banks as a source of funding for overseas projects has already been mentioned. The economic impact of global banks on the international monetary system extends beyond merchant banking, however. The global banking community directly influences, and in many cases controls, the purse strings and the economic vicissitudes of nations.

Understanding the basics of international finance is a prerequisite to entering the complex world of global trade. A global mentality requires management to measure the impact global banks have on government policies and on a market's ability to absorb, and pay for, a producer's products. Chapter 12 reviews the changing spectrum of international finance and the role global banking plays in the financing of direct foreign investment.

Two of the most profound global changes in the American banking industry brought about by global banking are the evolution of international ownership of banks and the ability of global banks to raise capital worldwide.

Banking has truly become an international affair. Foreign financial institutions now own large pieces of American commercial and investment banks, such as Marine Midland, First Boston, and Goldman Sachs. American institutions, such as Shearson Lehman and Prudential-Bache, in turn, own large chunks of foreign financial institutions. This cross-fertilization promotes the integration of global objectives and adds worldwide financial stability to otherwise erratic financial markets.

It also opens the doors of European and Japanese financial markets to small and midsize companies. These doors have heretofore been closed to all but the largest corporations. The British government's decision in 1986 to grant permission to foreign firms to trade in British securities, commonly called *Big Bang*, and the concomitant raising of capital through foreign financial institution participation for the privatization of many previously state-owned English firms, were the real beginnings of truly international capital markets.

A U.S. company, wishing to raise capital for expansion into a foreign country, no longer must rely on American banks or government agencies. Through global banking, American securities can be floated on exchanges in London, and eventually Tokyo, as well as New York. Bank loans can come from an English, Japanese, French, or German bank. Merchant banking now serves American firms domestically and overseas, as well as British, Japanese, and other foreign firms. Global banking has, in fact, opened the financial doors to everyone financing global trade.

Latin-American Debt Crisis

During the 1970s, most of the large American commercial banks, misjudging the opportunity to capitalize on perceived burgeoning economies, made substantial loans to Latin-American governments. Mexico, Brazil, Venezuela, and most of the rest of the countries in Central and South America, borrowed hundreds of billions of dollars from American banks, and others, to further their internal economic growth. Unstable economies, political upheaval, the collapse of the oil market, unreasonable protectionist trade policies, and widely fluctuating currency exchange rates, combined to bring Latin America one of the worst, and largest, debt crises ever known.

By 1982, few, if any, countries could even meet interest payments, much less return any principal amounts to the bank creditors. Loans were restructured; then restructured again. American banks reserved against 25 percent of the balance, found it wasn't enough, and have since reserved additional amounts. Plummeting bank profit margins and capital ratios raised the fear of collapsing U.S. money center banks. This drove federal regulators to the brink of hysteria by 1985. They properly recognized that if the banks failed, the federal government would have to pick up the tab, and this would be political dynamite.

The current status of the repayment of this debt remains unsettled, and many now doubt that it will ever be repaid. The final outcome may be many years in the future. Meanwhile, American exporters to, and investors in, Latin America must go forward with their trading.

Although from a political perspective, the risk for the small or midsize company desiring to locate facilities in many Latin-American countries (Peru, Chile, Colombia, and Nicaragua to name a few) remains questionable, the economic gains can be substantial. Latin America will undoubtedly be the next large market to open for smaller American companies. If U.S. banks can get their act together and resolve the debt crisis with these countries, Latin markets will probably explode. Current attempts at debt-equity swaps with private companies is one alternative that seems to be working, and others forms of restructuring will inevitably occur.

The International Monetary Fund

In 1944, as World War II was winding down, representatives from the Allies met to plan the international financial system that would be implemented after the war. At Bretton Woods in New Hampshire, the Allies agreed on the formation of the International Monetary Fund (IMF) to provide temporary financing to member countries in addressing short-term balance-of-payment problems. The Fund was also to provide support for a fixed rate currency exchange rate system. A sister organization—the World Bank—was also formed. Its purpose was to offer long-term loans for the reconstruction of infrastructures, and the development of other worthy economic projects. These institutions were, and are, owned by the member countries. Only the communist countries and Switzerland refused to participate.

The role of IMF has increased substantially over the years. Today it is one of the most powerful and important financial institutions in the world. Its main thrust in the modern age has been to support financial assistance to Third World countries for the development of their internal economies and infrastructures. Although the IMF continues to lend money to these countries, its major involvement is in approving specific projects and developers prior to the awarding of financial assistance by private or international development banks.

Critics of the IMF argue that to get this approval, a country must follow restrictive macroeconomic policies within its borders. In other words, the country must get its act together before the IMF will give its stamp of approval. Inflation rates must be reduced, budget deficits dramatically changed, money supplies curtailed, and political harmony, at least temporarily, stabilized. Leftist critics claim such policies lead to high unemployment and social unrest. Nevertheless, the IMF prevails.

These restrictive IMF financing approvals usually mean that a country is ripe for investment. It certainly reduces the risk of disruptive internal economic trade policies. It also gives the small or midsize company some comfort that potential free market forces will support their entrance. If a country cannot qualify for IMF approval, chances are good that a small or midsize company should not participate either.

The Eurodollar Market

In the late 1950s, the United States was having trouble defending the value of the dollar set at the 1944 Bretton Woods conference. Because of the substantial financial assistance funneled through the Marshall Plan to rebuild war-torn nations, a balance-of-payments problem occurred: More dollars were flowing out of the United States than into it. Most of these dollars ended up in Europe. The Europeans began using them to purchase U.S. gold. Reserves were being rapidly depleted and this made Americans nervous. The government enacted several regulations to reduce this exposure.

One of these measures restricted foreign borrowing in the U.S. capital market. It also required American companies to borrow offshore for their foreign investments. If a company wanted to build a plant in Mexico, for example, it had to raise its capital there, not through U.S. capital markets. As can be imagined, this had an enormous effect on the development of overseas capital markets. Europe was very liquid at the time, with substantial deposits of U.S. dollars in American and international banks located in London. This money remained from the balance-of-payments deficit that had not been used to buy gold. Eurodollar deposits were not regulated by any banking authority, either in the host country or from the United States. In 1960, Citibank invented the certificate of deposit, which turned these Eurodollar deposits into negotiable instruments. This major innovation led the way to the creation of the Eurobond, which in turn created a market for corporate securities denominated in U.S. dollars.

Eurobonds became, and continue to be, a major source of funds for American companies wishing to develop overseas facilities with non-U.S. funding. Floating issues of Eurobonds may seem like a complex method adaptable only by large corporations. It is not, however. A midsize company wishing to expand overseas, can utilize this funding method as easily as General Motors. Contacting one of the major U.S. investment banks, or foreign merchant banks, can get the ball rolling.

CONCLUSION

This chapter reviewed the major international economic factors requisite to an intelligent analysis of the risks and rewards of global transactions. Determining which specific economic factors might influence a particular decision for a given company under specific circumstances is a complex process. Each avenue, however, will probably affect to some degree at least the ease of entry, expected returns, level of risk, and growth potential for nearly all international traders.

No one set of criteria, calculations, or formulas exists that will yield the right answer for everyone. Selling to, or investing in, each country dictates a different set of circumstances. American and foreign trade policies keep changing. International financial markets are volatile. The directions of U.S. and foreign government programs for economic development shift like the rolling sands. Political upheaval, social unrest, and fundamental changes in political philosophy, continue to make global trade a risky endeavor. One can never be certain what political or economic influences will control the markets in a given country, or area of the world, during a specific time period. Even U.S. trade policies keep changing to reflect the current administration's perception of changing American advantages, and disadvantages, in the world's markets.

Nevertheless, the better one understands the vagaries of international economics, the clearer the decision-making process becomes. By defining the interaction of forces contributing to stability, or instability, in a specific foreign market, a company enhances its chances of making the right decision, at the right time. This chapter has set forth some basic rules of international economics. These rules should provide the uninitiated global trader a basic understanding upon which to formulate meaningful, risk/reward judgments.

Beyond the impact of international economic forces, the ramifications of U.S. and foreign tax policy also need to be reviewed prior to committing time, money, and effort to developing an overseas market. The next chapter examines the major tax regulations affecting American companies going global.

CHAPTER 3

TAX IMPLICATIONS OF GOING GLOBAL

MAJOR TOPICS

KEY POINTS

1. Foreign Tax Deductions and Credits. Whereas deductions and credits for taxes imposed by foreign governments afford some relief for American-owned foreign companies, the disparity in tax rates between other countries and the United States negates much of the benefit. Further limitations are imposed through the recapture of foreign losses taken in prior years, and the restrictive covenants of Controlled Foreign Corporation and Foreign Personal Holding Company regulations. Locating a facility in Puerto Rico has distinct tax advantages as well as unique financing possibilities.

2. Foreign Sales Corporations. Foreign Sales Corporations (FSCs) replaced the Domestic International Sales Corporation (DISC) as a mechanism to reduce taxes on export sales. Though the requirements of setting up and managing an FSC appear to be burdensome, it is really quite simple and inexpensive. The major deterrent seems to be that an FSC must be incorporated and have an operating office in a qualified foreign country. FSC management companies, however, can be utilized by the small and midsize company to avoid adding overhead personnel. Many foreign countries qualify as a location for FSC offices. The U.S. Virgin Islands, Belgium, Barbados, Jamaica, and the Netherlands, have the most ideal local requirements under which to operate an FSC. A small exporter doing $50,000 or less in export sales can still take advantage of FSCs by joining a shared FSC group.

3. International Acquisitions. The Tax Reform Act of 1986 severely restricted international acquisitions. The *basket* provisions for classifying foreign income penalize U.S. companies making foreign acquisitions, by limiting the effectiveness of foreign tax credits. On the other hand, Section 338 asset write-ups are still permitted for foreign acquisitions, even though the repeal of the General Utilities Doctrine disallows this for domestic deals. Nontaxable reorganizations can also be utilized for foreign acquisitions, but restrictive covenants must be closely followed. Because the tax ramifications of international acquisitions are so complex and far reaching, careful tax planning for preacquisition and postacquisition structuring is crucial.

4. Tax Haven Countries.   The use of tax haven countries to shelter foreign income has been severely restricted by the IRS. Nevertheless, with proper structuring of foreign holdings and careful documentation of sales transactions, tax haven countries can still be beneficial. It requires the use of trading companies, irrevocable trusts, and foreign reinvestment of earnings. Fortune 500 companies, who have used this tax shelter for years, have learned how to manage their offshore investments. They continue to utilize tax havens, in spite of IRS antagonism.

5. Foreign Partnerships and Joint Ventures.   Many countries, especially in the Third World and the communist bloc, have opened their doors to foreign investment opportunities by proclaiming tax-free periods while developing their economies. For an American company to take advantage of this opportunity, a national partner is normally required. To date, the U.S. government has not provided relief from restrictive foreign tax credit regulations to encourage American companies to enter this realm. A few have, however, in spite of IRS obstinacy, and from a nontax perspective, are doing very well.

6. Recent Developments in International Taxation.   Recent international tax developments include Soviet legislation to encourage Western investments, a new tax information exchange agreement with Mexico, an agreement with Hong Kong to give tax relief to shipping companies, and Australian legislation taxing employers for employee benefits granted.

The Internal Revenue Code (the Code) specifies that all American citizens—business entities as well as individuals—will be taxed on total income, from any source, earned or generated from any location in the world. Nearly every other country in the world with a national income tax law, taxes its citizens only on income earned in their home country, excluding income earned overseas.

American taxpayers, on the other hand, do not have this luxury. They pay income taxes on everything, regardless of its source or form. Furthermore, American taxpayers are taxed on worldwide income whether or not the country of origin taxes the same income. Obviously, this leaves plenty of room for double taxation—once by a foreign government and again by the U.S. Treasury.

The Code does allow some offsets and deductions, however. If a transaction is properly structured, in most cases, a U.S. corporation can avoid being taxed twice on the same income. Deductions and tax credits for income taxes paid to foreign governments alleviate the problem somewhat. As this chapter will describe, however, American companies still suffer disproportionately from inequitable taxation.

Granted, the Tax Reform Act of 1986 and the Revenue Act of 1987, together with slight variations in interpretations since then, have reduced the tax rate for all American taxpayers. At the same time, however, many economically viable provisions of the old tax laws have been abandoned. Preferential capital gains calculations, the General Utilities Doctrine, multinational restructuring and distribution rules, and a variety of other helpful provisions encouraging capital formation and international trade have been abandoned. They have been replaced by a cornucopia of so-called reforms that do little more than placate special interest factions from large corporations, financial giants, and vocal voter groups. In the meantime, several of these reforms have left small and midsize businesses even less competitive in the global marketplace than they were prior to 1986.

One of the interesting aspects of the American form of democratic capitalism is the paranoid distrust that exists between economic sectors: consumers and business, state and local governments and the federal bureaucracy, the public and the financial community, educational institutions and students, and especially between the business world and the federal government. In an attempt to catch American businesses lying, cheating, and defrauding the government, Congress has, over the years, enacted a multitude of legislation and regulations to limit the freedom of companies from competing effectively with foreign economic powers.

Though certainly not the only reason American producers are losing out to Japanese and European manufacturers, and perhaps not even the prime reason, restrictive legislation has certainly stymied American companies in many competitive areas. Examples of two such legislative acts are the Foreign Corrupt Practices Act of 1977 (analyzed in Chapter 7) and the Tax Information Exchange Agreements (TIEAs), otherwise known as *tax treaties.*

Tax treaties have been negotiated with many of America's trading partners, although several nations are excluded. The primary purpose of TIEAs is to provide the taxing authorities of both countries, but principally the IRS, free access to information and transactions of companies doing business in their respective countries. This is clearly an infringement on the privacy of American citizens and businesses who wish to enter the global arena. A TIEA assures the IRS that even without incurring much expense or effort, their auditors can track the worldwide income and expenses of American taxpayers. Since a basic assumption in government ranks seems to be that the business world is fundamentally dishonest and will cheat wherever and whenever possible, the enactment of TIEAs should not be surprising.

It should be noted that deductions and tax credits for income taxes paid to foreign governments are not affected by the inclusion of a country in TIEAs. Obviously, the intent in tax treaties is not to provide U.S. companies with tax breaks or other major assistance in international trade. TIEAs remain a vehicle to prevent U.S. taxpayers from cheating on their tax returns.

On the other hand, TIEAs do bring some benefits to U.S. corporations. If employees attend meetings or conventions in TIEA countries, the IRS allows a deduction for the expenses incurred during these trips without regard to the more stringent rules generally applicable to foreign conventions. But documentation to substantiate the expense still must be produced when a taxpayer's return is audited. Also, countries that have executed TIEAs qualify as a foreign location for a Foreign Sales Corporation (discussed later in this chapter).

Certain U.S. government-sponsored financial assistance programs mandate that the recipient country must have executed a TIEA. The Caribbean Basin Initiative program, for example, stipulates that a country entering into a TIEA may be eligible for project financing under Puerto Rico's Section 936 program (see Chapter 13).

FOREIGN TAX DEDUCTIONS AND CREDITS

A U.S. citizen, or a domestic corporation, may deduct foreign income taxes paid, or accrued, to a foreign government. Or it may choose a credit against its U.S. tax liability. If a company participates, or cooperates, in any way, with an international boycott, however, it loses the deduction and credit. Benefits such as those arising from the use of an FSC, or a foreign controlled corporation, will also be lost. The value of the lost deduction, or benefit, will be determined by the ratio of the value of the sales or purchases of goods or services arising from the boycott activity to the total value of foreign sales or purchases of the corporation.

Participation in, or cooperation with, an international boycott occurs when a company agrees not to do business with a specified second country (such as Israel), or with other companies doing business in specified countries. An agreement not to hire, or to refuse to do business with other companies whose employees are of a specific race, nationality, or religion also falls under the boycott rules. At one time or another over the past 20 years, Saudi Arabia, Libya, Oman, Lebanon, Bahrain, Kuwait, Syria, the UAE, Yemen, Iraq, Jordan, and Iran have all insisted that American companies boycott Israel, and other nations, as a prerequisite to doing business in their country. Taiwan and South Africa have also been subjects of boycott activity at one time or another.

Aside from the boycott provisions, any U.S. taxpayer is entitled to either a deduction for foreign taxes or a tax credit at the company's discretion. As long as the foreign tax paid or accrued represented an income tax, or a tax imposed in lieu of an income tax, it qualifies. Other types of taxes imposed by a foreign country are not subject to either a deduction or a tax credit. Unfortunately, as in every other provision of the tax code, there are exceptions and limitations here as well.

Limitations

With the reduction of tax rates under the Tax Reform Act of 1986, the equitability of foreign tax credits suddenly became illusory. An American taxpayer may not use foreign tax credits to reduce a U.S. tax liability on income from sources within the United States. As long as IRS rates were similar, or close to those imposed by foreign countries, this limitation made some sense. Now, however, with corporations paying a maximum U.S. rate of 34 percent, and other countries, such as Great Britain, imposing rates far in excess of this rate, a condition can easily occur wherein the tax credit will exceed the U.S. tax liability on foreign income. The following example illustrates the calculation:

Income from British operations	$100,000
Income from U.S. operations	200,000
Total worldwide taxable income	$300,000
U.S. tax rate	34%
Tentative U.S. tax	$102,000
Calculation of limitation—	
Foreign income of $100,000 divided by worldwide income of $300,000, equals	.3333
Multiplied by tentative U.S. tax from above	× 102,000
Tax credit limitation	$34,000

The tax credit is limited to $34,000, even though Great Britain, with a tax rate of 48 percent, imposed a tax of $48,000 on its host country income of $100,000. The difference between $48,000 and $34,000 ($14,000), can be carried back two years and forward five years. The carrybacks and carryforwards are still subject to the limitation test in appropriate years. Another quirk stipulates that foreign losses can only be used to offset foreign income, and cannot be deducted from U.S. source income. Other restrictions of a lesser magnitude also apply.

Recapture of Foreign Losses

An overall foreign loss sustained in any given tax year is subject to recapture in later years. An overall foreign loss is defined as the amount by which the sum of foreign expenses, losses, and other deductions, properly allocable to foreign source income, exceeds the gross income from these foreign sources. Generally, the amount of foreign loss recharacterized as income is limited to the lesser of the overall foreign loss for the year earlier, or 50 percent of the foreign source taxable income of the current year.

In other words, if an American company starts up a foreign operation, and sustains operating losses for the first few years, and then deducts these losses on its U.S. return, the losses will be reclassified as income in later years and taxed accordingly. It's the same principle as recapture of depreciation when the depreciable property is sold.

Any gain on the disposition of business property used outside the United States during the preceding three-year period will also be subject to the recapture rules, with minor exceptions. Therefore, a disposition of foreign business property may result in both a reduction of the limitation on foreign tax credit and an increase in the American taxpayer's income.

There appears to be no end to the ways an American company can be deterred from competing effectively in the global market. Overcoming these legislative obstacles often taxes even the most creative business mind. With competent tax advice and imaginative planning, some of these obstacles can still be overcome.

Locating in Puerto Rico

Puerto Rico is not considered a U.S. possession for purposes of qualifying as a foreign location for a Foreign Sales Corporation (described later in this chapter), although the U.S. Virgin Islands and other U.S. possessions do qualify. Just the reverse holds true for tax provisions under Section 936 of the Code. Under Section 936 American companies that derive a significant portion of their income from Puerto Rican income are considered *936 companies*. A 936 company is effectively exempt from U.S. income tax on income derived from Puerto Rican activities. If the company repatriates this income to the Unites States, a *tollgate* tax of 10 percent is imposed by Puerto Rico, but still nothing from the IRS. As long as the funds remain in Puerto Rican banks, or are reinvested in the Commonwealth, no tax is paid.

Clearly, for any company seriously considering international trade in the Caribbean, a location in Puerto Rico can be extremely beneficial. Not only will it get a significant tax break, it also becomes eligible for unique financing arrangements jointly sponsored by the U.S. and Puerto Rican governments called the *Section 936 Financing Program*. Chapter 15 describes the salient features of this program.

Credits for Taxes of a Foreign Subsidiary

If an American company chooses not to consolidate foreign subsidiaries with domestic operations for tax purposes, but does receive repatriated earnings from the subsidiary, these earnings are considered dividends by the IRS. The domestic corporation may then elect to take a tax credit for the amount of foreign tax levied against the foreign subsidiary's earnings that are the basis for the dividend. The tax base of ownership in the subsidiary is then adjusted by both the amount of the dividend and the tax paid by the subsidiary. Foreign tax credits may also be taken when a domestic corporation is required to include undistributed earnings of a controlled foreign corporation in its income.

A number of other special provisions relate to the inclusion or exclusion of foreign income and losses. The applicability of the foreign tax credit, excise taxes on transfers of property to foreign entities, and recognition or nonrecognition of gains on redemption of stock in a foreign controlled corporation further muddy the waters. These rules are far too complex to include in a book of this scope, however, and generally not of interest to the business manager; unless, of course, he also happens to be the controller of the company.

Competent tax advisers can readily describe the disposition of special foreign tax matters. They should obviously be consulted prior to engaging in any global transactions. There is one more subject relating to foreign income that may be of interest to business managers, especially owners of smaller businesses; that is, *controlled* foreign corporations.

Controlled Foreign Corporations

Controlled foreign corporation tax laws are another attempt by the U.S. government to catch taxpayers trying to shelter income in what are referred to as *tax haven* corporations. Where a foreign corporation is controlled for an uninterrupted period of 30 or more days by U.S. shareholders, such shareholders are taxed on some of the corporation's undistributed earnings, as well as earnings distributed in that year. A U.S. shareholder is any American individual, partnership, corporation, estate, or trust who owns 10 percent or more of the corporation's voting interest. A controlled foreign corporation is defined as one in which U.S. shareholders own more than 50 percent of the corporation's voting interest for at least one day during the taxable year.

A U.S. shareholder must include as taxable income, a proportionate share of the controlled foreign corporation's "subpart F income." It must also include previously excluded "subpart F income" withdrawn from investment in less developed countries. Any increase in earnings in U.S. property, exclusive of FSC income, is taxed as well.

Nothing in the tax code can be straightforward. Controlled foreign corporations are no different. Here, "subpart F income" is defined as the sum of the following:

1. Income from the foreign company.
2. Income from the insurance of U.S. risks.
3. Personal holding company income.
4. Income of the foreign corporation multiplied by the international boycott factor as determined under Section 999.
5. Any illegal payments paid by, or on behalf of, the foreign corporation to government employees or agents (an obvious attempt to enforce provisions of the Foreign Corrupt Practices Act).

These income items are included only for that portion of the taxable year during which a U.S. shareholder(s) held controlling interest. If it's one month, then one twelfth of the annual income items are included. To be eligible for the foreign tax credit, a U.S. shareholder must make the selection to be taxed as a domestic corporation on the undistributed earnings of the controlled foreign corporation.

When setting up a subsidiary in a foreign country, it is imperative to consult with competent advisers, not only conversant with local foreign tax regulations, but with the Code as well. IRS rules governing foreign holdings of American taxpayers can become extremely complex. Any American company going abroad for the first time should weigh carefully both U.S. and foreign tax implications of the expansion to be certain of taking advantage of all tax breaks allowed.

Foreign Personal Holding Company

A foreign corporation is classified as a foreign personal holding company under the following circumstances:

1. At least 60 percent (50 percent after the first year) of the company's gross income consists of dividends, interest, royalties, annuities, rents (unless 50 percent or more of total gross income), gains in stock and commodity transactions, income from personal service contracts, and other specified types of income.
2. More than 50 percent of the corporation's outstanding stock is owned directly or indirectly by five or fewer U.S. citizens or residents.

A U.S. shareholder of a foreign personal holding company is subject to a tax on both the distributed and undistributed income of the foreign company. The tax is imposed on all income as if it had been actually received as dividend income. Properly structured, however, the use of such personal holding companies can continue to provide a shelter for offshore income.

Dividends and interest received by the foreign personal holding company from certain related foreign corporations are exempt providing that: (1) the company paying the interest or dividends is related to the recipient, (2) it is created or organized under the laws of the recipient's country, and (3) it has a substantial part of its assets used in its trade or business located in the same foreign country. Tiered foreign subsidiaries meeting these requirements are excludable from foreign personal holding company rules but may be subject to the foreign controlled corporation rules.

FOREIGN SALES CORPORATIONS

In 1984, the Foreign Sales Corporation (FSC) replaced the old Domestic International Sales Corporation (DISC) as a means of reducing tax liabilities on export sales. Several members of GATT had become disgruntled with what they claimed was an unfair trade advantage for American exporters using a DISC. In 1976, a GATT panel decided that in fact, the use of a DISC was an unfair export subsidy. After years of debate, the United States finally agreed in 1982 to replace the DISC, and in 1984, FSCs were born. Under the Tax Reform Act of 1984, a portion of the FSC's income is exempted from tax. The act deems this exempt foreign trade income to be foreign source income, not effectively connected with a trade or business within the boundaries of the United States.

A major advantage over the old DISC, is that FSCs actually reduce the tax bite, whereas DISCs merely deferred taxes. Also, whereas the DISC was strictly a paper company, an FSC must be incorporated outside the United States, have a legitimate office, and maintain accounting records.

As long as the FSC is established in a qualifying country, and both the FSC and the domestic parent corporation comply with the rigid requirements for documentation imposed by the Code, using an FSC can save up to 15 percent of taxes on income generated through export sales. Unfortunately, as in everything else Congress tries to do to help private enterprise, the complexities of operating FSCs preclude many smaller companies from using them. Still, for those who embark on an export program, FSCs prove helpful and a legitimate tax saver.

An FSC is a separate company formed by the exporter (or others under contract). It must be incorporated in a qualified foreign country with an operating office in that country. Theoretically, this is an administrative and bookkeeping office. It prepares invoices to foreign customers for the exporter's sales and deposits collections in a local bank. By employing complex formulas, an exporter can exclude certain percentages of income generated by export sales from taxable income.

Qualifying Foreign Countries

Currently, the list of countries qualifying for FSC incorporation and operation include:

American Samoa	Ireland
Australia	Jamaica
Austria	Korea
Barbados	Malta
Belgium	Morocco
Canada	The Netherlands (but not the
Cyprus	Netherlands Antilles)
Denmark	New Zealand
Dominica	Northern Mariana Islands
Egypt	Norway
Finland	Pakistan
France	The Philippines
Germany	Sweden
Grenada	Trinidad
Guam	Tobago
Iceland	U.S. Virgin Islands

The foreign countries in the above group have also signed TIEA treaties. The United Kingdom and Italy have not been included because apparently their national laws do not give the IRS sufficient freedom to attach records. Bermuda, St. Lucia, and Costa Rica will probably be added to the list shortly.

Pragmatically, those countries that offer the best opportunities for establishing an FSC office are all of the U.S. possessions, plus Barbados, Belgium, Ireland, Jamaica, and the Netherlands. These countries have enacted legislation to eliminate or substantially reduce any local taxing of FSCs. The Tax Reform Act of 1986 further amended qualification requirements by establishing that not only must the Secretary of the Treasury certify that the tax treaty signed with a specific country includes a satisfactory information exchange program, but also that the program includes FSCs. Paranoid distrust of the business sector continues to permeate the halls of Washington.

To Qualify as an FSC

There are both large FSCs—used by nearly all of the Fortune 500—and small FSCs. To be classified as a small FSC, annual export sales of the parent company must be $5 million or less. To encourage smaller exporters to use FSCs, Congress has simplified administrative procedures and reporting requirements. From a practical perspective, however, an exporter with less than $50,000 in export sales will find it too expensive to set up and maintain his own FSC. Several state and trade organizations have recognized this disparity and started their own FSCs called *shared FSCs* to fill the void. This way any business, with any amount of export sales, can now take advantage of this tax saving device.

To qualify as an FSC, a corporation must meet the following criteria:

1. It must be incorporated in a qualified foreign country or in a U.S. possession (excluding Puerto Rico).
2. There must be no more than 25 shareholders.
3. It can have no preferred stock.
4. It must maintain an office in the qualified foreign country or U.S. possession, as in (1) above.
5. A set of accounting records must be maintained at this office, and certain other records must be maintained in the United States.
6. There must be at least one non-U.S. resident on its board of directors.
7. It cannot be a member of a controlled group of corporations of which a DISC is a member.
8. It must have elected FSC status by unanimous consent of the stockholders within the 90-day period preceding the taxable year for which the election is made.

In addition to these qualifying requirements, an FSC must meet two other criteria. The first is the "Foreign Management Test." To meet this requirement, the following conditions must be met:

1. Only income which is classified as *foreign trade income* qualifies for exemption from income tax. It is defined as the gross income of the FSC attributable to foreign trading gross receipts.
2. The management of the FSC must take place outside of the United States. In other words, the FSC must be managed by someone other than a U.S. resident.
3. All shareholders and board of directors meetings must be held outside of the United States.
4. The FSC's principal bank account must be maintained outside of the United States.
5. All dividends, legal fees, accounting fees, and salaries of its officers and directors must be paid from these offshore bank accounts.

The second qualification specifies that the *economic process* of an FSC must take place outside of the United States. The test for foreign economic process takes two forms: sales participation tests and direct costs test. To meet the sales participation test, the contract relating to a sales transaction of the FSC must have been solicited, negotiated, or made outside of the United States. This is fairly straightforward and merely means that an exporter (or his agent, when using an export management company) must communicate with the customer and agree to the terms of sale in a location other than the United States.

The direct costs tests are a bit more complex. Either one of the following meets the direct cost test:

1. The foreign direct costs incurred by the FSC, or its agent, are at least 50 percent of the total direct costs of the transaction.
2. At least 85 percent of the direct costs incurred with respect to at least two of the following activities are foreign direct costs.
   a. Advertising and sales promotion.
   b. The cost of processing of customers' orders and arranging for delivery of the product.
   c. Transportation costs from the time of acquisition of the product by the FSC to the delivery to the customer.
   d. The cost of the determination and transmittal of a final invoice, or statement of account to a customer, and the receipt of payment.
   e. The assumption of credit risk.

There are two major advantages that a small FSC (one with not more than $5 million per year in export sales) has over a large FSC. The direct cost tests can be met with costs incurred in the United States. A large FSC must incur these costs overseas. Second, a small FSC may pay all administrative expenses out of a U.S. bank account. A large FSC must use an offshore bank.

It's important to note that either the FSC itself, or its duly authorized agent, may satisfy the requirements of these economic process tests. This agent could be an export management company or other company providing sales and processing assistance. It could even be the parent company itself. The economic process tests must be met on a transaction-by-transaction basis. The invalidation of one transaction does not invalidate other FSC business. On the other hand, the foreign management test must be met at all times during the taxable year.

Customer collections deposited in a foreign bank may be repatriated to the U.S. tax free, and are treated as an exempted dividend by the parent company. Furthermore, from a practical perspective, the FSC office does not have to prepare customer invoices on site. These can be prepared in the United States through a company's normal accounting activity. A monthly summary of paid customer invoices is then forwarded to the FSC and maintained as an accounting record in its office.

Smaller exporters find that it is not practical to set up a foreign office, staff it, and maintain local accounting records. There are many FSC management companies in all qualified foreign countries to handle these administrative details at a very low cost. Most large U.S. banks, law firms, and accounting firms with foreign offices provide the service. There are also independent FSC management companies located in nearly all qualified countries. These are normally managed by Americans. The fees charged by an FSC management company are usually quite low. They range from $1,500 to $5,000 a year, depending on the volume of transactions handled and whether the FSC is a small or a large one.

Shared FSCs

Shared FSCs have become popular for exporters with a sales volume of less than $50,000. The state of Delaware has taken the lead in passing legislation to encourage the formation of shared FSCs to help small companies establish export programs. Under a shared FSC, up to 25 exporting companies may form a single FSC without having to issue separate classes of stock to each of them. The effect is to share the costs of operating an FSC, but still reap the 15 percent tax benefit. A shared FSC still requires a foreign presence, however, and all other tests described above must be met.

INTERNATIONAL ACQUISITIONS

Chapter 11 describes the mechanics of making a foreign acquisition. The Tax Reform Act of 1986 also raises some serious tax questions about the structure and methodology of foreign acquisitions. The basic problem focuses around two features of the Code: the classification of income baskets for purposes of utilizing the foreign tax credit, and the treatment of dispositions of foreign assets.

The Tax Reform Act of 1986 severely restricted a U.S. company's ability to utilize the foreign tax credit. An earlier example pointed out what happens when the tax rate in the foreign country—in that case Great Britain—is higher than the U.S. rate. Part of the foreign tax credit cannot be utilized during the current year and must be either carried back, or forward, to offset foreign income from other years. But there is an even more significant obstruction relative to acquiring a foreign company; that is, the basket effect.

To prevent American taxpayers from moving their income offshore and engaging in other tax savings efforts, Section 904 of the Code requires the application of foreign tax credits separately to certain classifications of income called *baskets*. Each basket consists of income from high withholding tax interest, financial services, shipping, dividends from noncontrolled 902 corporations, certain dividends from DISC corporations, certain Section 923(*b*) foreign trade income, and certain distributions from FSCs. The two most important categories, however, relating to foreign acquisitions are the passive income basket, and the general income basket.

The passive basket consists of income from interest, dividends, and gains on the sale of passive assets. The general basket consists of all income not classified in one of the other baskets. General business income is normally the largest component of the general basket. Dividends, rents, interest, and royalties paid by a controlled foreign corporation to a U.S. parent retain the same characteristics as with the foreign company and do not take on the character of the current distribution. This feature prevents a U.S. parent from reclassifying distributions into lesser used baskets—such as the passive basket—and forces such income into the general basket.

Since the foreign tax credits limitations are limitations per basket, not in total, any excess credit from the general basket cannot be used as an offset to the passive basket. Furthermore, it is unlikely a U.S. corporation will ever have excess foreign tax credits from one item of income in the passive basket to offset the residual U.S. tax on another item of passive income. The *high tax kickout* rule sees to that. This rule specifies that passive income which is subject to a foreign income tax rate greater than the U.S. 34 percent rate, is reclassified as general basket income.

The basket rules about foreign tax credit limitations sound complex—and they are. However, the rules have a significant impact on structuring a foreign acquisition. If the seller is a U.S. company, it will obviously try to minimize the foreign income taxes imposed on the transaction, and maximize the application of the foreign tax credit against the U.S. tax liability. The buyer, on the other hand, should try to minimize the foreign taxes on income generated after the deal closes by obtaining a stepped-up depreciation basis for assets in countries with high tax rates.

The Implications of Section 338

Section 338 of the Code states that a corporation which purchases at least 80 percent of the stock of another company may elect to treat the acquisition as a purchase of assets. The target company is then considered to have repurchased these same assets at a price equal to the amount the buyer paid for them. This in turn, provides a new, higher depreciation base for future years.

The repeal of the General Utilities Doctrine, under the Tax Reform Act of 1986, prohibited a company making a domestic acquisition from taking advantage of tax write-offs through this method. The repeal of the General Utilities Doctrine had no effect on international acquisitions, however.

When the acquired company is a foreign corporation, not engaged in a U.S. trade or business, and sold by an American corporation, Section 338 write-ups are still permitted. The gain on the sale must be recognized by the selling corporation and also may result in the inclusion of "subpart F" income in the seller's taxable income. This is in direct contrast to buying an American corporation where the tax liability falls to the buyer. For an international purchase from a U.S. seller, a Section 338 election passes the burden of taxation to the seller. Obviously, if the seller is another foreign corporation, such tax matters are moot.

Nontaxable Foreign Acquisitions

Although in the past several years most international acquisitions have involved a cash purchase of stock of the acquired corporation and have been taxable transactions, foreign acquisitions can also take the form of tax-free reorganizations. Assume that an American corporation, XYZ Corp., purchases the assets, or stock, of French Products, a French subsidiary of another American corporation, ABC Corp. The tax to the seller, ABC Corp., on the gain from the sale is deferred until it disposes of the property received in the transaction—presumably stock of XYZ Corp. The buyer, XYZ Corp., then obtains a carryover basis in the acquired stock of French Products. To qualify for this treatment, international acquisitions must not only meet the requirements of tax-free reorganizations for domestic acquisitions, but also the provisions of Section 367 of the Code.

Section 367 includes four distinct rules governing the qualification of an acquisition transaction as a tax-free reorganization:

1. It permits the nonrecognition of gain treatment if property transferred to the foreign corporation is used by the foreign corporation in the conduct of business exclusively outside of the United States. Inventory, accounts receivable, installment obligations, foreign currency, and certain leased property (all considered *tainted assets*), depreciated property used in the United States, or intangible property, are excluded from this exemption, and if these are transferred to the foreign corporation the tax-free reorganization provisions do not apply.
2. If assets are transferred to the foreign corporation from another foreign branch that has reported operating losses, these losses are recaptured.
3. The exemption is also lost if the stock, or securities of another foreign corporation that is a party to the transaction, is transferred to the acquired corporation.
4. Section 367(a)(5) specifies that certain outbound transfers of property, from the United States in connection with reorganizations will be taxable unless the transferor is a closely held corporation.

A complete explanation of the mechanics of applying these provisions is far too complex for inclusion here. However, an American company considering the acquisition of a foreign corporation should be aware that tax-free reorganization provisions are possible. Competent tax counsel can advise if such a scheme fits with the specific transaction under consideration.

Tax Planning and International Acquisitions

A number of matters enter into effective tax planning when buying a foreign company, both before the actual sale closes and after the acquisition. Basic questions center on how to minimize foreign taxes in the host country, and how to maximize the foreign tax credit for the deduction of U.S. taxes.

Financing a foreign acquisition with leveraged debt also must be weighed against potential tax effects. Frequently, an intermediary foreign holding company acts as a holder of the acquisition debt to benefit from an interest deduction in the holding company's host country. This could invalidate the deduction for U.S. tax purposes. The IRS could also recharacterize the interest payments into a different basket for foreign tax credit limitations. Financing a foreign acquisition, or a foreign start-up operation, presents a series of interesting and complex tax questions.

The entire subject of tax planning prior to entering into an acquisition agreement for a foreign company is wrought with pitfalls. It is so crucial to the type of acquisition financing, the management and capital structures of the acquired company, intercompany pricing policies, and the potential future disposal of the company, that this subject is examined in its entirety in Chapter 11, as part of the decision-making and planning process involved in foreign acquisitions.

TAX HAVEN COUNTRIES

Not too many years ago, the use of *tax haven* countries as depositories for foreign income was a popular way for entrepreneurs, and others, to build a retirement nest egg with income from foreign sources. The IRS did not, and does not now, have TIEAs with these countries. The tax haven countries prospered, secure in the knowledge that American and other foreign taxpayers would never have to worry about a bank or government agency revealing business transactions or monetary holdings to any taxing authority, including the IRS.

The IRS, the Department of Justice, the FBI, and a variety of other government agencies have attempted to penetrate the security of these countries over and over again. So far, at least, they have been successful in destroying this business for Bermuda, the Bahamas, Switzerland, Luxembourg, and the Netherlands Antilles. These former tax haven countries have buckled under to the American taxing authorities and Department of Justice investigators, and therefore, are no longer secure for American investors.

The future of tax haven countries as legitimate terminals for American foreign investment income remains in doubt. Several U.S. government agencies continue to try to put pressure on these oases to enter the fold of taxing bureaucracies. So far they have resisted. The use of foreign tax haven countries by American citizens and corporations is still possible, and legal, but it takes substantial planning, some cost to set up and to maintain, and a degree of loss of control over investment portfolios.

Although the specific procedures vary somewhat depending on which country the foreign income comes from, the approach many foreign corporations use is similar. It would be wise, however, to use tax havens only for income from foreign businesses not located in TIEA countries. Also, the following procedure normally only works for products exported from the host country, not those sold domestically.

1. The first step is to set up a trading company in a tax haven country.
2. Customer orders are recorded on the books of the trading company, which also receives a sales commission from the producing company for marketing services rendered.
3. The trading company then places orders on the producing company for products to be drop-shipped direct to the end customer.

4. When the producer ships the products, it invoices the trading company at cost, plus a small profit.
5. The trading company then invoices the customer directly with instructions to remit to the trading company's lockbox in the tax haven country.

The end result of such a maneuver means that the manufacturer has recorded a small profit on the sale, and a commission expense to the trading company. To the extent that there is taxable income, a tax would have to be paid in the manufacturer's country of origin. The trading company pays the manufacturer for the goods at his invoiced price. The bulk of the profit on the sale gets recorded on the trading company's books. Since it is located in a tax haven country, of course there is no tax to pay there.

Before trying such a scheme it would be wise to recognize a few caveats:

1. The trading company should be owned by a trust, set up in the tax haven country, and administered by an appointed agent— usually a lawyer. The trust must be irrevocable, and the manufacturer should not be the beneficiary.
2. The trading company should be superficially managed by the trustee, although it can have employees, managers, and sales personnel on its payroll.
3. The commissions paid to the trading company should not be paid in cash. They can be offset against what the trading company owes the manufacturer for the products shipped.
4. The cash earnings of the trading company cannot be repatriated to most host countries without incurring a tax liability. Therefore, these earnings should be invested offshore (or in the tax haven) so that income from the investment will also flow back to the tax haven country.
5. An American company, owning a foreign company under this scheme, must be careful to avoid constructive receipt of the earnings, either in the foreign manufacturer's country or in the United States. Of course, the trading company cannot be a controlled foreign corporation or a foreign personal holding company, as defined in the Code. This obviously requires very careful planning.

Although the IRS sees red when a company operates in this manner, most of the Fortune 500 do it. And they do it within the constraining laws of the Code. It's not a surefire way to shelter all foreign income, but, judiciously managed, a tax haven company can be beneficial to anyone with foreign investments. It is perfectly legal, providing an irrevocable trust owns the trading company, and the earnings are not repatriated.

FOREIGN PARTNERSHIPS AND JOINT VENTURES

Many countries, especially in the Third World, Eastern Europe, and the communist Far East, have structured local laws to provide Western investors significant tax breaks and shelters in exchange for investing in these countries. Many times a local partner, either an individual or a national company, must be involved as a partner in the ownership of the business. Sometimes, it is necessary to let a national have a hand in the management of the company also. The benefits of such arrangements to the host country are obvious. Not only do they get much needed technical advice, and engineering and manufacturing technology, Western investors also bring into the country hard currency, which can then be used to acquire much needed imports.

With all local tax burdens eliminated, it can be equally advantageous to a foreign company starting up a business. It is truly unfortunate that the federal government hasn't recognized the political, economic, and social benefits, not only to developing nations, but also to the future of American trade, by allowing companies investing in such countries to exclude at least a portion of earned income from taxation. So far, however, this is not the case. Even though the host country doesn't impose a tax, a foreign subsidiary's earnings will be taxed in the United States; only in proportion to U.S. ownership of the company, however. From a business perspective, such expansion generally means extra profits to an investor, even after taxes.

RECENT DEVELOPMENTS IN INTERNATIONAL TAXATION

Although it is impossible to predict the outcome of the recent changes toward the opening and restructuring of Eastern European economies, the Soviet Union has already begun to encourage foreign investment through joint ventures with Soviet businesses. Under recent decrees, three liberalizations of foreign participation have occurred:

1. Foreign partners can set up companies in the Soviet Union with their share of capital as high as 100 percent.
2. Chairpersons of a joint venture no longer need to be Soviet citizens.
3. Joint ventures with foreign partners enjoy a complete tax holiday for two years.

These early indications certainly bode well for Western companies considering future trading with the Soviet Union.

A tax information exchange agreement was signed with Mexico in November 1989. Theoretically, the exchange of such proprietary information is subject to various safeguards designed to protect taxpayers' rights. Again theoretically, this information must be kept confidential and can be used only for tax purposes. In addition, information about deposits in U.S. banks will be reported to Mexican authorities only on specific request when there is evidence of tax noncompliance in Mexico.

The United States and Hong Kong have executed a double tax agreement whereby income derived from the international operation of ships is exempt from taxation. The ships must be operated by individuals who are residents of Hong Kong, or by controlled corporations which are managed or controlled in Hong Kong. This was enacted in response to changes in the Tax Reform Act of 1986, specifying that to be exempt from American taxation, these conditions must exist.

Australia has enacted a fringe benefit tax payable by employers in Australia on the fringe benefits provided to employees. Included are such mundane benefits as office Christmas parties and gifts to employees from the employer.

CONCLUSION

This chapter has reviewed the major U.S. tax implications of American companies doing business overseas. Each topic reflects the current interpretations of the Code and subsequent regulations, and rulings through mid-1990. Regulations, Tax Court decisions, interpretations, and rulings, as well as complete changes in the Code, continue to keep U.S. tax legislation in a state of flux. As the federal government begins to accept the nature of a global economy and the concomitant requirement for American businesses to be allowed to compete openly with foreign competitors, more sophistication in taxing provisions will likely occur.

The execution of tax treaties with American trading partners reflects ominously on the ability of government bureaucrats to ever really trust American business motives. Consequently, while Japan, Germany, the United Kingdom, France, Italy, and other countries have already recognized the desirability of meaningful tax laws, the United States continues to insist on taxing the worldwide income of American corporations.

An overview of the major factors to be considered by small and midsize companies contemplating an entrance into the global markets has been examined. The fundamentals of international economics have been reviewed, and major U.S. tax regulations affecting global trade have been summarized. As new entrants develop strategies to cope with the vicissitudes of global economics and tax impediments, creative trade tactics and organization structures will surely mitigate some of the uncertainties caused by these barriers.

CHAPTER 4

CULTURE CRUNCH

MAJOR TOPICS

KEY POINTS

    1. People Relationships. When doing business overseas, customary American male/female relationships must be adjusted to local customs. Many countries, especially developing nations in the Middle East, Southeast Asia, and Latin America regard the role of women in business distinctly differently than that of the United States. Businessmen must also be careful not to offend local relationship customs.

    2. Societal Norms. American acceptance of religious freedom and nondiscrimination because of race, color, creed, or sex, is not practiced globally. Regardless of personal beliefs, an American businessperson must be careful to grasp local customs before entering into business transactions. The use of cigarettes, liquor, and drugs overseas differs radically from American norms. Double standards permeate most cultures.

    3. Business Protocol. A clear understanding of the specific business practices in the host country is essential to global success. Even large corporations such as Hewlett-Packard and ITT have been forced to retrench because of a lack of understanding or acceptance of local business protocol.

    4. Tips on International Travel. A listing of 16 tips is presented to make international travel a little less tiresome and hazardous to the business traveler.

Harry Macauley, vice president of finance, and Sara Rinwalt, vice president of product development with Mirror Images, Inc., a $55 million producer of electronic health care diagnostic equipment were on their way to negotiate a $15 million contract for their new line. Neither had traveled outside of the United States before, and both were excited at the opportunity to see the legendary home of Sinbad the Sailor near Muscat, the capital city of the Sultanate of Oman. The customer was an Omani government agency responsible for managing Muscat's two hospitals. Financing was pretty well worked out and all that remained was contract language.

The travel agent had booked them through London's Heathrow terminal which made the total trip about 20 hours, including a layover. The two executives were certain they could wrap up the negotiation in three days and had booked their return flight accordingly. The plane landed at midnight in 100 degree heat. After two more hours of dealing with obstreperous customs and immigration officials and a dusty cab ride to their hotel (which Sara later claimed bred 12-inch roaches as pets), the travelers had a fitful two hours of sleep.

At 7:30 A.M. a driver showed up to take them to the government official's office. Negotiations began by 8:15—but not for Sara. Courteous but firm, the official told Sara she was not allowed in the negotiating room and should wait in the lobby, which had plenty of English magazines (and a part-time working air conditioner). Stunned, Sara complied. At noon the driver returned to take Harry and Sara back to the hotel. No one had bothered telling them that all stores and offices in Muscat closed between noon and 4:00 P.M.

By this time Sara was furious and Harry didn't feel much better. The government official seemed to talk in circles, in broken English, and nothing had been accomplished all morning. After lunch the two Americans decided to spend some time at the hotel pool, but Sara was informed that women were only allowed at the pool between 9:00 A.M. and noon. the afternoon was for men only. By this time Sara was seeing red and told the hotel manager where he could put his hotel, his regulations, and his country. Harry returned alone to negotiate the second shift from 4:00 to 8:00 P.M.

The next two days were just as bad. Harry was unable to resolve even one issue. Sara spent both mornings in a filthy, open-air bazaar near the hotel and afternoons sulking in her room. Friday morning finally arrived and even though negotiations had barely started, Harry and Sara were ready to leave for the airport. After all, they had their return flight already booked for that day. But once again they were uninformed. In Arab countries the sabbath was celebrated on Friday—not Sunday—and of course their driver never showed up. They finally rounded up a taxi.

When they started through customs, an official signaled Harry to wait in a holding room while his passport and exit visa were checked. Sara was led by a leering sergeant to a different room, without any explanation. Five minutes before flight time both travelers were led to the plane through a corridor of machine gun-toting soldiers. Once on the plane Sara burst out crying, "I have never been so humiliated, embarrassed, and frightened. I'll never return to this godforsaken country." Harry didn't feel much better, returning to his boss without a signed contract.

This anecdote might seem harsh, even unreal, but it is a true story. Such episodes occur frequently to Western business travelers who are unversed in the culture, customs, and business practices of the host country. While it is true that many Third World countries have radically different customs than developed nations, the latter can also be difficult for Americans. Horror stories abound from first-time business travelers returning from England, Italy, or France unable to conduct the business they had set out to do. People from other nations might have similar problems traveling to the United States, but few are as naîve as Americans, and few suffer as severe a culture crunch as Americans do. If their goal is to effectively conduct business overseas, American business travelers must learn the basic rules of their host country.

Each culture holds certain conventions, relationships, business practices, and customs sacrosanct. Many are based on religious beliefs. Others emanate from centuries of learning pragmatic survival. Some derive their existence from pressures from the outside world. But all must be adhered to if a person expects to be able to communicate effectively with the local populace. The basic customs, practices, and beliefs affecting business dealings can be grouped under three classifications: people relationships, societal norms, and business protocol. The failure of Harry and Sara to make any progress during their stay in Oman illustrates mistakes they made in each of these areas.

PEOPLE RELATIONSHIPS

With an increasing number of American women earning major roles in business organizations, the number directly involved in global trade is also escalating. Business travel for women is never easy, but internationally it can become a nightmare. American relationship customs seldom hold overseas. Even in the most developed nations of Western Europe, female participation in business practices remains minimal compared to the United States. The interaction between women and men in many business areas continues to reflect what Americans consider antiquated prejudices.

Outside of the United States, Canada, and perhaps the United Kingdom, the women's movement has had little impact in the business community. In Japan, the Philippines, Nicaragua, and a scattering of other nations, women have earned high posts in government. Some have risen to the top. But little progress has been made in the business world compared to the United States. Traditional male/female roles continue to be the norm. Although it is understandably difficult for American businesswomen to accept these out-dated relationships, to flaunt personal business success in most of these countries will only bring misunderstandings and perhaps failure.

American businessmen must also learn a new set of relationship rules when doing business overseas. In many countries women are revered and protected far beyond American customs. The cavalier attitude toward casual male/female relationships in present-day America marks an American male as untrustworthy and perhaps a bit jaded in many Islamic and Asian countries. What may be passable behavior with women in American business circles invariably brings hostility and rejection overseas. Americans of both sexes must learn new relationship rules when conducting business at the global level.

Male/Female Relationships

No one doubts that American women have made significant strides in the business world during the last 20 years. Many are now respected executives and managers of major corporations. Many have contributed significantly to the growth and profitability of American businesses. Though prejudice still exists, increasingly women are attributed their rightful places alongside, or over, their male counterparts.

Few would argue in this day and age that women are just as capable as men to perform virtually any activity. Some would argue that they are far superior in certain disciplines. In a short period of time women have achieved remarkable progress in banking, insurance, advertising, fashion design, public relations, broadcasting, journalism, and many other industries. Also, most men are pleased with women's success and are supportive in that they have succeeded in overcoming prejudices.

On the other hand, just because equality of the sexes exists in America doesn't mean the same is true throughout the world. In fact, there is a wide discrepancy between women's rights in this country and their positions in most of the rest of the world. For example, Sara was upset with her treatment in Oman. She thought she was being discriminated against because of her sex. She was. But not with malice. In Oman, Saudi Arabia, Iran, Iraq, Libya, North Yemen, Morocco, and many other Islamic countries, women are treated with the utmost respect. So much respect, that they are not allowed in environments where their reputations or character could be sullied.

Business is considered a man's world. Raising children and taking care of the living quarters, female work. Women's faces and their bodies are afforded the utmost respect and for this reason they are not allowed to bathe, swim, or to be seen, other than fully clothed, by strange, unknown men. So when Sara was not allowed to attend negotiations, and when she was not allowed at the pool with Harry, these rules were in deference to her honored position as a woman, not because of any put-down or disrespect.

It doesn't do any good for American women to object to this treatment. When in Rome, do as the Romans do. Like it or not. In the global community the sooner Americans learn that their way is not always the only way, the faster they will achieve a global mentality.

On my first trip to Saudi, I committed just the reverse blunder. One morning with a couple of hours to kill, I wandered into an open-air food market in Jizan, a small desert town near the North Yemen border. Thinking it was a good opportunity to pick up some fresh fruit to bring back to the project camp, I tried to negotiate with one of the vendors. When I had ventured into the market it was teeming with women, all busily chattering and carrying on with the stall vendors.

As I moved through the throngs, and especially when I began talking to the vendor, I noticed a strange quiet come over the crowd. The vendor wouldn't answer me but he did break out in a wide smile, and soon laughter. He finally made it clear that I didn't belong in the market. This was a woman's place and it was a woman's job to purchase the foodstuffs. Confused and sheepish, I was escorted out of the market by the vendor. Needless to say, I never again tried to buy from an open market in Saudi, or in any Arab state for that matter.

The feminist movement has not reached Latin America, the Middle East, parts of the Indian subcontinent and Southeast Asia, nor many countries in Africa. Anyone doing business in these regions of the world should be certain they know the male/female rules or they will surely stumble.

First-time female business travelers will always be accepted more readily if they do not travel alone. A male business associate is the best choice, if possible. Otherwise two women from the same office should travel together.

Sexual Mores

Published guides to help Americans cope with overseas travel and international trade tend to ignore variations in sexual mores as a crucial element in global success. Yet more American men and women fall prey to faux pas in this area of cultural differences than any other.

The predominance of Judeo-Christian ethics and democratic capitalism have fostered an American culture founded on the rights of the individual, male or female, to act according to personal desires. Divorce, birth control and abortion, casual sex, pornography, and sexual polygamy spring from the individual's right to self-determination. In the global community, however, individual rights and desires are often restricted by government decree or social norms. As a visitor to a foreign country, the violation of acceptable behavior patterns makes it impossible to be effective in business transactions.

While over 50 percent of American marriages end in divorce, the number is closer to 10 percent in Europe, and less than 1 percent in the Far East and Latin America. The family remains an important aspect of social life in nearly every country except in the United States. When a divorced American flaunts this fact in front of Argentinians, Japanese, Italians, or East Indians, business transactions very often fall apart. More progress can be reached by remaining mute on the subject.

Similarly, in many countries married women are treated with great respect while single Western females are looked upon as targets for improper advances. In several South American countries a woman sitting by herself, or even with another woman at a bar, is considered fair game. A male companion signals marriage, or at least "stay away," to local Casanovas.

Birth control and abortion are seldom discussed openly overseas. In some countries birth control and abortion are both prohibited, as in Romania prior to the recent revolution. In other countries, birth control is actively encouraged by the government, as in China. Predominately Catholic nations in Latin America frown on either. In several African nations, the more children a woman bears the higher her social status—but never out of wedlock.

Casual sex as practiced in the United States is verboten in most Third World countries and in the Far East. In many parts of America, casual sex between unmarried people is frequently acceptable behavior or at least acknowledged as a widespread practice. Overseas, such a practice can often cloak a woman in the veil of an outcast and degrade a man's honor. In most Middle East countries unescorted women are not allowed on the streets or in restaurants. In many Latin countries public displays of affection are frowned upon. In the Far East, open touching—holding hands, hugging, kissing—between men and women is regarded as demeaning, tasteless, and embarrassing to observers.

On the other hand, in many Western European countries such as England, the Netherlands, Germany, and Denmark, casual sex is not only acceptable behavior but licensed by the government. Although local custom does not frown on casual sex, it is never openly discussed or practiced in formal business dealings.

Pornography is generally considered distasteful in most non-European societies. When traveling to the Middle East, the mere possession of locally defined pornography can bring prison terms. On my first trip to Tripoli, Libya, from Rome, I picked up an Alitalia Airline magazine that included an article I wanted to finish in my hotel room. Upon searching my briefcase, the customs inspector saw the magazine, thumbed through it, noticed an article about a beach in Sardinia with a photograph of a girl in a modest swimsuit, and the fireworks began. My briefcase and luggage were dumped on the floor, my passport was confiscated, and of course the magazine disappeared. Only a last minute intervention by a Chinese business partner saved me from experiencing first hand the *luxury* of a Libyan jail.

With some exceptions, the Judeo-Christian culture sanctifies monogamous male/female relationships. This is not always the case overseas. In Arab states it is not uncommon for a man to have several wives. The same holds true in several central and western African republics. It can be perfectly acceptable behavior for a Colombian or Ecuadorian male to have several sexual encounters while supporting a single wife and family. On the other hand, it is never acceptable for a woman to have anything other than a monogamous relationship.

While understanding a country's sexual mores might seem to be beyond the scope of a global mentality, it is not. Most foreigners visiting or doing business in the United States are careful to grasp which sexual mores are acceptable and which are not in American culture. The same should be true when Americans deal in the world markets. The more one understands about a host country and its cultural sanctions, the more successful that person will be in business transactions. Figure 4–1 lists major relationship points valid for Americans conducting business anywhere in the world.

SOCIETAL NORMS

Many attitudes and beliefs of Americans emanate from our constitutional heritage. The individual right to religious freedom and the separation of church and state, for example. Others have been legislated either through the courts or by Congress. The banning of discrimination because of race, color, creed, or sex has been upheld by the U.S. Supreme Court time and again. Congressional legislation against smoking in public places and the criminalization of illegal drugs are well-known laws. Still other customs have evolved by public acceptance over the years. En-

FIGURE 4–1
Relationship Protocol

Do

1. Extend traditional courtesies.
2. Graciously accept traditional courtesies.
3. Travel with a companion, if you are a woman.
4. Wear a wedding band..
5. Emphasize strong family ties.

Don't

1. Criticize a male-dominant society
2. Emphasize the role of American women in business.
3. Express opinions on birth control and/or abortion.
4. Talk about or express opinions pro divorce.
5. Engage in casual sex.
6. Carry magazines, books, or pictures advocating sexual freedom.
7. Criticize polygamous cultures.
8. Display affection in public.

glish as the national language and proper dress codes for business and in public places, for example.

Just as Americans have their own lifestyles and customs, so do citizens of other countries. Many have some of the same customs as Americans; in others, laws and customs are radically different. To be successful in the global sphere, an American businessperson must take the time and make the effort to comprehend the societal norms of any country in which business will be conducted. And then these norms must be followed. The "ugly American" already has a bad global image to live down. Businesspeople can do a great deal to help erase the perception.

Religion, Creed, and Color

Americans have generally been brought up to honor religious freedom and racial equality. Our Constitution and Bill of Rights speak to these freedoms. Our courts have consistently ruled in favor of freedom to practice openly any religion we choose. Our federal courts and legislature have mandated racial equality in every walk of American life. Sometimes we forget the value of such freedom. All it takes to appreciate how great these freedoms really are, however, is to experience first hand the cultures of many Third World and authoritarian countries.

To this day, a passport with an Israeli stamp, or a Jewish sounding name, will keep a traveler out of most Islamic countries. For many years, black Americans were not welcome in South Africa. White European or American citizens still get hassled by customs officials, the police, and hotel and restaurant owners in many countries in central Africa. Hispanics continue to be denigrated in some Caribbean countries.

Because a certain nation practices bigotry shouldn't dissuade Americans from doing business there, however. Social activists have tried for years, somewhat successfully, to prevent Americans from conducting business in South Africa, but they still do. Currently, there is a hue and cry against American firms doing business with China, but they still do. American tax regulations penalize firms complying with Arab boycott rules against the Israelis, but boycotts continue.

Clearly the choice is up to the individual whether to do business with nations practicing unsavory racial or religious policies. The fact remains, however, that to be truly global, a company must look at markets that present the best opportunities for competitive advantage. And that means that a business owner or manager must understand and comply with the religious and racial customs of the host country if he plans to do business there.

Language and Dress Idiosyncrasies

It is definitely not necessary to learn the language of every nationality involved in the global market. It isn't even necessary, though at times it can be desirable to know more than the English language. Knowledge of Spanish, French, German, Italian, Russian, or Japanese is helpful, but not required. English is and will probably remain the universal language of global business. In those few instances when a knowledge of a local language or dialect is crucial, interpreters can always be found.

On the other hand, to successfully engage in international trade, a person should come to grips with some of the basic phrases and words of the host country, just to smooth the waters in business dealings and social meetings. A few words in Spanish or Portuguese will get a person by in most of Latin American. Some catch Japanese phrases and names will suffice in Japan. A few French phrases seem to serve fairly well throughout Western Europe. Nothing impresses a host more than an American who has taken the time to learn some basic words in his native tongue. It almost always pays off.

Local dress codes are more crucial to business success, especially for women. Short skirts, sheer blouses, and tight sweaters are always in poor taste and universally frowned upon. A conservative, clean-cut business suit is always acceptable. Shorts, halters, or T-shirts should never be worn away from the beach in Latin-American or Southeast Asian countries. Modestly long summer dresses are the preference.

Women are universally respected providing they look and dress the part, and don't encourage male advances. Slacks or pants of any kind should be left at home. Because of local laws or customs they might not always be allowed to participate in certain business dealings, but women are always respected.

Men, on the other hand, usually have to earn respect through business acumen and appropriate appearance. Business suits are always appropriate in temperate climates. Slacks and a dress shirt, without tie or coat is appropriate attire south of the border. Typically American leisure clothes such as loud sport shirts, shorts, or tennis garb are verboten everywhere in the world, except the United States.

Unisex look-alike fashions have not infiltrated the rest of the world. In the business realm, women should always look feminine and men should look masculine. Both should always give the appearance that they are there on business, not as tourists.

For leisure-time activities, both men and women should avoid bikini swimsuits. Women should always dress for dinner. In warm climates long dresses are the mode of the day. Men should wear coats and ties for dinner except in warm climates when open-neck sport shirts and slacks are acceptable. In Latin America, popular Guayabera shirts take the place of coats and ties for more formal wear.

Smoking, Liquor, and Drugs

Except for regulated America, a man can smoke cigarettes, cigars, or a pipe anywhere in the world. Women are more restricted. In European countries it's OK: in the Middle East it's not. Women in New Guinea and Borneo smoke but most men don't—even though it's permitted. Latin-American countries don't care one way or the other, although in some situations it is impolite for a lady to smoke. Other than in some Middle East countries, smoking per se is generally ignored. Airplanes, hotels, restaurants, office buildings, government offices, and nearly every other public place allows smoking without regard to who or where they do it. Apparently the intense concern regarding antismoking so prevalent in America has not yet infected the global community. The only real restrictions are how many cigarettes a person can take through customs, and that varies with each country.

Liquor and drugs are another matter entirely. Throughout Southeast Asia, including parts of the Indian subcontinent and China, opium remains the drug of choice. Although illegal in many areas, its use continues. Foreigners are usually welcome to partake if they can find a den. Marijuana, cocaine, heroin, and other mind-altering drugs are not predominant either in the Orient or in the rest of the world. Even though many of the local populace in South and Central America smoke marijuana, in Turkey shoot heroin, and in Europe use anything available, an American bringing drugs into or out of a foreign country risks imprisonment nearly anywhere in the world. Everyone knows how closely most customs officials look for drugs.

In the world of international business, drugs are not prevalent. As a matter of fact, marijuana and cocaine usage remains far more common in the American business community than overseas. Regardless of a person's individual beliefs about drugs, none should ever be carried while traveling overseas. Discussions about drugs should be avoided. Most international businesspeople believe that taking drugs slows their mental faculties, and business is too important to lose a battle because of a foggy mind. It's also good practice to decline their use if offered after business hours. A person will never be chastised for not partaking: he may if he imbibes.

Liquor is trickier. In many countries, alcoholic beverage consumption is far greater than in the United States—even in business circles. Wines are a staple in France, beer and whiskey in Germany, beer, gin, and scotch whiskey in England, saki in Japan, rum and Mexican beer in the Caribbean, local wines and beer in South America, and so on. It's difficult to do business overseas without running into alcohol at least once a day. The exception, and its' a strong exception, is anywhere in the Arab states. Under Islamic law, liquor is forbidden. To consume any alcohol, or even to have it in one's possession, is a serious crime punishable by imprisonment. Obviously a smart business traveler will not carry any alcohol in luggage or a briefcase when traveling to the Middle East.

It goes without saying that overconsumption of alcohol—drunkenness—must be avoided at all costs. It's all right for a host to get intoxicated; it's not all right for an American guest to do the same. American businesspeople are expected, the world over, to be on their best behavior at all times. They represent the most powerful country in the world. An American businessperson who falls down drunk is, in the eyes of a foreigner, insulting his or her own homeland. And that is bad.

The Double Standard

We frequently criticize ourselves for practicing double standards in the American culture; that is, different standards for men and women, for whites and minorities, for labor and management, for rich and poor. Many other countries practice double standards far more diligently than Americans. Double standards relating to male/female relationships, religious and racial bigotry, and natives and foreigners have already been examined. The biggest discrepancies, however, seem to be between the *haves* and the *have-nots*.

In Latin America, Pacific Basin countries, Africa, the Middle East, Eastern Europe, the Soviet Union, Caribbean and Central American countries, and even in several Western European cultures, a middle class as we know it in America doesn't exist. Two-class systems predominate; that is, educated business and government officials and uneducated, impoverished workers and peasants.

The cultural and moral practices of the elite class differ little from those Americans accept as normal. However, differences do exist in how openly subjects such as divorce, abortion, birth control, casual sex, and substance abuse are discussed. In the United States such topics appear in newspaper headlines and TV broadcasts. In most other countries they are kept private.

These same societal norms for the working classes differ markedly, however. Religious and cultural barriers restrict such activities to those regarded as inferior, or outcasts. When public disclosure brings such activities to light for someone in the elite class, cries of indiscretion ring out. When the same cultural aberrations are practiced by a person in the working class, fines, imprisonment, even death are frequent penalties.

A global mentality dictates that Americans understand these double standards and quickly learn how to deal with them. In the global arena, very often it is not *what* is done, but *how* it is done that influences success or failure in a business transaction.

Figure 4–2 lists the major points commonly practiced for respecting local societal norms.

BUSINESS PROTOCOL

As with people relationships and societal norms, every country practices a different set of rules and customs for conducting business. Many seem outmoded to Western businesspeople. Others appear to be totally unreasonable and even unbusinesslike.

FIGURE 4–2
Societal Norms

Do
1. Make an effort to learn local customs that are different from American.
2. Learn local laws affecting individual rights.
3. Be conscious of racial dissimilarities.
4. Learn a few common phrases in the local language and use them.
5. Dress modestly at all times.
6. Follow local customs for business and leisure-time dress codes.
7. Learn how to deal with double standards in cultural practices.

Don't
1. Express opinions about race or color.
2. Express opinions about religious practices or philosophy.
3. Violate racial or religious barriers.
4. Expound American mores about racial or religious equality.
5. Try to converse or conduct business in local language without an interpreter.
6. Smoke in public, if a woman.
7. Overindulge with alcohol.
8. Use drugs of any kind (marijuana, cocaine, heroin, and so on) even if offered.
9. Carry alcohol or drugs in luggage or on person.

In Southeast Asia, for example, most business continues to be conducted under ancient Chinese customs. Family businesses and close familial ties between companies lend a certain mystique to trying to conduct rational business transactions based on profitability and return on investment. Government dictatorships in South America control economic activity from the top. Most officials expect to be personally compensated for arranging meetings, granting licenses, and other activities. Monarchical governments in the Middle East cling to traditional *handshake* contracts. When broken, imprisonment or even death can be the punishment.

The American businessperson in these countries must learn what protocol is expected before entering into a business transaction. Too many have not done this and been forced to retrench. Even the largest corporations make this mistake. Hewlett-Packard, Quaker Oats, and ITT are a few examples of major corporations failing in global transactions because their representatives did not understand local business protocol. Perhaps the most difficult non-American custom to accept has to do with time constraints.

Schedules and Time

American businesspeople are always in a hurry, as anyone can observe during the noon hour at Broad and Wall Streets, 57th and Fifth Avenue, Madison Avenue and State Street, or Union Square. Decisions are rapid. Schedules are set and adhered to. The clock controls our business life. When we take a business trip, the travel agency always writes round-trip tickets for returning flights. When meetings are called for 9:00 A.M., attendance is expected at that time. If the parties to a business luncheon for 1:00 P.M. don't show up until 1:30, their table is given to someone else. If a person misses the 6:04 commuter train and gets to the office half an hour late, the boss has a fit. Time limits, schedules, appointment commitments, and regulated days seem to dignify promptness and penalize tardiness. Perhaps this rat race has something to do with the high incidence of ulcers, heart attacks, and nervous breakdowns in the United States.

In the global economy such hustle and bustle is generally unheard of. Northern Europeans are the exception. Germans, especially, are noted for their punctuality. And yes, there are occasions when train, plane, and conference schedules must be met just to keep things moving. But in most cases, business is conducted at a much slower pace than in America.

> The point was brought home clearly during my first trip to the other side of the globe. I had arranged a meeting with a bank manager in Colombo, the capital of Sri Lanka to negotiate a construction loan for a hotel development project on the island nation. The flight from New York took 22 hours and I lost track of the time zones. The meeting was set for 10 A.M. the morning after my arrival the night before.
>
> Somehow I dragged myself out of bed and strode into the bank office at 9:55. The manager showed up at 1:30—just in time for lunch. I was furious but controlled my temper. "Good afternoon Mr. Tuller," was his opening remark. "I checked the airport and noticed your flight didn't arrive until 2100 hours. I didn't expect you at my office until tomorrow. My German friends are the only people I know who keep their appointments on time. Most travelers from the States require at least 24 hours to recuperate." Needless to say I postponed my return flight, returned to the hotel and slept for 24 hours.

There are three rules that nearly every seasoned international business traveler follows (except harried Americans who seem to insist on following New York rules):

- When a trip takes more than four hours flight time, never attend a business meeting without at least eight hours sleep.
- Expect the other parties to a meeting or appointment to be late, prepare for it mentally, and don't get upset.
- When conducting business overseas, never schedule a return flight until after arrival in the host country. Have a return ticket, but keep it open.

Negotiating Protocol

Most international business transactions require some type of negotiation. Price, delivery, financing, payment terms, performance standards, and so on are frequently negotiated on a case-by-case basis. Whether these negotiations are conducted in the United States or overseas, negotiating with non-American businesspeople is a different ball game. To effectively conduct a negotiation overseas, observing the following protocol almost always results in a satisfactory conclusion.

THE TEN RULES OF NEGOTIATION

1. *Location.*   If in the United States or your facility overseas, negotiate in a formal office. If on the opponent's territory, let your

host choose the location such as his office, hotel lobby, restaurant, or airport lounge.

2. *Equal numbers on team.*   Be sure to have the same number of participants as your opponent, and with the same qualifications; such as lawyers, accountants, engineers, and marketing people.

3. *Ending time.*   Do not establish an ending time for negotiations. If you planned on three days and it extends into three weeks, let it be.

4. *Courtesy.*   Always be supercourteous, regardless of the demeanor of your opponent. If he gets angry or excited, stay cool and calm. Be unflappable.

5. *Don't be in a hurry.*   Set a starting time, but if the meeting begins later, let it happen. Each day should begin with lots of small talk. Let your opponent decide when to begin negotiating. Be patient.

6. *Maintain your position.*   Don't try to maneuver from one negotiating position to another. Don't start with a high number expecting to come down. Don't begin with onerous terms expecting to restate your position later on. Once a position is taken, stick to your guns.

7. *Clarify the meaning of words and phrases.*   American clichés are just as confusing to the other party as his colloquialisms and language idiosyncrasies are to you. Clarify the meaning of every word that may cause confusion later on. Reduce each point agreed upon to writing.

8. *Keep it formal.*   Do not maintain an informal atmosphere. Wear appropriate business attire. Do not become jovial, humorous, or light hearted. Stick to business.

9. *Socialize while negotiating.*   If your opponent suggests dinner, the theater, lunch, or other social events agree. It probably means he wants to negotiate in a less formal atmosphere. But be careful of becoming too relaxed. If the social event is in the United States or in your location overseas, you pay. If it's the reverse, let your opponent pay.

10. *Don't oversell.*   When negotiations are completed leave. If you feel you've come out ahead, don't get the big head. Imply that there will always be a next time. Be humble. If you are unhappy, don't show it. Let the negotiation end when it ends.

Following these rules won't win every negotiation, but adherence to them will enhance the chances for success.

Legal Requirements

Trying to get something accomplished that violates the laws of a host country sounds obtuse. However, dogmatic, profit-oriented Americans often forget this simple rule. We wouldn't expect a Pakistani to start up a business in Massachusetts without obtaining a license to do business in the state and filing for a federal E.I.N number. When an American starts a business in Pakistan he must be aware of, and comply with, the laws of that country. Each country has its own peculiar laws affecting businesses. Some require work permits and visas, others don't. Some prohibit hiring labor from outside of the country, others encourage the practice. Many require a business license, a few don't.

Every country has its own peculiar labor laws—some written, some informal. In Trinidad, for instance, labor unions are very popular. Foreigners starting up a business or a project normally employ a labor consultant to avoid problems with the union. Banking laws, currency exchange and repatriation laws, and tax laws differ with each country.

The most bothersome and misunderstood laws, however, generally have to do with individual rights. Under what conditions can a foreigner be put in jail, or thrown out of the country? Possession of pornography, as seen earlier, is just cause in several Arab states. Theft of property can cause lengthy incarceration in many countries. In Saudi Arabia the amputation of fingers and hands can be enforced as punishment.

In many regions of the world, women's rights are significantly different from the United States. In the Congo and Angola, women cannot own property. In most Arab states women have no voice in the government. Until recently, women were not allowed to vote or hold office in Pakistan. In Morocco, women can be sentenced to death for having an extramarital affair.

When considering an overseas investment in a business or development project, or even when conducting negotiations, a thorough grasp of the laws as they affect business dealings and individual rights is crucial.

Business Etiquette

In addition to the points already covered dealing with schedules and time, negotiating strategy, male/female relationships, and managing alcohol and drugs, there are four major topics of business etiquette that should be recognized when involved in the global community.

- Courteous conduct.
- Accepting and giving gifts.
- Eating and drinking.
- Body language, color, and slang.

While most of us appreciate interacting with anyone who treats us with common courtesy, most of us are not too quick to reciprocate. We are even less apt to initiate a courteous gesture, word, or action. Business manners tend to be forgotten in the race to succeed in a competitive business climate.

This is a major error when living and doing business in the global community. Good basic manners, polite conversation, and courteous actions always encourage the same in return. Amicable relationships tend to be smoother and more advantageous to everyone involved. A brusque, self-centered attitude nearly always creates animosity and friction. When people of two diverse cultures try to conduct a business transaction to benefit both parties, courtesy on both sides can ease an already difficult situation.

Exchanging gifts is a little more difficult to manage. Americans have been indoctrinated by bribery scandals and the Foreign Corrupt Practices Act against giving or accepting a gift in connection with any business dealing. This makes doing business overseas extremely awkward. Nearly all businesspeople in all parts of the world (except the United States) expect to give and receive gifts in appreciation for courtesies rendered. It doesn't have to be an expensive gift—although sometimes it is. Usually a classy bottle of champagne or liquor, a gold pen and pencil set, or a set of earrings for the boss's wife is sufficient. But there must be something.

In most global circles it is considered extremely rude and unbusinesslike to refuse a gift—whatever it may be. It is just as rude not to reciprocate—regardless of what our congressional leaders say. To be successful in the global arena, a way must be found to give and receive gifts gracefully, and still remain within the law. It's always done, and probably always will be.

A third problem many Americans have when doing business abroad is dealing with the local food and drink customs. A person raised on steak and potatoes usually has difficulty with raw fish and oysters. An orthodox Jew can't eat pork. Regardless of background, most Americans have trouble swallowing the eyeball of a goat, which is exactly what happened to a good friend of mine. Derek, an executive with Northrop Corporation, was sent to Iran to supervise the construction and opening of a new aircraft manufacturing plant that resulted from a countertrade agreement between Northrop and the Shah's government.

On the opening night, his Iranian hosts invited Derek to a ceremonial dinner. As guest of honor, Derek sat at the head of a long table with 30 Iranian business and government officials. The waiter placed the appetizer in front of Derek. Closing both eyes and tilting his head back, Derek gulped the eyeball so fast he didn't taste it.

Hopefully, most people will not be required to swallow goat eyeballs, but other local delicacies will undoubtedly be presented from time to time. Though it is always possible to refuse, the time inevitably arrives when such a refusal will be taken as an insult and a business deal lost. Developing a global mentality means more than merely addressing business transactions!

The final topic of etiquette is often the most difficult to deal with because the rules of the game are not spelled out. Body language, slang words, and idioms, even plain vanilla English words have different connotations and meanings in different countries. There are even differences between the Queen's English and Americanese. A car trunk in America is a boot in England. Gasoline is petrol. A traffic circle is a roundabout. In America you pay your check in a restaurant. In England you pay the bill. Beer and scotch here are lager and whiskey across the pond. And a truck is a lorry. If Americans and their British cousins can't agree on the same language, what hope is there to understand the rest of the world?

Writing dates can cause all kinds of problems. In America, 7/10/90 means July 10, 1990. In England and Europe it stands for October 7, 1990.

Colors also confuse. In America white symbolizes life and virginity: in Malaysia and Indonesia it means mourning. In several African countries red signifies death, as it does in Turkey. Red means danger in the United States: in India it signifies life.

Global variations in body language could fill an entire book. Bowing means hello and goodbye in Japan. Shaking hands is meaningless. Yes is indicated by shaking the head from side to side in parts of Africa and Asia. Standing in line is unheard of and considered impolite in Latin and Arab countries. The thumbs up sign is pure vulgarity in many Third World countries.

"How are you?" is taken literally throughout Europe and demands a lengthy explanation. "See you around" is also translated literally. Say "This really bugs me" in Micronesia and your host will send for the exterminator. The one common phrase throughout the world, however, that means the same no matter where a person goes, is, "I love you." Don't say it unless you mean to marry.

It's always a good idea to check on local etiquette norms before you leave home. Since that doesn't always help, an even better idea is to be very careful with what you say and how you say it, as well as what you wear and how you hold yourself. When all else fails ask your host what a word, gesture, or color, means to him. It's always preferable to admit ignorance rather than commit a faux pas.

Adversary versus Cooperative

The American form of democratic capitalism implies an adversary relationship between labor and management, government and the public, financial institutions and business enterprises, and above all, between competitors. Whereas adversary competitiveness may work in the United States (although many believe this is the principal cause of impending doom), it will not fly throughout the global community. Adversary competitiveness occasionally arises in socialist capitalism, such as practiced in England, France, Germany, and Australia. It is the antithesis of good business practice in Japan, the Eastern Bloc, the Middle East, India, Southeast Asia, and most of Africa. In these cultures, oligopolistic and social welfare states promote cooperative relations within the business and government spheres.

Everything considered, this is probably the major difference between the way business is conducted in the United States and the way it is done in the rest of the world. This dichotomy is also the root cause of much of the difficulty Americans have in adjusting to business practices in other nations.

To achieve a true global mentality American business owners and managers must recognize this difference in cultural styles. They must structure policies and strategies to incorporate both forms in an integrated model. It is crucial to achieve this integration because only in a cooperative model, tempered by a competitive, aggressive spirit can American business begin to stress long-term achievements rather than short-term gains.

To match the Japanese, and soon the Germans, businesses must be

FIGURE 4–3
Business Protocol

Do
1. Understand local business practices in advance.
2. Keep your word.
3. Be patient, slow down.
4. Be courteous at all times.
5. Follow the Ten Rules of Negotiation.
6. Comprehend and follow local laws.
7. Accept and give gifts graciously.
8. Learn the local slang.

Don't
1. Make promises you can't keep.
2. Try to stay on schedule.
3. Carry a return flight reservation.
4. Conduct business the first 24 hours after arrival in a country.
5. Refuse local dishes if offered.
6. Become an adversary.

more concerned with global market share and long-term capital formation than with short-term earnings per share and dividend payments. An integration of cooperation and adversary aggressiveness should provide an unbeatable combination to achieve these ends. By integrating the best of both worlds, American small and midsize businesses should be able to more than hold their own in the global economy. Figure 4–3 outlines the major points of business protocol.

TIPS ON INTERNATIONAL TRAVEL

Every frequent traveler has horror stories to tell about near misses in the air, crazies on the plane, lost luggage, hotel reservations that vanished, and many more. Frequent international travelers seem to have these experiences and them some, such as bribing a customs inspector in Ghana with a gold pen, or getting drunk on two martinis and a bottle of wine crossing the Atlantic, or a lost engine causing a diversion to Guam on the way to Tokyo, or being too ill to get out of bed during a three-day stay in Tanzania, or arriving home in Chicago while the luggage finally showed up in Cairo, Egypt. International travel is a never-ending tale of woe. The more experienced one becomes, the worse it seems to get. A 5-hour trip from New York to Los Angeles is duck soup compared to 25 hours to Bombay.

Experienced international travelers have all sorts of tricks and gimmicks to cope with long flights, stifling airports, horse roaches in hotels, and rancid food. Following are a few tips I can offer from years of trying to find a way to survive a truly global headache.

TRAVEL TIPS FOR SURVIVAL

1. Schedule a flight to arrive in the evening. Airlines seem to think people prefer to fly all night so they can work the next day. This is crazy. There is usually at least one daytime flight from New

York to Europe. South America is less of a problem. The Far East is too far to matter.

2. Sleep at least 24 hours after arrival. Don't leave the hotel, and by all means, don't conduct any business for the first 24 hours.

3. Don't drink alcohol or eat heavy meals while flying. Both will rob energy and potential sleep.

4. Try to use only carryon luggage. Overseas airlines object to this, but be creative. As a minimum, carry enough to get you through three days. The odds are high it will take at least that long to get the baggage back from Antarctica.

5. Carry your own medicine chest. A letter, duly notarized and officially stamped from your doctor will get the drugs through customs. Include lots of aspirin, band-aids, insect repellent, calamine lotion, sunscreen oil, scissors, gauze, tape, safety pins, rubber bands, and paper clips—also some glue.

6. Be sure to get all recommended vaccinations before you leave home—and some for preventive medicine that are not recommended. Carry an IAMA vaccination card and a booklet from IAMA listing names, addresses, and phone numbers of recommended English-speaking doctors in all countries.

7. Carry an international driver's license (available from your state motor vehicle bureau).

8. Don't drink tap water, anywhere, for the first two days, regardless of who says it's potable. Use bottled water, even to brush your teeth. Also stay away from local milk.

9. Don't eat seafood if you are going inland. Don't eat meat anywhere in the world for the first two days—unless it's frozen and imported from the United States or New Zealand. Don't eat fresh fruits and vegetables in a Third World country. Do drink local beer, wine, and liquor—they are much safer than local water.

10. Carry mosquito repellent and roach food to the Third World.

11. Always carry on your person a written letter explaining who you are and who to contact in the local country and at home in case of emergency. It should also list any medicine you are allergic to or drugs you cannot take, along with blood type and any other information someone might need if you are incapacitated.

12. Always have room reservations for that night before you leave the plane. Check ahead to find out how much the approximate taxi fare will be to your hotel. Be prepared to negotiate with local taxi drivers who don't speak English.

13. Try to carry a small amount of host country currency with you from home.

14. Convert only a minimum amount of dollars to local currency at the arriving airport. Banks have much better exchange rates.

15. Contrary to American Express advertisements, always carry some good old American dollars—in addition to traveler's checks.

16. THIS IS THE MOST IMPORTANT TIP OF ALL. Carry dollars, coins, gold pens, cigarettes, and inexpensive jewelery to bribe

customs officials in Third World airports. This is essential. Forget your morals and what Uncle Sam says. Bribes are a way of life overseas. In many countries it's the only way to get out of the airport.

With these tips anyone should be able to survive at least a few weeks in any country in the world. As you get more experienced, other steps will become obvious.

One final word about business travel overseas. There is nothing that denigrates an American business traveler more than appearing to be a tourist. Forget the sights and sounds of a strange new world. A business traveler is there to do business. Get the business out of the way first and then take time to see the sights. Most hosts are more than eager to show off their country, providing the business transactions have been completed. The country bumpkin who comes to New York for the first time and keeps staring at the skyscrapers until he gets hit by a taxi is definitely not the impression a global businessperson wants to portray.

SECTION II

GETTING READY TO GO GLOBAL

CHAPTER 5

PRIORITIZING GLOBAL MARKETS

MAJOR TOPICS

KEY POINTS

1. **Developed and Developing Countries.** Identifies countries that fall under each of four classifications: developed, newly emerging or Third World, those previously under communist domination, and totalitarian regimes still closed to global trade.

2. **Free Market versus Government-Controlled Economy.** Analyzes the pros and cons of doing business in free, social welfare, and tightly controlled markets. Market characteristics and potential for U.S. investment are described, along with probable risks.

3. **Markets and Competition.** A market grouping matrix lists 19 broad product classifications. The matrix shows the highest probability of success for each of the product classifications in each of three market classifications, and China. Infrastructure projects in developing nations attract special attention.

4. **Government Policies.** Trade barriers might restrict the importation of materials or labor. Conversely, governments may offer subsidies to attract investment. American policies place restrictions on the export and import of certain products and specific countries. The Arab boycott of Israel presents peculiar problems. Policies concerning trade with China are ambivalent. The U.S. government encourages trade with Caribbean nations.

5. **Macromarket Checklist.** A checklist helps quantify and prioritize political and economic factors influencing decisions to enter global trade.

> The CEO of a $20 million metal furniture manufacturer began our meeting with the following dissertation. "I've been reading about global markets and international trade and I certainly agree that's the way to go for the future. My company has exported a small amount to Europe over the past few years and it looks like our next step should be our own foreign manufacturing plant. I don't think Europe is the best place for us, though. Too much competition from other furniture manufacturers. Japan, the Caribbean, Argentina, West Africa, and India seem to be viable choices, but I don't know enough about these areas to make a commitment. And what about financing, communications, the stability of the local governments, and local business practices? I'm not going to jump into anything without more information."
>
> Listening patiently, I finally suggested that there were plenty of sources of information he could use, but before embarking on lengthy, and costly, data gathering sojourns, we should analyze the pros and cons of some of the blossoming global markets in terms of his company's objectives. This chapter describes the analytic approach we used to advance to the next rung in deciding to become a major player in international trade.

All global markets are not advantageous for all businesses. The media would like us to believe that everyone should jump on the EC bandwagon. The federal government would like companies to invest in Eastern European economies. President Bush favors China as a new market for American private industry. The IRS wants companies to stick with countries already in the TIEA fold. Large American banks would like to see private investment flow into Latin-American countries to bail them out of their debt crises. General Motors and Chrysler see Japan as the place to put their money.

On the other hand, Union Carbide probably rues the day it ever ventured into the Indian subcontinent. ITT couldn't figure out how to stay competitive in European telecommunications. Westinghouse's gas turbine division finally gave up trying to compete with German and Italian firms in the Middle East. United Fruit took a beating in Guatemala, and Anaconda is sorry they ever tried to do business in Chile.

Conflicting directions from Washington bureaucrats, both good and bad experiences of multinational corporations, worldwide political and social unrest, and enormous changes in the global economy expected in the next decade, leave the small or midsize company in a quandary when trying to assess opportunities in international trade.

How does a company determine which market offers the least risk and the greatest opportunity? Frequently the two goals are conflicting. What U.S. government policies affect investment decisions? Where can a company get reliable information about the legal, tax, customs, and licensing requirements of foreign countries? What regions and nations offer the best risk/reward projections? How can a person get the right answers without knowing what questions to ask? In other words, what criteria should be considered in making global decisions? Also where can a company get the detailed information necessary to form intelligent judgments?

This chapter, and those that follow, provide analytic techniques and sources of information to help define the what, where, and how to become a global player, either through exporting or by investing directly in a foreign business, or both. Assuming a company has a choice about which country to invest in or export to (its products are truly global and serve markets in more than one country), the first step should be to establish a set of decision criteria designed to meet the company's objectives.

This can be accomplished by viewing the world market from four dimensions and then weighing the advantages and risks of each:

1. A market-controlled economy versus one which is government controlled.
2. The market demand, market growth potential, and competitive forces for a company's products.
3. Restrictive or supportive U.S. government policies.
4. Host country trade policies.

The evaluation of each of these factors cannot be done independently. Each factor influences actions in the others. In developing an analytic technique, however, dealing with each topic individually clarifies the decision-making process.

A global mentality mandates that a company export to, import from, or make direct investments in those markets providing the best competitive advantage in pricing, deliveries, cost of production, sourcing of materials, and strategic trade-offs. A specific market may not be especially attractive as the focus of an investment, yet to gain strategic global position, such an investment may be required. The Glostar case is a perfect example.

In 1985 Glostar Knitting Mills, a $12 million manufacturer of women's sport sweaters, scarves, caps, and other outerwear decided to confront its Korean competitor head-on. The Korean company, with extremely low labor and overhead costs could sell its exported sweaters in the United States for less than the direct costs at Glostar. Though the CEO and his chief financial officer felt that the Far East market was weak, Glostar decided to meet Korean competition on its home turf.

The American company opened a plant in Seoul and began selling direct to the South Korean and Japanese markets. This competition ate into the Korean competitor's cash flow. Eventually the Korean company was forced to slacken off in the United States and to concentrate its efforts protecting its home markets. Two years later, while addressing a trade group in Boston, the CEO of Glostar commented that if his company had not risked opening their Korean plant, they would probably be out of business in the American market by now.

DEVELOPED AND DEVELOPING COUNTRIES

Western Europe (including Scandinavia), the United Kingdom, Australia, Japan, Canada, South Korea, and Taiwan are considered developed nations. Under certain conditions Israel and South Africa can also be considered as developed, although their special circumstances deny complete entrance to the closed group of industrialized nations. Close relationships between the United States and Canada, including the recent opening of trade barriers and the easing of communications and movement between the two countries, place our northern neighbor in a unique position as well.

Developing countries are more difficult to define. There are really three types of developing nations:

1. Those new or emerging nations commonly referred to as the Third World.
2. Those countries under previous domination by communist governments and closed to Western trade but now emerging as viable trading partners.
3. Those countries continuing under totalitarian rule and remaining closed to global trade.

The Third World includes all of South and Central America, Mexico, the Caribbean nations, most of Africa (except Libya, South Africa, and a few smaller countries under communist domination), the Middle East, the Indian subcontinent, Southeast Asia, and most of the Pacific Basin nations.

The former communist bloc nations are Poland, Czechoslovakia, Hungary, Bulgaria, Romania, Yugoslavia, the USSR, and China—although China requires a somewhat different evaluation than the others. Many of these former communist bloc countries support highly developed economies traceable to the Middle Ages and certainly cannot be considered new or emerging nations.

China remains a basically agrarian economy. If not communist controlled it would be included in the Third World classification. Those countries remaining closed to global trade include Cuba, Albania, Libya, Vietnam, Angola, and a few smaller nations scattered around the world.

The purpose of categorizing countries into these groups (i.e., developed, Third World, former communist bloc, and closed) is to better define the opportunities and hazards for a foreign company entering their markets.

FREE MARKET VERSUS GOVERNMENT-CONTROLLED ECONOMY

A free market economy is really a misnomer. Total freedom to trade doesn't exist in any civilized market. Trade barriers, monopolistic regulations, government subsidies, and politically expedient economic policies, all place restrictions on demand, supply, the movement of goods, prices, and the role of imports and exports. The enormous political clout exercised by Fortune 100 corporations, trade unions, and other special interest groups preclude the United States from ever having a free market economy.

Democratic capitalism, however, does foster markets as close to free as possible in our current definition of a civilized world. Several European economies have come close to free markets at one time or another: France before Mitterrand nationalized its major industries; Germany, except for American political meddling and financial regulations imposed by the Bunderstaat; Great Britain, once the privatization of previously nationalized industries is accomplished; Canada and Australia, except for socialist subsidies and remaining trade barriers.

From the perspective of entering and competing in the global economy, one should look at all markets as being government controlled to some degree. The major differences are in the types of controls, the degree of enforcement, and the penalties exacted. The next two chapters look at the predominant economic characteristics of each of the major markets of the world. Therefore, an in-depth analysis here would be redundant. General parameters can be constructed, however, under each of the captions listed above.

Developed Nations

Developed or Western industrialized nations are certainly the easiest to do business with for a small or midsize company. Language synergism (or at least familiarity) fosters negotiating procedures and other selling methods not dissimilar to American tactics. Effective communication networks enable rapid, clear transfer of information. Nominal travel and work restrictions, sophisticated global banking and financial systems, and hard currency make doing business with, and in, these countries relatively straightforward.

Most developed nations tend toward social welfare economies. Economic activity is controlled by a relatively small number of suppliers. In some nations, such as Italy and France, the largest suppliers are government owned; for example, transportation companies, basic industries providing steel, coal, and oil, the communications industry, and so on. In other countries, such as Canada, Australia, and Great Britain, oligopolistic industries are being privatized. Regardless of ownership, however, a social welfare economy whose main thrust is to provide for, and safeguard, the social well-being of its populace places limitations on competition from major foreign suppliers.

On the other hand, an oligopolistic social welfare state, intent on owning and managing those companies with a major impact on social programs, leaves the competitive door open to an array of noncritical industries. These markets offer unusual opportunities for smaller firms. Nearly all nonmilitary, high-tech industries remain open to private enterprise. Consumer products continue to be supplied by a host of smaller companies. Machine tools, agricultural equipment, and health care products and equipment are a few of the many industries open to market competition.

A number of American companies have been successful in competing effectively in Japan with consumable products such as foodstuffs, pharmaceuticals, cosmetics, and health care supplies. Japan is certainly a premier oligopolistic economy. Smaller foreign electronics, electrical, and plumbing suppliers have successfully opened manufacturing and distribution facilities in Great Britain, Belgium, and the Scandinavian countries.

The policy of keeping social support industries in the government fold has enabled smaller foreign companies to compete more effectively in submarkets than if these industries were privatized. Although government-owned companies tend to be cumbersome and weighted down with bureaucracy, once a supplier learns how to penetrate the veil of self-serving bureaucratic protectionism, selling to these behemoths can be extremely profitable. Under government subsidies, prices are usually higher and margins wider than in a free market economy.

The advantages and risks of doing business in or with developed nations can be summarized as follows:

Advantages:

1. Language symmetry.
2. Familiar marketing procedures.
3. Relatively open travel and work laws.
4. Modern banking systems.
5. Hard currency.
6. Large market for nonmilitary hardware, consumer goods, high-tech products, machine tools, agricultural equipment, health care products.

Disadvantages:

1. Limited competition within nationalized industries.
2. Cumbersome bureaucracies with which to contend.
3. Extensive competition from large multinational corporations.
4. Heavy competition from Japan and other developed nations.
5. High cost of labor and, in some cases, overhead structures.

The Third World

If Western Europe can be defined as oligopolistic, the Third World carries the emblem of monarchistic or socialistic. Most of these poorer nations go a step further than oligopolies. Government bureaucracies exert significant influence over which companies are allowed to compete in which markets within their borders. Stringent price controls, market entry requirements, and compliance reporting dictate a different approach when selling to these markets. Many countries require majority government ownership of private companies. Payoffs, kickbacks, and bribes are commonplace. Local partners are frequently necessary to cut through bureaucratic red tape.

On the other hand, because these nations require such a vast array of imported goods and services, opportunities for both exporting and direct investments are greater than with developed nations. Third World countries are either rich, such as the Middle East and Southeast Asian oil nations, or poor, as in most of South and Central America. Demand for external goods and services remains high throughout the Third World, however. Between the International Monetary Fund and the World Bank (both of which rely principally on U.S. funding) and the U.S. government itself, financing imports or supporting direct investments is seldom a problem for these nations.

Lower operating costs and high demand tempt many Western companies to enter Third World markets, either as a buyer or a seller. Buyers encounter less opposition from host country governments than sellers.

Without exception, all Third World countries recognize the need to develop an internal economy to provide jobs and political stability. They also desire hard foreign currency for trading purposes. In poorer countries, hard currency is also sought for debt service payments. A foreign company finds little opposition to establishing a physical presence in those industries considered critical to the development of an economic base. In many cases the U.S. government even foots the bill through its U.S. Agency for International Development (USAID) program.

Sellers are less fortunate. Most Third World countries do not have sufficient hard currency to support any significant import program, except for those commodities deemed essential for political and social stability. An attempt to export compact discs to Ecuador will probably fail, for example. Exporting agricultural implements should succeed. Unless a countertrade agreement can be reached, however, getting paid from Third World countries can be a real headache.

Following are the pros and cons of doing business in government-controlled Third World economies:

Advantages:

1. High demand for most products and services.
2. U.S. financing assistance for direct investment.
3. Inexpensive labor, materials, and overhead structures.
4. Local governments encourage the development of in-country industries.
5. Local and U.S. government-sponsored export programs.

Disadvantages:

1. Stringent government control over prices and market entry.
2. Local laws requiring national majority ownership of businesses.
3. Government control over what products or services are allowed entry.
4. Difficult communications, travel, and work permits.

Former Communist Bloc Nations

Economies in Eastern Europe and the Soviet Union present a unique opportunity over the next few years for Western companies. The complete economic failure of tightly controlled markets has created a pent-up demand unequaled in the rest of the world. Arbitrarily depressed price structures, deplorable quality of manufactured goods, and a virtual abandonment of nonmilitary research and development efforts have left these economies in ruins. As governments experiment with socialistic capitalism, privatization of industries will undoubtedly open the door to competitive markets for a variety of products. Consumer products, capital goods, technology development, and agricultural commodities should all be in high demand.

The universal goal of these nations is to develop an infrastructure of private businesses which will eventually permit a high degree of economic self-sufficiency. Without hard currency or free market management know-how, these nations offer unusual opportunities for direct foreign investment. Countertrade agreements have already begun to bring

Poland and Hungary much needed products to shore up their social structures. Grain and other raw foodstuffs continue to be imported by the Soviet Union. Czechoslovakia and Yugoslavia have both called for private foreign investment to rebuild their economic bases.

Even though U.S. government guarantees minimize the political risk of investing in former communist bloc countries, small and midsize companies should be aware of the inevitability of severe economic swings in the years ahead. The enormous pent-up demand for all goods and services, together with comparatively low operating cost structures, will cause prices and corresponding margins to rise significantly in the short term. As internal production capabilities and financial systems begin to materialize, however, supply and demand forces will most likely drive prices down and costs up. This indicates that the next few years should be the best time to take advantage of these markets.

Just as the Marshall Plan permitted West Germany, Japan and, to a lesser extent, Italy, to recover rapidly from economic desolation after 1945 and become global economic powers, so will the U.S. government and private investments speed socialistic capitalism down the road to recovery. It's hard to say when, but there is little dispute that in the future, global competition will come from private enterprise in these countries as surely as it has from Marshall Plan recipients.

The principal advantages and disadvantages of doing business with or in countries formerly closed to world trade are:

Advantages:

1. Enormous pent-up demand for industrial, consumer, and technical products and services.
2. U.S. government guarantees against political risk.
3. Local governments eager for private capital.
4. Low operating costs.
5. High sell prices.
6. U.S. financing.
7. Skilled labor force.

Disadvantages:

1. Lack of in-country management know-how.
2. Shattered communications.
3. Financial systems in disarray.
4. Bureaucratic obstinacy.
5. Eventual cost increases and prices decreases.
6. Heavy competition from Western Europe and Japan.
7. Eventual intense in-country competition.

China

The economic system in China bears separate analysis. China is the only hard-line communist country considered an active trading partner of the United States. A totally government-controlled market always brings the greatest risk to competitive participants. Potential nationalization of companies or industries, artificially fixed prices and operating costs, and ubiquitous laws regulating market supply and demand make direct investment in China at this time a risky business for the smaller producer.

MARKETS AND COMPETITION

Global markets can be viewed in eight industry groupings:

1. Consumer products.
2. Capital goods.
3. Chemicals.
4. Travel and leisure services.
5. Health care.
6. Infrastructure.
7. Agricultural products.
8. Technology.

Each of the global politico-economic regions exhibits different characteristics of supply, demand, and growth potential for each of these industries. A new entrant into global markets should attempt to choose those markets yielding the lowest getting-in and operating costs together with the best product longevity and growth prospects for his specific product line. A judicious examination of these market conditions prior to entry certainly increases the likelihood of establishing and maintaining a globally competitive position.

One way to view the matchup of a country's or a region's economic characteristics and market demand is with the matchup matrix in Figure 5–1. To use the matchup matrix find a product/service category that best fits your business. Then use the pros and cons of each market grouping from the previous section to evaluate where the best competitive advantage might occur.

The predetermined choices inserted in Figure 5–1 illustrate a broad interpretation of the most likely matchups providing first-time entrants the best combination of market size, high margins, and the least competition. When using the matchup matrix, management should incorporate its own judgment of best fit combinations.

Certainly developed countries with hard currency, stable political environments, and sophisticated consumers offer the largest customer base for many products and services. The ease of entry and familiar business practices encourage new entrants to try their hand in these markets. In terms of market growth, however, developing markets present the greatest potential for the future. With pent-up demand in Eastern Europe and China and burgeoning populations in Latin America, these regions must offer market growth superior to Western Europe, Canada, or Japan. Entry in these markets is riskier. Many smaller companies will be dissuaded from competing. But this makes the markets all the more lucrative for those with foresight and staying power.

During the next decade, infrastructure projects in several African nations should offer significant market growth for contracting firms willing to bid them. Although hotel and resort development has been going on for several years in the Middle East and parts of South America,

FIGURE 5–1
Matchup Matrix

Product/Service	Developed Economies	Third World	Former Communist Bloc	China
Consumer Products:				
Necessities		×	×	
Luxuries	×	×		
Capital goods:				
Machinery		×	×	×
Off-/on-road vehicles		×		
Spare parts	×	×	×	×
Chemicals			×	×
Travel and Leisure:				
Hotels/resorts/spas		×		
Restaurants			×	×
Recreational products	×			
Health Care:				
Cosmetics			×	
Pharmaceuticals		×	×	×
Infrastructure:				
Roads		×		×
Power and water plants		×		
Schools and hospitals		×	×	×
Communications		×	×	×
Agricultural products:				
Raw foodstuffs			×	
Consumer goods	×		×	
Fast-food			×	×
Technology		×	×	×

there are plenty of Third World countries relatively backward in the travel and leisure area. As political and social stability evolve, economic development will call for an increasing emphasis on travel accommodations and eating facilities.

Large corporations have been selling pharmaceuticals and chemicals to developing nations for years. As global financial systems stabilize in the 1990s and populations continue to grow, these markets will expand sufficiently to encourage new entrants.

A great variety of capital goods are needed to rebuild Eastern Europe and even the Soviet Union. Although government-to-government assistance will be directed principally to help large corporations, there should be more than adequate market demand for smaller firms supplying components, subassemblies, and spare parts.

New schools and hospitals are desperately needed throughout the world. Contractors as well as suppliers to these industries should realize significant market growth. American financial aid is already flowing to African countries, the Middle East, and Southeast Asia to improve these social necessities.

Major American, Japanese, and European corporations are firmly entrenched in many industrialized countries and in some lesser developed nations. Obviously, it is difficult for the small or midsize producer to offer much competition to the big boys. To bid against Bechtel or Fluor for a power plant in Malaysia would be foolish. To compete with IBM for supplying personal computers to companies in Great Britain would probably lead to failure. There is no logical reason to take on Squibb, Wyeth, and Warner Lambert in Western Europe.

However, the mere fact that these industry giants are already entrenched creates submarkets for aggressive smaller companies. Spare parts are always needed. Market niches requiring rapid distribution can be tapped. Subcontractors with special skills are always in demand by prime contractors.

No small or midsize business should be deterred from entering a global market merely because an industrial giant is already there. Picking the right market niche, providing personal customer service, and offering top of the line quality products always enables a firm to compete globally. The trick is to pick the right global market as a beginning. The worst thing a new global entrant can do is to become engaged in an economic war before gaining some experience in the international sphere.

THE EFFECT OF U.S. GOVERNMENT POLICIES

Other than the few countries remaining under totalitarian rule and therefore closed to global trade, the trade barriers erected by foreign governments have little bearing on the decision to enter a given market—with some notable exceptions. In some countries specific products may not be imported, such as women's bikini swimsuits in Saudi Arabia. In some cases unreasonable tariffs preclude competing with in-country producers, such as import duties on Coca-Cola and other soft drinks in some Latin countries, or California wine in France. Japan has also erected stiff tariff barriers to prevent importation of a whole array of consumer products.

There are two types of local trade barriers that must be considered, however, before a company moves toward a direct foreign investment. In addition to technical and management know-how, both of which can be transferred from the United States, any company establishing a facility overseas must be assured of an adequate supply of materials and parts, and a qualified labor base.

Few, if any, developing nations have a sufficiently developed industrial base to manufacture all the parts and subassemblies needed to make finished products. Most do not have basic steel, aluminum, and rubber industries. Parts, subassemblies, and basic raw materials must be imported from other countries. It is essential that trade barriers to such imported products do not prohibit a company from operating its facility efficiently.

Skilled labor is also in short supply in many developing nations. Most countries encourage foreign investment specifically to develop internal production capabilities, which in turn provides jobs for its populace. Therefore, many nations restrict the importation of skilled labor, either through denial of work permits or union membership requirements.

If a company opens a manufacturing plant in a country without skilled labor and labor importation restrictions exist, the only option is to train local labor. This could take a long time and delay getting the facility on line. While in most cases the host country government—or the U.S. government—subsidizes the cost of labor training, this won't help get the facility operating any sooner. Therefore, just as with material and parts, a company planning a foreign facility must be certain that the acquisition of skilled labor doesn't conflict with government trade barriers.

Nevertheless, assuming that a company's products are not specifically outlawed and it obeys local laws and regulations, most governments do not prevent foreign companies from trading with or in their countries.

The U.S. government isn't as obliging. Military hardware or weapons, research technology, and any product or service that the government deems proprietary to national security cannot be sold overseas without the express permission of the appropriate federal agency. This policy has been in existence for many decades. Everyone knows about it. Companies have learned to live with the restriction because it seems reasonable. Other government policies may not appear as reasonable.

For example, any American firm that knowingly or unknowingly takes part in, or sanctions in any way, the Arab economic boycotts of Israel will be penalized by the disallowance of foreign tax credits. Furthermore, at the government's discretion, fines may be levied against the company and its officers. Recent economic sanctions against South Africa fall into the same category. Until recently, trade of any type with the Soviet Union or its satellites had to be cleared through Washington. Penalties equally severe apply to a company violating the Foreign Corrupt Practices Act forbidding bribes, payoffs, and kickbacks to foreign firms or representatives.

The federal government also restricts American companies from importing certain materials, components, parts, or products from specific countries as Chapter 19 discloses. This further restricts American firms in global competition.

Extraordinarily restrictive barriers exist to the importation of certain garments and other textile products. These were established to protect the American textile industry and to save jobs—neither of which has materialized. Trade barriers also failed to protect the steel industry.

Unreasonable tariffs and quotas on Japanese cars, motorcycles, machine tools, semiconductors, and other electronic products prevented the American producer from acquiring low-cost materials, components, and parts. This forced American firms into a noncompetitive global position. But the restraints did little to aid the industries they were supposed to protect.

Federal government trade policies with China remain in a state of flux. It is unclear at this time how far the government will go to encourage American producers to enter Chinese markets. It is equally uncertain how many restraints will be enacted to prevent market entry. Clearly, a company considering exporting to or establishing a direct investment in China must estimate independently what impact current and future federal policies might have on its decision.

Conversely, the federal government has been more than eager to influence positive trade with Caribbean and Latin-American countries. The Reagan administration's Caribbean Basin Initiative program released substantial federal funds to promote and assist American investment in that region. Investment advice can be obtained from half a dozen different agencies. The identification of product and market opportunities for American companies is abundantly available. Even federal tax deferrals and reductions exist for those companies willing to invest in specific Caribbean countries.

Similar encouragement to American investors permeates the government's policies toward several Central and South American countries. Federal negotiators recently convinced the IMF and the World Bank to begin the bailout of Mexico's debt obligations. Technical assistance and financing aid are available to companies investing in Guatemala, Costa Rica, Bolivia, and Uruguay. Signals from Washington indicate that before long U.S. tax incentives will be granted to companies willing to invest in industrial and agricultural enterprises in Colombia and Peru.

Whether it surreptitiously attempts to protect American industry with import trade barriers or whether it actively fosters American private investment in the economic development of our neighbors, the policies, programs, and active participation from the American government are probably here to stay. As such, it behooves anyone beginning the global journey, or any company anticipating expansion or contraction of overseas markets, to ascertain what current and anticipated government policies might apply.

MACROMARKET CHECKLIST

This chapter has outlined the four macromarket factors that should be assessed prior to going global. They were:

1. Identify the type of economy offering the best market potential.
2. Analyze market demand and potential market growth for your specific product or service.
3. Evaluate global and local competitive conditions.
4. Examine the current and anticipated policies of foreign and U.S. governments relating to trade barriers or trade assistance.

This assessment won't assure a company success in the global marketplace. On the other hand, ignoring these four basic market parameters will certainly hinder an effective global entrance. The checklist in Figure 5–2 should prove helpful in determining the priority of political and economic factors influencing a company's decision to enter global trade.

FIGURE 5–2
Macromarket Checklist
For _____

	Very Important	Moderately Important	Not Important	
Country:				
Administrative:				
1. Language symmetry	___	___	___	
2. Familiar marketing procedures	___	___	___	
3. Easy to travel to and within	___	___	___	
4. Work permits easy to arrange	___	___	___	
5. Modern banking systems	___	___	___	
6. Hard currency	___	___	___	
7. Easy and effective communications network	___	___	___	
8. A developed infrastructure	___	___	___	
Local government:				
9. Cumbersome bureaucracies	___	___	___	
10. No restrictions on importing materials	___	___	___	
11. No restrictions on importing skilled labor	___	___	___	
12. Nonrestrictive export regulations	___	___	___	
13. Low taxes or tax forgiveness	___	___	___	
14. Encouraging development of in-country industries	___	___	___	
15. Eager for private capital	___	___	___	
16. Control over prices and market entry	___	___	___	
17. Laws require national majority ownership of businesses	___	___	___	
Business base:				
18. Substantial industrial base	___	___	___	
19. Skilled labor available locally	___	___	___	
20. Materials and parts available locally	___	___	___	
21. Low-cost labor	___	___	___	
22. Low-cost material	___	___	___	
23. Lack of in-country management know-how	___	___	___	
Market Size, Market Growth, and Competition:				
Market demand and growth potential:				
24. Large consumer population	___	___	___	
25. Local market demand for consumer products	___	___	___	
26. Local market demand for industrial products	___	___	___	
27. Local market demand for agricultural products	___	___	___	
28. Local market demand for technical services	___	___	___	
29. Major customers are the government or government-owned companies	___	___	___	
30. Major customers are private companies	___	___	___	
31. High sell prices	___	___	___	
32. Government defined markets	___	___	___	

FIGURE 5-2 *(continued)*

	Very Important	*Moderately Important*	*Not Important*	
Competition:				
33. Competition from nationalized industries or local firms	____	____	____	
34. Competition from large American multinational corporations	____	____	____	
35. Competition from Western Europe and Japanese companies	____	____	____	
U.S. Government Interference or Assistance:				
36. Federal financing assistance	____	____	____	
37. Government guarantees against political risk	____	____	____	
38. Technical assistance available	____	____	____	
39. Identification of investment opportunities	____	____	____	
40. Restrictive import barriers	____	____	____	
41. Foreign Corrupt Practices Act	____	____	____	
42. Boycott laws	____	____	____	
43. South Africa sanctions	____	____	____	
44. China policy	____	____	____	

CHAPTER 6

OVERVIEW OF MAJOR DEVELOPED GLOBAL MARKETS: JAPAN, EUROPE, AND CANADA

MAJOR TOPICS

KEY POINTS

This chapter examines the trading opportunities in each of four major developed nations/regions. These opportunities are evaluated under six criteria.

1. Trade characteristics.
2. Economic needs.
3. Currency restrictions.
4. Political future.
5. U.S. government support/restrictions.
6. The probability for success by an American company.

A summary of the advantages and risks of doing business in each country/region appears at the end of each section.

The following chapter looks at developing nations under these same criteria.

The Bush administration trade policies leave much to the imagination. In the same vein as smoking restrictions, auto emission controls, safety regulations, cholesterol levels in food products, and farm crop selection, the American government continues to insist that the rest of the world conduct business as done in the United States. Ours is the best and only way to run a country, and hence a business. Threats of severe retaliation face any nation not agreeing to play the game our way.

In early 1990, Carla A. Hills, U.S. trade representative, was assigned to head the American trade delegation negotiating new trade policies with the world—and specifically those nations who seem to be getting the better of American producers; that is, Japan, Taiwan, Hong Kong, and Korea. She returned from talks with the Japanese "frustrated and concerned" by Japan's refusal to do it the American way. She blatantly announced that she would use "a crowbar where necessary" to force Japan's market open to U.S. exports.

The problem is relatively simple. Japan's internal economic and political systems enforce rigid controls over foreign participation in Japanese markets. They do this through high-import tariffs, quota restrictions, an incestuous interlocking of industrial and financial cartels, complex distribution networks, extensive government subsidies, and close supervision by state ministries. Since 1945, Japan has overtly structured exporting, and later direct foreign investment, as its main economic strategies. The Japanese public has accepted this policy as the best way for Japan to grow and become self-sufficient.

Until recently, the Japanese exhibited little demand for Western-style commodities. Truly global American firms understand this cultural dissimilarity and have turned Japan's idiosyncrasies to their advantage. Campbell Soup, McDonald's, Boeing, and Du Pont are examples of companies profiting enormously in Japanese markets. Of course, nonglobal American firms dislike the Japanese because they can't strategize how to conquer this lucrative market. Pointing a finger at "unfair competition," these firms have turned to the federal government to solve their own ineffectual marketing policies.

On the flip side, several congressional leaders, such as Senator John Heinz of Pennsylvania and Congressman Mel Levine of California, argue that the federal government should make American businesses more competitive with subsidies, tax breaks, import quotas, and other trade regulations. Of course, whenever the government has become involved in protecting American companies from foreign competition, such as steel, textiles, semiconductors, and automobiles, it has failed miserably. Not only have these policies not stopped foreign competition, they have contributed to a substantial increase in selling prices to the American public.

So far, the Bush administration, advocating trade policies from the Reagan era, has taken the position that the answer to global competition is for all countries to eliminate trade barriers and let American companies export whatever they want. And just like Reagan, Bush and his economic advisers miss the mark.

A global mentality continues to escape government economists and trade advocates. They continue to view the world as *us* versus *them*. They refuse to acknowledge that efficient, well-managed global companies, of any size, left to their own devices, can compete effectively in any market economy. It is the inefficient, poorly managed companies that cry for protectionist help. Since the majority of American companies that employ the majority of the voting public seem to fall into the latter category, the economic immaturity fostered in Washington is probably not surprising.

The trade war isn't over. Many industrialized countries, in addition to the United States, sport a predominance of inefficient, poorly managed businesses. And they are crying "uncle" as well. During 1989, trade representatives from the United States, Canada, and the European Community met at Hakone, Japan, to forge a common strategy to present during the 107-member nation meeting to negotiate new features of the General Agreement on Tariffs and Trade (GATT).

One feature of GATT that the "Big Four" would like to see changed is the ending of all barriers to trade in service industries, such as banking and insurance. Developing nations oppose this position. They argue that by allowing the entrance of mammoth financial institutions into their markets, their own fledgling financial service companies would be threatened.

The Big Four would also like to see an end to what they call the piracy of intellectual property such as patents, trademarks, and copyrights. Developing nations oppose this view because many are havens for pirates who manufacture videos, records, and pharmaceuticals (among many other products) without paying royalties.

The United States wants the Japanese to allow importation of more agricultural products, specifically rice. The American delegation also wants EC nations to stop subsidizing agricultural production.

Throughout the four-year Geneva-based Uruguay round talks, little resolution was reached. Meanwhile the United States continues to try to badger the Japanese and others into helping inefficient American producers. Current indications are that the Japanese, at least, are having none of it and skirt the issues with promises of long-term studies. As the EC begins flexing its muscle in 1992, the result will probably be the same from them.

Meanwhile, small and midsize companies must press forward toward penetrating global markets with or without governmental interference.

The analysis of macromarket factors reviewed in the previous chapter is an essential starting point to evaluate global markets with the highest potential for your company. This chapter and Chapter 7 take the process one step further through a detailed evaluation of major world markets offering potential for small and midsize companies. A grasp of these political, social, and economic variations between markets helps a company fine tune its best opportunities for product or service offerings worldwide. The six components reviewed for each market are:

1. Market trade characteristics.
2. Economic needs.
3. Currency restrictions.
4. Political future.
5. U.S. government support/restrictions.
6. The probability of an American firm succeeding.

JAPAN

Japan seems to be of the most imminent concern at this time and certainly manifests an opportunity for global market penetration in a variety of industries. A substantial population, financial and political stability, and enormous pent-up consumer demand for a variety of goods and services make Japan a desirable market for years to come. Several hurdles must be overcome, however: language and cultural dissimilarities, government-erected barriers, and monopolistic marketing structures, to mention the most prominent.

Language normally does not present an insurmountable problem. Even though learning to speak, read, and write Japanese could be a herculean task for many, the close military, political, and business ties with America for 45 years has brought the English language into most business transactions. Interpreters are plentiful in Japan. Even if a negotiation or other business transaction must be accomplished in Japanese, an American shouldn't have too big a problem understanding what is happening.

The Japanese culture is another matter, however, as many American companies have learned to their dismay. Current Japanese consumer appetites are a far cry from Western tastes.

Trade Barriers

Government trade barriers can be a formidable hurdle to overcome. However, regulations affecting the Japanese consumer and industrial markets are really no greater than those in many other countries, notably the Middle East and China, and in many cases less severe. Murky rules and market regulations, fair trade laws that limit sales promotions, complex import procedures, and onerous import duties reflect to a large extent cultural differences from the West. To a lesser extent, they mirror government economic policies still in existence from the post-World War II reconstruction era. Protectionism certainly prevails. Furthermore, it seems likely that many of these government-imposed trade barriers will remain for some time to come, regardless of what Ms. Hills has to say.

Of course the alternative to exporting products to Japan is direct investment. Several companies have found this means far superior to coping with government import controls. Most industrial companies have found joint ventures with Japanese firms the best entry. Du Pont is doing very well in Japan. Japanese employees regard this company as a premier place to work. Recently, Du Pont through its two subsidiaries, Du Pont Japan, Ltd., and E.I. du Pont de Nemours International, agreed with Matsushita Electric Industrial Co. to jointly develop materials for the electronics industry. Avon did relatively well with its 60 percent-owned Avon Japan mail-order company, until its recent sale.

Distribution

The extremely complex and tightly controlled distribution system is probably the biggest stumbling block for American companies trying to enter the Japanese market. Layering from the many sectors of the distribution system can easily increase the price of imported goods four or five times. Some status-type consumer products are much worse. For example, the wholesale price of a bottle of Hennessy's VSOP cognac is about $7.00. By the time it gets to the store shelves it is priced at $77.50! Or take the ladies' scarf purchased by the import agent for $30. He sells it to the wholesaler for $60, who sells it to the department store for $90, who sells it to the consumer for $160. Just finding someone to distribute a company's products can be a problem because of long-standing, exclusive relationships between wholesalers and retailers.

American ingenuity has proven the distribution maze can be beaten, however. Amway is doing a booming business in Japan. It imported its own distribution system. Household items, toiletries, and cookware are sold by over 500,000 Japanese distributors—direct from their homes. Nomura Research Institute reported that Amway, with $500 million in sales, is the fastest growing foreign firm in Japan.

Blue Diamond Grocers broke into the Japanese markets with their California almonds by utilizing Coca-Cola's Japanese distributors selling to 1.2 million outlets. Tiffany & Co. struck a deal with Mitsukoshi Ltd. to be its sole distributor and increased sales 38 percent in 1988. Even the German company BMW solved its Japanese distribution problem. With astronomical land costs, BMW did not want to waste such an asset for car lots. Instead, the company hired Japanese citizens who already owned land to be dealers using their land for the lots.

It's not easy, however. To start up a new company in Japan, whether national or foreign, is a difficult undertaking. A recent study sponsored by the American Chamber of Commerce in Japan and conducted by A.T. Kearney concluded that the incestuous distribution system creates built-in discrimination against any new company—Japanese or foreign.

U.S.–Japan Trade Negotiations

Much has been written lately in the newspapers, trade magazines, government publications, and even books, about how unfair the Japanese trade barriers are. We let them come into the United States but they won't reciprocate. There are always two sides to any argument, however, and it helps to understand the major points of contention on both sides. What do we want the Japanese to do? An entire list of concessions; although the major ones falls under eight groupings. The United States wants the Japanese to:

1. Open the distribution system to more imports.
2. Enforce antitrust laws more vigorously.
3. Stop overpricing imports with high tariffs.
4. Overhaul their land-use policy.
5. End bid-rigging and other collusive practices that shut out imports.
6. Stop the restrictions on Japanese government purchases of U.S.-built supercomputers and satellites.
7. Eliminate standards that shut out processed lumber products milled in America.
8. Allow the importation of rice and other banned agricultural products.

On the surface these seem like requests that would certainly help American companies enter the Japanese market. But what do the Japanese want in return? The Japanese want the United States to:

1. Move more aggressively to reduce the budget deficit.
2. Increase savings and investment by Americans and American companies.
3. Improve education and training of the workers to make the U.S. work force more competitive.

These requests don't seem too onerous either. Interestingly, their achievement would probably help the American economy a lot more than Japanese interests. The Japanese seem to be interested in improving American markets and stabilizing the American economy so that they can sell more goods and make more profits for Japanese companies located in the United States—which is certainly a global outlook. The U.S. government, on the other hand, continues to express the "us" and "them" philosophy by addressing principally export/import concerns, not direct investment—which is certainly not a global view.

In all, Japanese negotiators have pushed 80 proposals that they would like the United States to implement, many just as sweeping as those proposed by the Americans. In addition to requests that are obviously beneficial to the American economy, several matters the Japanese would like resolved are clearly opposed by American public opinion. To reduce what the Japanese consider to be excessive American consumption and to boost savings and investment, they would like the U.S. government to:

1. Put a stiff tax on gasoline.
2. Limit the number of credit cards Americans have.
3. Levy a national sales tax.
4. End tax deductions for home mortgage interest.
5. Encourage American business schools to teach the Japanese language and business-management courses.

It should go without saying that such proposals are ludicrous and will never be accepted. Yet, the Japanese claim their requests are no more far-fetched than those proposed by American negotiators to change the Japanese social structure.

In mid-1990, a joint communiqué by Washington and Tokyo announced agreement on mutual changes by the two countries to improve trade relations and reduce the Japanese surplus with the United States. With much hoopla on both sides of the Pacific, the agreement, in fact, sidestepped definitive action on all major issues. Under the so-called Structural Impediments Initiative, the following promises were made:

Japan agreed to:

- Continue to make narrowing its trade surplus a top priority.
- Increase spending for public works over 10 years to $2.76 trillion, and to make $162 billion in capital investments in Nippon Telegraph & Telephone Corp. and Japan Railways, which have been privatized.
- Simplify its import process and make it easier to open large retail stores that could import foreign products.
- Make antimonopoly policy stricter and raise fines for illegal cartels.

- Change its foreign exchange law to invite more foreign investment.
- Within two years, allow consumers not to pay off bank credit card balances all at once—which presumably will stimulate spending and reduce saving.

In return, the United States agreed to:

- Continue cutting its trade deficit.
- Seek to eliminate the federal budget deficit and reduce the government's outstanding debt.
- Urge Congress to enact the Savings and Economic Growth Act of 1990—which presumably would stimulate private investment and savings.
- Seek to ensure that Japanese investors are given nondiscriminatory treatment under the U.S./Japan Tax Treaty.
- Seek legislation to ease antitrust regulations on joint production ventures in the United States—presumably to enhance competition (it remains unclear what the negotiators had in mind by "enhancing competition").
- Improve education and worker training programs.

Both sides agreed to these grandiose schemes without the power to make them happen. The respective legislatures must take the action first. However, private enterprise in Japan and the United States must agree to support such legislation. Both conditions remain in doubt.

Financing

One big advantage of doing business in Japan, other than the enormous demand for goods and services, is the stable, sophisticated financial system. With the Japanese yen a hard currency, conversion is never a problem. Although restrictions against foreign membership on the Tokyo Stock Exchange have kept American and European investment banks from actively pursuing new public issues of foreign companies located in Japan, the time will inevitably come when an event similar to the British "Big Bang" hits Tokyo. In the meantime, with the 10 largest banks in the world headquartered in Japan, financing business transactions is normally not an insurmountable problem. Also, with Japanese branch banks throughout the world, money transfers and letters of credit are easy to arrange.

Politically, Japan is becoming more like the United States every day. Ethical and sex scandals rock political leaders. Relatively free speech and a free press debate national issues and denounce political gerrymandering. And now, for the first time, free multiparty elections. Although the incumbent party easily won the majority, many new seats were picked up by the opposition.

As Japan continues to move toward a true multiparty political base, more progressive economic policies will most likely be forthcoming. As this occurs, many of the traditionally difficult barriers to foreign participation in Japanese markets will probably also be eased, making global companies more welcome than now.

Even with the difficult distribution system and onerous government trade barriers, imports and foreign direct investments are beginning to flood the Japanese markets—contrary to the picture portrayed by Washington. The Japanese minister of finance announced in early 1990 that Japan's trade surplus had decreased steadily through most of 1989. In January 1990, the current account, the broadest measure of trade in goods and services, registered a trade deficit for the first time in six years. The trade deficit totaled $636 million compared with a $2.51 billion trade surplus in January 1988.

Through most of 1990, the ministry continued to report monthly trade deficits rather than surpluses and cumulative surplus shrinkages. Analysts regularly report that these decreases are caused by a weaker yen, higher oil prices, or slowing auto exports. This should certainly give heart to those fearful of Japanese trade supremacy.

Many American firms have found a way to do business in Japan, just as they have in every other country of the world. Those still leery of attacking Japanese markets should not be deterred by propaganda from Washington reflecting the loud voices of major American corporations too inefficient or poorly managed to compete globally. Although it is difficult to predict what schemes will be forthcoming from our nation's bureaucrats, short of an outright boycott of Japan, future opportunities for American firms in Japanese markets look promising. Such a boycott seems highly unlikely with Japan currently supporting the U.S. Treasury markets.

Summary

Trade Characteristics:

1. Government-controlled entry through extensive trade barriers.
2. Internal distribution network difficult to penetrate.
3. Extremely high land values and tight controls over land sales.
4. Highly developed financial system including the world's largest stock exchange.
5. Skilled labor force and qualified management technocrats.
6. Heavy local competition in some products, especially electronics and basic capital goods.

Economic Needs:

1. Westernization of consumer tastes creates an enormous potential market for consumer goods and services.
2. Large population concentrated in cities affects distribution and retailing.
3. Concentration on developing an export economy has neglected consumer needs.
4. So far at least, the government has not been willing to relax import or foreign investment restrictions.

Currency Restrictions:

1. The yen is a hard currency, easily convertible to dollars.
2. Anticipated influx of foreign investment in Japanese companies

foreshadows an increasingly close tie between the yen and the dollar.

Political Future:

1. Democratic capitalism well on the way.
2. Stable, elected government.
3. Two-party system beginning to develop.

U.S. Government Support/Restrictions:

1. United States pushing for more open markets.
2. Supports increased exporting to Japan as well as direct investment by American companies.
3. Current trade imbalance a major problem for Washington.

Probability of Success:

1. With perseverance and the right product, small to midsize firms should consider Japan as an export customer.
2. Probably too costly for many firms to make direct investment.
3. The Japanese culture is difficult to adjust to for the first-time global entrant.
4. Over the long term Japanese markets are vital to the prolonged success of a global company.

WESTERN EUROPE

If Japan frustrated American politicians and influenced the shape of American trade in the 1980s, most signs indicate that Western Europe will do the same in the 1990s. By the time the Single European Act, signed in February 1986 by the 12 European Community (EC) member nations, becomes a reality, Western Europe will represent a single market of more than 320 million consumers. They will be well-fed, well-heeled, and ready to shop until they drop. According to government estimates, a unified Europe will have a gross national product of $4.5 trillion, nearly equaling the $4.8 trillion of the United States.

Skeptics argue that too many difficult changes must be resolved between the countries to make 1992 a realistic starting date for the EC. If it does take until 2000 so much the better. A prolonged planning and conversion period offers American companies a heretofore unrealized opportunity to participate in the major marketing frontier of the decade.

Current membership in the EC consists of: Belgium, Denmark, France, Greece, Ireland, Italy, Luxembourg, the Netherlands, Portugal, Spain, the United Kingdom, and Germany. When all the measures envisioned in the Single Europe Act are implemented, citizens of these countries will have unrestricted access to goods produced anywhere within the 12 member states. These revolutionary measures range the gamut of the economic spectrum from mutual recognition of professional qualification and status between states, to the equalization of indirect taxation, and to the standardization of technical specifications for everything from electric outlets to automobile safety.

It certainly is not yet clear what specific impact the EC will have on the importation of American-made goods. Several of the same American corporations screaming loudest about unfair Japanese trade practices are sounding the alarm that the EC may try some of the same strong-arm tactics to keep out non-European goods and services. Most of these fears are groundless for those already firmly entrenched as global companies. For those companies relying exclusively on exporting rather than becoming directly involved in a foreign investment, however, concern should be genuine.

Although the EC has agreed to abide by commitments agreed to in GATT, some important service industries fall outside the GATT provisions, notably banking and financial services. As noted earlier, the United States, Canada, and the EC have been arguing among themselves, and with the Japanese, over this issue for years.

In October 1988, Willy de Clerq, external affairs commissioner for the EC, broached a potentially serious problem in the banking area. He hinted that non-EC banks may be restricted from operating in Europe unless "mirror image" relationships are agreed to. This means that all EC banks would have the right to operate within the United States, as American banks operate in Europe now. Some protectionists believe this would wreak havoc on the extensive state-level banking controls existing in the United States today. Others, more globally oriented, view such a change as welcome and beneficial to the American public. They argue that such entrants would open up true global competition in the banking industry—something this country has never experienced.

American Participation

How will the implementation of the EC program help small and midsize businesses? One significant way is by reducing the cost and administrative hazards of dealing with 12 separate sets of customs, tax regulations, labor codes, and product specifications. With just one set of standards and rules, market doors swing wide.

The European Commission (an agency with the EC), has developed a type of *marriage brokerage*, a noncommercial service to bring businesses in member nations with complementary needs together. Expanding businesses will continue to look for acquisition and joint venture candidates in the United States, predominantly among small and midsize companies. This, in turn, opens the door for smaller American companies to do the same in Europe.

Many companies, large and small, are taking steps to get their foot in the door while it is still open. David Michael & Co., an $18 million Philadelphia flavor manufacturer is already searching for a joint venture partner in France and England. Hunt Manufacturing Co., a midsize graphics art company has agreed to acquire three similar businesses from Bunzi PLC of Great Britain. Kelly Services, Inc., has acquired temporary help companies in the Netherlands and New Zealand. Siemens AG and IBM have agreed to jointly develop a 64 million bit memory chip to be produced by factories in America and Germany. Du Pont is building a factory in Asturias, Spain, to produce its Nomex fiber products for use in protective clothing and filters.

In an effort to "facilitate the restructuring of European industry," the European Commission has also announced plans to make corporate takeovers in the EC easier. Among other things, the commission wants to strengthen the voting rights of shareholders and force corporate bidders to outline their takeover plans. It is felt that such disclosure will not only provide common grounds for the EC to veto unfavorable takeovers but also simplify the procedures for friendly acquisitions.

The plan would give the Commission exclusive powers to regulate mergers between companies with worldwide revenues of $5.5 billion or more. It appears that such regulation will be a major deterrent to industry monopolistic tendencies common in several industries in the United States (shipbuilding, telecommunications, pulp and paper, and so on). Conversely, this high approval limit makes acquisitions by smaller and midsize companies more likely.

Some major hurdles must be overcome before the EC can become a reality, however. A few of the unresolved issues that continue to impede its implementation are:

- The reconciliation of bank secrecy laws in Luxembourg.
- Agreement and conversion to a common EC currency.
- Equalization of personal and corporate income tax laws.
- Homogenization of sovereign political extremes.
- Elimination of the abuses of EC provisions that exempt public administration from the principle that all Europeans are eligible for jobs throughout Europe.

Strong trade union opposition to proposals for common wage rates throughout the EC could further delay implementation.

Not surprisingly, the establishment of a common EC currency is already causing consternation in some circles—notably Great Britain. In the face of intense criticism by those fearful of losing the stability of the pound sterling, the British government continues to try to talk up the value of sterling in anticipation of joining the exchange rate mechanism (and at the same time drive down a double digit inflation rate). The exchange rate mechanism (ERM) is built into the European Monetary System (the common currency system to be implemented in the EC) and limits the fluctuations of 9 of 12 European Community currencies. So far, Britain, Greece, and Portugal remain outside the ERM, although the English are poised to make the leap.

Timing and Investment

Although the timing of EC unification remains questionable, most authorities agree that in the end there will be a European common market. Exporting into this market may be more difficult for American firms but it will certainly be more cost effective. On the other hand, direct investment in European businesses and facilities will undoubtedly offer significant global advantages to small and midsize firms.

It seems likely that the EC will enact protectionist legislation for some industries, at least in the beginning. For this reason, expansion plans in Europe should begin immediately. Establish a presence before the door closes.

In addition to getting in under the wire of protectionist legislation, there are two tactical reasons for moving rapidly. First, by waiting until massive distribution and retailing chains are established by European firms, outsiders will have a difficult time breaking into the system—similar to the dilemma in Japan. Second, the economies of scale that American industries have enjoyed for decades will encourage European competitors in basic manufacturing, processing, transportation, and construction industries to merge, thus creating even stronger monopolistic competitors.

Price competition will inevitably come next and create an even greater barrier to entrance by a smaller firm. Higher prices paid for American export products to cover additional shipping and export handling costs will no longer be tolerated. If you are not already established on European soil, market entrance will become increasingly difficult and costly. Perhaps businesses in niche markets won't be as severely limited, but even that is uncertain.

Regardless of the specific industry or product, the opportunity presented by a very large and burgeoning market requires serious strategic planning. This should be started immediately. A global perspective indicates the need for serious consideration of relocations, mergers, business acquisitions, and business start-ups on European soil now, not five years from now when everyone else has made the move.

Summary

Trade Characteristics:

1. An enormous market of over 300 million people.
2. Current trade barriers can be overcome relatively easily.
3. Common cultures encompass most American product and service demand.
4. The time to move is now since the implementation of the EC will probably invoke protectionist trade barriers to foreign investment.
5. After the EC implementation, exporting will be more difficult but also more cost effective.
6. The world's largest base of skilled labor and management talent.

Economic Needs:

1. No special needs although with 300 million people and a thriving industrial base, consumer and capital goods similar to those sold in the United States should be welcome.
2. After the EC implementation, public transportation vehicles, advanced communications equipment, computers, construction and construction equipment, and a variety of replacement parts for standardization should be good markets.

Currency Restrictions:

1. Currently none. All nations deal in hard currency.
2. If EC implements common currency, exchange fluctuations will be minimized. Until then, the pound, French franc, deutsche mark, and guilder float at approximately the same levels.

Political Future:

1. Short of another major war, political stability from elected governments should prevail.

U.S. Government Support/Restrictions:

1. Currently trade between Western Europe and the United States is as free as any in the world. After the EC, if protectionist measures are taken, the United States will certainly reciprocate.
2. Little financial aid or assistance from the U.S. government.

Probability of Success:

1. For a smart company, entering the European market before EC implementation should assure a promising future.
2. After the EC becomes firmly entrenched, competition will be severe and protectionist measures may preclude entrance.

EASTERN EUROPE AND THE SOVIET UNION

Gorbachev's *perestroika* and the unraveling of the Eastern Bloc raise questions in three major areas affecting the global strategies of American companies. First, what relationship will exist between Poland, Czechoslovakia, Hungary, Bulgaria, Romania, and the Baltic states, and Western Europe after the implementation of the EC common market in 1992? Will these nations be invited to join at some point in the future? If so, how will their soft currencies be integrated and converted to EC hard currency and what impact will this have on the banking community? What roles will EC and American private industry each play in the reconstruction of Eastern Europe?

Second, the entire German unification question raises serious doubts about the integration of East German commerce into the EC. Will West Germany stand off until full East German integration is a fait accompli? What impact will unification and the reconstruction of East Germany have on the booming West German economy? What role, if any, will private industry from other European countries and from the United States play in rebuilding East Germany? What long-term impact will the conversion of ostmarks to deutsche marks have in the global financial markets?

Third, how rapidly and to what extent will the Soviet Union encourage American participation in its rebuilding efforts? Will the Soviets permit significant American direct investment in private businesses or will outside participation be limited to the importation of specific goods, services, and technology? What will the Soviet position be on free travel within the country by American businesspeople? How much will American companies have to rely on countertrade measures to sell in the Soviet economy? Will efforts be made to harden the Russian ruble?

On the other side of the coin, will the United States open its borders to Soviet technicians and businesspeople to learn how democratic capitalism works? If so, what impact will that have on joint ventures in the Soviet Union by American firms, either with complementary Soviet firms or EC companies? Will the EC be given preferential trade treatment over the Americans?

Obviously, at this stage there are more questions than answers. Some trade matters are beginning to crystallize, however. There is little doubt that Eastern Europe will need massive financial and trade assistance from the West in the short run to rebuild their economic base and to convert from controlled to market economies. Poland has already made arrangements with American private venture capital funds to invest in Polish businesses with OPIC (Overseas Private Investment Corporation) guarantees.

The Polish and Hungarian Experiments

Cable television has already come to Poland. A joint venture, 70 percent owned by the American investor, David T. Chase, and cable TV-consultant, Norval D. Reese, has been formed as Poland Cablevision B.V. These investors are also financing the project to the tune of $900 million. The other 30 percent is owned by Potelkab, a Polish company whose shareholders are various government ministries and agencies.

The Polish American Resources Corp. of New York has invested an initial capitalization of $7.5 million to start the first American bank in Poland. The joint venture includes four Polish state companies.

General Electric will invest $150 million in a joint venture with RABA, the Hungarian manufacturer of trucks, axles, and diesel engines. They plan to build a plant in Szentgotthard, Hungary, with operations beginning in 1992.

The Soviet Experiment

Investment moves by American companies in the Soviet economy are even more staggering, considering the range of unsettled questions facing Western business participation. A consortium of Western firms headed by Combustion Engineering has made a deal with Tobolsk Petrochemical Co. (owned by the Soviet government) to build and run a $2 billion petrochemical complex in western Siberia. A three-way venture between Tabard Farm of Middletown, Virginia, and two Soviet agricultural cooperatives was formed to make and distribute potato chips in the Soviet Union. Pepsico closed a countertrade deal with the Soviets to sell them Pepsi-Cola syrup in exchange for exclusive rights to distribute Stolichnaya Vodka in the United States plus three freighter ships.

Furthermore, as reported by the Soviet Tass news agency, 1,284 foreign firms (many of them American) have created joint ventures with Soviet partners requiring initial capital of over $3 billion. Half the Western investment went into light industry and service businesses, 20 percent in industrial services such as marketing, engineering, and maintenance, and about 15 percent in heavy industry and machine tools. Western commercial attachés have warned that, so far at least, the Soviet business climate remains hazardous for all but the biggest and most patient foreign firms. One Western diplomat was quoted by Reuters Wire Service as stating that because of the shortage of hard currency, the opportunities for smaller firms are limited because they normally cannot afford to wait for long delays in payment or engage in complex countertrade deals. Complicating the picture is the fact that Soviet items easily sold in the world markets are already supplying Moscow with some hard currency. Products left over for barter or countertrade are frequently difficult to market.

One midsize American firm wouldn't take no for an answer, however. Taking advantage of the hesitancy by IBM, Apple, and AST to get involved in countertrade arrangements, American PC Corp., a division of Phoenix Group International, Inc., signed an $8 billion order with the Soviets. Over a period of years, American PC plans to ship 3 million computers for Soviet businesses and 3 million for Soviet schools. A shipment of 770 computers has already left. The agreement also calls for technology transfers allowing the Soviets to eventually manufacture and service their own computers. In payment, American PC will receive commodities such as oil, scrap metal, and uranium. These commodities will then be sold for hard currency outside the Soviet Union.

Eastern Europe Trade

All is not a bed of roses in the former communist bloc. A meeting of the 10-nation communist trading bloc, COMECON (Council for Mutual Economic Assistance), in Sophia, Bulgaria, pointed up some glaring difficulties to a smooth conversion to market economies. The COMECON nations are comprised of the Soviet Union, Poland, Romania, Hungary, Bulgaria, Czechoslovakia, Vietnam, Mongolia, and Cuba.

A compromise agreement was reached that all COMECON trade by 1991 be done at world market prices and in hard currency. Eastern European countries, long dependent on Soviet energy supplies contended that such a fast liberalization would be disastrous for their economies already strapped for hard currency. However, the Soviets prevailed. Even though the representatives felt that most trade in the future would be bilateral, the rapid switch to world market prices on a hard currency basis will take place within the bloc.

Currently, COMECON trading practices are based on barter and artificial currency exchange rates. Poles, Czechs, and Hungarians are planning to implement hard currency transactions quickly while other members continue to use fixed rates. Warsaw and Prague will link their currencies in a direct rate, bypassing the ruble, COMECON's nonconvertible accounting unit. East Germany has already broken with COMECON and converted their ostmarks to West German deutsch marks.

The U.S. government has agreed to a gradual easing of trade restrictions with Eastern Europe. This is especially relevant in high-technology areas. The government has agreed to allow American companies to sell Eastern Bloc nations computers up to six times more powerful than those now permitted. It is also relaxing restrictions on exporting fiber-optic cables and some sophisticated machine tools.

But so far the Bush administration has refused to relax restrictions on more sophisticated technology such as transmission equipment needed to set up the fiber-optic network or digital switches such as those needed by Poland and Hungary for modernizing their telecommunications systems. What other barriers will be removed in the near future is uncertain, according to administration officials.

There is one encouraging note for foreign firms needing financing to invest in the Eastern Bloc. Thirty-four countries have taken the first steps toward forming a new development bank to help finance ventures in Eastern Europe: the European Bank for Reconstruction and Development in Eastern Europe. The 34 nations are expected to contribute $12 billion. This will make it the largest regional assistance program since the Marshall Plan. The bank plans to provide loans, loan guarantees, economic and technical assistance, and make equity investments in Eastern Bloc businesses.

From a global market perspective, pent-up consumer and industrial demand after 50 years of government-controlled markets presents a promising future for those businesses with the courage to participate. Eventually, it seems logical that close ties with the EC will have to be established. Companies with a foothold in Eastern Europe at the time will certainly have a competitive advantage over newcomers. The only real question for smaller and midsize companies is the assistance and/or restrictions mandated by Washington. If the U.S. government is serious about helping Eastern Europe and the Soviet Union rebuild their economies, new financial and technical assistance programs should be forthcoming in the next two to three years.

Summary

Trade Characteristics:

1. There are really three markets: (*a*) Poland, Czechoslovakia, and Hungary, (*b*) the rest of Eastern Europe, and (*c*) the Soviet Union. Each has its own trade restrictions on Western imports and direct investment.
2. Although the dust is not yet settled, Poland, Czechoslovakia, Hungary, and Yugoslavia have already expressed eagerness for American private investment and have eliminated most restrictive barriers.
3. Joint ventures with Soviet companies appear to be the only viable means to penetrate the vast USSR market.
4. Most countries have an adequate skilled labor base but lack management talent and modern technology.
5. Financing programs for Western investments in Poland are already under way.

6. Eventual interaction of Eastern Europe with the EC and the impact of German unification are important unsettled matters affecting investment decisions.
7. Both Eastern Europe and the Soviet Union will experiment with the workings of a market economy. Moving from a state-controlled economy will take time and a learning curve.

Economic Needs:

1. Nearly 50 years of deprivation in Eastern Europe and 70 in the Soviet Union create an enormous pent-up demand for consumer, technical, and capital goods.
2. Infrastructures throughout Eastern Europe must be rebuilt and modernized, including telecommunications, roadways, public transportation, waste disposal, public utilities, schools, and hospitals.
3. Construction of factories, living quarters, shopping centers, and tourist facilities should be booming for many years to come.

Currency Restrictions:

1. Only Poland, Czechoslovakia, and Hungary are moving rapidly toward hard currency. Eastern Europe has virtually no cash reserves.
2. The Soviet Union has begun steps to harden its currency. Substantial gold reserves should make the job easier.
3. All countries want and need dollars and other hard currency.
4. Countertrade will continue as a viable way to enter Eastern European and Soviet markets, at least for a few years.

Political Future:

1. This is the big unsettled question. No one can predict what the next 10 years will bring to the political arena.

U.S. Government Support/Restrictions:

1. Severe U.S. trade restrictions remain in effect but the government is beginning to gradually relax prohibitions against American business involvement.
2. Political-risk guarantees support financial investment in Poland.
3. The Bush administration is still trying to understand what has happened to the Soviet Union and the communist bloc. It may be several years before the fog clears.
4. Eager participation in these regions by Japan and Western Europe will probably force Washington to substantially relax trade regulations, financing support, and travel restrictions within the next few years.

Probability of Success:

1. Although the political and currency risks remain high, any American company that can get its foot in the door before the EC is formed should be in a promising competitive position for years to come.

CANADA

Canada remains the most compatible trading partner for the United States. American companies export twice as much to Canada as they do to Japan. The United State is also Canada's largest trading partner. Direct investment from both sides of the border has resulted in a homogeneity in U.S.–Canadian firms to such an extent that it is virtually impossible to distinguish nationality. New trade agreements bring even greater emphasis for cross-fertilization.

On January 1, 1989, the U.S.–Canada Free Trade Agreement (FTA) came into being. This created a plethora of opportunities for manufacturers and exporters on both sides of the border. American exporters have especially benefited from the lower U.S. dollar. Tariff cuts, easy cross-border movement of personnel, and synergistic cultures make this an ideal time to enter Canadian markets. The fact that the Canadian economy is approaching a recession at a much slower pace than the United States adds fuel to the fire.

The furniture industry presents one example of how lowering tariffs have helped American exporters. Furniture tariffs had been running 6 to 16 percent and precluded many small and midsize U.S. furniture manufacturers from competing in the Canadian market. The FTA caused these tariffs to drop by one fifth in 1989 and on a sliding scale to be completely eliminated in five years.

Jake McGill, CEO of a $35 million diversified manufacturer in upstate New York, decided to take advantage of these new markets for his chrome furniture division.

Jake had wanted to take advantage of the company's proximity to Canada for many years but because of high tariffs couldn't compete with European and Asian firms. After FTA passed, Jake bit the bullet and set about learning the complicated rules of the accord and how to handle the rules of origin provisions. The FTA requires exporters to complete certificates of origin to ensure that only products made in the United States or Canada, or containing significant North American content, qualify under FTA. Prior to 1989, McGill's company stayed out of Canada completely. In 1990, exports of over $6 million will be realized.

In addition to furniture, five other product sectors have been identified by the U.S. Department of Commerce as hot prospects for exports to Canada: medical equipment, textiles and apparel, sporting goods, building materials and products, and laboratory instruments.

While the FTA eliminates all tariffs on goods produced within the United States or Canada by 1998, certain industries have requested immediate or accelerated removal. In the first half of 1990, duties came off trade worth $5 billion affecting some chemicals, electronic components, telecommunications equipment, aluminum products, printed circuits, diesel locomotives, and many other goods.

New travel rules now allow personnel registered with U.S. or Canadian firms to cross freely between the two countries. No work permits are needed. This means that American firms can test the Canadian market directly from their home base or through a U.S. representative.

Direct Investment

Direct investment is also accelerating appreciably. Ferro Corporation is adding Canadian branch plants to strengthen its use of Canadian natural resources for increasing sales in the United States. Other companies may find that Canadian plants can be used for shorter run, or niche market products. This leaves American facilities which generally have lower wage rates, for higher volume, labor-intensive production. Major investments by American companies have included a $1 billion aluminum refinery in Quebec by Alumax, Inc., and another $1 billion worth of new plants for Pratt & Whitney, General Tire, General Electric, and Reynolds Metals.

As a result of the FTA, government screening of U.S. business acquisitions or new investments in Canada is being progressively reduced. Beginning in 1990, only investments totaling more than $50 million required government review. By 1992, this level will be increased to $150 million, effectively removing government interference in small and mid-size business acquisitions. Low energy costs, access to raw materials, and a highly skilled work force should encourage American companies of all sizes to look to Canada as an ideal location for beginning their global expansion.

Summary

Trade Characteristics:

1. Close geographic and cultural ties have fostered substantial trade between Canadian and U.S. firms for years.
2. Highly skilled work force, management skills, and a modern infrastructure makes Canada probably the most attractive trading partner in the world.
3. Passage of the FTA has already lowered many trade barriers, and in the next five years nearly all will be gone.

Economic Needs:

1. The needs of Canadians are the same as those in the United States.
2. With the Canadian economy declining at a slower rate than the United States, proportionate markets should improve across the border.

Currency Restrictions:

1. The Canadian dollar has always been as stable as the U.S. dollar, in fact at times more stable.
2. There are no restrictions to the free movement of either currency.

Political Future:

1. With a parliamentary government the Canadian political picture should be as stable as the United States—unless Quebec starts another secession movement.

U.S. Government Support/Restrictions:

1. As much as the federal government can support anything, it supports open trade with Canada.

Probability of Success:

1. For small and midsize companies, Canada offers the best, easiest, and least expensive way to enter the global arena. If a company can succeed in the United States, it can make it in Canada.

CONCLUSION

For many small and midsize companies, entering the global arena through a developed country might appear easier and more straightforward than plunging into an export program to, or a direct investment in a developing nation. In many cases this is probably a good analysis. For others, however, markets in developed nations are already highly competitive and structured. Many major American corporations are already firmly entrenched. Joint ventures may be about the only way to resolve this issue. On the other hand, it is entirely possible that the best global entrance could be through a less competitive and faster growing developing country. The next chapter looks at characteristics of several of these markets.

CHAPTER 7

OVERVIEW OF MAJOR DEVELOPING GLOBAL MARKETS: THE CARIBBEAN, LATIN AMERICA, MIDDLE EAST, PACIFIC BASIN, ASIA, AND AFRICA

MAJOR TOPICS

KEY POINTS

This chapter continues the examination of trading opportunities in Third World and developing nations and regions. As in the previous chapter, these opportunities are evaluated under six criteria: (1) trade characteristics, (2) economic needs, (3) currency restrictions, (4) political future, (5) U.S. government support/restrictions, and (6) the probability for success by an American company. A summary of the advantages and risks of doing business in each country/region appears at the end of each section.

Entering through a developed country with synergistic cultural and economic goals may be the easiest and quickest route to attack global markets but not necessarily the most profitable. Entering by the backdoor through a developing nation, or one without a welcome mat for American participation is an entirely different matter. The risks are higher, but then so are the returns.

Even though a newly industrialized nation, such as Singapore, Taiwan, Hong Kong, or even South Korea, has a historical base of trading and financial systems upon which to build for the future, protectionism and favoritism proliferate these countries. Each of these nations has built its economy around exports similar to Japan's. Each zealously guards its trade borders against any deterioration in its trade surplus. Overcoming favoritism usually requires gifts, informal side agreements, and a willingness to reciprocate favors with monetary payments. The Foreign Corrupt Practices Act has caused more than one American company to stumble badly when trying to do business in the Far East.

Less developed nations such as Indonesia, Mexico, North Yemen, or Gambia present a somewhat different set of entrance barriers. Many are politically unstable. The probability of internal wars, nationalization of industries, or other government expropriation of property makes a direct investment a gamble. Others are so economically poor, have such a drought of labor or raw materials, are so politically corrupt, or are so oppressive, that smaller companies find it extremely difficult and risky to set up a facility or even to sell export products in the country.

Still others remain under totalitarian rule and operate as closed societies with strict government control over all economic activity. There are a few countries whose past acts against humanity, and specifically against Americans, bring a cry of moral outrage from the U.S. government and the American public whenever trade is considered.

However, as we all have witnessed in the past few years, political and social institutions have a way of changing. The cold war is over. America is not engaged in a drawn-out shooting war with any nation. Economics is winning out over ideologies in Europe, Asia, South America, and Africa. So what might seem to be a poor choice for direct investment or trade today, could easily turn out to be the burgeoning market of tomorrow. For this reason, it is desirable to grasp at least the bare essentials of the political and economic structure of countries such as Burma, Mongolia, and Vietnam. Although not viable trading partners now, one or more could easily become substantial markets in the not too distant future.

This chapter looks at some of the more promising developing global markets for small and midsize companies either now or in the foreseeable future. Some major markets have been omitted because internal conditions make it extremely unlikely that they will become viable for smaller companies in the next 10 years. India, Pakistan, Afghanistan, and Sri Lanka have been omitted because their geographic distance from the United States, internal labor, financial or consumption restraints, or endemic warring factions make reasonable trade decisions difficult and costly.

Australia and New Zealand have not been included because of the high cost of market entry, barriers to foreign investment, uncontrolled inflation (Australia has been experiencing an 18 percent rate) and intense local competition. Large corporations can do very well *down under* but smaller companies would probably do better elsewhere. Cuba has been omitted from consideration because of current trade boycotts by the American government. Should conditions change, however, the pros and cons of doing business in other Caribbean nations will become applicable here as well.

Because of feared trade barriers from the European Community and a continuing lack of overt trade cooperation between Pacific Basin countries, a meeting was held in Canberra, Australia, in November 1989, between 12 East and Southeast Asian countries and the United States, Canada, Mexico, Australia, and New Zealand to begin discussions leading toward economic cooperation in the area. Representatives even gave themselves a name—Asia-Pacific Economic Cooperation (APEC) and agreed to meet again in Singapore in 1990 and Seoul in 1991. The Singapore meeting resulted in more name-calling than constructive progress (even reporters from *The Wall Street Journal* were chastised). Hope abounds that Seoul will be more productive.

The growth of the Pacific Basin in the 1980s belies any assumption that this area is not an economic force to be reckoned with in the 1990s and beyond. Whereas the Atlantic and the Mediterranean have been the principal focus of world trade for centuries, conditions are changing. In 1989, 40 percent of world trade took place across the Pacific. The countries bordering the Pacific produced 44 percent of total world gross national product.

Opportunities to exert economic leadership in this area are rapidly slipping from the grasp of American companies. Not the least bit hesitant, Japan continues to invest billions of dollars in the region while American companies continue to be enamored with European economies and American financial resources crumble under the weight of a deteriorating banking system. Perhaps the pendulum will swing, but as of 1990, America has a lot of catching up to do to become a sustaining economic power in the Pacific.

The International Institute for Management Development in Lausanne, Switzerland, and the World Economic Forum based in Geneva, announced a new ranking of countries with the most attractive business conditions. The study was based on 326 criteria such as labor costs, political climate, social progress, and government support (or nonsupport) for private enterprise. Of countries classified as developed nations, the list reads in the following order: Japan, followed by Switzerland, the United States, Germany, Canada, and Sweden. Of the developing nations, Singapore led the parade followed by Taiwan, Hong Kong, South Korea, Malaysia, and Thailand. Clearly the gong has sounded for American businesses of all sizes to recognize the long-term importance of active participation in the future economic development of the Pacific Basin.

The proximity of the Caribbean and Central America, however, and the intense interest by the U.S. government in developing economically viable and politically stable neighbors make these developing regions potentially an easier, quicker, and more profitable way for smaller companies to enter the global marketplace.

THE CARIBBEAN AND CENTRAL AMERICA

The Caribbean and Central American markets are a drop in the bucket compared with Japan, the EC, or Eastern Europe. However, because of their close proximity to the United States, clear cultural similarities to many Americans, and active support from the U.S. government, the Caribbean can be an ideal jumping off point for the small or midsize new entrant to global markets.

In 1983, Congress passed the Caribbean Basin Economic Recovery Act, commonly referred to as the Caribbean Basin Initiative (CBI). This program has provided a unique impetus to the development of trade and direct investment with 21 Caribbean countries. These 21 countries are:

Antigua/Barbuda	Haiti
Aruba	Honduras
Bahamas	Jamaica
Barbados	Montserrat
Belize	Netherland Antilles
British Virgin Islands	(Bonaire and Curaçao)
Costa Rica	St. Kitts/Nevis
Dominica	St. Lucia
Dominican Republic	St. Vincent
El Salvador	and the Grenadines
Grenada	Trinidad and Tobago

Six additional countries are eligible for inclusion but have not requested admission (with the exception of Guyana): Anguilla, Cayman Islands, Guyana, Nicaragua, Suriname, and Turks and Caicos Islands.

The initial purpose of the CBI was to stimulate economic development in these nations by permitting duty free imports into the United States. Since its inception, however, CBI assistance has extended far beyond this limited goal. The program now includes:

1. U.S. economic assistance to aid private sector development through direct financing programs, development banks, chambers of commerce, skills training programs, and foreign trade zones.
2. Self-help efforts to improve local business environments and support investors and exporters.
3. Deductions for convention expenses for U.S. companies holding meetings in CBI countries to promote tourism.
4. Promotion programs, including trade and investment financing, business development missions, technical assistance programs, and a special government access program for textiles and apparel.
5. Encouragement of support from multinational development institutions such as the IMF, Inter-American Development Bank, and World Bank.

The CBI program encourages American companies to make direct investments in Caribbean businesses as an alternative to the Far East. It cites comparatively low labor rates, high productivity, ease of access, and cultural synergism. CBI officials report that through 1989, companies investing in the following types of businesses in the Caribbean have had the greatest success:

- Apparel and other made-up textile items.
- Electronic and electromechanical assemblies.
- Data processing/keystroke operations.
- Handicrafts, giftware, and decorative accessories.
- Wood products, including furniture and building materials.
- Recreational items, sporting goods, and toys.
- Tourism.
- Seafood.
- Tropical fruit products.
- Winter vegetables.
- Ethnic and specialty foods—sauces, spices, liqueurs.
- Ornamental horticulture.
- Leather goods.
- Medical and surgical supplies.

Before embarking on a CBI investment, it's a good idea to get an advance ruling on the eligibility of products with potential for import into the United States. Such a ruling can be obtained by writing the U.S. Customs Service at: Value and Special Classification Branch, Classification and Value Division, U.S. Customs Service, 1301 Constitution Ave. NW, Washington, DC 20229.

For those companies interested in exporting to the CBI, the Department of Commerce will help locate Caribbean buyers and distributors. It will also assist in publicizing new products in these international markets. Sources of joint venture partners and other direct investment assistance can be obtained from the Caribbean Basin Information Center: (202) 377-2527. General information about investment climate, local political and commercial regulations, and other data for a specific country can be obtained from Commerce Department desk officers (see appendix). In-country advice and assistance is provided by commercial attachés stationed in all U.S. embassies.

There are no currency restrictions in CBI countries. American dollars are freely translated to and from local currency. Most currencies are pegged to the dollar to avoid wide exchange variations.

Political Change and the Role of American Business

From a political perspective, nearly all Caribbean and Central American governments are relatively stable and eager for American participation in building their economic infrastructures. With Chamorro winning control in Nicaragua, Noriega behind bars in the United States, the Salvadoran massacre heading in a downward spiral, and Jamaican radical nationalism subsiding, many experts confirm that building the economic base in these countries is the surest way to ensure future political stability.

These rapid political changes point to the need for radical alterations to U.S. trade and assistance policies over the next decade, especially for Central American nations. If history is any indication of the effectiveness of federal bureaucratic achievement in the economic rebuilding process, however, any meaningful, long-lasting economic assistance must come from the private sector.

Over the past 50 years, the only significant private sector development has been by major corporations such as United Fruit, Anaconda, and the oil companies, eager to exploit natural resource reserves with little attention paid to building a solid economic base. Nationalist politics have proven this era to be over. The emphasis in the next decade will be on building infrastructures and transferring technological and management expertise to the local populace.

Small and midsize companies can make major contributions in these areas. By taking advantage of U.S. government aid programs, companies can make investments in the Caribbean with very little equity. They can also invest with little risk or start-up cost. And they can do it quickly without lengthy negotiations to reduce local trade barriers.

Summary

Trade Characteristics:

1. Most countries have limited trade barriers and welcome U.S. investment and products.
2. Unskilled labor is plentiful and cheap. Management talent is lacking.
3. Financing assistance is plentiful.
4. Most countries maintain market economies with few government controls.

Economic Needs:

1. Most countries have large populations at the poverty level.
2. Technology and capital goods of all types are needed.
3. Basic consumer goods are also needed.
4. Luxury items or high-priced consumer goods should be avoided.

Currency Restrictions:

1. The U.S. dollar is welcome in all Caribbean and Central American countries.
2. Local currencies are usually tied to the dollar and therefore are readily convertible.
3. Black markets in U.S. dollars flourish.
4. There are few restrictions against the repatriation of U.S. dollars.

Political Future:

1. Some nations such as Costa Rica and Barbados are very stable.
2. Governments in other countries such as Jamaica, Grenada, or Guatemala can change radically and rapidly.
3. All countries are trending toward more stable, freely elected governments. Some, such as Haiti, are not yet there.

U.S. Government Support/Restrictions:

1. The Caribbean Basin Initiative program illustrates how much the U.S. government wants to stabilize the area.
2. Panama and Nicaragua are good examples of how far the United States will go to get its way.
3. There are virtually no trade restrictions from the United States.

Probability of Success:

1. For most small or midsize companies, this region offers almost as great an opportunity as Canada, with much less competition.
2. Cheap labor, U.S. government subsidies, and synergistic language and cultural bases should help even the smallest company get established.

SOUTH AMERICA AND MEXICO

Other Latin-American nations not included in the CBI present a different set of economic considerations. Enormous debt obligations, continued political instability, nationalistic philosophies, and essentially agrarian populations (except Argentina), make South America a questionable investment opportunity for the small or midsize company at this time. Newly elected governments in Brazil, Argentina, Chile, and Peru, are faced with enormous internal economic problems. It's too early to know what improvements might be achieved.

President Fernando Collor de Mello in Brazil, for instance, must face up to a monthly inflation rate of more than 70 percent. Argentina's president, Carlos Menem is encountering the worst inflation rate (80 percent per month) in his brief tenure. For the year 1989 the Argentinian annual inflation rate was over 12,000 percent! With such currency instability, foreign investment just doesn't make much sense. Aside from the horrendously restrictive monetary policies enacted by the governments of Brazil and Argentina to bring some semblance of order to the financial markets, the two countries have also agreed to implement a mini "common market." By December 31, 1994, it was agreed that all barriers to bilateral trade between the two countries would be lifted. A gradual phasing-in between now and 1994 should begin to stabilize at least a portion of economic trade in these countries.

The Role of Private Investment

Past exploitation by large American natural resource companies has left a bad taste in Latin mouths for American business practices. Many of the majors continue active business in South America, however. General Motors, General Electric, Union Carbide, R.J. Reynolds, Dow, Xerox, Goodyear, and Johnson & Johnson all conduct business throughout the continent. Large and small American construction companies continue to engage in building infrastructures, commercial complexes, and hotels. A few midsize companies have taken advantage of the Latin debt crisis by engineering debt-equity swaps for industrial and commercial property.

For the most part, however, South America remains virtually untouched by smaller firms. Most have opted for participation in the more secure and less volatile nations of Western Europe or the Far East. While exporting has given many firms an entry into South American markets, few have followed up with direct investment. The Japanese have not been so gun-shy, however. Recognizing the huge potential for developing industrial and consumer demand, the global Japanese have not been hesitant to invest in manufacturing, retailing, and distribution businesses throughout South America.

There remains a substantial demand for American products in the consumer, agricultural, and some industrial markets. For those companies willing to cope with Latin business and political idiosyncracies, South America might be a reasonably good opportunity, especially for those companies already exporting to the region. To make a successful investment in plant and equipment, however, a company must look at long-term competitive global advantage. Not short-term return on investment.

Many global thinkers recognize that laws of economics will eventually resolve the debt crises, even if American banks remain obstinate. The IMF and World Bank are beginning to step up to the problem in Mexico. In 1990, the World Bank extended a loan of $1.26 billion to Mexico as support for its debt restructuring agreement with commercial banks. This loan, plus another $1.27 billion from the IMF form part of a total $7.3 billion restructuring package to relieve Mexico of its unmanageable debt burden.

It also seems likely that Washington will begin to recognize the desirability of allowing the private sector to bail out Latin economies. When this occurs, government-sponsored initiatives, similar to the CBI, will be forthcoming for many countries in South America. Those small or mid-size companies poised to take immediate advantage of these policy changes obviously stand to gain the most. Once the American public tires of allowing the South American production of cocaine and other narcotics to overshadow logical, reasonable, and necessary government trade policies, the pendulum should swing.

The Mexican Experiment

Mexico is the first Latin country to begin taking major steps to resolve its economic calamity. By systematically dismantling the country's trade and investment barriers, the government of Carlos Salinas de Gortari has opened Mexico's baroque doors to the winds of competition. As an example, Bell Atlantic International, Inc., has entered into a joint venture with a Mexican firm, Industrias Unidas, S.A. in a bid to provide cellular telephone service in Mexico. The venture, Telecommunicaciones del Pacific S.A. will build and run cellular networks in three regions that include the cities of Guadalajara, Tiajuana, Culiacán, and Hermosillo. As further inducement, the Mexican government is awarding 20-year franchises to private companies for telecommunications services in eight regional markets.

Disincentives still abound, however. Prevalent interest rates hovering around 40 percent are a strong discouragement to local investment in capital-intensive industries. Capital through Mexican sources is almost impossible to arrange. However, this leaves the door open to American firms with non-Mexican financing to take advantage of the extremely low wage rates in Mexico and the close proximity for travel and shipping. Chapter 19 examines current and projected trade agreements that make Mexico an even more attractive investment.

Summary

Trade Characteristics:

1. Extremely high foreign debt obligations with no foreseeable way to liquidate it, short of outright default.
2. Nationalistic governments retain pesky protective barriers to foreign investment, but most can be managed.
3. Japanese are investing heavily throughout South America and Mexico.
4. Corrupt government officials demand payoffs for approvals of everything from hiring labor to transporting goods.
5. Some countries have skilled labor base—most do not.
6. Inflation totally out of control.

Economic Needs:

1. All countries below the poverty level.
2. Technology, modern factories, and capital goods are needed most.
3. Basic consumer goods must now be imported.
4. Agricultural products in high demand.

Currency Restrictions:

1. All countries desperately need foreign exchange.
2. Soft currency often convertible to dollars only within the country. Many have restrictions against currency repatriation.

Political Future:

1. Most countries are politically unstable but do have elected governments.
2. Poverty levels, foreign debt, military strongmen, and definitive class systems support continued instability.
3. No resolution in the foreseeable future.

U.S. Government Support/Restrictions:

1. Verbally supportive of political stability and economic development, but not much action.
2. Aid continues to flow, but not enough to make a major difference in most countries. Should be more in the future.
3. Few restrictions for imports to the United States.
4. Cocaine trafficking continues as predominant government neurosis.

Probability of Success:

1. Mexico seems to offer the best prospects.
2. High-risk venture in most countries, but for those willing to gamble, the long-term payoff can be enormous.

THE MIDDLE EAST

The Middle East can be loosely defined as Israel and the Arab countries of Saudi Arabia, Oman, United Arab Emirates, Bahrain, Kuwait, Dubai, North Yemen, Syria, Jordan, Lebanon, Iraq, and Iran. During the 1970s and early 1980s the Middle East offered fertile ground for American investment. Major construction projects to build infrastructures, manufacturing and distribution facilities to provide Western-style goods, military buildups for national defense, and the development of transportation and communications networks provided American investors enormous new markets.

Strong ties between Israel and the U.S. government created special opportunities for exports to and investment in Israel. Government-to-government mutual support agreements between the United States and Saudi Arabia, Oman, the UAE, and Kuwait assured a warm welcome to American businesses. The Iraq-Iran war in the Mid-1980s encouraged additional outside investment in several Arab countries, notably Saudi Arabia, and importation of much needed military materiel. On the other hand, the Lebanese civil war, the hostage issue, and political antagonism with Syria, Iraq, and Iran have stopped any significant private trade with these countries.

Most of the basic infrastructures have now been built, however. Competition between American suppliers and European private enterprise has begun to make Middle East trade more treacherous for smaller firms. The first development wave has been completed. Gargantuan profits reaped by early investors are no longer feasible. Opportunities continue to exist for many products, however, notably in agribusiness, military goods and services, and replacement parts for infrastructure projects. But the ease of entry and profit margins have changed.

As the 1990s begin to unfold, the Middle East seems curiously out of step with the rest of the global community. Israeli-PLO struggles continue unabated with nothing new being offered by either side. Lebanon remains locked in suicidal internal conflict leading nowhere but to more death and destruction. Iran wrestles with consensual agreement for a national identity. Iraq seems bent on suicide. Saudi Arabia, the UAE, and other oil-producing states languish in the aftermath of their bloated power surge in the 1970s, but seem unwilling to advance beyond the parochial aims of their feudal leaders.

As internal wars obliterate previous economic gains, and apathetic leadership hopes for renewed American interest in their internal affairs, the infrastructures of Middle Eastern countries, so tenuously developed in the 1970s and early 1980s have begun to crumble. Eventually, much of the roadways, communication networks, public utilities, hospitals, and education facilities will have to be rebuilt. For the present, however, the mañana attitude seems to have relegated such infrastructure rehabilitation to the back burner.

Business Practices

Most business in the Middle East is conducted or tightly controlled by local government agencies. Customers are rarely private businesses. Payments for imported goods and services nearly always require government approval. Banking and financial services are also tightly controlled by the respective governments. Skilled labor is nonexistent in several countries and must be imported from Pakistan or other nations. Management talent, though improving in places, such as Saudi Arabia and Israel, remains unsophisticated in current techniques.

Other than oil and a few other natural resources, production raw materials are scarce and must also be imported. Special licensing requirements, stringent business-structure regulations, unsophisticated financial and banking systems, and cultural anomalies make the Middle East a difficult place as an initial investment opportunity for western companies.

Without a working knowledge of Middle Eastern business practices and special government contacts, it is becoming increasingly difficult for smaller companies to gain a foothold in either the Arab countries or Israel. As the region begins to settle down politically, the Israeli-Palestinian issues are resolved, the American hostages freed, the Iraqi debate settled, and the Lebanese civil war ends, business opportunities are sure to open up. Meanwhile, most small or midsize companies can probably find better global opportunities in other regions.

Summary

Trade Characteristics:

1. Heavy state involvement in business practices.
2. Barter supports local economies.
3. Except for Israel, small populations of unskilled workers and no management talent. Israel just the opposite.
4. Rich in oil reserves but import nearly all consumer and capital goods and technology.
5. The oil states have enormous trade surpluses.

Economic Needs:

1. Basic consumer goods, capital goods, agricultural commodities, foodstuffs, and technology are needed throughout the Middle East.

Currency Restrictions:

1. Currencies are soft, but convertible in major trading centers.
2. Repatriation of funds can be sticky in some countries.

Political Future:

1. Lebanon, Iran, Iraq, and Syria—uncertain.
2. Israel elected parliament seems to be working, albeit stumbling.

3. Arab kingdoms are ruled by family monarchies which will continue to hold power.
4. Potential is high for an all-out war in the region.

U.S. Government Support/Restrictions:

1. Continued heavy subsidies and moral support for Israel, including close trading ties.
2. No official trade ties with militant nations.
3. Huge military technology and weapons support for Arab states—especially Saudi Arabia.
4. Eager to give any support requested to keep oil lanes open.
5. Intent on stopping Saddam Hussein.

Probability of Success:

1. This is not the time for smaller companies to enter Middle East markets for the first time.

THE PACIFIC BASIN AND ASIA

Many small and midsize companies have found the Pacific Basin an excellent market in which to flex their global wings. Diverse cultures, vast unexploited natural resources, burgeoning populations, relatively stable political climates, and an encouraging financing ambiance have afforded many western companies the opportunity to enter local markets with relatively less risk than in other global economies. The vastness of the Pacific Basin makes it difficult to generalize. The best way to learn of specific possibilities is through the American trade representative responsible for your specific area of interest.

There are some major markets, however, that are worth looking at. Singapore, Taiwan, Hong Kong, South Korea, New Zealand, and Australia are the more developed countries. Indonesia, still in the developing stage, can best be evaluated as a Third World market. At the other end of the spectrum, many Asian countries remain firmly entrenched in Leninist political and economic philosophy.

Association of Southeast Asian Nations

The Association of Southeast Asian Nations (ASEAN) consists of Thailand, Malaysia, Singapore, Indonesia, the Philippines, and Brunei. Although this grouping reflects similar cultural, political, and security traits, the stage of economic development in each of the member countries varies considerably. At one end of the spectrum, Singapore has been eminently successful in fostering internal development and global trade. Brunei, with its vast oil reserves and Japan as the only customer, has become a wealthy nation. At the other end, the Philippines and Indonesia, though practicing market economics for some time, have yet to reach their full potential.

ASEAN members have several common concerns that often conflict in the pragmatic world of global trade: rising nationalism, export economies, economic interdependence, and a recognition that the United

States must continue to provide for the security of the region. Though some of these concerns result in conflicting results—throwing out American military bases is inconsistent with the United States providing military security to the region—ASEAN looks to the future as an economically self-sufficient region.

A further consensus among member nations is that the United States remains essential to the development and stability of the region as these countries grow in economic and political strength. No other major nation is seen as a reasonable substitute for American economic and military support.

Malaysia

Since 1986, when the last general election was held prior to 1990, Malaysia has experienced remarkable economic growth, even though its political scene has been fraught with turmoil. Rubber and tin have long been the mainstays of this predominantly export economy. In recent years timber, oil, and palm oil have joined the ranks of major export commodities. Manufacturing has also risen in importance and now accounts for a significant portion of total annual exports. The recession of 1985–86 drove many banks and cooperatives out of business. By 1989, however, most of these problems were being put in the past. In 1989, the Malaysian gross domestic product (GDP) increased 8 percent, just a shade below 1988, according to the *Far East Economic Review*.

Malaysia has been and continues to be receptive to foreign investment. It offers several incentives to encourage foreign investment in production facilities. In fact, it was foreign investment that bailed the country out of the last recession. The 1988 increase in foreign investment was reported by *Asiaweek* to be three times the increase of a year earlier. Manufacturing has been the major segment benefitting from foreign investment.

Minister of Trade and Industry, Datin Padukah Rafidah Aziz, predicted that growth in manufacturing will be 34 percent of GDP by 1995. In 1988 it was 24 percent—a rise of over 15 percent from the previous year. Manufacturing in 1990 makes up about one half of total export value while primary commodities, exclusive of oil, represent only 20 percent. A decade earlier, the proportionate shares were reversed.

Electronics and electronic components make up about 15 percent of the exported products. Various textiles and textile products are also a significant factor. As reported in *Asiaweek*, the Malaysian trade ministry firmly believes that the favorable combination of skilled labor and the low wage rates encourages the manufacture of high value-added products. Clearly this could be a very attractive global investment opportunity for western companies.

To date Americans have not recognized this opportunity. During the first nine months of 1989, Japan, Taiwan, and Singapore were the leading investor countries. Japan alone invested M$2 billion during this period—principally in timber production.

Malaysian exports to other ASEAN members exceeded M$190 million in 1989. New markets have been opened in South Korea, Iran, and

China for its palm oil. Malaysia now ranks in the top five of the world's producers of cocoa.

All is not rosy however. The lack of capital goods production and consumer products led to a net trade deficit for the year 1989. Malaysian officials expect their overall trade surplus to decline again in 1990. Unemployment is running at 8 percent and the inflation rate hovers around 4 percent. As reported in the *Asian Wall Street Journal*, the finance minister's budget for 1990 reflected no tax changes to compensate for this mixed economic bag. It did, however, include import duty reductions for some household items, sporting goods, and motorcycles. It also reflected a reduction in taxes on hotel and tourist services.

Although trade barriers and government restrictions on import volume are similar to Japan's, they are not as severe nor as widespread. With a strong developing economy and vast natural resources, Malaysia appears to be an excellent avenue for direct investment by smaller companies. Strategically located in Southeast Asia, Malaysia could well serve as a focal installation for providing raw materials or components for final production or assembly in other locations.

Thailand

Thailand politics have gradually democratized over the past 15 years. Today Thailand provides strong evidence of how a traditional feudal society can evolve into institutionalized capitalism. The king remains in control. Internal conflicts between religious, nationalistic, and monarchal groups continue. To date, however, none have been of sufficient thrust to disrupt the democratic evolution of a market economy, albeit still in the developing stage.

As Clark D. Neher reports in the March 1990 issue of *Current History, A World Affairs Journal,* the Thai economy has undergone a remarkable expansion since 1986, averaging nearly 10 percent per year. For the past 30 years, the economy has grown an average of 7 percent per year in spite of global recessions. The nation now ranks near the top of the world's economies in terms of growth performance.

As an exporter, the results are even more spectacular—25 percent growth each year from 1986 through 1989. Manufactured products are at the heart of this growth and now account for a greater share of GDP than agriculture. Foreign direct investment has been the catalyst to make this growth possible. Through 1989 countries leading the investment parade in descending order were Japan, Taiwan, the United States, Hong Kong, and South Korea. Additionally, tourism brought in over $3 billion in 1989 and now accounts for the largest segment of Thailand's foreign exchange.

The current Thai government professes a dedication to maintaining a free-market, export-drive economy. It welcomes foreign investment in productive industries. The labor base is large and reasonably well trained. There are a number of technocrats eager to train for managerial positions. Thailand has been and continues to be a viable location for a small or midsize company wishing to enter the Southeast Asia market.

Indonesia

As Indonesia launched its fifth five-year economic plan (1989–93) indications from Jakarta were that the government would place significantly greater reliance on the private sector to provide economic growth through additional capital and structural changes. The government also expects the private sector to realize significant improvements in productivity. This economic sector is being helped by a series of public reform packages. These reforms are directed toward three specific areas of trade:

1. The deregulation of trade and foreign investment.
2. Improvements in the effectiveness of banks and other private financial institutions.
3. The phasing out of government intrusions into economic matters.

These reform packages reflect the government's attempt to radically change the rules of doing business in Indonesia. This is especially true in banking and finance, trade and industry, and foreign investment. It is too soon to tell how effective these reforms will actually be. On the other hand, such a sincere attempt at a market economy should be welcome news to potential foreign investors.

In the banking and finance area the most important change involves the elimination of restrictive licensing provisions for the formation of new banks. This should permit the formation of new Indonesian banks and the entrance of foreign banks to joint ventures with Indonesians. Bank Indonesia, the central bank, has made it clear that insolvent banks can no longer look to it for bailouts.

Free trading on the Jakarta Stock Exchange also opens the door to foreign participation. Foreign investors are now permitted to purchase shares directly in Indonesian companies and can own up to 49 percent in any Indonesian company except banks. Foreign participation in joint ventures are even less restrictive. In 1988 Taiwan and West Germany each invested about $1 billion. American companies invested $672 million. Japanese investment totaled $256 million.

Deregulation and privatization continues, although the first big wave has now been completed. Competition will inevitably become fiercer. A sound labor base with low wages, an active financial market, and an avowed government policy of encouraging foreign investment, should make Indonesia another strong candidate for direct investment by smaller, global-oriented firms.

Burma (Myanmar)

The Burmese government officially changed the name of the country to Myanmar in June 1989. Political turmoil continues to exist. It may be some time before Myanmar becomes a relatively safe investment. Faced with an underlying economic crisis, the government is trying to encourage private sector development as the answer to its problems. Unfortunately, there are many obstacles, not the least of which is the high value of its currency, the kyat.

The Myanmar government did take a step in the right direction in 1988 when it legislated a new foreign investment law—the Union of Burma Foreign Investment Law. Under this new law, foreign investors may form either wholly owned businesses or joint ventures in which the foreign company must own a minimum of 35 percent. Producers of goods to be exported are favored.

To date, several joint ventures have been formed with private companies from Malaysia, Singapore, Thailand, and South Korea. Few American firms have ventured into this potential hornets' nest. Coca-Cola is one who did brave the move and plans to open bottling facilities in Myanmar during 1990–91.

The most significant change in Myanmar occurred with the granting of 5-year onshore oil exploration and 20-year joint production agreements to Japanese, South Korean, Dutch, Australian, British, and American companies. It is widely held that Myanmar holds substantial oil reserves and other natural resources.

Foreign debt continues to hamper the development of this country. Although no new debt has been added since 1987, the balance of $4.35 billion at that time has increased substantially by omission of interest and principal payments.

Summary

Trade Characteristics:

1. Enormous natural resource reserves.
2. Foreign investment generally encouraged.
3. Import barriers very lax.
4. Skilled workers in Malaysia, the Philippines, and Indonesia.
5. Although nationalism is increasing, foreign businesses are welcome in all countries.
6. Currently, Japan and Taiwan have made the greatest investment inroads.
7. Countertrade continues a viable vehicle for entrance.

Economic Needs:

1. All developing countries need consumer goods, technology, and capital goods to build their economic base.
2. Infrastructure development required in Myanmar, Indonesia, and parts of Malaysia.

Currency Restrictions:

1. Hard currency needed.
2. Repatriation rules vary.
3. Convertible to dollars in Southeast Asia but difficult to convert in the United States.

Political Future:

1. Most are now politically stable. Myanmar is still questionable.

U.S. Government Support/Restrictions:

1. Not yet awakened to the economic advantages in the area although minimal financial aid is flowing.

Probability of Success:

1. Excellent opportunity for smaller firms to get in on the ground floor through direct investment.
2. Significant financial assistance from the Asian Development Bank.
3. Strategically located for exports to Japan and China.
4. Rich in natural resources.

NEWLY INDUSTRIALIZED NATIONS

Singapore, Taiwan, and South Korea continue to enforce stringent trade barriers similar to the Japanese. All three countries run significant trade surpluses and discourage the opening of import markets. On the other hand, the governments are relatively stable, currency exchange is never a problem, and highly skilled labor and management personnel are available. These conditions make foreign investment very attractive, especially to American firms. Many companies have invested in these industrialized nations already, and there will undoubtedly be many more to come.

Taiwan is especially attractive. Merrill Lynch and Shearson Lehman have been given permission to open the first foreign brokerage offices on the island, giving these firms an entry into the high-flying Taiwanese stock market. Smaller American companies are also taking advantage of this lucrative market. One example is Voith Hydro, Inc., of York, Pennsylvania.

Voith Hydro, Inc., is a private manufacturer of large pumps, valves, turbines, and other hydraulic equipment with sales of about $100 million. As reported by Jennifer Lin in the *Philadelphia Inquirer* the company won a contract for $82 million for a hydroelectric plant in Taiwan. In 1987, the government-owned Taiwan Power Co. (Taipower) announced it was building a hydroelectric station in the center of the city of Mingtan. The station will be designed to generate electricity from a water cascade. At night, pumps move the water back up to the top reservoir. This was a big project for Voith Hydro. Its president, Goetz Pfafflin, wanted to win it.

In the beginning, the company followed the normal bidding procedures called for in the bid package. After a year of traveling to Taiwan and a series of meetings and negotiations, it became clear to Pfafflin that regardless of what the Taiwanese were saying about wanting to improve U.S. trade, they favored a handful of Japanese suppliers who had been handling the utility's business for 25 years. Pfafflin also believes that the Foreign Corrupt Practices Act forbidding American firms from offering or accepting gifts or payments in return for business, put the company at a severe disadvantage in dealing with both the Taiwanese and its Japanese competitors—who have no such scruples.

Frustrated, Pfafflin turned to political clout to win the contract. He sought help from the U.S. Commerce Department, the U.S. trade representative, and the U.S. government office in Taipai. He enlisted the support of two American senators, two congressmen, and one governor. He obtained endorsement letters from the U.S. Army, the Department of the Interior, and the Tennessee Valley Authority. Finally, Pfafflin petitioned the Taiwanese Ministry of Economic Affairs, Ministry of Foreign Affairs, the Council for Economic Planning, and its U.S. representatives in Washington. Eventually clout won out over the Japanese.

If there is one lesson Goetz Pfafflin learned about doing business in Taiwan it was that political clout can often outweigh the merits of technology in winning a project.

Although the newly industrialized Asian nations offer large, well-financed, and profitable markets, global competitors also recognize this. Until a company can gain experience in international trade, it's probably safer to start somewhere else.

Hong Kong is a separate case. It has not been included in this analysis because of its planned reversion to the People's Republic of China (PRC) in 1997. Conditions created by this drastic change are too unsettled to even guess what the post-1997 Hong Kong economic scene will look like.

Many foreign companies have invested in facilities in Taiwan, South Korea, and Hong Kong for several years. Trade barriers are substantial, however. A smaller company just getting started in global trade will have a difficult time of it here.

INDOCHINA

The winds of change are blowing in Indochina. The 1989 withdrawal of Vietnamese troops from Cambodia (albeit without formal validation) and the implicit support from Washington for the installation of a moderate Khmer government, point the way toward increasingly normalized trade relations with Phnom Penh. American government sources expect the new Khmer government to encourage private enterprise, work with indentifiable noncommunists, and restore Buddhism to the country.

Whether or not the new government can bring the murderous civil war under control remains uncertain. Until that happens, U.S. trade policy toward Cambodia remains dormant. American private enterprise should benefit, however, by watching developments during the ensuing months closely. If political instability moderates, American companies should be prepared to look at Cambodia as a viable global market.

Poverty remains Vietnam's central problem. Federal government officials estimate a per capita annual income of between $200 and $300 in 1988. This makes Vietnam one of the poorest countries in the world according to economist's "poverty index." It has virtually no hard currency reserves and owns one of the world's worst trade deficits.

There is no love lost between Moscow and Hanoi. The Soviets can ill afford to continue much longer their military and economic aid package totaling more than $3 billion annually. Obviously, they would like the United States to share this burden. This seems highly unlikely, however, without major ideological reforms from Hanoi—which seem just as improbable. Vietnam wants Washington to remove its opposition to international loans and lift the embargo on American trade. Yet in the near term there is little likelihood of this policy evolving either.

Just as Cambodia will probably offer trade opportunities in the long term, so will Vietnam. In modern history, no government has succeeded indefinitely under a blanket of economic disaster. Vietnam will probably be no different. If Americans can get over the moral implications of trading with Hanoi, eventually significant trade opportunities will unfold for companies of all sizes.

Laos remains politically tied to Vietnam, but economically attracted to Thailand. Trade relations with the United States can be defined as limited but hopeful. As economics continue to drive the political aspirations of Laotian leaders, it is possible that trade will begin to approach normalcy in the next decade.

CHINA, NORTH KOREA, AND MONGOLIA

Efforts continue by the Bush administration to maintain long-term economic ties with the People's Republic of China (PRC) while preaching moral disdain for the Tiananmen Square massacre. In spite of the administration's prodding, the foreseeable future for private enterprise participation in the Chinese recovery from Maoism appears questionable.

There remains an underlying sentiment of the American public for Washington to maintain *moral policies* in relation to economic interaction with the PRC. Human rights violations in the aftermath of the Tiananmen incident remain vivid memories of the risks of doing business with an oppressive regime. Federal actions such as providing sanctuary to Fang Lizhi and his wife, cutting off all military sales, expressing opposition to international loans, suspending high level official contacts, and issuing advisory notices against American tourists traveling to China, seem to support the *people's revolt*. But it's hard to tell how much opposition is real and how much just window dressing.

As with other attempts at economic sanctions, the administration's efforts to thwart the PRC leadership seem to have failed. In 1990, the World Bank granted the PRC a 40-year loan of $60 million at 1 percent interest. American businesses continue to do business with and within China. Fast-food chains, cosmetic manufacturers, hotel chains, and many other large and small American businesses still prosper on the China mainland.

The PRC has assured foreign banks and governments that it will be able to repay its debts. China's foreign ministry announced in 1990, that China boosted its trade surplus from $800 million in 1988 to more than $5 billion in 1989. During 1989 Chinese exports rose by 6.5 percent to over $43 billion, while imports fell 3.9 percent to just over $38 billion. It seems clear that even with the global outrage expressed at the Tiananmen incident, economic trade continues to overshadow ideological and moral differences.

Over the long term, strategic economic needs will probably persuade

Beijing that its best interests lie in strengthening economic ties with both Japan and the United States. These two nations are clearly in the best position to provide the key products, capital, and technology essential for the long-term development of China's economic base. Even though other sources are available through Taiwan, South Korea, and Western Europe, the United States remains in the forefront of state-of-the-art technology and strategic reach. Most importantly, it poses no political or military threat.

It seems highly improbable that China will convert to a democratic free market anytime in the foreseeable future. An autocratic government with a pluralistic economy is a very real possibility, however. Although it is difficult to postulate the direction of Sino-American political and formal trade relations in the near term, over the long haul American private enterprise support of a developing China seems highly probable. The exact nature of this support, the role of smaller American companies, and the incentives or barriers from the PRC remain unclear. Certainly, a global mentality requires a close watch over future developments in the relationships between Beijing and Washington.

North Korea and Mongolia

A progressively widening gap exists between the economies of North and South Korea. Pyongyang is well aware of this disparity. In spite of continued adherence to hard-line communist dogma, North Korea is learning that archaic Stalinist economic strategy and enormous military expenditures take their toll of the country's economic base. With its staunchest supporters, China, Vietnam, and the USSR, in economic disarray, little help can be expected from these sources in strengthening trade relations. Talks with the Seoul government continue in a halfhearted effort to resolve ideological and economic differences leading to a Korean unification. Currently these talks bring little hope for success in the near future.

Dialogues between Washington and Pyongyang have been minimal. However, recent invitations to certain politically mainstream Americans to visit North Korea may begin to bridge what is currently an unbridgable ideological gap. Any opportunities for American business participation in the North Korean economy in the near term appear remote.

The U.S. government has made few attempts at the normalization of relations with Mongolia. Lack of interest by the American people in this remote region are reflected in the avoidance of any direct trade talks with the Mongols. With the rapid changes in the Soviet Union, Mongolia's closest trading partner, and with the increased opening of world trade, Mongolian leaders are preparing to expand their contacts with the outside world. Quite naturally, Japan is stepping forward as the likely candidate to offer economic assistance. It is possible, although at this time somewhat improbable, that the United States will seek a similar role in Mongolian development.

Summary

Although China has opened its trade doors somewhat to American businesses, recent political developments make definitive planning for market entrance by smaller firms precarious. Cambodia and Vietnam will eventually open up, but for the foreseeable future, active trading with U.S. companies will be very limited. This is not the region in which to learn international trade; at least not right now.

AFRICA

Muslim North Africa, the black middle belt, and racist South Africa are probably the global markets least understood by American business. The diversity of cultures, ideologies, and primordial economic policies tend to frighten off potential new entrants into the dark continent's markets. Libya, Chad, Angola, and Ethiopia are presently impervious to American business investment and to the development of U.S. trading partners. The decaying economic strata of Nigeria, Zaire, Somalia, Niger, and the Central African Republic presents impenetrable obstacles to all but a few basic American goods. The U.S. government, yielding to the moral outcries of special interest groups, implemented economic sanctions against South Africa. Such boycotts effectively remove this rich country from further American business participation—at least for the moment. Efforts by Mandela and de Klerk toward dialogue aimed at resolving the apartheid question, including visits to the United States by the two leaders, may hasten the return of global trade normalcy.

Market-Oriented Countries

On the plus side, the Ivory Coast, Senegal, Gambia, Kenya, Tanzania, and Zambia have stabilized their political base and are moving rapidly toward market economies. Egypt, Morocco, and Zimbabwe also offer markets adaptable to American global interests. Wyeth Labs, the pharmaceutical subsidiary of American Home Products, has participated successfully in these African markets for years. Political upheaval, economic disasters, currency machinations, and the U.S. government's hyperanxieties about spreading communism, have not deterred this global firm. Wyeth has managed to develop a stable market base in many African countries in the east, west, central, and northern part of the continent. The company has even found ways to maintain market ties with Libya!

Zal Holdings, a Zambian company which grew out of the vast copper mining industry, is a good example of how far some African companies have progressed in the world market. Zal is currently active in a variety of products and services in engineering, manufacturing, air and sea cargo, construction, travel and tourism, and personnel recruitment. The company has sales of nearly $100 million, a staff of 600 in its London office, 2,000 in Zambia, and 400 in its far-flung operations in Tanzania, Zimbabwe, Mozambique, Kenya, Malawi, and Ghana. Zal has significantly influenced the flow of hard currency into Zambia. It provides the country with a sound foundation for developing further international trade.

Gambia is another small African country coming out of the economic doldrums. Tourism blossoms on its small coastline as several European developers have built first-class resorts and hotels. Kenya, a progressive market economy by African standards, has long offered excellent opportunities to foreign investors, including American. Recently implemented business development incentive programs in Malawi and Liberia (once civil war ends) present interesting possibilities. As the politics in Namibia settle down, enormous amounts of aid from the United States and European nations will inevitably offer opportunities for significant infrastructure projects there.

Risks Prevail

There are definite risks for any foreign company engaging in African trade. Nationalism permeates nearly all nations on the continent. Many are extremely poor and wracked by political and military corruption. Others maintain tribal customs with a myriad of dialects, cultural aberrations, and rudimentary business practices. Soft currency predominates the lesser developed countries. Market economies such as Zambia and Kenya, still have a long way to go to offer significant expansion opportunities for foreign investment. And of course, the one country with a developed economic base and wide possibilities for profitable foreign investment—South Africa—is currently off-limits to American companies.

A brief note on South Africa provides a glimmer of hope, however. International trade has a way of overcoming ideological and moral dichotomies. In spite of the U.S. government ban on the importation of South African steel, a $91 million bridge at the Houston Ship Channel is being built with steel girders from South Africa. Importers get around the ban by convincing administration officials that girders are a fabricated product, one step removed from raw steel, and therefore not subject to the boycott laws. The Bush administration agrees!

Another way many companies are avoiding the South African boycott is to export to South Africa through subsidiaries located in Canada, Europe, or other countries. They also import through the same channels. This is all perfectly legal in the eyes of the Bush administration. It just goes to show that economics always prevail. Even federal laws can't prevent traders from trading.

Summary

African market-oriented countries offer potentially good opportunities for smaller or midsize global companies. Abundant natural resources, pent-up demand for consumer products, capital goods, and Western technology present an excellent environment for developing manufacturing and distribution facilities. Although European firms have been competing in these countries for several years, the Japanese are still minor role-players.

Several large American corporations have entered into countertrade arrangements with these nations. But significant market opportunities still remain for smaller entrants. The major drawback is the prevailing American ignorance of African culture. This makes companies unwilling to gamble on the unknown. For those willing to learn, however, market-oriented African nations afford a lucrative avenue for global trade.

CHAPTER 8

SOURCES OF INFORMATION

MAJOR TOPICS

KEY POINTS

1. **U.S. Government Agencies.** Department of Commerce, Eximbank, and other federal agencies maintain computer data bases and hard copy reports covering various aspects of global economic trends and market opportunities. Country desk officers can be especially helpful in alerting a company to opportunities in developing nations.

2. **State and Local Assistance.** Every state and nearly every large city maintain trade commissions specifically to assist local companies engage in local trade. Foreign trade zones exist in most states and can be helpful for importing or transshipping.

3. **Private Sector.** Universities, trade associations, large accounting and consulting firms, banks, and large multinational corporations are all helpful sources of global information. A listing of major publications is presented as an additional aid.

4. **Personal Contacts.** Casual acquaintances and friends can often point a person in the direction of information sources. An anecdote describes how.

5. **Staffing.** Even the smallest firm must establish minimum staffing to handle international transactions. A minimum organization is recommended for an American home office and one for a foreign office of a growing global company.

''I know we have to change our thinking from worrying about the Northeast and Midwest to looking at global markets. I'm sick and tired of running up against Kawasaki and Honda every time we call on a customer in Boston or

Detroit or Cleveland. If the Japanese can sell into the United States there's no reason we shouldn't sell into Japan—or Korea, or Germany, or Kenya, for that matter. Our engines are as good or better than Kawasakis or Hondas. My problem, Larry, is that I don't know how to get started, how to take the first step without spending a lot of money and time."

My good friend Hank Ewing was serious. He really wanted to go global with his small, single-stroke engines. I suggested he might want to start with a less restrictive country than Japan. We ran through the list of data sources together. I then recommended Hank contact the U.S. trade representatives for Kenya and Korea and get their input about trade barriers and market conditions in those countries. I also suggested he talk to Toro Manufacturing whom I knew had experience selling power equipment overseas. A month later I received a call from Hank, "Great advice, old buddy. I did what you said, one thing led to another, and now I'm deluged with data for four African countries, France, Italy, and Mexico. Korea just won't work. Too restrictive." Hank was off and running on his first global venture.

Deciding to enter the global marketplace and actually doing it are two entirely different matters. The former requires a specific mind-set; the latter takes work. Getting started in international trade frequently results in frustration. Without hard preparation, it leads to costly errors and wasted time. Managements from more than one small company have started to go global only to find that they don't know how to do it. The next step is a retreat into their isolationist shell. In the end, they lose.

To maximize the probability of success in global markets, the business owner or manager must arm himself with as much information as possible in six major areas:

1. Market opportunities.
2. Personnel recruitment.
3. Legal, accounting, and tax information.
4. Financing alternatives.
5. Selling and delivery procedures.
6. Risk management.

A wealth of information exists about each of these subjects. The sources can be logically grouped under seven headings. Figure 8–1 identifies which sources should be approached for each of the six major operations categories.

This chapter explains where and how to get information about market opportunities and technical assistance. It also passes along some tips on minimum personnel staffing for beginning international organizations. The following two chapters detail how to obtain information about specific countries or projects by conducting country surveys. Financing sources are examined in Chapters 12 through 15.

Before assessing the pros and cons of entering the global arena, it's helpful to review the wealth of information available through U.S. government agencies. Whether beginning an export program or investing in overseas facilities, federal agencies can provide more data, about a greater variety of topics, than any other source. Ideally, gathering global

FIGURE 8–1
Types of Information by Source

U.S. Government Sources:
- Market opportunities and technical assistance.
- Selling and delivery procedures.
- Financing alternatives.
- Risk management.

State and Local Government Agencies:
- Market opportunities and technical assistance.
- Financing alternatives.
- Personnel recruitment.

Trade Associations and Trade Groups:
- Market opportunities and technical assistance.
- Selling and delivery procedures.
- Financing alternatives.

Private Sector:
- Market opportunities.
- Financing alternatives.
- Risk management.
- Personnel recruitment.

Professional Advisers:
- Selling and delivery procedures.
- Financing alternatives.
- Legal, accounting, and tax information.
- Personnel recruitment.

Personal Contacts:
- Market opportunities.
- Legal, accounting, and tax information.
- Personnel recruitment.

Active Solicitation through Promotion and Advertising:
- Selling and delivery procedures.

data will be completed prior to spending money on international travel or hiring people to staff an international activity.

U.S. GOVERNMENT AGENCIES

The most voluminous sources of information about global market opportunities and technical assistance reside in the Department of Commerce. Within that department two organizations are dedicated to providing businesses with intelligence and assistance for attacking overseas markets: the International Trade Administration (ITA) and its sister organization the United States & Foreign Commercial Service agency (US&FCS). Reports, periodicals, computer data banks, books and other reference material can be obtained for a nominal charge, or free, from any one of 48 district offices and 19 branch offices nationwide. Each district office trade specialist can provide information about:

- Trade and investment opportunities abroad.
- Foreign markets for U.S. products and services.
- Services to locate and evaluate overseas buyers and representatives.
- Financing assistance.
- International trade exhibitions.
- Export documentation requirements.

- Foreign economic statistics.
- U.S. export licensing and foreign nation import requirements.
- Export seminars and conferences.

Most district offices maintain an extensive library containing all of the latest reports. They also work closely with 51 District Export Councils (DECs). These are groups of over 1,700 business and trade experts ready to help American firms enter the export field.

Economic trends and foreign sales leads are compiled by on-site US&FCS officers stationed in 126 offices around the world. These officers have been hired directly from the private sector. All should understand firsthand the problems of U.S. companies trading abroad.

Additionally, the US&FCS employs over 500 nationals around the world to assist in gathering and assimilating data for commercial programs. These programs include background information on foreign companies, market research, business counseling, assistance in making appointments with key buyers and government officials, representation for companies hurt because of trade barriers, seeking out trade and investment opportunities that can benefit American companies, and identifying overseas sales reps for U.S. companies. Bid listings, the current political and economic status of countries, market intelligence, new projects coming up, and many other types of information are available. This information is disseminated through the Trade Opportunity program (TOP).

As of 1988, worldwide ITA offices utilize the computer-based Commercial Information Management System (CIMS). All CIMS data is classified by Standard Industrial Classification (SIC) codes. Any ITA office can now provide market, product, and geographic information on any subject merely by pushing a button and generating a computer printout. The following samples indicate the type of information the Department of Commerce has available to identify and assess the advisability of entering foreign markets for specific products. Although not an inclusive listing, these seem to be the data and reports most requested.

Project Opportunities

One of the biggest headaches for overseas construction companies is to determine where the next bidding opportunity will exist for major projects. Bechtel, Fluor, Brown & Root, and a few other international engineering firms keep their market intelligence flowing through their own people stationed in every outpost of the world. For a smaller firm, however, such an undertaking would be unrealistic. Through the CIMS, smaller contractors can get reports and analyses of projects coming up for bid in any country. Reports analyzing marketing opportunities in specific countries can also be obtained.

Overseas Business Reports

Overseas Business Reports (OBRs) are broad-based reports that present an overview of market conditions in specific countries. They are written from a general business outlook. They do not include analyses for specific products or industries. Prognostications and analyses vary by country but most OBRs contain information about important market conditions and trends. They also identify current economic and commercial profiles for major regions of the world economy. Semiannual OBRs include six-month projections for U.S. trade with specific countries.

Global Market Research

Global market research, so necessary to comprehend potential shifts in demand, competitor strategy, and pricing tactics, can literally take a growing company forever to prepare. Therefore the results would always be out of date. The ITA has done much of this tedious work already—and keeps it current. The wealth of information ITA has compiled for global markets makes this a good place to begin understanding the characteristics of a specific industry in a specific country; say, medical electronics in Italy. Global market research facts, figures, and analyses are available for 50 key industry groups. They range from communications and electronic components, to packaging equipment, machine tools, and recreational equipment.

Reports can be generated for practically any market research subject desired. Some of the most widely used reports include information about market size, distribution channels, forecasted market potential, business customs and practices, customer analyses, trade barriers, competitive environment, and specific trade contacts.

Many smaller companies find OBRs the best starting point in analyzing which country or region to pinpoint. Not only do OBRs touch the broad issues, for some countries they also include data about tariff regulations, channels of distribution, and local legal restrictions governing foreign direct investment.

Export Trends

The ITA and US&FCS data base is enormous. Without such broad coverage, company personnel could spend weeks pouring through reams of paper, charts, analyses, tables, and a variety of other statistics. Now all this data has been translated to computer instant information. A trade specialist will be happy to extract whatever statistics a person may want. Historical trends can be printed out for the past five years showing, for a single industry, the amount of U.S. exports by generic product and by importing country. Tabular printouts of competitive information and potential future trends of each generic product group can also be obtained.

Trend analysis reports highlight data such as the future prospects for a specific industry, the industry's performance over the past five years, and the identification of its highest volume products. All subgrouped SIC code industries are not available; but all the basic, major classifications are.

Statistical tabulations can also be obtained to analyze export data for specific countries in manufactured and agricultural products. Using these separate data base sorts, a comprehensive picture can be painted for the past five years and the immediate future. These statistics are prepared at the gross levels. They may not be available for specifically defined second and third tier SIC code groupings. But at least this is a good starting point.

Foreign Economic Trends

Foreign Economic Trends (FETs) provide much the same information as OBRs, but more detailed. They deal with specific countries and include a detailed review of current business conditions. They also present an indepth analysis of the future economic prospects for the country. The prognostication for importing U.S. products does seem skimpy at times. By supplementing this report with an OBR, however, the user can get a fairly clear picture of the potential market for his product lines.

Industry Statistical Profiles

Depending on a company's product offering, statistical profiles of specific industries might prove helpful. As with any government report, the forecasts and projections of market conditions or political winds must be tempered with common sense. Government projections tend to be based on historical statistics and the current political philosophy in Washington, both of which can be misleading for the future. Industry statistical profiles present an overview of world demand and the prospects for market interest in U.S. exports. They also include a statistically compiled export rating chart, which may or may not be useful.

ITA's Trade Development unit compiles these statistics. The organization is grouped into seven sectors: aerospace, automotive affairs and consumer products, basic industries, capital goods and international construction, science and electronics, services, and textiles and apparel. The Trade Information and Analysis unit pulls data from each of these sectors to develop market intelligence. It then disseminates international trade and direct investment data as requested by specific inquiries.

Industry specialists plan international marketing programs directly with their industry groups, trade associations, and state development agencies. They also assist in developing policy statements aimed at reducing trade barriers. Their respective product groupings are promoted through marketing seminars, foreign buyer groups, business counseling, and executive trade missions. They also provide information on market opportunities in their respective countries.

Custom Research Service

For a small fee, a company may request an ITA to compile a personalized research study for any one of a select group of countries. Currently, this list includes the United Kingdom, Italy, France, West Germany, Canada, Brazil, Colombia, Mexico, Singapore, Indonesia, India, the Philippines, South Korea, and Saudi Arabia. More countries may be added at any time. Reports generated from this customized research include key marketing data for a specific product line in a specific country. This data may consist of several or all of the following data, depending on the product and country:

- Sales potential.
- Entry and distribution.
- Trade barriers.
- Names of competitors.
- Qualified purchasers.
- Comparative prices.
- Customary promotion practices.
- Leads for local joint ventures.
- Leads for direct sales representation.

Country Desk Officers

The country desk officers in ITA's International Economic Policy unit probably constitute the best source of general information for a company wishing to enter new or unfamiliar foreign markets. Separate desk officers, all located in Washington, cover Africa, China and Hong Kong, Canada, USSR, Eastern Europe, Caribbean Basin and Mexico, South America, South Asia, Pacific Basin, European Community, Japan, Near East, and Israel.

The responsibility of desk officers includes maintaining up-to-date information for each country in each desk's region. Such information includes all economic and commercial conditions. It specifically identifies legal regulations, tariffs, economic and political developments, business practices, trade data and trends, market size, and market growth. These officers develop and recommend trade and direct investment policy positions of the Department of Commerce. They also conduct government-to-government discussions of relevant issues. In this role desk officers participate in negotiating trade and investment agreements with their assigned countries. They also work with ITA district offices in counseling businesses and arranging seminars on trade and overseas direct investment opportunities.

Foreign Certification and Standards

A company starting to sell in global markets must be certain its products meet the specific certification standards of the host country. The National Center for Standards and Certification Information (NCSCI) is the central depository for foreign standards information. A quick check with this office can save months of wasted effort trying to get qualified in a specific country.

Small Business Administration

The Small Business Administration (SBA) maintains a program that coordinates with Eximbank for export financing. Some larger SBA offices also offer business counseling to firms starting an export program. For a variety of reasons the SBA has been unable to attract qualified people with global experience to fully staff international trade offices. Most of the advice handed out comes from inexperienced advisers. This can do the neophyte global manager seeking market or product information more harm than good. It's usually better to start with an ITA office and wait for the SBA to catch up in the future.

STATE AND LOCAL ASSISTANCE

Nearly every state and many larger cities maintain active trade commissions composed of representatives from local businesses and government. The purpose of these trade commissions is to foster state and local business activity through increased exporting. Most provide business counseling services, information gathering departments, federal export program coordination, technical assistance, and financing advice and assistance. Some states, such as Illinois, are very active in soliciting foreign direct investment to stimulate the job market. Others push for increased imports of components and assemblies to be fabricated into finished goods in their respective states.

State and local trade commissions work closely with industry trade associations and private trade groups. A company can work through a local group without incurring the aggravation and at times unmanageable bureaucracy of federal agencies. As a minimum, local groups are a good place to begin researching potential global opportunities in Europe and Japan. Some states offer local financing programs as well. This saves an enormous amount of paperwork required when dealing with Eximbank or other federal financing sources.

In major metropolitan port areas such as New York, Chicago, Los Angeles, Houston, and Philadelphia, local trade commissions can also assist in identifying freight forwarders, trading companies, and export management firms. They also offer assistance in setting up a foreign trade zone (FTZ) or in identifying those that are already established in the area. Chapter 19 describes the workings of FTZs more fully in relation to importing and transshipping.

PRIVATE SECTOR

A number of sources of market intelligence and technical assistance exist in the private sector. The advantages of avoiding government agencies should be clear to anyone who has worked through bureaucratic red tape—for any purpose. Private sector sources quite often have as much or more information about future global market development than many federal offices. The private sector generally is less than helpful in providing technical assistance, however. The best private sector sources are:

- Universities.
- Seminars and publications.
- Big 5 accounting/consulting firms.
- Banks.
- Large multinationals.

Almost every major university offering a business curriculum has now added at least one course covering international trade. This means that even those without graduate business programs maintain library reference works. Some graduate business schools now offer a degree in international business. They have a wealth of library material and other reference works.

A few forward-thinking schools even offer evening and noncredit courses in international trade. Information originating from universities about global market opportunities or technical assistance does tend to be less practical than that available from other sources. On the other hand, some schools, such as the Wharton School at the University of Pennsylvania, are quite attuned to the needs of the business community.

Attending seminars and reading publications is the least expensive, easiest, and quickest way to source market opportunities through the private sector. The American Management Association puts on some good seminars as do many university business schools. Occasionally seminars sponsored by one of the Big 5 accounting firms or major law firms heavily involved in international work can be helpful.

There are excellent publications available dealing with global trade topics. Aside from sporadic articles in *The Wall Street Journal, Business Week,* and *The New York Times, The Economist* is definitely worth the subscription price. Figure 8–2 lists some of the others that are dedicated to international developments.

These are all must reading to keep up on the general conditions in world markets. To get more detailed information on specific countries or regions try the following:

> *Background News.*   From the Bureau of Public Affairs, Department of State.
>
> *Operational Information on Proposed Projects.*   From the Asian Development Bank.
>
> *United Nations Development Business.*   Included in the Business Edition of the Development Forum and reviews the Inter-American Bank's monthly operations.
>
> *International Business Outlook.*   Covers monthly activities in the global banking and finance area and includes the World Bank monthly operating summary.

The Big 5 accounting firms will be most happy to send you monthly newsletters and course offerings on international trade. Some, such as Price Waterhouse, do an excellent job in nonmarketing areas. It produces a monthly newsletter for clients that highlights recent changes in economic, tax, and legal conditions in targeted countries. They don't offer much in the way of market-oriented data, however. A single phone call to the nearest office of one of these firms will get you on the mailing list. You don't have to be a client or use their services in any way. Of course, they hope you will in the future.

Money center banks such as Chase, Citicorp, and Chemical, with large international departments, periodically send newsletters to their customers covering current developments both in the United States and overseas. These topics normally relate to major shifts in economic policy, ex-

FIGURE 8–2
Publications Specializing in Global Trade

World Trade. This bimonthly magazine is probably the best resource available for beginning global companies.

Current History: A World Affairs Journal. An excellent monthly magazine specializing in articles about political and economic changes, by country, throughout the world.

Foreign Policy. A quarterly publication of the Carnegie Endowment for International Peace. Deals mostly with international political and social changes.

Foreign Affairs: America and the World. Published five times a year by the Council on Foreign Relations, Inc. In-depth analyses, by country and region—economic and political.

Finance and Development. A quarterly put out by the International Monetary Fund and the World Bank.

Financier. A monthly journal of private sector policy.

World Bank Annual Reports.

The World Development Report. An annual from the World Bank.

Economic and Social Progress in Latin America. An annual from the Inter-American Development Bank.

Bulletin. A quarterly magazine from Crédit Suisse (the Swiss Bank).

EX-IM News. A weekly report covering the activities of the Eximbank.

change movement, and financial regulations. Once again, however, they are short on marketing data. A phone call or letter to their international department is sufficient for most major banks to get on their mailing list. If that doesn't work, your local banker can make the contact for you.

Large multinationals that have been successful in the global arena are normally more than willing to meet with the owner or manager of a smaller company to discuss opportunities overseas. I have had the best reception going directly to the corporate vice president in charge of the group handling the products I'm interested in rather than an international department. Even though these companies all have substantial international staffing, an introduction from a group vice president smooths the waters for further meetings down the line. Clients have found General Mills, Exxon (before Valdez), Gillette, Du Pont, Dow Chemical, and Boeing to be most helpful in providing general descriptions of market opportunities.

PERSONAL CONTACTS

It's truly amazing how much information can be gathered from friends and acquaintances. Most people are more than willing to give advice if asked. Everyone likes to show how much he or she knows. Casual conversations at dinner parties, sporting events, vacation trips, at golf or tennis clubs, charity fund-raising events, or just chatting on the telephone can yield an enormous amount of information about potential market opportunities.

I was trying to gather some information about market opportunities in the Western Caribbean, (Guatemala, Honduras, Belize, Nicaragua, Panama, and eastern Mexico) for a client who manufactured small generator sets. Having completed a thorough search through the normal government channels and trade associations, and interviewing two good friends at Dow and Du Pont, I thought I had enough data to write a fairly comprehensive report. I was ready to recommend a country survey in Guatemala, and perhaps Honduras as the next step.

In casual conversation with one of our foursome during a golf game I happened to mention my interest in the current status of construction development in Guatemala. "I just returned from Guatemala last month and I can assure you that there is nothing of any significance going on in the construction industry now. After the election in 18 months, the government may settle down and start building some roads and possibly a hospital or two in the northern sector, but right now there is nothing."

This insight proved invaluable. I changed the report to recommend shelving any plans for a distribution center for at least two years. The Guatemalan government did start a few road building projects in a couple of years and at that time we made the investment. Any earlier would have been a major strategic mistake.

As a follow-up to that experience, I compiled a list of all the people I knew with international experience, and I keep it updated continuously. Now I always cross-check information from other sources with someone who has been to the country recently.

MINIMUM INTERNATIONAL STAFFING

A very real hazard in developing a strategic global plan is the lack of qualified management personnel with experience in international trade. This will surely change as Americans become more worldly. At the same time, however, greater demand for such people will probably make it just as difficult to locate them in the future as it is now. The biggest mistake a company can make when entering the global marketplace is to do so without experienced personnel. No company, large or small, can effectively compete in the global arena without at least some management expertise in international trade.

As a minimum, either the financial manager or the marketing manager should be comfortable dealing in the global arena. Even a small export program, with no overseas travel, requires knowledge of how to ship the goods, how to arrange the financing, and how to collect from the customer. The performance of these functions is substantially different from dealing with domestic transactions. To stumble around trying to get the order, shipping the order, and then collecting on it can be an extremely expensive learning process—for anyone. It's far better to get someone on board who knows what he or she is doing.

As later chapters disclose, to successfully compete in the global arena, a company should not make a choice between exporting and direct foreign investment. A global mentality requires that steps must be taken whenever and wherever required to compete effectively either within the United States or overseas. The choice cannot be: Should I start exporting, or should I locate a plant overseas, or should I import components? The only rational decision is all of the above, whenever and wherever called for. That being the case, it behooves every company to staff up as soon as possible to be able to make these moves.

Through many years of observing mistakes American companies make when entering the global marketplace and making a few myself, I came up with the organizations shown in Figure 8–3 as minimum requirements for any company, regardless of size, getting into international trade.

With only a U.S. home office, marketing managers will be on the road most of the time. If a company plans to get orders from more than one region, extreme global distances mandate a salesperson for each region to be covered. It is virtually impossible for one person to solicit business in Europe and the Middle East; South America and the Caribbean; or Indonesia and Japan. Therefore, if a company decides to utilize its own people to make sales calls and book orders, there must be at least one salesperson per region—preferably two.

Similarly, with a plant in France supplying products to West Germany, England, Italy, and East Africa, one person could never do it. At least two salespeople should be assigned to each region: one to do the marketing and research, one to make calls on customers. Most companies find that at least one of these two should be a national from the same country as the facility.

David Ries, CEO of Hy-Pro Electronics, Inc., Tampa, Florida, disregarded my advice and that of his son who ran a small machine shop in the south of England. David purchased a small electronics distributor located near Naples, Italy, to service Europe, the Middle East, and North African markets. The acquired company, Pieno Batiste, used sales reps exclusively to cover these markets. Soon after the deal closed, David terminated all the reps. He then hired an Italian sales manager to work out of Pieno's Naples facility. He assigned the sales manager responsibility for entire market coverage. Twelve months later, with sales plummeting from Rome to Egypt to Lebanon, the sales manager quit. David asked me to interview him on his last day in Naples. "I'll tell you why I quit," he thundered. "There was no way I could be in Beirut, Rome, and Cairo at the same time, but that's what Ries wanted. Some day he should try flying that route and see if he can do it!"

It almost always works better to hire a national as general manager for an overseas location. An American in this position often brings hard feelings and animosity from employees and customers. On the other hand, many have found that a British or French general manager can be effective anywhere in Europe, the Middle East, or Africa. An Italian, Portuguese, or Spaniard does well in Latin America. An American should be able to handle the job in the Caribbean and in several countries in the Far East, however. Japanese or British also do fairly well there.

The finance manager stationed in an overseas facility, regardless of where it is, should be an American citizen. This is crucial for three reasons: he must be knowledgeable of U.S. tax laws, he must understand the U.S. banking system, and he must speak clear English with all the idioms and cliches the home office personnel are accustomed to using. Also,

FIGURE 8–3
Minimum Organization Staffing for Managing Global Trade

Without Overseas Location:
  At U.S. Home Office:
    Finance manager   (1)
    Traffic manager   (1)
    Secretary-administrative manager   (2)
  Traveling Overseas:
    Marketing manager   (1) per geographic region
With Overseas Location:
  At U.S. Home Office:
    Finance manager   (1)
    Traffic manager   (1)
    Traffic clerk   (1)
    Secretary-administrative manager   (1)
    Clerical   (3) per $2 million sales
  At Overseas Location:
    General manager   (1) per location
    Finance manager   (1)
    Traffic manager   (1)
    Sales manager   (1) per product line
    Marketing manager   (1) per geographic region

for internal control reasons, he should not have any proprietary interest in local political or social relationships that might jeopardize his independence. Obviously, the home office finance manager must have some exposure to international trade.

The secretary-administrative manager is a crucial position at the home office, with or without an overseas location. This person should have a second language. Travel arrangements, conference calls, banking relations, and contract administration activities are performed more efficiently by someone with an ear for languages.

The above personnel constitutes a *minimum* international staff. In most cases additional people will be required. This configuration will get most companies started in global trade, however. The next question is where to find these people. Most of my clients have recruited international expertise from the following sources:

1. International contractors: Bechtel, Fluor, Brown & Root, and a score of smaller contractors.
2. Large oil companies with sound management: Occidental, Shell, Texaco, or Aramco (Arabian American Oil Co.).
3. International groups of large multinationals: GE, the aerospace companies, United Technologies, Du Pont, and Dow are some of the best.
4. Universities with strong international graduate departments: the Universities of Chicago, Kentucky, and Pennsylvania; Georgetown, George Washington, Johns Hopkins, American University, and the University of Southern California have excellent departments.
5. International departments of Big 5 accounting/consulting firms: Arthur Andersen, Ernst & Young, Price Waterhouse, Peat Marwick, Coopers & Lybrand.

6. International departments in overseas branches of major banks and investment banks: Chase, Citicorp, Goldman Sachs, J. P. Morgan, Barclays, Chemical, Hong Kong and Shanghai, and European American, are good starting places.

Although there are undoubtedly some extremely qualified people working in government agencies, the only luck either I or my clients have had is recruiting from the U.S. Agency for International Development (USAID), or the Peace Corps. Somewhat surprisingly returning Peace Corps volunteers of all ages seem to do an excellent job in the business world, although it's difficult to sell them on a business career after all they have experienced.

CHAPTER 9

THE COUNTRY SURVEY: ADMINISTRATIVE SEGMENT

MAJOR TOPICS

KEY POINTS

Most of the administrative segment of the country survey can be accomplished from your home base. Some items may require traveling to the host country. The chapter describes what to look for in this data gathering process under eight subject headings. At its conclusion, the chapter includes a listing of all the questions that should be answered before proceeding with an in-country detailed investigation.

Tim McGee, vice president–marketing for a midsize Chicago manufacturer, was exuberant over winning the bid on a $10 million Colombian order for generator sets. Now that delivery was expected in three months, Tim panicked and called in his controller, Barry Golder. "Now what do we do, Barry! Ten million dollars worth of gen sets to be shipped, moved a hundred miles overland, and assembled at the job site. Do we need a license? How about tax clearance? What are the rules for hiring local labor? We're supposed to be paid in Colombian pesos: How do we get the money out of the country? My friend, you better buy a plane ticket and get down to Bogotá."

Barry returned from Bogotá three weeks later with a case full of applications, forms, tax data, names and phone numbers of local attorneys and accountants who spoke English, and a contact at Chase Manhattan Bank in Bogotá. Two days before the shipment was scheduled to leave, approvals came through from the Colombian government for a business license, a tax ID number, banking authorizations, and instructions for obtaining work visas. If only Barry had done the survey earlier, the cost of this administration investigation could have been included in the bid price. Now it was too late.

Large corporations involved in global trade for many years have little difficulty with the mechanics of doing business in a new country. Worldwide political and trade connections and several overseas bases, produce a vast reservoir of global knowledge. Successful multinationals easily absorb the intricacies of peculiar tax laws, legal and audit requirements, living conditions, trade barriers and the myriad of other details affecting a smooth transition into a new market.

Growing companies, new to the global arena, aren't as fortunate. A company may be in the export business for years without ever grasping the underlying logistics of setting up a facility, managing a project, or otherwise making a direct investment in a foreign country. To attempt such a venture without a thorough grasp of the peculiar rules and regulations inherent in doing business in that country will most certainly result in confusion and loss of profits. At worst, ignorance can doom the project to failure before it ever gets off the ground. Smart managers make sure that they have enough information about the host country's business practices to make intelligent investment decisions. This gathering process is called *a country survey.*

Country surveys consist of two distinct parts: the administrative segment dealing with general and national policy matters, and a more detailed investigation relating to the specific investment. These surveys involve a series of information gathering steps. Most of the administrative data can be obtained before leaving home. Detailed information relating to a project investment must be gathered on location.

The topics to be included in the administrative survey are:

1. Political/economic climate.
2. Business structure.
3. Audit, tax, legal and licensing rules.
4. Banking affiliation.
5. Communications.
6. Professional advisers.
7. Personnel matters.
8. Insurance coverage.

The topics covered in a detailed investigation consist of:

1. Language interpreters
2. Safety/security.
3. Trade barriers—import/export.
4. Government subsidies.
5. Marketing practices, distribution, and controls.
6. Materials, supplies, and equipment.

7. Labor/management resources and controls.
8. Shipping and transport.
9. Local utilities.
10. Living accommodations and health care.
11. Education and social facilities.

This chapter looks at each of the sections of an administrative survey and lays the groundwork for the detailed investigation covered in the next chapter. The major objectives in both parts of a country survey are: (1) to gather enough hard data about doing business in a specific country to make intelligent investment decisions, and (2) to obtain facts about local customs and business practices and to identify appropriate governmental and private contacts for the smooth implementation of the project.

POLITICAL AND ECONOMIC CLIMATE

Once a country or region is chosen as a possible candidate for a direct investment, detailed information about its current and projected outlook for political stability and economic potential must be gathered and analyzed. A wealth of data and expert prognostications exist for many developed nations. Obtaining information about England, Germany, Japan, Australia, and so on is relatively simple. A call to the appropriate consulate or federal agency brings literally volumes of brochures, statistics, political analyses, economic trends, future growth plans, and a variety of other useful data. Country desk officers can furnish up-to-date information about a country's political and economic climates. Daily newspaper and trade magazine accounts do a fairly good job of reporting current political conditions.

Political and economic data about developing nations is not quite as easy to come by. It requires some digging. A host country's trade office, consulate, embassy, or even its tourist bureau can yield some information. To get a complete picture, however, a trip to the host country will usually be necessary. Even then, many nations do not keep accurate or current statistics on economic trends or business data. Most have nothing available in print about the political climate. The best sources for this data are either the host country office of the American Chamber of Commerce, or management personnel of other American companies already operating in the country. Foreign branch officers of American banks are especially helpful.

Questions to Ask

Questions to be answered, either directly or by inference, and the data to be gathered about a country's political and economic climate are:

1. Does the country have an elected government or is it run by a dictator, monarch, or other form of central control?
2. If elected, when is the next election? What is the prognosis for change?
3. What is the general attitude toward Americans? Good? Bad? Indifferent?
4. What are current relationships with the U.S. government?

   5. Are there other American companies doing business in the country? If yes, then which ones?
   6. What is the official attitude toward foreign investment?
   7. What is the unofficial attitude?
   8. What is the country's main economic base? Imports? Exports? Self-sufficient?
   9. Are there statistics available showing economic growth or decline (e.g., annual capital expenditures, imports, exports, wage rates, inflation rates, and interest rates)?
  10. What are the demographics of its population?
  11. Are major businesses owned or controlled by the government?
  12. What are the trade barriers to foreign investment, import quotas, and internal distribution systems?

BUSINESS STRUCTURE

The laws of many countries, especially developing nations, prohibit foreign control of local businesses. Some countries decree that local businesspeople or local companies own at least 50 percent, and sometimes 51 percent, of a foreign investment. Others require that the government itself own 50 or 51 percent. Still others are content to participate in equity ownership with less than controlling interest. Before making a firm investment commitment, a company must be certain of the peculiar business structure laws within the host country. If local partnership is mandated, it must search out and negotiate an agreement with a local participant.

The form that shared ownership takes varies between countries also. Some require a business to be incorporated in the host country. Others prefer a formal joint venture. In still other circumstances, a normal partnership arrangement is acceptable.

Except in the case of joint ventures, most local parties will assume an inactive role in the management of the business. Management and policymaking are normally left to the foreign investor. As long as local laws are followed, a passive partner won't interfere in the running of a business. In fact, one of the primary purposes of requiring a local partner is to ensure that the foreign company does follow local laws and regulations. Of course the host country government, or local partner, expects the company to be profitable. It also expects to receive a proportionate share of these earnings. If a foreign investor operates the company at a loss, it can anticipate a more active role by the silent partner, as Matt Doolan of Reckotech Electronics learned.

> Reckotech Electronics had sales approaching $24 million. The company designed and manufactured a line of components for use in telecommunications switch gear. Mike Madison, vice president of marketing, was responsible for opening a new assembly plant in the sultanate of Oman. He made arrangements with a local trading company, Al-Ahfed, Ltd., to be a silent partner owning 50 percent of the operating company. Mike also planned to use Al-Ahfed, which was partially owned by the sultan, as his marketing agent within Oman and for exports to India and Pakistan.

Everything went smoothly for the first two years. The plant was constructed, labor hired, a British manager installed as managing director, and sales followed the growth plan. Although Mike had difficulty justifying various "miscellaneous" disbursements to several government agents and shipping intermediaries, Al-Ahfed convinced him that this was the way business had to be conducted in the Middle East. His boss at Reckotech, however, objected to these payments as being contrary to the Foreign Corrupt Practices Act and therefore had to stop.

During the third year, even though sales continued to grow, profits trailed off. The following year, the company was operating at a loss. Mike was notified "through channels" that because the sultan was unhappy with the plant's progress, Al-Ahfed would begin approving all labor hirings and all disbursements over 1,000 Omani rials (approximately $2,500). When the CEO of Reckotech heard Mike's explanation he was furious. He quickly ordered the sale of Reckotech's share of the Omani company to Al-Ahfed.

The final result was not pleasant. With a $2 million investment in the subsidiary, Reckotech took a loss on the sale of $1.7 million! This was the last time Reckotech ventured into the Middle East. It was also the only time the company made a direct investment in a country prohibiting a foreign investor from keeping controlling interest in a business.

Reckotech had a bad experience, but only because the CEO didn't understand the ground rules. Rules governing the business structure of foreign investments in any country obviously must be followed in order to do business there. A foreign investor must also adhere to local business practices. If these conflict with home country standards and the company still wishes to do business in the host country, local management must find a way around the problem.

Joint Ventures

Very often, a joint venture with another Western company already situated in a host country can be the easiest and cleanest way to cope with local customs. On the other hand, if a local partner must be used—either a government agency or official, or a private individual or company—it always works out best to let the partner know right up front, before dollars are committed, what standards your company must follow. Not infrequently, if he knows what your rules are, he can either smooth the way with other nationals and government bureaucracy, or teach you how to cope with local requirements.

Rules governing the structure of a foreign business in any country can easily be obtained through that country's consulate or trade representative. U.S. trade representatives can often offer sound advice, but it's always better to get the official word from host country representatives directly.

If a local, nongovernment partner is required, the best way to locate a reputable one is through a lawyer or consultant in the country of choice. It usually involves interviewing several candidates before judging which makes the best fit. Obviously, if a government agency or official will be your partner, you'll have to take what is offered.

Questions to Ask

Questions to be answered about business structure are:

1. What are the foreign business ownership laws?
2. Can a business be operated as a corporation or a partnership? Should tiered corporations be used?
3. What are the restrictions on each form?
4. Must a foreign company have a local partner?
5. If yes, must it be the government or a government agency, or can it be a private individual or company?
6. Are partners passive or active?
7. If a local partner is required, what ownership shares are mandated by law?
8. Even if the law does not specify local partnership interests, could it still be advantageous to form one?
9. Should the local company have the parent's name or be completely divorced from it?
10. How much graft must be managed and who will do it?

AUDIT, TAX, LEGAL, AND LICENSING REQUIREMENTS

Although many questions about local laws, business licensing, government audit requirements, and tax regulations can only be answered by experts in the host country, much information can be gathered before getting on a plane. At this stage of the survey, international law firms and accounting firms with offices in a nearby city (e.g. Washington, New York, Philadelphia, Miami, Chicago, Los Angeles, San Francisco, or Dallas) can be a good starting point. Although data gathered from these sources will be general and very broad, at least it provides a base for further investigation.

Audit and Tax

Any Big 5 accounting firm (previously the Big 8) can be especially helpful. If local personnel aren't familiar with the broad regulations of a specific country, they can readily obtain the information from one of their foreign offices. Most already have the data you'll need at this stage, however. It is usually compiled in pamphlets or newsletters and sent to clients. Price Waterhouse, for example, sends out a monthly newsletter with current developments in audit and tax laws in countries throughout the world. Coopers & Lybrand also does a good job, as does Arthur Andersen. This information is normally free. A simple call to any Big 5 office will get the ball rolling—at least as far as audit and tax matters are concerned.

Questions to Ask

In the audit and tax area, the following questions should be answered:

1. What are the quarterly or annual audit requirements?
2. If an audit is required, must it be done by a local audit firm?
3. Must the firm be certified?

4. How extensive must the audit be?
5. What other financial reports must be submitted or certified by an independent accountant?
6. Is there a list of government-accepted auditors in the country?
7. Which ones are correspondents of, or in partnership with, a Big 5 firm?
8. Can the audited financial statements be consolidated with the parent?
9. If not, how will results be reported on the parent's statements?
10. Has the country signed a Trade Information Exchange Agreement (TIEA)?
11. What are the corporate and personal income tax rates?
12. Is worldwide income taxed or reported?
13. Are there any tax incentives for foreign investment?
14. How are intercompany transactions with the parent taxed?
15. Does the country qualify for a Foreign Sales Corporation?

Legal and Licensing

Answers to foreign legal questions are a little harder to come by. Because of the vast array of peculiar corporate legal requirements throughout the world, few, if any, Western law firms have a comprehensive knowledge of any one country—with the exception perhaps of other Western countries such as England, Belgium, France, or Germany. However, they should at least be able to provide broad advice about business structure, licensing, and labor laws.

In addition, all international law firms have correspondent firms in many countries where they do not have offices—just like the Big 5 accounting firms. Most are more than willing to put you in touch with one of these correspondents either by telex or by arranging a direct meeting in the host country.

With the advent of the European Community(EC) and the predominance of Japan in the global community, nearly all large law firms have established overseas offices in these regions. Many midsize firms are also hopping on the bandwagon. Nearly all major law firms with Washington offices have strong international connections. Baker & MacKenzie is one of the largest. If you don't know of an international firm in your area, your legal counsel can certainly steer you in the right direction. Don't be surprised, however, if the really important legal questions can't be answered without a foreign visit.

Questions to Ask

Legal and licensing matters that should be resolved at this stage of the country survey are:

1. Which correspondent firms are recommended?
2. What business licensing laws must be complied with?
3. What import or export licensing is required?
4. What ethical problems can be expected in dealing with foreign law firms?

5. What are the prevailing incorporation laws?
6. Are there any restrictions for joint ventures or partnerships?
7. Are there unique features in litigation laws pertaining to Americans?
8. Are there any stringent visa or work permit laws to worry about?
9. How will actions of nationals hired as employees affect the parent company's liability for compliance with the Foreign Corrupt Practices Act?
10. What other U.S. laws require compliance overseas?
11. What are the preferred means of handling U.S. boycott provisions?
12. Which legal counsel will review contractual documents?
13. Who will handle legal counsel for arbitration cases?
14. Can this law firm be of help in overseas contract negotiations conducted either in the U.S. or in the host country?
15. What Washington connections does the firm have to smooth the road for financial or technical assistance, or to cut through red tape?

BANKING

It is impossible to do business in the global economy without an affiliation with at least one U.S. bank. Whether exporting or establishing a direct foreign presence, a bank located in the United States must be used for wire transfers, L/C (letters of credit) issuance and confirmation, exchange conversion, and a multitude of other activities. It is important to locate the *right* bank, however; one that has an established track record in handling international transactions. The wrong one can delay receipt of funds, confuse L/Cs, and generally add significant cost and effort to any global transaction.

Even though the tendency is to use the same bank that handles the parent company's checking account and short-term borrowing needs, this often results in the wrong choice. If at all practical, the best choice is one of the 10 or 12 largest banks with complete facilities for handling international transactions. Many have sizable branch offices in different regions. One should be within reasonable proximity for most businesses.

Foreign Banks

If you can't locate a major bank in your area, try a foreign bank with U.S. offices. On the West Coast, banks such as Sumitomo (Japan) or Hong Kong & Shanghai (Hong Kong) do an excellent job throughout the world. On the East Coast, Barclays (Great Britain), National Westminster (Great Britain), Deutsche Bank (Germany), Crédit Lyonnais (France), Bank of Nova Scotia (Canada), Banque Indosuez (France), and Algemene (the Netherlands) all do credible work. The idea is to pick a bank that has major branches or correspondent banks in the country in which you intend to do business. It makes the job a lot easier to have a *home* bank for references, guarantees, and to assist in foreign money transactions.

When choosing a home-base international bank, be sure it has the capability to serve your needs over the long haul. Maintaining a long-term relationship with a single bank is far more beneficial than continually changing. The home-base international bank should have a large, fully staffed international department with the ability, and the track record, to handle L/C issuance and confirmation and money transfers worldwide. Its name should be recognizable in the global financial community (for reference letters). It should be willing to support you with bank guarantees. And it should maintain a network of branches or major correspondent banks worldwide.

Regional Familiarity

Since some banks are more proficient in one part of the world than others, try to locate one predominant in the area you are going into. For example: Bank of Nova Scotia and Chase are excellent for the Caribbean; Chemical is strong in Central America; Sumitomo and Citicorp are good in South America; Hong Kong & Shanghai is known throughout the world and especially effective in Southeast Asia—as is Sumitomo. Barclays, Chase, and Citicorp are all proficient in the Middle East; Banque Indosuez, and Crédit Lyonnaise, along with Barclays and NatWest are well known in most of Africa; and Deutsche Bank has the inside track in Eastern Europe.

Although your local banker might be put out that you want to do business with a different bank, with a little pressure he should be willing to produce a letter of introduction to one of the majors. This is critical for the smaller, less publicly known business. A letter of introduction is about the only way to get the attention of a major bank.

Questions to Ask

When a home-base international bank looks promising, the following questions need to be answered:

1. Where are the bank's U.S. branches located?
2. What U.S. correspondent banks are used?
3. Can the international department respond within one day for the issuance of L/Cs and within two days for confirmation?
4. Will the bank handle verification of shipping documentation?
5. Will the bank issue reference and introduction letters?
6. Will the bank handle guarantees?
7. How long does a money transfer take? (It should never be more than four days going or coming.)
8. Who is the international bank manager assigned as liaison officer?
9. Can the bank handle currency conversion and exchange arbitrage?
10. Will the bank provide a listing of worldwide branches and correspondents?

11. What is the cost of issuing L/Cs, money transfers, guarantees, and bankers' acceptances?
12. What communications can be established with your local bank to transfer moneys and verify documents?
13. Will the bank participate in federally funded financing programs, such as Eximbank guaranteed loans, SBA guarantees, USAID assistance, CBI programs, and so on?
14. Do all foreign branch managers speak English?
15. What type of communication system is in use for corresponding with branch or correspondent banks? Telephone, telex, courier, or what?

COMMUNICATIONS

When doing business in Western Europe or Japan, communications are never a problem. Cable and telex systems are in place and working. Courier services compete for business. First-class telephone systems permit direct dialing for international calls. Regular mail delivery can usually be accomplished within seven days. Efficient and frequent air transport to and from these regions makes emergency deliveries commonplace. A wide range of ocean shipping lines is available. Even computer telecommunications service can be utilized for instantaneous communications.

In the rest of the world, however, communications can be a severe problem, even within the country itself. Many developing nations do not have business or residential telephones connected to international operators. To make an overseas call, a person must stand in line at the telephone company office for one of the few international trunks. In Guyana or Zaire, placing a local call can take as long as waiting for an international trunk line—often hours, sometimes days.

Courier Service

Courier service isn't much better. Recently, at the foot of the Río Dulce in Guatemala, I urgently needed to sign some legal documents prepared in Philadelphia. Having used DHL for years, and more recently Federal Express, to deliver and receive documents all over the world, I did not anticipate a problem. Upon investigation, however, I learned that the only delivery point in Guatemala was at the DHL office in Guatemala City—some five hours away by local bus or auto.

Unusual Solutions

In many cases, there isn't much a person can do about antiquated communications networks, other than to be aware that such problems exist. Sometimes this information isn't available without a trip to the host country. But many times enough data can be gathered before leaving home to lay out a plan for coping with deficiencies. One of my clients, McAllister Construction Company handled its problems in the following way.

Edwin O'Shannessy, CEO of McAllister, landed a multimillion dollar contract to build two schools and a hospital in Ecuador, near the Peruvian border. While I was busy performing the detailed survey, Ed assigned his controller, Harry Bartholomew, the task of researching communications facilities. The primary concern was to be able to communicate with the two jobs sites high in the mountains of southeastern Ecuador.

A quick call to the Ecuadorian consul in Washington convinced Harry that extraordinary measures were called for. He learned that Ecuador did not have direct dial international telephone service. He also found that the supply of electricity to the town in which the construction would take place was unreliable and frequently down for two to five days at a time. Furthermore, Guayaquil was the closest city of any size—150 miles away over mountainous roads.

Harry eventually came up with a unique solution to this complex communications problem. His plan included the following three steps:
1. The site manager would install portable telephone switching gear (similar to today's cellular systems) at the job site. Electricity would be supplied by generator sets used on the job site for power tools.
2. The site controller would be equipped with a personal computer loaded with telecommunications software and a small printer, both of which would run off the generator set. This, together with the telephone gear would enable rapid and confidential communications with the home office.
3. An on-site fax machine, hooked into the telephone gear, would provide the final link in a complete communications system, independent of Ecuadorian networks.

The controller arranged for all of the appropriate gear to be delivered to the home office before the project began. It was then hand carried to the job site as the engineers and supervisors made their initial trips.

In many cases, especially in out-of-the-way places such as the McAllister job site, it may not be possible to resolve communications problems from the United States. In that case, they will have to be handled during the detailed survey. Most of the time, however, with Yankee ingenuity, a person can identify communications glitches and reach at least tentative solutions during the initial administrative survey without ever getting on a plane.

Questions to Ask

During the communications phase of the administrative survey the following questions should be answered. Rather than merely asking questions, quite often "test run" phone calls, courier deliveries, and sample mail yield answers faster than relying on someone else's estimates.

1. Does the country's telephone service operate on direct dialing for international calls?
2. If not, are local operators or central AT&T operators used for placing international calls?
3. Can overseas calls be placed from private phones or must a central telephone office be used?

4. What is the cost of calls to the United States?
5. Can U.S. telephone credit cards be used to call out of the country?
6. Is telex used extensively for international communications?
7. How reliable is the electric system?
8. Are computers in use for telecommunications?
9. What pickup and delivery points are used by DHL and Federal Express?
10. How many days delivery service do the couriers guarantee?
11. Is postal service reliable?
12. What is the cost of mailing to and from the United States?
13. How many days delivery time for mail to and from the United States?
14. What is the reliability of telephone, telex, courier service, or postal service between the host country and non–U.S. locations?
15. How reliable are these services when used within the host country?

PROFESSIONAL ADVISERS

Part of the administrative survey should be to determine which professional advisers can be relied upon to answer questions, to deal with especially sticky business problems in the host country, or to maintain close ties with Washington bureaucrats. Once again, larger multinationals have little difficulty coping with the idiosyncrasies of foreign governments, customers, banks, or labor unions. Years of experience have established relationships between the U.S. corporation and appropriate advisers and officials in host countries. Neither do these experienced global traders have much trouble from Washington. Most have Washington bureaus on their payroll. Many engage full-time consultants or international lawyers who do nothing but grease the skids with federal agencies.

Small companies don't have these luxuries. They must either use their own resources and ingenuity or engage outside professionals to provide assistance. What type of assistance does international trade require that domestic business does not? For companies without an experienced international staff, the following activities can be nearly insurmountable if attempted on their own:

1. Putting together bid packages for foreign projects.
2. Negotiating contracts with international buyers or government agencies.
3. Acquiring real estate or production facilities overseas.
4. Preparing appropriate export shipping documentation.
5. Managing U.S. and foreign customs requirements.
6. Coping with provisions of the Foreign Corrupt Practices Act and boycott regulations.
7. Gathering data and then arranging financing assistance through Eximbank, the SBA, or other federal and state agencies.
8. Setting up and managing a foreign sales corporation for exports.

9. Arranging with USAID officials for technical, bidding, and negotiating assistance.
10. Preparing U.S. compliance reports.
11. Opening the doors to congressmen, senators, governors, the military services, U.S. trade representatives, and other federal and state officials for soliciting political clout.
12. Opening the same doors when onerous federal trade policies must be skirted to get the order.
13. Assisting in the selection and interface with advisers in the host country.
14. Keeping abreast of changes in U.S. government trade policies, tax laws, financing subsidies, and political exigencies.

These are only a few examples of the types of administrative matters unique to global trade. Each individual case is different. Each has its own set of requirements. Most companies would be well advised to engage professional advisers for assistance in these matters rather than trying to go it alone.

Types of Advisers

There are four types of advisers that can be helpful in assisting with the intricacies of doing business overseas:

- Lawyers and legal firms.
- International public accounting firms.
- Industry lobbyists and international trade assistance groups.
- International management consultants.

Most firms getting started in global trade find that using all four sources is not only the least expensive, but also the fastest way to get going.

A major step in the administrative survey is to identify which advisers to use for the specific country and task at hand. Clearly, a high-powered Washington lawyer with connections in the Department of Agriculture is not needed for building a distribution center in France. On the other hand, he could be most helpful in arranging financing for shipments of farm produce to Ethiopia. An international consultant will do little good if the company plans to export wooden ladders to Canada. He could, however, make a big difference in preparing a complex bid to open a series of quick print shops in Eastern Europe. An industry lobby group can be extremely helpful in soliciting political clout when a foreign company competes for an order. The same lobbying effect might be useless in negotiating a construction contract with the government of Bolivia.

Qualified international advisers do not advertise. They are contacted through references. A good starting point can be through readily accessible Big 5 accounting firms. They all have management consulting divisions and international staffs. Most are more than willing to provide referrals of qualified international lawyers and consultants. Another good source is the International Law Institute, 1330 Connecticut Avenue, NW, Washington, DC 20036 (202) 463-7979.

Trade associations can also be helpful. If your industry association doesn't have a formal international lobbying group, its director should be able to point the way to at least one Washington contact. Large university business schools offering international courses are another source. Executives from other companies already engaged in global trade are usually willing to pass on references of qualified professionals. If all else fails, the top management of an international department in a major bank can point out qualified accountants or lawyers.

Questions to Ask

When making the initial contact, specific information about the person's qualification to handle your specific job should be garnered.

1. What experience does the individual have in your specific areas of interest?
2. What other companies has he represented? Talk to the executives in these companies. Find out if the professional knows what he is doing.
3. What type of fee structure does he charge? A minimum of $1,000 per day should assure you of qualified credentials.
4. What specific government agencies does he work with?
5. What countries does he specialize in?
6. When he is out of town, who in his organization can handle your matter?

These criteria are certainly not inclusive, but if you get positive responses, the person is probably qualified and details of the engagement can be worked out later.

PERSONNEL

One of the biggest mistakes companies make when beginning their global expansion is to try to do it without experienced personnel. Major differences between doing business globally and domestically necessitate different management qualifications. Assigning the recipient of a Salesman of the Year award for domestic sales the responsibility for marketing the same products in Italy, Egypt, or Malaysia will surely result in failure. Putting a controller who is a whiz at computer-based cost systems, cash management, and monthly financial statements in charge of arranging supplier credit for a buyer in Peru will only create confusion and eventually higher cost. A production manager may be able to handle union grievances and sophisticated production control systems but more than likely will fall flat recruiting, training, and managing a work force of unskilled West Indians in Grenada.

Recruiting International Managers

The company that tries to implant American business practices overseas without the experience of dealing with foreign customs generally fails. As a step in the administrative survey, the smart company will begin a campaign to recruit appropriate management personnel with international experience. These personnel will staff the home office activities that coordinate with a foreign facility or customer. Key management personnel for a foreign facility should be recruited overseas—except for the financial manager who should be an American citizen.

There are many reputable international employment services in the United States. Some specialize in engineers and construction managers; some in financial, production, or marketing personnel. Any large city phone book lists such agencies. An even better source, especially for personnel to manage foreign locations, is international employment agencies in the United Kingdom. Again, many companies service this market. The best source of information is the *London Sunday Times*.

Passports

Once the recruiting process begins, other personnel matters must be dealt with. Everyone knows a passport is required for overseas travel, right? Wrong? On Monday night Mark Flanagan, CEO of Wearsit Rubber Company left for England for a meeting the next day with a potential partner of a joint venture in the Netherlands. Tuesday afternoon he walked into his New Jersey office. "What happened? Why are you back so soon?" asked his secretary. "Who ever thought I'd need a passport to get into England? No one ever told me!"

Another surprise awaited Larry McComber when he took a 22-hour flight to Sri Lanka for a meeting with some government officials. Without a passport, he sat at the nonair-conditioned Colombo airport for 10 hours waiting for a flight back to the United States.

Passports are easy to get from any county courthouse, by mail, or through one of several passport services in any major city. An original birth certificate, two passport-size portrait photos, a completed application form, a check for the appropriate fee, and any American citizen can get a passport within 30 days.

Driver's License

An international driver's license is also handy, although not necessarily required. Any American Automobile Association office will issue you one for a small fee, as will a state bureau of motor vehicles.

Medical

Several medical matters should be coordinated at this point. All personnel traveling overseas should get vaccinations against local diseases before they leave. If there is any question about what shots are required or advised, contact the host country's consulate office in the United States. Most hospitals maintain a listing of what shots are recommended by each country. Most hospitals or clinics also provide an official vaccination card showing what shots a person has had and the dates administered. For some countries, showing this card to an immigration official is a prerequisite to entrance.

Overseas travelers should also carry a medical kit for emergencies—especially when traveling to lesser developed nations.

A physician should prescribe what drugs to carry. In any event take aspirin, band-aids, diarrhea medication, and something to relieve the pain from toothaches. Because of the worldwide concern about cocaine, heroin, and other illegal substances, be sure to retain copies of any prescriptions filled by a pharmacist—complete with his official stamp, if possible. Of course, any personnel traveling overseas either temporarily or on permanent assignment should be required to pass a complete physical examination.

The same doctor, hospital, or clinic that provides vaccinations for international travelers also maintains a listing of recommended English-speaking physicians in the host country. This can be an invaluable assist in emergencies. Also, it doesn't hurt to carry a membership card from the IAMA, the international medical assistance organization.

Financial Emergencies

During the initial phases of the administrative survey, it's always a good idea to make appropriate plans for financial emergencies hitting international travelers. Financial emergencies also happen to parent company personnel permanently stationed overseas. Experienced global businesspeople find that carrying a letter of credit from a U.S. bank is extremely helpful in financial emergencies. With such an L/C, any recognized bank in the world will permit cash draws up to the amount specified in the document.

> Bob Porvel kept himself out of jail in the Philippines with the L/C he carried. Driving to his apartment in Manila one night after a meeting with local businesspeople, Bob was forced off the road by a speeding Philippine army truck. When the local police arrived, Bob was immediately blamed for reckless driving and endangering army personnel. Hauled off to jail, the magistrate demanded a $500 payment or Bob could plan on spending the next week in jail. Bob agreed to make payment the next morning. Posting a letter of credit from Chase Manhattan that he always carried with him as collateral, he was allowed to return to his apartment. The next morning he collected his L/C, contacted a local bank, and arranged for the $500 payment.

It is also a good idea to provide management personnel with an internationally recognized company credit card. American Express is the best, but a Chase, Citicorp, or Chemical Bank, VISA or MasterCard will also suffice. All airlines and most hotels, at least in developed nations, will honor a credit card. Those in developing nations often want cash. Credit cards not only conserve cash, they allow more freedom of movement. This can be essential in conducting global business.

Travel

The final step in the personnel area is to find out which airlines service the host country and what the lowest fares are. When traveling to Europe or Japan any major airline will suffice. I have found, however, during more around-the-world business trips than I care to recount, that American carriers are my choice when flying to and from developing nations. The planes are newer and better maintained. They generally fly closer to schedule. And after spending weeks in an unfamiliar and sometimes hostile country, there's something about boarding an American plane, with an American crew, and all the idiosyncrasies of American service that seems especially welcome.

Others feel differently. Many experienced travelers prefer British Airways throughout the world. Either Singapore or Cathay Airlines in the Far East; and Swissair, KLM, or Lufthansa for Europe and Africa are also popular choices. Regardless of which airline is used, planning to do business overseas requires a knowledge of air fares and schedules.

INSURANCE

To round out the administrative survey, a company should know which existing insurance policies cover mishaps overseas. If deficient, new riders should be added. As Chapter 18 describes, insurance coverage for both commercial and political risk can be obtained from the Foreign Credit Insurance Association (FCIA). However, private policies may be more inclusive, cheaper, and cover a wider range of risks.

There are five types of insurance coverage that should be investigated at this stage of the survey:

- Personnel emergencies.
- Shipping damage or loss.
- Property casualty.
- Product liability.
- Auto and rental cars.

Group health, life, and accident insurance policies carried by most domestic companies may not be effective for overseas travel or living. American hospital and medical plans can seldom be used in foreign hospitals or for treatment by foreign physicians. Life and accident policies may or may not cover flying or political insurrection.

As part of the administrative survey a company should be sure that what it carries will apply overseas. If it doesn't, change coverage so that it will. Worker's compensation policies never include offshore locations. This type of protection will have to be obtained in the host country, if available.

A number of marine insurance companies cover loss or damage to goods during ocean shipping. Most domestic transport or fire and casualty policies do not. If you can't locate a marine carrier in your area, ask the state insurance commission for a list of companies. If that doesn't work, try one of the maritime states, California, New York, or Florida, for a listing.

Property located offshore is hardly ever covered by domestic policies. New policies, and perhaps different carriers, will have to be located to cover an overseas facility. Most international banks can be helpful in locating a carrier for your particular area. If all else fails, Lloyds of London will certainly help, although their policies are expensive.

Product liability insurance for goods manufactured and/or sold overseas is generally not included in domestic policies either. In developed countries, such coverage can be readily obtained locally. In less developed countries, it just isn't available anywhere. For those companies that feel strongly about product liability coverage, thorough investigation with existing carriers should provide leads to offshore companies (perhaps Lloyds) that, for a price, cover anything.

Automobile insurance policies may or may not include driving overseas. A quick call to either the underwriter or an agent can determine if the host country is included in present policies. Also, it's a good idea to include foreign rental car insurance in the basic fleet policy. This can save a bundle of money. Many overseas rental car companies insist that coverage be taken unless the lessee can provide proof that an applicable company policy is in force. And the rates are exorbitant. For a $10,000 liability coverage, $10 to $12 a day is not unusual.

CONCLUSION

Most of the administrative survey can be done at home before visiting the host country. Some leads naturally result in additional investigation on arriving overseas. Figure 9–1 summarizes the data to be gathered in the administrative part of the country survey by seven major classifications.

That finishes the administrative survey. The next chapter examines the steps involved in performing the detailed investigation for a specific project and country.

FIGURE 9–1
Summary of Administrative Survey Data to Be Gathered

Political/Economic:
1. U.S. and host country trade barriers to foreign investment, imports, and exports.
2. Form of host country government (elected, monarchy, dictator, militant) and projected changes in the future.
3. Explicit and implicit attitude toward Americans/Westerners.
4. Host country's major imports and exports.
5. Economic indicators showing growth or decline in economic base.
6. Controlled or free market.
7. Ownership of host country businesses—private or government.

Business Structure:
1. Foreign business ownership laws.
2. Requirements for local business partners—government or private.
3. Laws governing percent ownership with local partner.
4. Pros and cons of structuring the host country facility as a division or subsidiary of the parent company versus keeping it entirely separate.

Audit, Tax, Legal, Licensing:
1. Lists of correspondent law offices and accounting firms.
2. Business licensing requirements.
3. Recommendations for coping with local political graft.
4. Unique laws affecting Americans or other Westerners.
5. Work permit or visa restrictions.
6. Compliance requirements for pertinent U.S. laws.

FIGURE 9–1 (concluded)

7. Availability for assistance in host country legal matters.
8. Connections in Washington or host country to cut red tape.
9. U.S. and host country audit and financial reporting requirements.
10. TIEA status of host country.
11. Personal and corporate income tax rates and special tax provisions of host country.
12. Tax or other incentives for foreign investment.
13. Host country qualification for location of Foreign Sales Corporation.

Banking:
1. Listing of branch and correspondent banks and names of managers.
2. Ability of U.S. bank to handle wire transfers, L/Cs, shipping document verification, currency conversion, and exchange arbitrage.
3. Cost and timing of each of the bank's services.
4. Bank reference letters and assurance of guarantes.
5. Communications network with local U.S. bank.
6. Participation in federal financing and assistance programs.
7. English-speaking branch managers.
8. International communications systems employed.

Communications:
1. Stage of development of telephone service to and from the host country.
2. Cost of telephone service and calls.
3. AT&T or other telephone company international credit cards.
4. Status of telex communications systems in the host country.
5. Reliability of electric service and telephone service for computers.
6. Courier companies serving host country.
7. Pickup and delivery points for courier service and time interval for sending and receiving.
8. Status of reliability and timing of mail service to and from the host country.

Professional Advisers:
1. List of Washington lawyers to assist in dealing with federal bureaucracy.
2. List of lawyers in host country that can do the same.
3. List of international management consultants.
4. Host country data from Big 5 accounting firm.
5. Services performed by appropriate trade association.
6. Trade association lobbying effectiveness.
7. Interview appropriate advisers before contracting.
8. References from other American companies doing business in host country.

Personnel:
1. Names and addresses of U.S. and United Kingdom employment agencies listing international managers.
2. Staff all international management activities, at home and at foreign location, with personnel experienced in global trade.
3. Be certain everyone has a passport.
4. Secure international drivers' licenses.
5. Required and recommended vaccinations for everyone.
6. Record of vaccinations to be carried by overseas travelers.
7. List of English-speaking physicians in host country.
8. Medical kits for everyone.
9. U.S. bank letters of credit for financial emergencies.
10. Company credit cards, preferably American Express and money-center bank Visa or MasterCard.
11. Airline schedules and fares.

Insurance:
1. Review group health, life, and accidental policies for overseas coverage.
2. Add new policies where appropriate.
3. Compare rates from private carriers with FCIA for political and commercial risk.
4. Include company-owned or leased foreign cars in domestic policy, if possible.
5. Also include short-term rental cars for temporary travelers.

CHAPTER 10

THE COUNTRY SURVEY: DETAILED INVESTIGATION

MAJOR TOPICS

KEY POINTS

The previous chapter dealt with the administrative segment of the country survey. This chapter covers the detailed information that must be gathered for a specific project. A summary listing of all the questions to be answered resides at the end of the chapter.

Only so much data gathering can be accomplished from the United States. Most of the information affecting a specific project must be assimilated directly from the host country. Such varied matters as labor availability and wage rates, sources of materials and supplies, transportation, distribution networks, living conditions, marketing practices, and government liaisons can only be dealt with in the host country itself.

Once the administrative survey has exhausted all sources of information accessible at home, the detailed investigation begins. The detailed survey may be of short duration or very lengthy. In either case, long-term success depends upon taking whatever time may be necessary to plan the specific implementation of the project.

It helps to send someone who previously has been to the specific country. The job can be completed in much less time and the information gathered will probably be more accurate. Most companies don't have this luxury, however, and must begin from the beginning. It is always best to have in-house personnel do the detailed survey. However, if no one has the time or ability to get the job done, an outside international management consultant can fill in; although these people are expensive.

If you go this route, be sure to clearly define the specific information the consultant should obtain. The more specific the assignment, the less it costs. Also, outside consultants can be far more effective if the entire administrative survey is completed first. Names and addresses of sources of information in the host country can then be turned over to the consultant before he or she leaves. This saves many days of expensive time.

> I was called upon to perform a detailed survey in Sri Lanka. My client was so anxious to get going that he insisted I leave in the middle of the administrative survey, without a list of local contacts. I had no knowledge of the culture, business practices, labor laws, banking regulations, or living conditions in Sri Lanka. Arriving at the Colombo airport at 9:00 A.M. after an all-night flight from Bahrain, preceded by an 8-hour flight from London and a 7-hour flight from New York, I checked into a local hotel and slept fitfully for 24 hours.
>
> The following morning, my first stop was to see the British manager of the local branch of the Hong Kong & Shanghai Bank. He directed me to a local Indian attorney who spoke fluent English. There my luck ran out.
>
> The Indian lawyer was on holiday and his assistant wasn't the least helpful. The bank manager next directed me to a local chartered accountant, who was less than helpful. From there the trail led to the head of a local labor group, an importer of Filipino laborers, a Sri Lankan trading company, the Electricity Board, and eventually to the customs office.
>
> After two weeks of hit-or-miss meetings, I returned home with a bare minimum of data for my client. The trip cost him $20,000. If he had arranged for my contacts and meetings ahead of time, the cost would have been half as much. More important, I would have obtained twice the amount of data in the same time.

The moral is clear: do your homework before spending money to send someone overseas.

Data to be gathered during the detailed segment of a country survey consists of three categories. How much emphasis is placed on each depends on the specific country and the company's project. To some extent, however, each of these topics applies to nearly all global investments:

General Business Information:
1. Language interface—interpreters.
2. Safety/security—persons and property.
3. Trade barriers—import and export.
4. Banking and permits.

Project Information:
1. Marketing practices, distribution, and controls.
2. Government subsidies.
3. Sources of raw material and supplies.
4. Labor/management resources and restrictions.
5. Shipping and transport.
6. Utilities—electricity, water, telephone.

Personnel Information:
1. Living accommodations.
2. Transportation.

3. Education facilities.
4. Social opportunities.

GENERAL BUSINESS INFORMATION

In many parts of the world the language barrier is the first hurdle to overcome. Although English may be the common business language in many parts of the world, it definitely is not in others. In parts of Africa, Asia, and South America, business and government officials insist on using native tongues. In rural Eastern Europe, the Soviet Union, Japan, and even some corners of Western Europe, local dialects prevail. Since second languages are seldom required in our education system, most American businesspeople remain language poor. If you can't speak the host country language, and business and government officials do not speak English, an interpreter must be found—in a hurry!

Interpreters are normally available for a reasonable fee in most locations. The best way to locate one is through the local office of the American Chamber of Commerce. Other American companies located in the host country can also be of enormous help: perhaps recommending the same interpreter they used. Branch offices of American or British banks also know how to find interpreters. Local officers of USAID know who might be available. Peace Corps volunteers stationed in the country can also point you in the right direction.

Finally, if all else fails, contact the local office of the government agency responsible for internal commerce—similar to our Department of Commerce. Needing to communicate with Western banking and government officials, local commerce agencies always keep interpreters handy. Of course, it is much better for at least one company employee to learn the local language before the project begins.

Safety and Security

The safety of company personnel while traveling or living in the host country should always be a major concern. Each country obviously has different laws regarding a person's right to protect himself and his property from harm. Few individual rights exist in dictatorial nations. In westernized countries there are more.

At least in the beginning, employees traveling to, or living in, the host country will be unaware of their personal rights. Can, or should, he or she carry a gun? Must the doors of a personal residence be barred and chained? What happens if an employee gets stopped or picked up by the local police? Where can he or she get help? These and many more personal safety questions must be answered before company personnel descend on the host country.

Three liaisons should be established as soon as possible after arriving in a foreign country:

1. *The American Embassy.* Let them know where you will be staying, for how long, and who to contact in the United States in the event of an emergency.

2. *The local office of the American Chamber of Commerce.*   Give them the same information.
3. *The local police department.*   Let them know who you are, why you are in the country, where you are staying, and who to contact locally and in the United States for emergencies.

American embassies seldom provide assistance in making business contacts or resolving disputes with government bureaucrats. They can be helpful, however, if an American citizen has a serious personal emergency. The best sources of help in an emergency are other American expatriates and local legal or public accounting professionals. Another essential safety measure is to always keep a typed letter on your person (preferably in English and in the local language) identifying who you are, your U.S. telephone number and residence address, company affiliation, and at least three local phone numbers to be contacted in an emergency.

Security protection for a company's property can also be a problem—just as it is in the United States. Even before my client began constructing his facility in Sri Lanka, I advised him to fence off his site with a 10-foot security fence topped with barbed wire, and to hire 24-hour guards. In Third World countries this is almost always a necessary precaution. Private security companies offering round-the-clock guard service are available in most countries. Whether building a new facility or project, or leasing a building, security precautions make sense, even in developed nations.

Trade Barriers—Import and Export

Regardless of a company's specific product lines, both importing and exporting play important roles. Some materials, supplies, or equipment not available locally, will most likely be imported. Shipping goods either to the United States or to another country involves exporting protocol. Every country has restrictions, duties, or regulations regarding either imports or exports, and usually both.

Learning the applicable rules is one of the first matters to attend to during the detailed survey. A competent local attorney should provide this information. If you can't get it there, go directly to the government agency responsible for foreign commerce.

While on a consulting job in Bermuda, my client tried to ship a car to the island for use by company personnel when traveling back and forth to the airport. When the boat docked, the customs official politely refused to allow the car to be unloaded. Bermuda has very strict regulations governing how many autos can be on the island at any one time. My client never thought to ask the question of me or the Bermudian government.

In another instance, we wanted to bring some lumber into Guatemala for constructing a building. Upon investigation we found that since lumber is a Guatemalan export product, the duties to bring it in were totally prohibitive. As pointed out in Chapter 6, Japan's restrictions on imports are some of the most stringent in the world. Taiwan, Australia, and South Korea aren't much better.

Exports can also cause a problem. If a direct investment is planned to produce goods for export to other countries, it's a good idea to find out what duties, customs restrictions, and shipping bottlenecks exist before commiting funds. Also, don't be surprised to learn from other Western companies that the only feasible way to get anything in or out of the country is to grease the palms of those in charge. It happens all the time, around the world.

Banking

Once a U.S. bank has been selected, introductions to the local branch or correspondent bank should be made. One or more accounts should be opened immediately. In many countries it can take up to two months to use the account, so it's always a good idea to open one as soon as possible.

A resolution from your board of directors will be required authorizing the opening of the account and the signatories. Reference letters of introduction from your U.S. bank will also be necessary. Since it can take up to 60 days to clear a check on a U.S. bank, a letter of credit should be presented when opening the accounts. Then wire transfer funds directly from the home bank.

Banking in Western Europe, Japan, Canada, and other developed countries is relatively straightforward. Many banking systems operate at a level of sophistication at least as efficient as in America. Many operate more efficiently. Wire transfers, L/Cs, short-term loans or overdrafts, deposits, bank drafts, and check writing are simple procedures.

Banking in the Third World or other developing nations, especially in Africa and Latin America, is a different matter entirely. Many of these countries remain as cash economies, either because of rampant inflation or because the people don't trust checks. Banks in some countries are notoriously corrupt and inefficient. The less money left on deposit, the less probability of loss.

Wages are usually paid in cash; bills settled with cash; and collections made in cash. This necessitates very close ties with, and daily trips to the local bank. So try to find a bank close enough to the new facility to permit easy daily transport. Third World banking also requires much closer internal control over cash than Americans are accustomed to.

A corollary problem arises in some nations with the repatriation or conversion of the host country's currency. Normally, a foreign company must obtain specific approval from the ministry of finance to remove local currency from the country or to exchange local currency for U.S. dollars. The mechanics of this must be resolved during the detailed survey, including an application to the appropriate agency for conversion/repatriation permits.

At the same time, any tax identification number, business license application, labor hiring clearance, or other government permit to do business in the country should be obtained.

PROJECT INFORMATION

After taking care of these general matters, the next step is to gather operating data for the specific project. Again, each company has slightly different priorities. To some extent, however, information about all of the following business matters should be assimilated.

Marketing Practices and Control

Not every company planning a direct foreign investment expects to market products in the host country. Some may establish a facility exclusively for exporting back to the parent company. Some projects service customers already identified by the home office marketing team. Contractors build projects for customers already known. Countertrade arrangements usually preclude the necessity of establishing a local marketing arm.

On the other hand, companies planning to produce products in local facilities for sale in the normal course of business, either within the country or exported around the world, need to organize a local marketing activity. They must also understand the types of restrictions and controls placed on these activities by local regulations.

A local trading company understanding the influence of explicit or implicit government control of marketing activities can get a foreign company up to speed faster than any other source. Since trading companies do business throughout the world, chances are excellent that at least one will be resident in the host country. If one can't be located, try the sales manager of an American or English company doing business in the country. They probably have coped with the same problem and found the solution.

The distribution of goods can be another major marketing headache. Some countries require goods produced locally, as well as those imported, to be distributed through predetermined distribution channels. These are normally controlled by a few, hand-picked local companies with close ties to government officials. Even to break into the system, appropriate *favors* must be discreetly granted to government agents and distributor officials.

Trading companies know the ropes. They know how to make the right contacts necessary to get a distributor to carry a new line of merchandise. A new American company frequently can handle its own sales calls or customer order taking, but be stymied by the distribution system. By the way, as helpful as American Chamber of Commerce offices are in other regards, they seem to be of little assistance in this area.

A third marketing challenge involves product pricing. A government may not issue formal declarations controlling what prices can be charged for specific goods, but the informal chain works just as effectively: especially in discount pricing, as Hans Junkel learned.

Hans Junkel was a marketing manager with Esto Chemicals, Inc. He was responsible for West and Central Africa. When Hans took the new assignment, he quickly learned that although the company's products were sold by company sales personnel stationed in each of the countries, the pricing in each market was substantially different. All products were sold through distributors to retail outlets and industrial firms.

> Hans found that the custom in Senegal was to grant a 50 percent discount for volume purchases (some of which was obviously funneled back to appropriate *interested* parties). The discount was 42 percent in the Ivory Coast, 10 percent in Morocco, and 63 percent in Zaire! According to home office intelligence, the discounts were supposed to be the same in all countries.

Government Subsidies

Many countries sustain a myriad of subsidies to encourage investment, reduce unemployment, and generally to further economic growth. The form of subsidy ranges all over the lot: from reimbursing the company for labor costs; to granting tax free incentives for 10 or more years; to providing low interest, long-term financing; to waiving import custom duties on production materials; to providing rent-free housing for company management. Some of these subsidies are widely announced and easy to ferret out. Many have probably already been revealed during the administrative survey. If not uncovered earlier, a quick trip to the local finance ministry usually produces good results.

Some subsidies are not granted across the board, however. They must be negotiated between company representatives and government officials. Negotiating with any government bureaucracy is at best difficult, even in the United States. At its worst, the uninitiated find it a nightmare. A local attorney can usually be very helpful in this area. He should know which government agencies control what subsidy programs. He should also have enough clout to get favored treatment before a meeting ever takes place. And of course he can also arrange a meeting with the right person.

American Chambers of Commerce or even other American companies doing business in the country don't seem to be much help in this area. Negotiations with government officials are usually too nefarious for outsiders to get involved. That's one reason you need a competent local attorney. If he does his job, formal negotiations should be merely window dressing. The deal will already have been cut by the time company representatives show up.

For a variety of reasons, it seems that the less developed the country, the more government subsidies and favored treatment are available. It's usually hard for Americans to do business this way. We have great difficulty knowing when or what to do or say. We do a terrific job managing a business. With our underlying moral compunctions, however, we have difficulty bringing ourselves to conduct business under informal and somewhat questionable rules.

A true global mentality demands that we learn. Standards of morality vary throughout the global business community. To be locked into the traditional American way only leads to confusion and missed opportunities. Rather than engaging in discrete negotiations with government officials themselves, many companies hire competent international consultants to do it for them. This is also a very clean way to cope with the Foreign Corrupt Practices Act.

Sourcing Materials, Supplies, and Equipment

Manufacturing companies often find that some or all of the materials and supplies needed in production must be imported. With rare exceptions, at least some of the equipment necessary to set up the production line, or vehicles to transport or move materials and product must be brought into the country either from the United States or from foreign suppliers.

One of the intentions of building a facility might be to assemble finished products for export around the world. This means that parts and components must be imported to the plant. Some countries, such as Malaysia, Venezuela, or Zambia, are rich in oil, copper, magnesium, timber, and other natural resources, but have no machine tool industry. Equipment and spare parts must be brought in. Industrialized nations, such as Norway, Taiwan, or Belgium, are capable of supplying machine tools but must import raw steel or aluminum. Problems arise when import restrictions and quotas make the cost of importing these materials uneconomical. In some cases they are not available at any price.

During the detailed survey, a company representative should ascertain what materials and equipment need to be imported to set up and operate the facility. He should also determine where they will come from and what barriers exist to efficient and cost-effective importing.

Usually it is fairly easy to get this information from local government bureaucrats. Many import restrictions can be ascertained during the administrative survey. Trading companies or import/export managers in the host country can also shed light. If another foreign producer uses similar materials and equipment, he can explain how his company gets the materials in and how much duty—or basheesh—they pay. As in other business transactions, unofficial import constraints are often the most powerful, as I learned in Trinidad.

My client was building a water purification plant near Port-of-Spain. During the civil engineering segment, several acres of underbrush and trees had to be cleared. All construction equipment on the island was committed to two other government-sponsored projects. Therefore, we contracted with a Venezuelan leasing company to rent several graders, dozers, and a crane. When the boat entered port, the longshoremen refused to unload the equipment, citing loss of jobs by native Trinidadians. It wasn't until I guaranteed three "nonwork" jobs to the union boss, and offered him a private office with a secretary on the job site, that the equipment touched land.

Before starting construction, buying or leasing property, or finalizing investment plans of any type, a smart producer takes the time to verify that all required materials and equipment can, in fact, be obtained at a reasonable cost.

Labor/Management Resources and Restrictions

A country's labor base can range from highly skilled (Germany) to partially skilled (Jamaica) to unskilled (Honduras) to nonexistent (Yemen).

One of the major elements of the detailed survey is to determine which classification the host country falls under. If you want to set up a labor-intensive electronics assembly plant and skilled workers are in short supply, either an elaborate training program must be set up (hopefully with government subsidies), skilled labor must be imported, or another location chosen. On the other hand, opening a facility requiring substantial numbers of unskilled laborers in Sweden or the Netherlands probably means paying exorbitant wages.

A survey of other companies requiring similar types of skilled workers yields a good indication of the labor base. Local vocational training schools, colleges and universities, and government training programs are usually excellent sources of trained workers. If all of these sources fail, skilled labor probably isn't available. Since local union officials eagerly broadcast a strong labor contingent, the lack of such a formal labor group is also a sure sign of a deficient skilled labor force.

If appropriate labor isn't available in the country, it must be imported. Businesses in Middle Eastern countries with small populations have imported foreign labor for years, principally from Pakistan and the Philippines. Labor brokers flourish in these countries. Any labor broker will gladly arrange for importing an appropriate number of workers with skills needed to do the job. A broker charges up to 25 percent of total payroll cost for this service, but it's still cheaper than for a company to try to import labor on its own. Also, be aware that wages are paid in cash, to the broker. He is then responsible for distributing wages to the workers. This is one reason most labor brokers tend to be wealthy.

Management talent is another matter. Nearly any developed country has management talent equal or superior to that found in the United States. Foreign managers may be less decisive, less attuned to so-called modern management techniques (mainly developed in America), and demand better fringe benefits than their American counterparts. As an offset, however, they are generally better trained in technical skills, communications, and direct supervisory abilities. They also tend to be more loyal to an employer and earn substantially lower salaries than American managers. Employment agencies and help wanted ads in major city newspapers are two of the best ways to attract these managers.

Management talent in developing nations is another story. In most nations, it is nonexistent. Managers and supervisors must be brought in from the United States, Canada, Europe, or Pacific Basin industrialized nations.

Shipping and Transport

A number of arrangements must be made to move materials, equipment, and products into and out of the facility. Moving goods usually involves three means of transport: ocean shipping to and from the host country, air freight, and inland transport. Shipping arrangements for components, material, or equipment from the home office should be handled from that end. This activity can be performed more efficiently and cheaper there than in a host country. Carriers can be identified, containerization arranged, insurance coverage purchased, and shipping documents prepared at the home office. Customs clearances at the port of entry, on the other hand, should be arranged locally.

Ocean shipping out of the host country should also be managed locally. Even in the smallest and most backward nation there should be at least one shipping company or freight forwarder to work with. At this stage of the survey, shipping rates, documentation requirements, export customs duties, and schedules of departing ships need to be assimilated. Any local company in the import/export business can help. Or the data can be obtained directly from dock or terminal officials.

During the administrative survey the names and schedules of airlines serving both the parent's home country and the host country were gathered. Although expensive, sometimes one has no other choice than to ship material by air. While shipments to the job site may be arranged out of the home office, local air freight must be handled within the host country. As part of the survey, the same information should be gathered from air carriers on this end as was done in the administrative survey.

Inland transport gets slightly more complicated. Trucking companies are nearly always locally owned. Developed countries have tariffs established for shipping virtually any product. This gives some uniformity to the trucking industry. Most Third World countries haven't reached this stage yet. Trucking companies must be identified. Schedules, routes, and containerization requirements ascertained. Negotiations conducted to establish shipping rates. If the facility will be located in an out-of-the-way place, miles from a major city, it's entirely possible that negotiations should include arranging for permanent truck assignments to the company.

A Western company could, of course, purchase its own trucks and hire its own drivers. In some locations this is the best way. In others, however, notably in South and Central America, the roadways are so poorly maintained, liability exposure to personal injury so severe, and lack of company loyalty so pervasive, that it is usually safer, in the beginning at least, to arrange for a contract carrier.

Electricity, Water, Fuel, and Telephone

Efficient, reliable utilities of every sort available in the United States spoil us. In almost every other country, including Western Europe and Japan, utilities are at best a thorn in the efficient operation of a business. Failures occur in all systems and rates can be exorbitant.

In Third World countries the situation is much worse. Many parts of Africa do not have an electric power plant and must use generators, or do without electricity. Potable water is practically unheard of in many parts of Central America, South America, and Asia. Even in the rain-filled Caribbean, it is a scarce commodity and guarded jealously. For a business requiring either large amounts of electric power or substantial quantities of fresh water, self-sufficiency is the only answer.

When Morton Plastic and Rubber Company opened its new processing plant in Alexandria, Egypt, the local utility company could not provide either sufficient electricity or fresh water required for the processing of the company's products. Morton solved the problem by installing its own oil-fired generator plant for electricity and desalination facility to convert the endless supply of Mediterranean salt water. Although very expensive, the company felt that over the long term, the strategic global advantages of being in this location far outweighed the initial cost of the two plants.

Another equally satisfactory, although less expensive solution is frequently employed in Caribbean locations with limited potable water and erratic electricity. Tie into the power utility, but keep a standing generator on the premises, set to kick in whenever the power fades or goes off completely. Portable desalination equipment as used by the U.S. Army can supply at least a reasonable amount of fresh water.

The lack of reliable electricity often precludes the use of computers, either in telecommunications or productive capacities. Prolonged upward or downward power variations can easily blow out the most sophisticated electronic equipment. Companies solve the problem by running computer equipment off direct current provided by one or more 12-volt batteries. An inexpensive converter converts DC to AC. The batteries can then be charged overnight, either with a standing generator or through the local power utility.

When power or water is scarce, you can be certain that the government controls its use. This means licensing. Although each country has different licensing laws, nearly all require rigid qualification procedures and substantial fees to get a permit to use public power and water.

Power and water shortages can be the most crucial deterrent to establishing a production facility. Coming to grips with these conditions during the detailed survey is mandatory. Applications must be filed with government officials to obtain appropriate licenses. Sharing power and water facilities with other manufacturing companies should be investigated. Quite often the licensing process requires an estimate of how much power and water will be used each month. Licensing fees are then based on how much you expect to use over the next year. If more than the estimated amounts is actually used, stringent penalties can be imposed.

PERSONNEL INFORMATION

What most companies regard as the final segment of the detailed survey should probably be completed first: determining the local conditions that affect company personnel stationed at the facility or traveling to and from the home office. There are four matters that normally concern either American or other foreign nationals stationed in a host country:

1. What type of accommodations will he and his family live in?
2. What type of local transport is available?
3. What are the educational facilities (for families with children)?
4. Are there other Americans or English-speaking expatriates nearby to socialize with?

The company also wants to know how much all of this costs.

Living Accommodations

Once again a wide disparity exists between expatriates living in Western Europe, Canada, or Japan, and anywhere else. Apartments, condominiums, even houses, are generally available either on lease or purchase in every country of Western Europe and Canada. At a cost substantially more than comparable dwellings in the United States, however. A two-bedroom apartment leased in Chicago, or Cleveland might run $1,500 per month base rent. In England, the same configuration could go for $2,500. Apartments and condos are also readily available in Japan, although there the cost is exorbitant. The same two-bedroom apartment could easily rent for $5,000 or more.

In developing nations the cost is always less, but then so is the selection. For a facility located in or near a major city (Buenos Aires, Kingston, or Kuala Lumpur), adequate housing for singles or families should be available without much difficulty. If located in the hinterlands, housing will probably consist of a hotel or a house owned by one of the upper class. There is almost always a real estate agent, or the equivalent, available to offer advice about housing. As an important step in the detailed survey, as much information as possible should be accumulated from these agents. It should include pictures of the types of housing, costs, lease arrangements, and availability.

Transportation

Management personnel relocating to a foreign facility need local transportation. Rail service works best in Western Europe and parts of Japan. Buses or autos are the primary means in the rest of the world. The local populace must also get around, so all countries have bus systems—some good, some horrible. In poorer countries, since most of the populace cannot afford cars, buses are the rule. Once an expatriate becomes accustomed to the heat, stench, and erratic schedules, buses become the preferred means for them as well; especially for cross-country junkets. While doing the survey, one should pick up published schedules of buses that run close to the facility. Also check on the cost—although it is always nominal compared to the United States.

Rental cars are the usual mode of transportation for visitors. Major U.S. and British car rental firms maintain rental depots throughout the world. Permanent managers, however, usually find that a purchase or long-term lease can be cheaper and more convenient than rentals. Densely populated cities such as Tokyo, Taipai, Singapore, and Seoul present a more difficult problem. Ordinarily, even if you can get a car, driving in these metropolises turns into a nightmare. Frequently, public transportation is preferable regardless of how bad or erratic it may be.

Driving laws in many countries can also be very strict. The last thing an expatriate wants to do is end up in a foreign jail for violating some inconspicuous driving regulation. Information about local driving laws, lease versus buy alternatives, cost comparisons, and availability of public transportation should all be gathered during the detailed survey. It may take some digging to get all the answers, but in the end expatriates moving to the host country appreciate the effort.

Education Facilities

Without school-age children in relocating families, this topic is irrelevant. On the other hand, personnel with families are vitally concerned about how and where their children will continue their education. Each nation has different school systems. Some support public education similar to the United States. Others rely on private schools, usually affiliated with a religious order for those who can afford it, and public schools or no school for the bulk of the population. Schools run by Americans for American expatriates have become very popular in many parts of the world. Also, some companies with large numbers of expatriate families provide their own American-type school, such as Aramco (Arab American Oil Company) in Saudi Arabia.

Colleges and universities have sprung up throughout the world during the past two decades. Primarily because of the large number of Western expatriates demanding higher education facilities, an increasing awareness of the value of further education has added impetus to the movement, even in developing nations.

The person assigned to perform the detail survey can readily obtain brochures, entrance qualifications, curricula, and cost of colleges directly from the institution. Information concerning public or private elementary and secondary education facilities can be gathered from appropriate government education ministries or from the local school administration office. And it certainly wouldn't hurt to ask managers from other American or European firms in the area about education systems. The American Chamber of Commerce office can also help.

Socializing

Although many companies ignore the need for leisure-time activities by their expatriate managers, the smart ones don't. No manager wants to get stuck in a remote foreign location with little or no opportunity for social contact. A company that thinks enough of its personnel to include this topic in its initial detailed survey inevitably gains tangible results from its people.

What type of leisure activities should be included? Descriptions of restaurants, bars, churches, and sports clubs seem to head the list. Golf or social clubs, libraries, athletic events, and other recreational facilities follow close behind. Resorts, historic structures, museums, the theater, and music festivals are important to many people for R&R vacations.

In addition to observing what is available, and picking up promotional brochures from tourist bureaus, invaluable information can be obtained from other expatriates. While meeting with managers of Western companies on other topics, it certainly doesn't hurt to get leads about leisure-time opportunities also.

Gathering information about personnel matters, and specifically the cost of supporting either a single expatriate or a family is not only helpful for the relocating employees, it is also necessary for establishing per diem payments or salary adjustments. If an employee must pay more to live overseas than he or she currently pays at home, the probability of relocating without some income adjustment is remote.

SUMMARY QUESTIONS

Although similar to the administrative survey in scope, the main objective of a detailed investigation is to assimilate enough information directly from the host country to enable a company's management to begin the process of establishing a foreign investment. Figure 10–1 summarizes the topics to be included in the detailed survey.

FIGURE 10–1
Summary of Data to Be Gathered during the Detailed Country Survey

General:
1. Arrange for one or more interpreters to work with company personnel.
2. Notify American embassy, American Chamber of Commerce, and local police of the identity of each expatriate in the country and his or her purpose in being there.
3. Arrange for security guard protection of facility.
4. Determine specific import/export restrictions for material, equipment, and products.
5. Open accounts with a local bank.
6. Make arrangements for permission to repatriate/convert currency.
7. Arrange with government officials for tax I.D., business license application, and other business permits.

Business:
1. Contact local trading company about marketing restrictions and practices.
2. Arrange with local trading company for distribution rights.
3. Talk with local Western firms about customary pricing structures.
4. Determine what formal government subsidies are available.
5. Use local attorney or international consultant to decipher and take advantage of informal subsidies.
6. Determine what materials, supplies, and equipment are necessary to start up facility, where they will come from, and what import barriers exist.
7. Determine adequacy of labor base and management talent, including cost and availability.
8. Contact local labor broker for importing labor.
9. Arrange with local employment office to source management talent.
10. Collect data about ocean shipping and air freight out of the country.
11. Negotiate arrangements with local trucking company for inland transport.
12. Determine licensing requirements and availability of power and water.

Personnel:
1. Collect data about expatriate housing accommodations and food cost.
2. Investigate public transportation and leased auto availability and cost.
3. Assimilate brochures, cost, and other data for family educational facilities.
4. Prepare collection of leisure time opportunities.

CHAPTER 11

ACQUIRING A FOREIGN COMPANY

MAJOR TOPICS

KEY POINTS

1. Why Buy an Existing Company?   There are five major reasons for buying a going business overseas rather than starting one from scratch: market presence, established networks, trained personnel, existing facility and equipment, and negotiated contracts.

2. Structuring the Buying Entity.   When planning a foreign acquisition, the structure of the buying entity must be carefully thought out. Should it be the parent corporation, a new corporation, a partnership, or a joint venture? Different countries dictate different rules for company ownership. Examples of several are provided. Joint ventures look like the only way to enter Eastern Europe.

3. Complying with the Internal Revenue Code.   The adequacy of tax planning prior to a foreign acquisition can determine the success or failure of the venture. Seven major structural and compliance considerations are examined.

4. Complying with Other U.S. Regulatory Laws.   The impact of nontax federal regulations on a foreign subsidiary must also be carefully weighed. The Foreign Corrupt Practices Act, Anti-Boycott Regulations, Trading with the Enemy Act, and the International Investment and Trade in Service Survey Act are examined.

5. Sourcing Foreign Targets.   Locating foreign companies to be acquired can be a tedious and draining task. Eleven proven sources are described. A matrix matching the best sources of assistance with major global regions provides a tool to begin the search.

6. Financing a Foreign Acquisition. This section examines seven methods for financing a foreign acquisition: merchant and clearing banks, international development banks (IDBs), government agencies, public debt issues, merger, buyer notes, and debt/equity swaps.

7. Due Diligence and Valuation. Lack of financial and market records coupled with informal contractual arrangements create a dilemma when trying to value a company. A suggested comprehensive checklist indicates what information should be gathered. All will not be available however, and common sense must prevail.

8. Negotiating a Purchase Contract. Unfamiliar language, contract methodology, and business practices, make third-party negotiators likely candidates to carry the ball. Disparate negotiating protocol in different cultures are shown as examples of some of the difficulties.

9. Special Employee Rights. The laws of most foreign countries grant employees far more rights than exist in the United States. The extremely high cost of employee benefits and peculiar dismissal rules in Europe could easily negate an acquisition there.

"If I had it to do all over again I would never waste time and money trying to start up a business from scratch. The three companies we acquired were on-line in one tenth the time it took to get one of the others rolling." Bob Latickilo, CEO of Worcon-Battle, a $22 million manufacturer of metal and plastic fasteners, addressed the local Kiwanis luncheon. He had just returned from closing his fourth acquisition deal, this one in Mexico. Latickilo went on to explain his company's phenomenal global growth over the past seven years. While domestic sales remained fairly constant at $3 to $4 million, business was booming in England, Norway, and Thailand.

By adding Mexico to the fold, he forecasted company sales of over $30 million by 1992. Although Worcon-Battle began its global venture through exporting, it didn't take long to realize that export sales were the tip of the iceberg. Distributors and processing companies were started from scratch in Trinidad, Venezuela, and Spain before the company learned that the acquisition route was a much faster and smoother road to foreign investment.

Once a company decides to enter global trade through direct foreign investment, the normal reaction is to look for locations favoring the start-up of a new company. Management begins one or more country surveys to learn about potential start-up opportunities. Possibilities for joint ventures with customers or domestic competitors are frequently explored. If a company has never made a domestic business acquisition, chances are high it won't begin global expansion by pursuing one overseas. In the beginning, it nearly always appears more cost-effective to start a foreign operation than to buy an existing company.

Other companies reject foreign acquisitions as being too difficult to finance. Or they worry about strange tax laws and legal requirements. In many cases, finance managers assume only the big boys have the muscle and resources to make a foreign acquisition.

For some industries, starting from scratch provides the only feasible way to enter a new market. Retailing, fast-foods, and personal service companies, for example, generally do not fit the acquisition mold. These businesses are so specialized that acquiring a similar company tends to destroy this uniqueness.

In most cases, however, and especially in manufacturing or distribution businesses, the acquisition of a going business provides the most cost-effective and timely way to become global. This chapter examines the major steps to accomplish a foreign investment in the shortest time frame and at the least cost. The procedures are similar to those employed domestically. Yet, there are enough differences to caution against proceeding down the same trail.

WHY BUY AN EXISTING COMPANY?

A variety of factors favor buying an existing company over starting one from scratch, especially in a foreign location. Each deal portrays somewhat different characteristics. Each country has its own foreign investment regulations to follow. However, the advantages of buying over beginning from scratch are fairly universal. They can be grouped under five headings:

1. *Market presence.* An existing business has already made the investment in time, people, and money to establish itself in a given market. Its products may differ from the buyer's, but by carefully sourcing the right target synergisms usually follow. Many times the target's product offering complements the buyer's and adds to overall sales volume.

2. *Established networks.* Distribution channels, a customer base, and supplier agreements should already be in existence and functioning. Many overseas companies already have marketing and distribution networks in other countries managing export product lines. Global supplier contacts for sourcing materials and supplies may already be in place.

3. *Trained personnel.* Management personnel in production, marketing, finance, engineering, and quality control are probably already on board. Locating capable local management talent is the hardest task when starting a foreign business. An acquiring company's management personnel, unaccustomed to local regulations and business practices, just can't perform at the same level of expertise. A trained labor base skilled in operating a company's machines and equipment, performing assembly operations, and managing administrative details eliminates the need for massive recruitment.

4. *Existing facility and equipment.* Arranging for the purchase or lease of facility space in a foreign location can be a nightmare. The high cost of importing machinery and equipment necessary for a start-up together with import restrictions can be equally se-

vere barriers. An existing business with production lines in place, inevitably comes on-line with a buyer's products more expediently.

5. *Negotiated contracts.* A number of contractual agreements must be negotiated when starting up a foreign company—some written, others verbal. Union contracts, sales representative agreements, supplier arrangements, negotiated pricing structures, leases, tax permits and licenses, pension documents, employment contracts, and a variety of other contractual arrangements are nearly always required to operate a business overseas. A business with contractual agreements already in place makes this phase easier and faster.

Most large corporations that have gone global successfully learned the hard way that acquiring a going business gets them into a new market faster, cheaper, and with significantly fewer headaches than beginning an operation from scratch. Many of these multinationals have also learned that buying controlling interest in a business can be much less expensive and require fewer local government approvals than acquiring 100 percent of a company. Joint ventures and minority partnerships, either with government or private participation, have become a favorite way of establishing a presence in new foreign markets. Ford, GE, and Du Pont are a few excellent examples of successful American multinationals that have acquired part but not all of foreign companies as a means of expansion.

Large multinational deals can become very complex. An acquisition transaction between Westinghouse and Siemens, A.G., or the Swiss manufacturer Brown-Bovari, for example, might include U.S. companies or divisions owned by foreign interests; branches in Singapore and Tokyo; distribution centers in Rio; and patents and trademarks registered in various countries.

Such a complicated acquisition might also encompass complex stock transfers; new equity or debt issues on any of the world's exchanges; and compliance with a multitude of U.S. and foreign regulatory laws, including the U.S. Antitrust laws. This type of acquisition is far beyond the scope of this book. These complex machinations, though interesting to follow, generally do not affect small acquisitions.

For even the smaller buyer, however, making a foreign acquisition involves several aspects not prevalent in domestic deals. The following sections review the most frequent variations. These variations fall under eight headings:

1. Structuring the buying entity.
2. Complying with U.S. tax laws.
3. Complying with other U.S. regulatory laws.
4. Sourcing foreign targets.
5. Financing a foreign acquisition.
6. Performing the due diligence investigation and valuing the business.
7. Negotiating the purchase contract.
8. Dealing with the special rights of employees of the acquired company.

STRUCTURING THE BUYING ENTITY

When making a domestic acquisition, a buyer usually looks at three possible acquisition vehicles: the buyer corporation, a new corporation owned by the buyer, or a partnership. Occasionally joint ventures enter the picture but these are becoming increasingly rare among smaller deals in the United States. Structuring the buying entity for a foreign acquisition can be slightly more confusing, depending on the host country and the financing arrangements.

In some countries, such as England, 100 percent foreign ownership is permitted. Normally, the buyer elects to use a new British corporation as a holding company for protection against lawsuits. Any British solicitor has access to a complete listing of existing shell corporations on file in government offices. For a few hundred pounds, a shell can be purchased, its name changed, and then used as a buying entity. It is already licensed by the government, has a tax identification number, and possesses operating permits. These are resident with the corporation regardless of name changes. Clearly, such a vehicle saves substantial cost and aggravation compared to incorporating anew.

Other countries, especially in the Middle East and Africa, prohibit 100 percent ownership by a foreign investor, American or otherwise. Some require a local government agency as a silent partner. Others allow private individuals or companies already registered in the country to become either minority or majority owners. In still other cases, especially with the privatization of nationalized industries, government bureaucracies may want to own minority shares in the beginning and then phase out over a period of years.

Regardless of the percentage split, in countries requiring local ownership participation, obviously a 100 percent acquisition is impossible. The best way around this is to structure the buying entity as a holding company. The holding company could be either a local tiered corporation or a straight partnership. Variations proliferate the landscape. The only way to be sure what the law allows is to check with a local attorney.

Partnerships, or joint ventures with local companies or government agencies are the way to go in Eastern Europe. Not only do such structures provide immediate access to local government bureaucrats, they permit a ready entry to existing markets. To date, American companies have been slow to pick up on the vast opportunities to acquire Eastern European businesses. Companies from Western Europe have not been so hesitant. The Department of Commerce reports that through mid–1990, there have been nearly 2,000 joint venture acquisitions by Western companies in Eastern Europe. Of this total only 216 have been from American companies. Figure 11–1 shows the breakdown.

COMPLYING WITH THE INTERNAL REVENUE CODE

Chapter 3 described the current tax legislation affecting the acquisition and operation of a foreign business. Competent international tax

FIGURE 11–1
Joint Ventures in Eastern Europe (Ventures with U.S. partners and all Western companies)

	Total	
Country	Western Deals	U.S. Deals
Poland	866	60
Hungary	600–700	140
East Germany	384	4
Bulgaria	60	10
Czechoslovakia	32	1
Romania	5	1

counsel will certainly emphasize the extreme caution that must be exercised when structuring a foreign acquisition. Planning steps to minimize both the U.S. and foreign tax bites for the buyer cannot be overemphasized. Foreign tax considerations must be weighed on a case-by-case basis with competent counsel from the host country and the United States.

From a buyer's perspective, tax planning for foreign acquisitions revolves around minimizing foreign income taxes and maximizing the use of foreign tax credits during the postacquisition period. Such tax planning involves seven major aspects:

1. Allocation of purchase price.
2. Capital structure.
3. Postacquisition structure of foreign subsidiary.
4. Licensing of intangible property (if applicable).
5. Management and technical services fees.
6. Use of base companies.
7. Intercompany pricing arrangements.

Allocation of Purchase Price

As with domestic acquisitions, the negotiated allocation of purchase price to the assets of the acquired company determines how much can be written off against income generated by the acquired company. The *basket* provisions of foreign tax credits create a more difficult environment than domestic tax issues. From a planning perspective, since most income will be classified in the general basket, the allocation of purchase price should have little, if any effect on categorizing types of income. However, judicious write-offs of the purchase price can reduce general basket income, and this is important.

Different countries have different tax rates. Some countries have different tax rates for different types of income. While the United States does not allow the amortization of certain intangible assets such as patents and trademarks, other countries such as Germany and Belgium do. Some countries define a profit on the sale of inventory as a capital gain. Under U.S. tax law it is ordinary income. Other countries do not allow a deduction for the depreciation of machinery and equipment.

Negotiations between buyer and seller will ultimately determine who gets what deductions. Generally, however, an American buyer will want to allocate as much of the price as possible to depreciable and amortizable assets, to inventory, and to those countries having higher tax rates.

Capital Structure

The major tax planning question involving capital structure focuses on which entity holds the acquisition debt and hence gets a deduction for interest expense. If the acquisition is funded with debt, or partially with debt, there are two advantages to being certain the debt resides on the foreign company's books, or on the books of a foreign holding company, and not with the parent company:

1. Foreign corporate tax rates, at least in developed nations, are usually higher than those in the United States. If the foreign subsidiary takes an interest deduction it reduces foreign taxes.
2. Prior to 1986, U.S. corporations could keep foreign acquisition debt on their books and lend the funds to a foreign subsidiary. This minimized the amount of interest allocated to foreign source income. After 1986, however, new rules dictate that interest expense be allocated on the basis of asset value, not gross income. This severely penalizes American corporations. As more than one acquisition gets added to the group, the rule becomes even more onerous.

In most cases, until the U.S. tax laws change again, an American company usually gains by keeping acquisition debt on a foreign subsidiary's books rather than at home.

Postacquisition Structure of Foreign Subsidiary

In those cases where a company owns more than one foreign subsidiary, postacquisition structuring may be done to take advantage of, or to avoid, TIEA countries. Forming a second corporation in a different country and funnelling income to it can play the TIEA rules to a company's advantage. It also might be prudent to combine the newly acquired company with another foreign subsidiary. Any number of structures are possible. The more foreign operations a company has, the greater the flexibility in planning postacquisition structures.

Licensing of Intangible Property

A buyer might consider purchasing intangible assets separately from the stock or assets of the target company. The parent could then license the patents, trademarks, or other intangible assets back to the subsidiary in exchange for royalties. If the foreign tax rates are higher than U.S. rates, this shifting of income could be most beneficial. Moreover, under the look through rules of Section 904(d), the royalties would fall into the general basket for foreign tax credit purposes.

Management and Technical Services Fees

Shifting income by charging management fees from the parent to a subsidiary is common practice in the United States. The same principle can be used overseas. If the host country's rates are higher than the United States', a parent benefits by moving income into the United States. Care must be exercised, however, to perform the actual management services overseas. If performed domestically, they end up as U.S. source income. Performing the services overseas qualifies the income as general basket foreign source income. Care must also be exercised to avoid subjecting foreign service fees to foreign income taxes.

Use of Base Companies

A buyer may consider establishing a *base company* to purchase products from the acquired foreign subsidiary and then to resell them to the acquired company's marketing subsidiaries. This reduces foreign income tax on the acquired operations. The base company could be organized in a low-tax nation, such as one of the tax haven countries, or in the United States. The income from this base company constitutes general basket foreign source income if the base company is owned by the parent. Little or no foreign taxes should apply. In order to give the base company substance, the parent may have to transfer assets, business activities, and business risks to the base company. With careful planning, however, income can be legitimately shifted to a base company practically tax free.

Intercompany Pricing Arrangements

Intercompany pricing should accomplish three conditions for tax purposes. It should be so structured as to meet the arm's-length standard of Section 482 of the code. It should meet comparable standards, if any, in foreign tax codes. And finally, it should be structured to maximize the parent company's use of the foreign tax credit.

COMPLYING WITH OTHER U.S. REGULATORY LAWS

Many countries require government approval to sell or buy either the assets or stock of a local company. Previous chapters have identified several. Mexico, Canada, most of the Middle East and European nations, and several countries in South American and Southeast Asia maintain such regulations. The biggest headaches in regulatory compliance, however, have nothing to do with foreign laws. They involve compliance with U.S. regulations, starting with the antitrust provisions.

Other countries do not have stringent antitrust laws. Restraint of trade is dealt with on a case-by-case basis. But in the United States, if products are purchased or sold within its borders, the antitrust laws come into play. If the Justice Department deems a company, domestic or foreign, violates these laws, injunctions and suits can be brought.

From a practical perspective, however, no foreign company, whether owned by an American company or not, would voluntarily subject itself to court action by the Justice Department. Another way had to be found. And the Justice Department did just that, by reissuing an updated version of the Antitrust Guidelines for International Operations.

In essence these Guidelines reiterate that the Justice Department will seek to prohibit any foreign merger or acquisition that would create, enhance, or facilitate the exercise of market power to the detriment of other American businesses.

Pragmatically, a small or midsize firm making a foreign acquisition should not have to worry much about the Justice Department's Guidelines unless it happens to serve a niche market with few competitors. These Guidelines were enacted primarily to stop giant corporations from monopolizing American markets. They have nothing to do directly with global markets.

The Foreign Corrupt Practices Act

The Foreign Corrupt Practices Act (FCPA) is surely one of the most insidious laws restricting American firms from global competition. The FCPA makes it unlawful for any American company to engage in or be a party to kickbacks, bribes, payoffs, or other payment or gift to influence a foreign official. The fact that companies from every other nation in the world make use of gifts and other payments just to survive in international trade has no bearing on the decision by Congress to keep American companies "morally right."

A second feature of the FCPA, and less widely recognized, has to do with recordkeeping. The FCPA mandates that every American company "devise and maintain a system of internal accounting controls sufficient to provide reasonable assurances" that its recordkeeping adheres to the generally accepted accounting principles (GAAP) devised by the American Institute of Certified Public Accountants.

Both rules apply not only to American-based companies, but to any company worldwide with American ownership. The U.S. parent will be held responsible for acts of all its subsidiaries, branches, divisions, and so on regardless of where they are located. Can you imagine telling a Saudi partner that he can't give or accept gifts? That is truly preposterous.

Other Restrictive Acts

The Anti-Boycott Regulations of the Export Administration Act also apply to American subsidiaries worldwide. Chapter 19 describes these provisions in detail.

The Trading with the Enemy Act prohibits unlicensed trade between American companies or persons and any other person or group resident within the territory of any nation with which the U.S. is at war. It also prohibits doing business with another company engaged in business within such enemy territory.

The International Investment and Trade in Service Survey Act of 1976 requires all U.S. companies investing overseas to file specific reports with the Department of Commerce. This keeps track of who is doing what overseas and gives the IRS and Justice Department one more means to keep watch over a company's activities.

SOURCING FOREIGN TARGETS

The hardest part of any acquisition, domestic or foreign, is to locate the right business to acquire. Sourcing acquisition targets in the United States has become a full-time job for hundreds of merger and acquisition consultants, business brokers, investment bankers, securities analysts, financial planners, lawyers, and public accountants. Some of these same people might be helpful in sourcing foreign acquisition targets, but it takes specialized knowledge.

Once a country or region has been identified for the target search, and the size, product lines, markets served, and management requirements have been defined, a number of sources can provide invaluable assistance. These items must be taken care of first, however. It makes no sense to engage sourcing assistance without first defining what you are looking for.

The effectiveness of sourcing techniques varies by country. In England and Western Europe, local offices of international Big 5 accounting firms are excellent starting points. Ernst & Young does especially well in Great Britain; Peat Marwick on the Continent.

When beginning a target search in the Middle East, branch managers of British and French banks can be helpful in recommending potential targets. If you can get to the right government official in a Middle Eastern country, he almost always knows of one or two possibilities.

The large international law firm headquartered in Washington, Baker & MacKenzie, often directs known prospective buyers to several local sources in South and Central America. Local offices of Arthur Andersen are also very obliging throughout Latin America. On several occasions, clients have been referred to potential acquisition candidates in Colombia, Ecuador, and throughout the Caribbean by branch managers of both Chase Manhattan and the Bank of Nova Scotia (Scotia Bank).

Sourcing acquisition targets throughout the Pacific Basin becomes trickier. The large number of family-owned businesses and their preference for dealing with people of Asian background, closes the doors to many Western buyers. On the other hand, the Asian Development Bank located in Manila can be extremely helpful in providing leads.

American government agencies such as the International Trade Administration (ITA), the Office of the U.S. Trade Representative, and Caribbean Basin Initiative program officials willingly provide leads to potential investment opportunities. Some are hesitant to identify specific companies available for acquisition. They will provide enough data and listings of companies in a specific country to get a search under way, however.

Competent international consultants and trading companies are two sources of acquisition leads applicable worldwide. Both deal with clients of various sizes and industry affiliation. Frequently, a client will inquire if a known buyer might be located. In other cases, for a fee, either a consultant or a trading company will conduct specific target searches.

FIGURE 11–2
Sourcing Acquisition Targets

	Western Europe	Latin America	Caribbean	Pacific Basin	Middle East
Big 5 accounting firms	×	×			
International law firms		×			
British, French and American bank managers		×	×		×
International development banks			×	×	
U.S. government agencies	×	×	×	×	
International consultants and trading companies	×	×	×	×	×
Merchant banks	×			×	×
American multinationals	×			×	
Foreign multinationals	×				×
Engineering contractors		×			×

Merchant banks, especially those with British affiliations, can perform the same type of target search investment bankers do domestically. County NatWest, Barclays, Charterhouse, and several others have offices in the United States. They are easy to contact and usually eager to take on acquisition searches. But they are expensive.

Don't overlook the possibility of acquiring a foreign branch of an American multinational. These corporations, accustomed to the merger and acquisition game, make frequent turnover of foreign divisions and subsidiaries a way of life. Try GE, Du Pont, Westinghouse, General Foods, Ford, Warner Lambert, and the tobacco companies. International engineering firms such as Bechtel, Fluor, and Brown & Root are also likely sources. Foreign multinationals willingly identify targets in specific countries to noncompeting firms.

The matrix in Figure 11–2 outlines which sources work best in different regions of the world.

FINANCING A FOREIGN ACQUISITION

Managements accustomed to using leveraged buyout (LBO) methods in the United States will be disappointed trying the same financing scheme overseas. Other than infrequent use in Great Britain, France, and Germany, very few LBOs are ever closed outside the borders of the United States. Foreign banks, merchant banks, government agencies, and business sellers seem to regard LBOs as strictly an American phenomenon. They see high risks of failure in such deals and most are unwilling to participate. Additionally, American banks shy away from foreign acquisition financing, at least for smaller companies. On the other hand, public debt issues by smaller companies, especially in the Eurobond markets, are more frequently used for acquisition funding overseas than in the United States.

The small and midsize buyer has seven principal sources of outside capital available for foreign acquisitions:

- Merchant and clearing bank.
- International development bank (IDB).
- Government agency.
- Public debt issue.
- Merger.
- Buyer note.
- Debt/equity swaps.

As in sourcing acquisition targets, potential financing sources vary by type and size of the deal, and country or region. Many times the same merchant banks or IDBs used to source targets can finance the deal. For European and Middle East acquisitions, British merchant banks provide financing directly and also help identify local sources. They also finance Pacific Basin acquisitions with participation from the Asian Development Bank.

Japanese trading companies and banks also handle deals in Southeast Asia, the newly industrialized Asian nations, and Indochina. Financing an acquisition in Japan poses special problems for smaller firms. A buyer can probably do better elsewhere, at least until the current U.S.-Japanese trade barrier donnybrook subsides.

The African Development Bank and Fund occasionally gets involved in providing financing assistance for African acquisitions. British merchant banks are also active in former British Empire countries in Africa. To date, however, few smaller companies have been able to source acquisition targets on the African continent as easily as elsewhere. The exception being South Africa. At the moment, however, expansion opportunities for American companies in this market remain dubious.

The newly formed European Bank for Reconstruction and Development in Eastern Europe has indicated that financing assistance will become available for joint venture acquisitions in Eastern Europe. To date however, the structure of such financing remains cloudy.

In Latin America, the Inter-American Development Bank headquartered in Washington offers to coordinate financing from local IDBs. It also provides limited direct financing for American acquisitions in South and Central America. Although announcements have not been made public, many American money centers and regional banks remain receptive to providing financial assistance for acquisitions in debtor countries. This usually takes the form of a private debt-equity swap to help the bank reduce defaulted Latin-American loans.

The Caribbean Basin Initiative program and the special Puerto Rican 936 program supported by the federal government can be very helpful in arranging financing for Caribbean acquisitions. Of all the regions open to global trade, an acquisition in the Caribbean is probably the easiest to finance and the fastest to close. Mexican acquisitions, whether in the border trade zones or elsewhere must be financed through U.S. sources. Increasingly, however, the Inter-American Development Bank has been offering sourcing assistance here also.

For European acquisitions, companies in growing industries with a significant, profitable history should have little difficulty floating small Eurobond issues on the London Exchange. The best way to investigate this possibility is through one of the major American investment banks handling Eurobond issues. Either Goldman Sachs, Morgan Stanley, Merrill Lynch, or First Boston can help determine if such funding looks feasible in a given situation.

If a company has already issued public stock, whether or not it is currently actively traded, it should be able to interest a potential foreign seller in a merger consisting of exchanging common shares. Once again, an American investment bank can be of enormous assistance in arranging such a transaction. Such assistance is normally well worth the steep cost. A smaller company trying to effect a stock merger with a foreign company usually finds it strenuous and fraught with pitfalls. An investment bank, or a British merchant bank, can easily provide the guidance to push the deal through.

Seller financing is seldom used in foreign acquisitions. Most foreign sellers regard taking promissory notes from a foreign buyer a risky business. There are exceptions, but they normally involve only very large companies, well known in global circles. One form of seller financing can be employed, however, when acquiring only a portion of a foreign company rather than 100 percent. Existing privately held companies that evolve into joint ventures normally take back a buyer's note on the assumption that as a partner, a seller has recourse on default.

Occasionally, the privatization of nationalized industries creates acquisition opportunities of smaller companies supplying parts or services within the industry. With the host country government as the seller, buyer paper cannot be used for financing. Under certain circumstances however, a government agency will allow a buyer to pay off the purchase price over a period of time. In essence, this makes the funding the same as paying off a promissory note.

Debt-equity swaps, as described in Chapter 12, are gradually becoming a unique way to finance acquisitions in certain Latin-American countries. Formal debt-for-equity conversion programs currently exist in Mexico, Costa Rica, Ecuador, Brazil, Argentina, Chile, and the Philippines. The process works as follows:

1. An American or other foreign bank creditor sells a portion of its debt from one of these countries to a private investor at a substantial discount from the debt's face value.
2. The investor redeems the debt from the foreign government, either at face value or at a lesser discount than granted by the original bank creditor. The redemption is made in local currency.
3. The investor then purchases a business in the foreign country using local currency.

This scheme involves an initial dollar cash payment to acquire the debt from the bank. Since the face amount has been substantially discounted, the foreign acquisition costs significantly less than if it were financed with U.S. dollars, and everyone wins.

DUE DILIGENCE AND VALUATION

Whereas due diligence investigations and valuation procedures are relatively straightforward for domestic acquisitions, this step can easily become a nightmare when buying a foreign company. Contracts, market and sales statistics, labor agreements, pension benefits, and financial statements are all unique to a specific country's laws and customs. Accounting requirements vary radically worldwide. Even in developed countries requiring financial compliance reporting, no two follow the same accounting conventions. Even between the United States and Great Britain, accounting terminology and acceptable financial reporting standards vary markedly.

Many less developed nations have no financial compliance standards except for annual tax returns. Financial records as Americans know them are practically non-existent. This makes it virtually impossible to determine the historical profitability of the business for valuation purposes. The value of many company assets and liabilities may also be unrecorded, so book value cannot be determined.

Market and trade statistics are seldom maintained as meticulously as in the United States. Since accrual accounting is virtually unknown in developing nations, trading performance is measured on a cash basis. Cash receipts become sales; cash expenditures expenses. The difference is profit or loss. Customer order backlog usually remains unrecorded. Market size and market share are seldom quantified.

Formal written contracts and agreements are also usually missing, unless required by government regulations. Many countries do have stringent employee laws, however. If formal agreements do exist, they usually refer to employee compensation or benefits.

Given this lack of formal recordkeeping, normal due diligence and valuation procedures must be modified to the circumstances. Establishing a reasonable price for a foreign company not currently owned by an American parent involves using bank accounts, tax documents, employee evaluations, contracts and agreements (to the extent available), competitor assessments, and Kentucky windage. Frustration and confusion normally follow the first assessment of a foreign company by an American buyer.

Unfortunately, no easy answer exists. Available records must be supplemented with commonsense judgment. The due diligence checklist in Figure 11–3 is the optimum. Many of these items will be unavailable. When specific data is missing, your judgment must prevail.

NEGOTIATING A PURCHASE CONTRACT

Whether the acquisition calls for a purchase of stock or assets, the negotiating price, terms of sale, and contract language should be handled through a third party fluent in the local language and familiar with local

FIGURE 11–3

Due Diligence Checklist for a Foreign Acquisition

A. Marketing:
  a. Customer order backlog reports: by customer and product line as of each quarter for the past three years and current year to date.
  b. Listing of orders received: by customer and product line for each month for the past three years and current year to date.
  c. Listing of shipments: by customer and product line for each month for the past three years and current year to date.
  d. Listing of outstanding customer contracts and outstanding customer bids: domestic and export.
  e. Listing and description of all sales representative organizations, agreements and commission schedules.
  f. Listing of export buyer sources.
B. Financial:
  a. Detailed operating statements and balance sheets by quarter (including annual reports) for the past three years and for each quarter of current year to date.
  b. All supporting schedules to above operating statements and balance sheets for the periods listed: that is, manufacturing overhead detail accounts, selling, general and administrative accounts, and detailed cost of sales. These schedules should be by major product line, if available, but as a minimum, separate schedules for export and domestic.
  c. Aged accounts receivable by customer as of each quarter for the past three years and for each quarter of current year to date.
  d. Physical inventory summary (if any) or detailed breakdown of inventory (raw materials, work in process—material, labor, overhead, and finished goods—material, labor, overhead) as of each year-end for past three years.
  e. Aged accounts payable by vendor as of each quarter for the past three years and for each quarter of current year to date.
  f. Listing of accrued expenses as of each year-end for the past three years.
  g. Income tax returns for the past three years.
C. Personnel:
  a. All employment contracts or agreements (oral or written), including any severance or termination compensation arrangements with salaried, hourly, or collective bargaining unit employees.
  b. All bonus, deferred compensation, stock option, profit sharing or retirement programs, or plans covering salaried, hourly, or collective bargaining unit employees.
  c. If there is a pension plan, all documentation, including compliance reports, actuarial reports, tax returns, Trustee reports, population census reports, funding requirements, unfunded liabilities, and so on, for the past three years.
  d. Schedule of hourly wage rates and number of personnel in each rate, by work center, department, and geographic location.
  e. Organization chart of salaried personnel, by location, showing function responsibility, tenure, age, salary, name, and title.
  f. All documentation relating to employee insurance coverages such as health, life, AD & D, and dental.
D. Contracts, Agreements, Appraisals, Insurance and Litigation:
  a. All contracts or agreements with vendors and customers.
  b. All contracts or agreements with employees.
  c. All contracts or agreements with collective bargaining units.
  d. All contracts or agreements with other third parties.
  e. All recent (within three years) appraisals of real estate or machinery and equipment.
  f. Listing of machinery and equipment.
  g. All insurance claims outstanding.
  h. All patents, copyrights, or license agreements.
  i. All noncompete covenant agreements.
  j. All lease or purchase agreements for machinery and equipment, autos, or real estate.
  k. Legal descriptions of all real estate including deeds, title reports, title insurance documentation, together with documentation of any lien thereon.
  l. Listing and description of all outstanding litigation or anticipated litigation.
  m. Is union contract transferable? If yes, then description of mechanics of making transfer, such as required approvals.
  n. Copies of all building and land leases.
  o. Copies of all warranty agreements.

FIGURE 11–3 (concluded)

> *p.* All outstanding bank loan documentation.
> *q.* All documentation for other debts outstanding.
> E. Corporate Documents:
>   *a.* Certificate of incorporation, including all amendments, name changes, and mergers.
>   *b.* Corporate bylaws.
>   *c.* Corporate minute book.
>   *d.* Corporate stock transfer record.

business contract practices. Few Americans making their first foreign acquisition have the background in local laws, customs, and business practices, not to mention contract terminology, to handle their own negotiations. Even when negotiating for an English, Canadian, or Australian acquisition, language dissimilarities often lead to confusion and frustration. It works much better to let a local contract attorney or management consultant do the negotiating for you.

Negotiating tactics vary substantially from those used in domestic business transactions. When dealing with the Japanese or Koreans, for instance, hard-nosed give and take tactics, vacillating positions, and meticulous clarification of contract language common in American negotiations will never fly. On the other hand, Dutch and German negotiators frequently spend more time clarifying language than they do on price.

Latins have no patience for formal schedules and try to encourage informal side agreements. Middle East negotiators prefer slow, informal, courteous, but verbal *understandings* to lengthy written contracts. They tend to be unrelenting on price.

Except in rare cases, it's useless to try to negotiate price based on finite calculations of present value or discounted cash flow. Only the more sophisticated have any idea what you're talking about. It's far better to use your own judgment about an equitable price and try to persuade the seller to adjust his thinking. Because of this disparity and many more, using a third party to handle negotiations is frequently the only way a deal ever closes.

SPECIAL EMPLOYEE RIGHTS

Employee rights in many foreign countries far transcend anything remotely possible in the United States. Many European countries with national collective bargaining agreements grant what appear to Americans to be unconscionable employee rights. Under these agreements, employees have the right to information and consultation when the management of a company contemplates major changes in operating procedure, stock ownership, or other significant plans or policies.

A set of employee rights called *codetermination* is common in several developed countries. In Germany, for example, codetermination grants employees the right to veto unpopular management policy decisions. Two boards of directors are required: one for strategy matters and one for operating policies. Employees sit on both. In the Netherlands, *works councils* made up of company employees must be consulted before implementation of termination, investment, or pension decisions.

In England, employees cannot be dismissed except under very unusual circumstances. British firms get around the law by calling layoffs *redundancies*. When a person's job has become *redundant* he or she is no longer needed by the company. Company-paid pension plans are mandatory. Employees in the Middle Eastern countries are often distant relatives to a ruling prince or other high government official. These employees have a right to a job for life.

Nearly all social welfare states place employee rights far above those of an employer. Substantial and costly benefit programs add significantly to employee wages. Dismissal is practically impossible. Even when an employee can be laid off, the company must continue to pay him compensation for long periods—often years.

Because of the high cost of sustaining employee rights, wage and employee head count ratios customarily used in American companies to judge the efficiency of an operation just don't hold water overseas. If an employee costs a company $20 per hour including benefits in the United States, a comparable rate could be $50, $60, or even $100 in Europe or Japan. Obviously, in judging the efficacy of making a foreign acquisition, the rights and costs of employees must be carefully weighed in the final decision.

CONCLUSION

Buying a foreign company may be the best or only way to effectively establish a global presence. The acquisition process overseas, however, presents challenges unmatched in domestic deals. Getting competent professional assistance from attorneys, consultants, public accountants, and officials from other American companies doing business in the host country is about the only feasible way for a company to close a deal.

On the plus side, buying a going business in a developing country can frequently be financed almost entirely outside the buying company. Federal agency funding, international development banks, and merchant banks all stand ready to provide financing assistance to the smaller company. This chapter has only skimmed the surface of a very complex subject. Significant research into the mechanics and difficulties of foreign acquisitions must be attended to long before starting down the trail to avoid costly, and often losing, efforts.

SECTION III

FINANCING GLOBAL TRADE

CHAPTER 12

GLOBAL BANKING

MAJOR TOPICS

KEY POINTS

1. The Role of Commercial Banks. American commercial banks and their foreign counterparts, clearing banks, must be used to move money, convert currency, and finance export transactions. Overextension of Latin-American credit has created a new global expansion opportunity through debt-equity swaps.

2. The Role of American Investment Banks. International investment banks such as Morgan Stanley and Goldman Sachs can help raise capital through the syndication of public issues on foreign exchanges. These giants manage investment opportunities for large pension funds. They also play a role in identifying foreign investment possibilities and foreign capital sources.

3. The Role of Merchant Banks. British, Dutch, and Japanese merchant banks play a major part in uncovering investment targets and coordinating financing with international development banks. Their reputation in supporting Eurobond issues and other foreign offerings can be a major assist for companies trying to raise capital. The role of merchant banks in identifying and bringing together foreign joint ventures and partnerships receives little publicity but is extremely vital to investments in certain regions.

4. The Global Financial Mentality. To be effective in the global arena a company must abandon its parochial attitudes about financial management. Financial management must be integrated with marketing and production activities. Foreign public issues are an accepted means of raising capital, even for the smaller company. Global expansion requires the utilization of integrated foreign financial resources. Financial managers must be trained in international finance. Guidelines are included for using the global banking system.

5. Global Banking in the 21st Century. To remain competitive in the next century, federal banking regulations must be changed to allow U.S. commercial banks to expand their international activities through the repeal of the Glass-Steagall Act. Larger banks should be allowed to acquire smaller ones to significantly reduce the fragmentation of the commercial banking industry. Financial advisory services from commercial and investment banks must be stressed. Archaic accounting and SEC regulations should be rewritten. Smaller companies should be encouraged to utilize public issues rather than bank debt to finance global expansion.

Michael McNally was a risk-taking entrepreneur of the old school. Determined, aggressive, self-confident, and more than a bit dictatorial, Mike had done very well over the past 20 years in the two businesses he owned. I came to know Mike when he hired me to assist him in selling his last company two years earlier—a $25 million manufacturer of automotive parts for the after market. It was a cash deal and Mike netted a cool $18 million. At 56 he decided to sail around Australia and New Zealand before retiring to a golf course in Florida. When he returned from his nine-month vacation, I heard from Mike again.

While cruising in the South Pacific sun, Mike made up his mind that he wasn't ready to retire yet. Although active in the stock market, he couldn't get excited about watching ticker tapes. He asked me to help him find another company to buy, preferably in Florida. It didn't take long to find a suitable candidate.

As we proceeded to put a deal together it became clear that traditional leveraged financing just wouldn't work in this case. The target lacked hard assets, cash flow had been erratic for three years, and foreign entries were beginning to penetrate the target's market. Chase, Citicorp, Chemical, First Interstate, and the rest of the larger U.S. commercial banks, embarrassed by recent Latin-American write-offs, still had their heads in the sand. The large U.S. investment banks, Merrill Lynch, Goldman Sachs, and Donaldson, Lufkin, weren't interested in such a small deal.

I contacted an old friend at Bear Sterns for advice. He suggested we try Charterhouse, a midsize British merchant bank currently pursuing U.S. investments. Structuring a debt-equity package including convertible warrants with Charterhouse, and a working capital line with the Bank of Credit and Commerce International (BCCI), a Luxembourg bank, Mike closed the deal.

Under Mike's tutelage the company prospered and regained its previous market position. Mike began exporting to the Caribbean and started looking for investment opportunities in South America. I exposed Mike to the possibility of buying Latin-American debt on the secondary market at a significant discount and swapping it with the Brazilian government for real estate and a plant. With the help of the Charterhouse gang Mike arranged just such a debt-equity swap to establish an operating plant in Brazil.

A year or so later, Mike received a call from a different British merchant bank in London suggesting he might be interested in acquiring an interest in a manufacturing company in Hong Kong. The company had recently indicated a need for a U.S.-based partner for western hemisphere distribution. He could use some of his company's pension funds for the equity investment and a Swiss bank was willing to raise the balance of the price through Euro-bonds. Mike jumped at the opportunity.

Other opportunities occurred for expansion into the global sphere. Today, from his base in Florida, Mike is happily running a true multinational company with facilities in five countries. He called me one day. "Larry, I just wanted to let you know how much I appreciate what you did to get me started with the global banking fraternity. It never occurred to me that so much money was available, in so many different forms, and in so many different locations. Next year we're planning a bond issue on the Seoul Exchange to raise capital for a new plant in South Korea. This has been a real eye-opener to the possibilities available through the global banking system. I can keep expanding this business forever!"

As long as executives think of financing business ventures only through commercial banks, a true global mentality is impossible. If foreign markets present burgeoning opportunities for products and services, global banking, with creative financing possibilities unheard of in the United States, paves the way for companies to take advantage of these openings.

Grants and loans from government agencies, private organizations, commercial banks, and asset-based lenders can help a business expand, to a point. American venture capital funds and investment banks can take the company over the next hurdle. But without utilizing the global banking system and its financial markets, a company places severe limitations on how far it can go, and how successful it will be in the global economy. A global mentality demands financial management encompassing global financial markets.

Global banking is best understood by looking at the roles played by the three major players: commercial banks, American investment banks, and international merchant banks.

THE ROLE OF COMMERCIAL BANKS

Everyone has dealt with commercial banks at one time or another. Even the corner grocery needs a bank for depositing customer receipts and clearing its own checks. Most companies use commercial banks for borrowing short-term working capital funds. Acquiring a company normally requires borrowing either short- or long-term debt from a commercial bank. Major New York banks are delineated between retail banks (Chase, Citibank, Irving, Chemical) and wholesale banks (Banker's Trust, J. P. Morgan). The latter act as banks for other banks.

One of the unique features of the American banking system is the proliferation of banks of all sizes located in every nook and cranny of the country. Every other civilized nation gets by with a central bank owned by the government (such as our Federal Reserve Bank) and a handful of banking institutions with branches throughout the country. Only in America does banking exhibit entrepreneurial characteristics.

To hold such a proliferation of banks together in one system, the nine largest have become known as money center banks. Except for Bank of America, they are all headquartered in New York. These banks act as clearinghouses for banking transactions of smaller banks. They set the prime rate. They manage most of the international business. They lobby in Washington for the banking industry. Because of the noncompetitive nature of the industry, major decisions and policies of the money center banks set the guidelines that control the industry.

International Business

Nearly all retail money center banks have branch offices in foreign countries. This can be very helpful to an American company entering a new country or region. In some countries, notably Egypt and most of the Middle East, government regulations require a national partner to hold controlling interest—usually the government itself. Top management of the bank normally falls to an American. In some cases, however, managers might be British or even local nationals. In any case, the English language is always spoken. This can be invaluable for a business traveler trying to find his way without a grasp of the local language.

When I conducted a business survey in Cartagena, Colombia, I didn't speak Spanish. Neither the hotel manager, the telephone operator, nor taxi drivers spoke English. My time was limited and I had to establish contacts with several subcontractors. I eventually located the American manager of the local branch of Chase Manhattan. My problems were solved. The bank manager was as happy to see a friendly American face as I was to find him.

Foreign branches of American banks are also helpful in exchanging local currency from and to dollars. They also make wire transfers and arrange Americanized short-term loans. This all makes doing business in a strange country much easier and faster.

Wire Transfers

As later chapters point out, the movement of money between countries is done almost entirely by wire transfer. Money center banks also act as clearinghouses for most wire transfers between an American bank and a foreign bank, or between a foreign bank and one in the United States. When the transfer involves two different currencies, one by the sender and one on the receiving end, it's important to use a bank that has the capability of making currency exchange at the lowest cost.

A client was working on a construction job in the desert of Saudi Arabia. The contract called for dollar payments to be made by the central bank, the Saudi Arabian Monetary Authority (SAMA). Contractual terms called for a direct transfer to my client's account in Banque François in Jeddah. Everything went smoothly until the final contract payment of $1,500,000. For reasons still unknown, SAMA reneged and insisted on paying in Saudi riyals. The French bank was more than happy to take the riyals, but wanted to charge my client a 10 percent fee for converting to dollars. It took a while but eventually I opened a new account at the Citicorp branch in Jeddah. SAMA made the final transfer to this new account and the conversion fee was only 0.75 percent.

On the receiving end, money center banks prioritize daily disbursements of transfers received from their correspondent banks. If a local or regional bank happens to be in an unfavorable position with its correspondent New York bank, it could take three, four, even five days to get the funds transferred. A favored correspondent can get the money in one day. So it pays to choose a local or regional bank carefully to avoid delays. By the way, no money center bank will ever admit to this practice, and few regional bankers know about it.

Currency Arbitrage

All money center banks, and many larger regional banks, maintain a special department responsible for currency arbitrage. The principles are exactly the same as arbitrage in the commodity markets. The idea is to buy and sell future deposits of foreign currency—or dollars on foreign exchanges—in anticipation of rate changes. While the banks do this for their own account, most are also willing to open accounts for customers who like to gamble. Currency arbitrage is definitely not for beginners. But it's helpful to know that currency hedging exists, if and when the need to protect against wild swings arises.

Export Financing

Commercial banks must be used for export financing. Whether the funds originate with the federal government or private sources, a commercial bank remains the focal point. If direct loans from Eximbank are used, the money flows from Eximbank to the commercial bank to the exporter or foreign buyer. Federal agency guarantees protect commercial banks against default on loans to exporters. Trade credit instruments always emanate from commercial banks. Collections from foreign customers flow through commercial banks. A commercial bank is involved in every aspect of export financing and cash management. Of course, the transaction efficiency and the cost to the exporter depend on which bank he chooses to utilize.

A commercial bank's expertise in handling international transactions is the most important criteria in choosing one. Companies located near a metropolitan area have no difficulty locating a bank with an international department. All major regional banks have them. Obviously, being located in or near New York makes it easier to use one of the money center banks.

The size of the bank isn't as important as its international expertise and the status of its working relationship with one of the money center banks, as the following example shows.

A client in the overseas construction business booked its biggest order ever, from Saudi Arabia. The company needed a bank guarantee to support a surety performance bond; a short-term unsecured loan to provide working capital until the progress payments began flowing; back-to-back letters of credit; and correspondent bank wire transfer capabilities with a branch of the British Bank of the Middle East in Jeddah.

First Jersey National Bank had been handling my client's accounts for several years, but did not have an international department. After stumbling through these international transactions for several months, the bank president informed my client that it just wasn't working and he better find a new bank. Under the gun from his customer to proceed with the project, my client panicked. He couldn't proceed without bank support.

Combing the countryside, we finally located another local bank, Commercial Bank of New Jersey. Although this bank also lacked international expertise, the senior vice president was eager to learn. He agreed to handle the company's account providing we would take the time to teach his people how to handle the transactions. Although this meant extra effort on my part, we agreed to go ahead because of Commercial's close working relationship with Chemical Bank in New York. Chemical happened to be the U.S. correspondent for British Bank of the Middle East.

As it worked out, within three months a new international department was formed at Commercial Bank and the transactions went forward. Three years and four major Middle East projects later, my client still used Commercial Bank. By that time it had grown into a major player in the global banking scene in north Jersey. We would have preferred to deal directly with Chemical, but in those days interstate banking laws prohibited a New York bank from doing business in New Jersey.

Collections, Payments, and Transfers

Even if a company doesn't use a commercial bank for financing overseas transactions, it still needs one to handle mundane collections, payments, and money transfers. Collections from foreign customers or payments of foreign invoices are seldom done with bank checks, as in the United States. Payments are nearly always made by wire transfer. A wire transfer is merely a mechanism banks use to debit a customer's account and credit a correspondent bank's account. No money actually changes hands.

Banks throughout the world maintain loose associations with other banks (correspondents) in other countries. Credit balances are maintained in money center banks in every major country, such as the United States, England, France, Germany, Japan, and several others. Periodic notification between banks of debits and credits against these balances are referred to as wire transfers. The system works as follows:

American Corp., with an operating line of credit at First National Bank, imports beef from New Zealand for $1,000 cash and uses its operating line to pay for it. First National reduces the operating line by a debit of $1,000 and credits its interbank account with Chase Manhattan for $1,000. Chase Manhattan debits the First National account for this amount and credits its correspondent bank in New Zealand—Commonwealth Bank of Auckland—at the current exchange rate for New Zealand dollars of, say, NZ$1,025. It then notifies the New Zealand bank of this transaction, along with all others at the end of the week. When notified, Commonwealth Bank debits its account with Chase and credits its customer's account for NZ$1,025. The New Zealand exporter can now draw out his money. Of course everybody charges a fee, and these fees reduce the amounts being credited and debited. Just the reverse would occur if American Corp. sells to a New Zealand customer.

This system works well throughout the world except in those Third World countries without correspondent relationships with American banks, such as Libya. In that case the transaction must flow through an intermediary bank, probably in England, France, the Netherlands, Switzerland, Germany, or Japan, which adds to the cost and time.

Exchange Conversion

Larger commercial banks also offer exchange conversion services. If possible, it's always a good policy to avoid taking foreign currency in payment of an account. Even with hard currency, the exchange differential and bank fees for making the conversion to dollars inevitably cut into profit margins. Sometimes it's necessary, however, especially when doing business in developing nations.

A developer contracted with Mitsubishi, the prime contractor, to install complex electronic assemblies for a new telephone network in the mountains of Colombia. Mitsubishi insisted on paying the developer half in dollars, transferred directly to an American bank, and half in Colombian pesos. The developer used as much of the Colombian currency as possible to pay local wages and buy local supplies for the job. At the end of the contract, Colombian pesos equivalent to over $200,000 remained in his account at the Bogotá bank. His only option was to take the pesos out and carry the funds back to the United States.

Upon delivering them to his bank in Chicago, he learned that yes, they would make the conversion to dollars, but he would lose the equivalent of $25,000 in exchange rates since withdrawing the balance in Bogotá. Additionally, he was stuck for bank fees of almost $7,500.

Even though most large American banks are willing to exchange most of the world's currency for dollars, there's no guarantee that it won't cost an arm and a leg! If an exchange must be made, it's usually preferable to do it with an American branch bank in the country of origin. Better still, use letters of credit drawn on an American bank in lieu of currency.

Some nations with soft currency prohibit repatriation of local currency. Eastern European countries are a prime example. In this case there is no alternative other than to use up local currency before leaving, or to insist on letters of credit or other noncurrency means of payment.

Letters of Credit

As described in Chapter 14, many transactions in the global community are handled through letters of credit (L/Cs). Commercial banks are the normal source and recipient of L/Cs. Banker's acceptances (BAs) and other debt instruments can also be used, but L/Cs are the most popular. Using an L/C as a payment vehicle means that a commercial bank charges the customer's account or line of credit for the amount of the L/C and associated fees. It then notifies the recipient bank that it is holding the instrument. Credits and debits are then settled between the banks, as described above, and the supplier may draw his cash out of his bank against the L/C.

The reverse occurs when an American company sells to a foreign customer on an L/C. The customer's bank notifies its American correspondent bank that an L/C exists. The American exporter then presents appropriate documentation to the American bank and draws his money. There are no exchange problems when using irrevocable L/Cs. There are no collection problems when the L/C is confirmed. And the seller gets his money as soon as he ships the merchandise.

Without a commercial bank that understands the use of L/Cs in international trade, this procedure almost always becomes garbled. This costs the seller valuable time in collecting his money. Therefore, when using L/Cs, just as with other facets of international finance, it's important to use a bank with an international department that knows what it is doing. Many don't.

Guarantees

Global trade almost always requires the use of guarantees; either guarantees of payment or guarantees of performance. Global banks perform this service admirably. If a customer's credit rating is high, a commercial bank may issue a standby L/C which in most countries can then be used as a guarantee. Without good credit, a company must utilize a portion of its operating line to secure the L/C.

Obtaining a surety bond to guarantee performance can be a costly and difficult undertaking, especially for smaller companies. Standby L/Cs answer the need. As long as a bank understands how the instrument works, there should be no difficulty in getting one.

Latin-American Loans and Debt/Equity Swaps

Large American commercial banks seem to have a propensity for making the wrong moves at the wrong times. As pointed out in Chapter 1, most sovereign loans made in Latin America during the 70s have never been repaid and probably never will be. Citicorp, Chase, Chemical, Bank of America and most major regional commercial banks have in the past, and continue today, to reserve significant portions of these loans on their balance sheets. They have not, however, written them off as uncollectible. Some day they must.

As an alternative, some banks tried to exchange part of their debt holdings with Latin governments for equity interests in local property and businesses. Since the banks were only interested in prime investment, and these are few and far between in Latin countries, this debt-equity swap program never really got off the ground. In the meantime, a small secondary market developed. This allowed banks to sell their debt instruments at substantial discounts. Private purchasers could then work their own swap with foreign governments. This program has been more successful, but most of the defaulted debt remains on the banks' books.

One example of how private enterprise can take advantage of the secondary debt-equity swap market was announced by Harvard University. The university has set up a unique scholarship fund that converts Ecuadorian national debt into grants to let students from Equador study at Harvard. It plans to devote $5 million to acquire Ecuadorian debt, worth approximately 15 percent of its face value, and donate it to an educational foundation in Ecuador—Funcación Capacitar. The foundation will then exchange the debt obligations in Ecuador's Central Bank for government bonds worth 50 percent of the debt's face value. The program will then provide scholarships and grants for more than 70 students and professors to attend Harvard over the next decade. In addition, the program will finance grants and internships for Harvard scholars to study in Ecuador.

If Harvard can figure out how to make money in the Latin debt/equity swap market, private companies should be able to as well.

In spite of such efforts, however, sooner or later, banks must deal with these enormous amounts of defaulted loans. A massive write-off could sink many of them and damage the entire financial system beyond repair. Continuing to carry the debt tarnishes their balance sheets and deteriorates their capital ratios. There appears to be no easy answer to the dilemma. An American executive, searching for the right commercial bank to link up with in global trade, should at least be aware of this debt crisis. He should try to choose a bank with the least amount to lose.

Some progress in easing the problem seems to be occurring, however. On March 10, 1989, at a meeting of the Bretton Woods Committee, Treasury Secretary Nicholas Brady announced a new plan for Third World debt reduction. The plan focused on encouraging banks to write off portions of their Third World debt, and exchange additional amounts for new debt backed by the World Bank, the IMF, and Japan. The Inter-American Development Bank would also play a role in backing the new issues.

After more than 10 months of negotiation, Treasury Undersecretary David C. Mulford announced that Mexico and its 450 creditor banks signed an agreement on February 4, 1990, to restructure its overall foreign debt along the lines of the Brady plan. Under the agreement, Mexican debt was reduced from $95 billion at the end of 1989 (half of which is owed to foreign banks) to about $80 billion. From 1989 to 1992, Mexico's annual interest payments will be reduced one third to $1.5 billion. Principal payments will also be reduced by $6.7 billion during the period. In addition, Mexico will receive about $1.5 billion in new loans from banks.

Costa Rica and the Philippines have also agreed in principle to new financing packages. Venezuela and Morocco are both pursuing active negotiations with their respective bank creditors. Although debt forgiveness is certainly a step in the right direction, one wonders at the sagacity of banks that continue making new loans, throwing good money after bad.

Foreign Banks

Any American company doing business overseas, whether exporting or operating a business in a foreign country, inevitably runs headlong into banking systems significantly different than in the U.S. For example, banks in England, Germany, Israel, Japan, France, and Italy have engaged in income-producing activities for years using off-balance sheet financing. American commercial banks, on the other hand, are restricted from this activity. Federal and state banking regulations specify minimum capital ratios and accounting requirements force compliance with archaic reporting procedures.

It's important for the novice entering the global arena to recognize the value of using foreign banks. Many times a foreign bank provides the best source of financing for a deal. In other cases it can be the only means to raise outside capital. Foreign banks also serve as depositories for local collections. Foreign banks can be utilized for transferring funds worldwide, issuing letters of credit, and a myriad of other functions. Foreign banks are generally easier to deal with, cheaper, and less inclined to hassle the customer, than their American counterparts.

Most of the larger foreign banks have branches, offices, or representatives in the United States. Appendix I lists the names and addresses of the most prominent.

THE ROLE OF AMERICAN INVESTMENT BANKS

Global investment banks are as different from commercial banks as night is from day. Even though the recent easing of banking regulations allows commercial banks to enter the fringes of investment banking, true investment banks such as Morgan Stanley, Goldman Sachs, Shearson Lehman Hutton, Bear Sterns, and PaineWebber continue to command this market. If the Banking Act of 1933 (also called the *Glass-Steagall Act*) is repealed at some time in the future this condition could change. But now, investment banks have the global investment business pretty much to themselves.

Investment banks became most effective in global banking by their globalization of financial markets. Globalization refers to the linking together of global financial markets into a common, worldwide pool of money. This pool is available to both borrrowers and lenders. It is not restricted to only large corporations. Any business may avail itself of these funds.

Probably the most effective way to define global investment banks is by comparing them to American commercial banks. Commercial banking is primarily concerned with deposit taking and lending. Investment banks specialize in securities trading and financial advisory businesses.

Commercial banks specialize in cash management activities; investment banks in the management of investments.

In recent years, many smaller firms sprang up under the guise of investment banks. Many of these are really venture capital firms concentrating on equity and debt investments in small or rapidly growing privately owned companies. Few provide true investment advisory services. None are active in securities placement and trading.

In the context of global banking, reference to investment banks always means the larger houses that specialize in raising capital for clients through securities markets and in providing financial advisory services for investment opportunities.

Investment banks welcome customers of any size. Even if a company has no plans to issue public securities, an investment bank can be very helpful in advising investment opportunities throughout the world. It also assists in structuring nongovernment financing to fund the investment.

Investment banks perform a variety of services in global banking but most can be grouped under five headings:

1. Syndicating debt and equity issues on foreign exchanges.
2. Managing pension funds.
3. Locating investment opportunities abroad.
4. Sourcing foreign money for U.S. investments (i.e., acquisition loans and private equity).
5. Offering general financial advisory services.

Syndication

Investment banks play a major role in syndicating public issues. If the issue is large, or diverse, an investment banker acts as lead manager and pulls in other support as underwriters. This activity is especially predominant in Eurobond issues.

Many companies may never think of issuing public securities in the United States. There isn't any need to incur the cost and aggravation as long as expansion can be financed through banks, venture capital firms, asset-based lenders, and smaller domestic investment banks. Going global requires a different mind-set, however.

To attain a true global mentality, one must think in terms of raising capital for worldwide expansion in the most expeditious, least expensive way. Acquiring a company, developing a large project, or starting up a chain of new distribution centers or manufacturing plants in several countries usually requires a fairly large amount of new capital. Because it will be used globally, restrictions prohibiting its use across national boundaries or for undefined purposes must be avoided at all costs.

American commercial banks can't help at all in these circumstances. Government funding may be available for some projects. International merchant banks can definitely help. But public issues provide the best means to raise large sums of capital for global use. A competent global investment bank not only provides financial advice about how, when, and where to make the issue, it also advises what amount to offer. For larger issues, it forms a syndication to get the issue to market.

Pension Funds

Most large investment banks manage investment portfolios of American pension funds. This provides another source of funding for investment in global enterprises. A company looking for long-term financing for an overseas project can often interest an investment bank in allocating part of its pension portfolio to the task. Though not widely advertised, several investment banks control millions of dollars of potential investment funds in pension portfolios.

Locating Investment Opportunities

One normally thinks of a banker's life as revolving about money, Treasury securities, and loan applications. This may be true of commercial bankers but it certainly is not applicable to investment bankers. Many executives of global investment banks have much broader backgrounds than just banking activities. Some come from the ranks of private industry. Other have put in time with government agencies. A few were entrepreneurs in their own right. Many came up through the securities brokerage houses. Hardly any rose through the ranks of commercial banking.

With such diverse backgrounds, and with a self-serving interest in global expansion, executives from the better investment banks serve as an invaluable source of information for locating the right country or region to set up a facility or start a marketing campaign. Keeping tabs on political and economic developments worldwide gives these global bankers a view of international opportunities seldom found in executives of industrial corporations. Financial advisory services offered by investment banks extend beyond the mere putting together of financing packages.

> The vice president of finance of Enroth Envelope Corp. asked me to help locate acquisition candidates in the Netherlands or Belgium for Enroth's next expansion move in Europe. Every target I turned up was either too large, too small, or unprofitable. I was ready to give up when I decided to ask an old friend at Bear Sterns for help. One of Richard's accounts had just completed a complicated countertrade deal that left the American client, who manufactured military vehicles, with a 70 percent equity interest in a Dutch paperboard manufacturer. This company had no desire to be in the paperboard business, and within six months my client completed the acquisition.

Though perhaps not the normal type of assistance global investment banks provide, my investment banker friend was a real help to me. Since then I have steered other clients to him for more extensive investment advice. Global banking is a broad arena; and investment bankers are some of the most versatile players in the game.

Sourcing Foreign Capital

As described in Chapter 13, financing expansion programs in foreign countries often invites participation by foreign banks, government bureaus, and private sources. Global investment banks play a major role in the latter case. During the rise of OPEC in the 70s, billions of dollars flowed into the Middle East. Saudi Arabia, Bahrain, Kuwait, the UAE, and Oman benefited especially well because of prior British, Swiss, and French interests already there. These interests provided Arab princes, sheiks, and other officials a vehicle to invest their newfound wealth in American and Western European property and businesses.

Much of this money has since turned over several times yielding even greater investment opportunities for the oil nations. Investment banks were slow to recognize this enormous capital flow. When they finally did, sufficient resources didn't exist to hop on the bandwagon. But then the British "Big Bang" caused global financial markets to begin opening. American investment banks suddenly became major sourcing vehicles for oil funds as well as other hard currency deposits.

Although such private capital normally remains hidden from smaller American companies, it exists nonetheless. Global investment banks know how to tap these resources. Debt, or even equity investments in businesses located in hard currency nations remain favorite repositories for private capital.

THE ROLE OF MERCHANT BANKS

Foreign banks are either clearing banks or merchant banks. The same bank might have two divisions, each performing separate activities. In other cases, clearing and merchant banks function as distinctly separate entities. Clearing banks engage in activities analogous to commercial banks in the United States. Merchant banks are similar to, but not the same as, American investment banks.

The largest merchant banks are located in the United Kingdom and Japan. Their activities range from assisting in the financing of international trade, to acting as underwriters for securities issues, to investing in operating companies for their own account. They form the backbone of international finance. A merchant bank should be the first stop an executive makes when initiating an international trade program. Many have offices in the United States, and are easy to approach.

A merchant bank is probably the best source of ready capital for investing in Western Europe, Japan, Korea, Hong Kong, or Taiwan. British merchant banks have been major players in global banking for centuries. They have contacts in virtually all countries. They overtly develop investment opportunities for themselves and their customers.

Though similar to investment banks, merchant banks are far more experienced in global banking. They represent the vanguard of financial advisory assistance. British merchant banks such as County NatWest, Barclays de Zoete Wedd, Midland, Charterhouse, and Warburg, together with the Hong Kong and Shanghai Bank, form the nucleus of opportunistic merchant banks. They are usually the best source of financing for the acquisition of a going business in developed countries.

In addition to sourcing acquisition capital, merchant banks can be helpful to the new entry into global markets in three other ways. Merchant banks coordinate activity with central international development banks; manage debt and equity issues on the London, Tokyo, and other foreign exchanges; and bring together Western companies and Third World private investors.

Coordination with International Development Banks

Merchant banks play an important role as intermediaries for small and midsize companies by identifying and coordinating the funding of projects benefiting developing nations. Merchant banks work with companies wishing to develop businesses in the Pacific Basin by coordinating financing through the Asian Development Bank. In Africa, they work through the African Development Bank and Fund. In Latin America it's the Inter-American Development Bank. The newly formed European Bank for Reconstruction and Development in Eastern Europe plans to utilize merchant banks as primary intermediaries.

A few global commercial banks, leasing companies, venture capital funds, and local development banks also function as intermediary development finance institutions (DFIs). So far, however, merchant banks dominate the field.

The purpose of central international development banks (owned by member country governments), is to encourage and fund projects helpful in accelerating economic and social growth in developing nations. In addition to matching priority development projects with private industry, merchant banks coordinate financing assistance from the development bank. This may take the form of loans from the development bank to the merchant bank, which in turn loans funds to private companies. It may also take the form of direct equity investments by the merchant bank with funds derived from the development bank. The latter method is used primarily for start-up businesses of small and midsized parent companies.

Merchant banks also serve as intermediary financial institutions for on-lending development bank funds. These funds can be used by small- and medium-size companies for balancing, modernization, replacement, or expansion of existing facilities. Finally, merchant banks assist development banks in identifying and funding the privatization of businesses owned by government agencies.

Merchant banks also act as syndicators for mobilizing the required domestic and external financing from other multilateral and bilateral agencies, private financial institutions, and private enterprises. This may result in direct participation in a project or in floating new debt or equity issues to raise required capital. In any event, as the project is completed, or the business becomes self-sufficient, the central development bank usually wants to get out of the arrangement by selling its interest to private investors. Merchant banks coordinate this effort through additional private investor sourcing or public issues.

Manage Debt and Equity Issues on Foreign Exchanges

Similar to investment banks, merchant banks can manage new bond and equity issues on the Tokyo, London, Paris, Frankfort, Pretoria, and other worldwide stock exchanges, either through syndication or by themselves. This can be an extremely valuable service to a company trying to raise financing for an acquisition or a business start-up when private venture capital funds are not available or are too expensive. Merchant banks are especially active in Euromarket issues.

By using a merchant bank as a financial and investment adviser to locate appropriate expansion opportunities, a company can easily parlay the relationship into the management of a public issue. In certain areas of the world, notably the Far East and South Africa, American investment banks do not have the contacts in financial markets that merchant banks enjoy. When raising capital in these areas, merchant banks remain far and away the best choice.

Coordinate Joint Ventures and Partnerships

With centuries of experience in bringing together and promoting trading agreements between foreign parties, merchant banks became adept at identifying and structuring joint ventures and partnerships between English, and now American companies, and governments or private enterprises from other nations.

An American farm equipment manufacturer wishing to source components offshore can utilize a merchant bank to locate and arrange financing for a joint venture with a Taiwanese assembler. A Malaysian rubber producer can join with a German gasket manufacturer through the auspices of merchant banks. Perhaps an American importer and distributor of Scottish bottled water wants to set up a distribution center in Venezuela. A merchant bank can help locate an appropriate Venezuelan partner and arrange financing for the joint venture.

A small American producer of emergency potable water equipment, Barsto Water Purifier, Inc., wanted to establish a presence in several Caribbean countries that experienced severe water shortages from hurricane-caused electric utility failures. The financial manager was having difficulty raising the $3 million necessary to open the first assembly plant in the islands. He couldn't interest his investment banking contacts. No commercial bank would touch the deal. And government financing wasn't in the cards.

Eventually he contacted the regional office of Barclays in Barbados. The Barclays representative arranged a joint venture between Barsto and government officials in Montserrat to form a joint venture assembly plant on the island. Barclays provided the required long-term debt financing. In three years, Barsto opened plants on two other islands as joint ventures financed by Barclays.

This type of coordination and financing assistance is probably one of the best resources available to smaller companies expanding overseas. Merchant banks are easy to work with, they understand the global marketplace, and they are capable of creative financing arrangements unheard of in the United States.

THE GLOBAL FINANCIAL MENTALITY

Parochial financial management must surely stymie even the most ardent advocate of international trade. Marketing managers may be eager to open new global markets. Production executives welcome lower cost, more efficient foreign labor. Distribution managers give a warm reception to cost-effective global distribution networks. Entrepreneurs and business owners look at the global economy as a burgeoning opportunity to expand their businesses. But none of these advantages in going global can occur without a new attitude toward the strategic financing of foreign trade.

Insular thinking about financing options must give way to a global financial mentality that recognizes and accepts capital sources and methods of raising capital heretofore untried. Small and midsize companies traditionally abhor the idea of going public. The extra costs of an initial public offering (IPO) along with increased operating restrictions and administrative regulations turn the heads of owners of closely held companies away from security transactions.

A global mentality, however, recognizes the need and desirability of integrating financial management with global marketing and resource management. Such an integration, at some point in time, demands recognition of public debt and equity issues on world exchanges as viable capital alternatives.

Similarly with banking relations. Although commercial banks will still be required, executives must seek out those with international expertise. They must begin to utilize investment banks and merchant banks as advisers in the global community. A global mentality does not fear the entrance of global competition but welcomes it. As such, companies must become familiar with and use foreign banks as much as they utilize American banks in handling daily transactions.

A global financial mentality is a prerequisite to opening foreign markets. Whether engaging in exporting, importing, or making a direct foreign investment, a company must master the global banking system to survive. To achieve this mastery, companies must begin to train their financial managers in international trade. Or they must hire new managers with experience in international finance. Either way, a high level of professionalism must be brought to financial management if companies of any size hope to attack the future by globalizing their markets and resources.

Clients and business associates frequently ask for specific suggestions for positioning their businesses to take advantage of global financial markets. Although the global banking system is a dynamic and ever-changing paradigm of creative funding and cash management techniques, instead of hit and miss answers to these questions I developed a set of guidelines as shown in Figure 12–1. Although the list must be expanded or changed as conditions warrant, it does provide a frame of reference.

GLOBAL BANKING IN THE 21ST CENTURY

Americans have a lot to learn to effectively utilize the global banking system as an asset. Business executives and financial managers must throw off

FIGURE 12-1
Guidelines for Using the Global Banking System

1. **The education process**   Get up to speed in international finance as soon as possible. Take a college course in international finance. Spend time with the head of the international department in a major regional bank. Tour the facility. Find out what law firm handles a major regional bank and meet with the lawyer in charge of international matters. Try the same tack with a Big 5 accounting firm. Hire a financial manager with international experience.

2. **Choosing a commercial bank**   Determine which local bank has an international department. Interview the department manager. Which money center bank is a correspondent? Get listings of foreign correspondent banks. Quiz the international manager on L/Cs, wire transfers, Eximbank support, and so on. How high in the management chain is the international manager? He should be a senior vice president, at least.

3. **Finding professional advisers**   Interview the international partners from all local Big 5 accounting firms. Do the same with the three largest law firms. Ask for a reference on investment bankers. Interview a senior international manager from at least two investment banks. Engage a lawyer, accountant and an investment banker on retainers.

4. **Know the sources of capital**   Prepare a list of all sources of capital in the areas of the world you expect to enter. Learn what special requirements apply to debt or equity issues on the nearest exchange.

5. **Engage a merchant bank**   Research two or three merchant banks active in the selected region or country. Do they have convenient branch offices? English-speaking managers? Interview at least two. Do they seem interested in dealing with a smaller company?

6. **Assign international responsibility**   Set up a small international finance department in the company—one person is enough. Be sure he has international finance experience. Let him make contacts with banks, investment banks, and merchant banks. Follow his lead.

7. **Experiment**   If the opportunity seems right, try a small public stock issue to become familiar with the regulations. Perhaps intrastate. Open a foreign bank account. Transfer small amounts back and forth. Try using L/Cs in domestic business.

8. **Global financial planning**   At the next strategic or operational planning cycle, introduce global financial sources in place of traditional bank financing. Use a foreign bank with U.S. offices for a working capital line. Incorporate exchange rate variances in forecasts—even if you have to use fictitious entries. Plan expansion moves with foreign financing.

9. **Conquer the "big boy" syndrome**   The more a person investigates global banking the more one realizes it is not just for the "big boys." Find out which competitors or customers use foreign banks, exchanges, or merchant banks, and ask their advice. Chances are good that at least one or two will be small or midsize companies. The more you know, the less there is to fear.

10. **Read, read, read**   The fastest way to learn about global banking and develop a global financial mentality is to read everything available on the subject: books about international trade, articles from trade journals, *The Wall Street Journal,* and *Barron's* articles, the Sunday edition of the *London Financial Times,* the *Economist* magazine, government publications, tax journals, and newsletters from Big 5 accounting firms. All of these sources should become regular, required reading.

the shackles of *thinking small* and enter the 21st century with as much global financial acumen as their foreign competitors. But business leaders can't do it alone. It will also take a global mentality from the commercial banking fraternity, the accounting profession, SEC regulators, and state and federal bank policymakers. To survive in the world of global banking four major changes must take place in American habits and policies.

Banking Regulations

American banks must be allowed to compete with their Japanese and European counterparts. The Glass-Steagall Act should be repealed immediately. Banks should be allowed to engage in international financial markets. They should be allowed to manage investment portfolios and public debt and equity issues.

The number of commercial banks must be decreased significantly. Interstate banking laws should all be abolished. Bankrupt or near bankrupt banks should be allowed to fail with the accompanying contraction of the domestic debt market. Depositor losses should be covered through the Federal Deposit Insurance Corporation (FDIC) with funding from the money center banks, which in turn will contract their domestic credit.

To compensate, money center banks and major regional banks should be allowed to consolidate with their weaker cousins. Smaller, local banks should be operated as subsidiaries. The assets of failed or failing savings and loans should be liquidated at auction immediately. These institutions should be closed and healthy thrifts allowed to engage in commercial banking transactions. Only money center banks should be allowed to support Treasury issues. Defaulted Third World debt should be written off and forgotten with a one-time allowance for reduced capital/asset ratios. Foreign investment in commercial banks should be encouraged. This brings dollars into the system and stabilizes capital ratios.

Financial Advisory Services

Commercial megabanks should enter the financial advisory services business specifically directed toward global banking. As more companies enter the global arena and begin asking global banking questions, two matters will soon become clear: (1) that this group of companies represents an untapped market for global banking services, and, (2) that they need help in structuring global financial management. Financial advisory services, long the private domain of investment bankers, should be incorporated into the business strategy of the megabanks. This in turn will make it easier for uninitiated producers to enter global markets.

Accounting and SEC Regulations

As the American financial community moves rapidly toward globalization, the accounting profession and regulators of the Securities and Exchange Commission (SEC) must change archaic rules of reporting transactions. Assets should be stated at cost or market, whichever is *higher,* not lower, as now required. Foreign investments should be recorded as a pooling of interests, not as equity investments. Currency conversion variances should be recorded as balance sheet items, not reflected in current period earnings. The accounting profession must move toward the standardization of accounting procedures between American, British, German, and Japanese practices. The SEC must release public companies from archaic disclosure requirements but implement more demanding standards for disclosure of foreign risk and debt conditions.

Encourage Public Financing

Small and midsize companies must learn that public debt and equity issues are for them as well as large corporations. They must accept the fact that to be truly global means sharing ownership. Private empires must give way to partial public ownership. The amount of leverage necessary to compete in the global market precludes the sole use of bank debt to finance expansion. Eurobonds and similar instruments must be used in conjunction with foreign and U.S. government funds.

It is unlikely that all of these conditions will occur in the next decade. We would all be better off if it were possible, but with the current state of the federal government's monetary, fiscal, and restrictive business policies, such changes seem unlikely in the near future. Eventually, however, political leaders must understand the global banking system or American companies will find themselves on the outside looking in, rather than leading the way to economic solvency.

CHAPTER 13

FINANCING DIRECT FOREIGN INVESTMENT

MAJOR TOPICS

KEY POINTS

1. **Foreign Banks.** Clearing banks can be beneficial in providing loans in amounts less than $1 million for local projects. Guarantees and export financing can also be arranged through clearing banks. Merchant banks should be used for foreign acquisitions.

2. **Overseas Private Investment Corporation (OPIC).** OPIC can be helpful in providing guarantees and financing for investments in developing countries. It also assists in the financing of international leasing arrangements.

3. **Private International Venture Capital Funds.** Comprised of American business and banking interests, these funds provide financing for investments in Poland and other Eastern European countries. Guar-

anteed by OPIC, similar funds will probably also sprout up for African and Latin-American investments.

4. U.S. Agency for International Development (USAID). Although USAID provides government-to-government aid to developing nations, an American company can benefit indirectly through AID political pressure. The agency also identifies investment opportunities.

5. International Development Banks (IDB). "Super" IDBs coordinate funding for investments in the Pacific Basin, Africa, and Latin America. A new reconstruction fund has been established for Eastern Europe. Local IDBs also finance projects of national benefit.

6. Other U.S. Government Agencies. The Departments of Commerce, Agriculture, and State have the wherewithal to assist in financing specific projects. The Office of the U.S. Trade Representative identifies financing sources and investment opportunities.

7. International Financing Institutions. Programs from three international financing organizations, similar to IDBs, are examined.

8. Far East Central Bank Financing. Direct investments and exports from several Far Eastern nations can be financed locally through central bank programs. Financing arrangements from Japan and South Korea serve as examples.

9. Joint Venture with Foreign Nationals. Financing may be obtained directly from a foreign joint partner, or established contacts can be used. Financing from foreign governments often requires a partnership with a national. The IESC helps locate joint venture partners.

10. Joint Ventures with U.S. Companies. Joining up with a large U.S. company benefits both parties. One provides the financing, the other the risk.

11. Bank Loan Debt/Equity Swaps. American bank loans to Latin-American countries purchased at a discount and then swapped with the sovereign state for local property or business provide an inexpensive method of financing direct investments.

12. Section 936 Financing. Investments in Puerto Rico and the Caribbean can be financed through this IRS-approved Puerto Rican program.

13. Debt and Equity Financing on World Exchanges. Companies may take advantage of opening foreign financial markets with public issues. This is the best way to raise large blocks of capital.

Mastery of cultural and language differences, marketing strategies, human resource development, and legal and tax regulations are prerequisites for success in the global marketplace. But without the proper financial support, other global activities can't succeed. Whether starting a facility from scratch, acquiring a going business, or contracting for a development project, without the right financing package any investment will surely be doomed to failure before it ever gets off the ground. Also the proper sourcing of funds is just as important to success as the amount of capital raised. Interest rates, payback terms, and lender/investor interference or support all play equally important roles.

Financing global trade falls logically under three headings: direct foreign investments, exports, and countertrade. This chapter examines options for financing direct foreign investments. The next chapter highlights major financing sources primarily geared to exporting. Chapter 15 describes the salient features of countertrade techniques.

There are four broad classifications of capital sources for direct foreign investment:

1. Foreign banks.
2. U.S. and foreign government agencies, private international development institutions, and international development banks.
3. Joint ventures, partnerships, and other business sources.
4. Debt and equity issues on the world's exchanges.

FOREIGN BANKS

As pointed out in the previous chapter, foreign banks operate differently from their American counterparts. Restrictive legislation and archaic accounting practices hamper U.S. banks. Foreign banks operate in a less sanitized environment and are able to structure creative packages for a variety of purposes.

While off-balance-sheet financing has been used by foreign banks for years without risking deterioration of the bank's capital ratios, American banks remain locked in their traditional roles as depositories of money from individuals, companies, and the government. Although it is true that the large money center banks are now involved in everything from soup to nuts (and want to be involved in more) their lack of creativity, outdated accounting principles, and government regulations continue to prevent the same level of assistance as available from foreign banks.

The previous chapter described the differences between foreign clearing banks and merchant banks. It also emphasized the use of merchant banks for financing business acquisitions, coordinating with development banks, managing debt and equity issues, and acting as a broker in bringing parties together for joint ventures. Originally formed by businesspeople, not bankers, to handle the credit and other financing of merchant customers and suppliers, merchant banks eventually found themselves doing more financing and investing than merchant trading. Although large American investment banks are trying to catch up, they still lag behind the major English, French, Swiss, and Japanese houses in global financing for major projects.

A word of caution in dealing with merchant banks, however. Leveraged buyouts (LBOs) are not as common overseas as they are in the United States. As pointed out in Chapter 11, if you plan to make a foreign business acquisition, be aware that typically American LBO financing will probably not be available. With the relaxation of the securities rules on the London Stock Exchange, and soon the Tokyo Exchange, creative security issues should probably fill the LBO void.

Short-term working capital funds or relatively lesser amounts of long-term capital can be raised through clearing banks. While few American commercial banks are willing to lend money for overseas projects, foreign clearing banks usually jump at the opportunity, particularly if the project is of local benefit. Working capital lines and overdrafts, performance guarantees, real estate mortgage loans, construction loans, and even participation in funding the acquisition of local businesses all fall within the province of clearing banks.

While some of the larger banks such as Royal Bank (Canada), Daiwa (Japan), or Standard Charter (United Kingdom) will consider financing packages for cross-border uses (usually handled through their merchant bank divisions) most clearing banks prefer to keep loans within their own countries, or at least close to home. For example, Banco Popular, the Puerto Rican bank, provides working capital and mortgage loans in nations throughout the Caribbean, but usually only if the borrower has some ties to Puerto Rico, or can demonstrate how the offshore investment will benefit the Commonwealth.

For companies seeking debt financing under $1 million, a local clearing bank is about the only available source. Large international banks won't touch such a small amount and there isn't enough income potential for merchant banks.

In some respects, collateral requirements of foreign clearing banks are less onerous than American banks. Foreign banks commonly use overdrafts in place of actual working capital loans. A company's reputation carries more weight than the value of inventory or equipment securing the loan. Cross-collateralization is seldom an issue, although compensating balances could be required. Many foreign banks are owned or controlled by the local government. The same personal contacts, *understandings,* and intermediary arrangements necessary to obtain licenses and permits as described in Chapter 10, influence the bank's willingness to finance projects, especially in developing nations.

Financing foreign direct investments through foreign banks is not the only or necessarily the best source of funding, however. A number of U.S. government agencies, private organizations, and other sources stand ready to compete with banks from any country. The following sections examine several nonbank sources that offer choices from a wide range of options.

OVERSEAS PRIVATE INVESTMENT CORPORATION

The Overseas Private Investment Corporation (OPIC) is a self-sustaining agency of the U.S. government. Though funded by the government at its inception in 1971, OPIC repaid all federal funds long age. It now finances its own operations as a private business—albeit within restrictive limits. OPIC promotes private sector economic growth in developing countries by offering assistance to American companies wishing to invest in these nations. Currently, there are approximately 100 developing countries eligible under OPIC's investment criteria. These are the only countries in which OPIC can offer assistance.

Several times each year OPIC reclassifies which countries qualify for assistance, depending on the current status of development within the country and what government-to-government trade agreements presently exist. Contact OPIC's Washington office directly for a current listing of eligible countries.

OPIC emphasizes assistance to smaller businesses rather than large corporations. In addition to an investor information service and a network of investor missions to assist smaller businesses identify foreign opportunities, OPIC provides medium- to long-term project financing and political risk insurance. It does not offer commercial risk coverage, as does the Foreign Credit Insurance Association (FCIA). However OPIC does provide coverage for currency inconvertibility, insurrection, civil strife, revolution, war, and foreign expropriation risks relating to an American company's investment on foreign soil.

Both the insurance and finance programs are available to new foreign ventures for U.S. businesses. They must be commercially and financially sound (OPIC prefers a 60/40 debt to equity ratio). The program also assists companies wishing to expand existing locations overseas. Two major stipulations exist, however. The project being financed or insured must assist in the social and economic development of the host country, and the project must be consistent with the current economic and political interests of the United States.

Financing by the Overseas Private Investment Corporation may be used only for projects or other ventures in which there is a significant equity and management participation by an American business. An American company utilizing OPIC assistance must have a proven record of competence and success in another business the same as, or related to, the one being financed. In other words, a contractor financing the building of a factory in Egypt must be able to submit evidence that he has built similar projects in other countries.

The American company must also have a significant continuing financial risk in the enterprise. *Significant* means 25 percent or more. Political risk insurance coverage is limited to the U.S. equity participation in the venture only.

OPIC Financing Programs

Three types of medium- and long-term projects are financed by OPIC:

1. Energy or energy-related projects (water systems, electric utilities, oil and gas drillings, processing products for local consumption, and alternate energy sources).
2. Projects offering significant trade benefits or development of the infrastructure for the host country.
3. Projects sponsored by small businesses or co-ops in those countries where the per capita income is greater than $3,800 (the current measure of the stage of development of the country).

All OPIC loans are nonrecourse; therefore, OPIC must be assured of the economic and financial soundness of the project, including, but not limited to, the ability of the company to repay the loan. Once OPIC judges a venture financially sound, with competent management, the company will not be required to pledge any additional general credit. This can be a real boon to smaller companies.

For example, if a company wants to start up a manufacturing plant in Gambia and puts up at least 25 percent of its own equity in the deal,

OPIC will coordinate with Eximbank and private foreign and U.S. banks to finance another 25 percent, usually requiring collateral. OPIC then finances the remaining 50 percent without additional collateral. Occasionally, OPIC considers nonproject financing and takes the role of a secured creditor, but it prefers the other route.

An American company can maintain complete ownership of the project, but OPIC encourages joint ventures or other participatory arrangements with local corporations or citizens. Wholly owned government projects remain ineligible. Even 51 percent government-owned projects are frowned upon. This makes it difficult to interest OPIC in projects specified by local law to have 51 percent local ownership. For expansion projects of existing businesses, OPIC loans up to 75 percent of the cost. For new projects, it limits its participation to 50 percent. These ratios vary depending on the country, political considerations, and current U.S. government policy.

Projects are financed by OPIC in two ways: by direct loans to the business, and by guaranteeing bank loans. Only projects sponsored by a small business qualify for direct loans. Currently such loans range from $200,000 to $4 million. Occasionally OPIC takes an equity position through a variety of convertible bond issues. It then sells these holdings to companies or citizens in the host country.

Most guaranteed loans are for major projects or larger companies. They can range up to $50 million—or even larger in some cases. Unless a small business participates with other American investors in a large project—such as taking a part interest in a manufacturing plant or participating in the construction of an electric utility plant—it probably cannot qualify for the guarantee program.

International Leasing

Chapter 14 examines leasing as a viable way to finance export sales. Rather than missing out on additional leasing profits, many larger companies elect to form their own leasing company to handle export sales. A small or midsize company can certainly reap the same benefits. An overseas leasing company is a natural adjunct to export leasing. Not only does OPIC provide political risk insurance coverage for leasing companies, similar to that for other projects, it also participates in the financing. It does this through both direct loans and guaranteed bank loans. OPIC's loan limit is $1 million with a medium-term maturity. Any American-owned or controlled foreign leasing company, defined as a small business by OPIC, can qualify. OPIC also guarantees foreign bank loans to foreign leasing companies having a significant American interest for up to seven years. The amount varies with the country and type of leases used.

Small Contractor Guarantee Program

Arranging a bank guarantee or surety bond to warrant performance against a contract can be a major problem for smaller contractors. Many American contractors fail to consider overseas projects simply because they cannot get such a performance bond/guarantee from a surety company. If they can get one, it is too costly. OPIC's Small Contractor Guarantee program fills the void. To qualify, the contractor must not be one of the Fortune 1000.

OPIC provides a performance guarantee to banks as collateral to a standby letter of credit. This L/C can then be used as a performance bond. All risks up to 75 percent of the credit are covered by OPIC. It is unconditional. Coupled with an OPIC insurance policy under the contractors and exporters insurance program, this percentage may be raised to 90 percent, leaving only 10 percent risk open for a bank or surety company.

PRIVATE INTERNATIONAL VENTURE CAPITAL FUNDS

As the political systems in Eastern Europe began to unravel in late 1989, the Polish government actively solicited Western private investment in Polish industrial and commercial enterprises. The idea was twofold: to attract foreign investment to shore up the sagging Polish economy, and to provide Poland with hard currency to purchase much needed goods and services from European and other Western countries. After investigating Polish opportunities, a group of 40 American businesses formed a venture capital group. Its mission was to provide private funding for the privatization of Polish industry and the start-up of new American businesses in Poland.

The venture program is structured after the African Growth Fund currently investing capital in poor countries in sub-Saharan Africa. OPIC agreed to guarantee the Polish ventures against political risk. In the event Poland reverts back to the orthodox socialist system, the venture capitalists get their money back from OPIC.

As the Eastern European countries, the USSR, China, and certain African and Latin-American nations continue the evolution to market economies, additional U.S. government-supported programs—similar to the Polish experiment and the African fund—will undoubtedly flourish. Any business that aligns itself with other companies anticipating the opening of these new markets should find itself in the driver's seat. Establishing close ties with OPIC is also a good way to get in on the ground floor when the next venture capital fund evolves.

U.S. AGENCY FOR INTERNATIONAL DEVELOPMENT

The mission of the U.S. Agency for International Development (USAID) is to assist foreign governments in economically disadvantaged areas to stimulate economic growth, promote higher standards of living, and improve foreign exchange earnings. As a government-to-government agency, it does not provide financing direct to American companies. In an indirect way, however, companies can benefit from USAID intervention in, and support of, a desired foreign investment. USAID programs are administered by 70 offices worldwide. Special private sector offices offer assistance to private businesses that includes:

1. Financial assistance to the host country for short-term stabilization and economic recovery by financing imports of raw materials and intermediate goods for the private sector.

2. Improving the business climate by supporting host country policy reforms and incentives to restore domestic business confidence, rationalize interest and foreign exchange rates, attract foreign investment, upgrade the infrastructure (roads, port facilities, irrigation projects, free zone facilities), and develop new trading programs.

3. Funding programs that upgrade human resource skills and managerial capabilities, overcome technical marketing and export obstacles, and capitalize financial intermediaries that provide credits to businesses in the host country. This includes capital for private sector development banks and other credit facilities for small and medium-sized businesses.

An American company can take advantage of USAID funding indirectly by investing in an area or in a project approved by USAID for financial assistance. Many times, with USAID money financing the local project, an American company will be given preference over other outsiders either at the bidding stage or otherwise trying to penetrate a specific market.

As related in *When the Bank Says No!: Creative Financing for Closely-Held Businesses*, one of my small contractor clients was a subcontractor on an electric utility project in North Yemen. Part of his contract was to provide most of the equipment (which was all manufactured by GE) to be installed at the site. When USAID learned that my client, along with several European firms, were competing for the project, they encouraged the North Yemenese to accept our bid since the equipment to be installed was American made and the installation would be done by an American company. We landed the job, and subsequently, when disputes arose concerning payments, USAID intervened, influencing the Dutch prime contractor to acquiesce to our requirement for L/C drawdowns.

Since 1984, USAID has been very active in supporting economic development of the private sector in the Caribbean and Central America under the Caribbean Basin Initiative program. Under this program, USAID, through its Private Enterprise Bureau (PEB), participates in medium- and long-term loans to joint ventures between an American company and a private company from the host country, or a government agency. These loans are specially tailored case by case. The PEB can be contacted directly for an application and current criteria. When considering an investment in this part of the world, by all means touch base with the Washington office of USAID to learn of current agreements.

INTERNATIONAL DEVELOPMENT BANKS

International development banks (IDBs) are active in many parts of the world. They provide funding for the economic development of a country's infrastructure and its private sector. Some of these banks are privately owned by large multinational commercial banks. Local businesses and local banks own others. Some are owned by host country governments. The Europeans and Japanese have utilized financing through IDBs for years, but smaller American businesses have yet to take advantage of IDBs in any magnitude. Though each IDB has different eligibility requirements and forms of financial assistance, they are similar.

In addition to local IDBs there are three *super* international development banks that offer direct financing to businesses as well as indirect funding to local IDBs. They are: the Asian Development Bank (for Asia and the Pacific Basin), the African Development Bank and Fund (for Africa), and the Inter-American Development Bank (for Latin America).

In May 1990, the European Bank for Reconstruction and Development in Eastern Europe was formed with $12 billion capital contributed by 42 nations. Its specific purpose is to help eastern European countries rebuild their economies and will be a "catalyst between the capital and know-how of the West and the businesses of the East," according to French President François Mitterrand. The bank is expected to begin operations in April 1991. At least 60 percent of the bank's loans will go to the private sector in Eastern Europe and the balance to public projects. European Community nations hold 51 percent controlling interest in the bank, but the United States is the largest single shareholder with 10 percent. Eastern European nations hold a 13.5 percent interest. The headquarters are located in London.

Though each IDB has slightly different programs, they are similar enough to use one, the Asian Development Bank, as an illustration of what can be done. Appendix J gives the addresses of these super IDBs as well as those of several local development banks.

The Asian Development Bank (ADB) was established in 1966 by a consortium of 47 member countries. Its purpose is to accelerate economic and social growth in the Pacific Basin by promoting financial and technical assistance for projects contributing to the economic development of the region. The ADB provides funding indirectly to private businesses and private banks and also directly to the private sector through intermediaries (financial institutions who provide medium- to long-term financing as their principal endeavor, such as local development banks, some commercial and merchants banks, leasing companies, and venture capital firms).

Direct financial assistance consists of medium- to long-term loans, without government guarantee, together with the underwriting of, and investment in, a company's equity securities. Grants are also awarded to private sector companies for project-related feasibility studies. Direct assistance to local banks and sponsors of projects involving venture capital, leasing, factoring, investment management, and commercial finance is encouraged. Indirect assistance to intermediaries consists of credit lines for small- to medium-sized new ventures and expansion of existing businesses. ADB also provides equity lines to intermediaries to facilitate their equity funding of new businesses.

Eligible projects include new or expansion productive facilities in energy, manufacturing, transportation, forestry, fisheries, mining, tourism, health, and agriculture. Projects geared to provide luxury items might be eligible if these products are produced primarily for export. The projects should use domestic raw materials, provide local jobs, and employ modern management techniques. Export products, or those which stimulate additional foreign investment, are favored. The applicant can be locally or foreign owned. It can be partially owned by a government, but must be run on a commercial basis. Financing is also provided for the privatization of government-owned businesses.

Total financial assistance in a combination of loans and equity contribution from the ADB cannot exceed 25 percent of the total cost of the project. A loan may range from $2 million to $30 million, except under unusual circumstance. Participation by intermediaries increases the amount. ADB equity investment cannot exceed 25 percent of the capital of the business; but neither can it be less than $100,000. The ADB refuses to be the largest single investor. The ADB also assists in structuring syndicated and cofinancing arrangements.

Security collateral must be provided for all loans. Commitment fees are 1 percent per annum on the undisbursed loan balance. Front-end fees and legal fees are also charged. The repayment period may not exceed 12 years. Interest rates based on the London Interbank Offer Rate (LIBOR) vary, as do currency denominations. Upon completion of the project, the ADB will sell its equity investment, at a fair price, preferably to nationals.

Nonregional member countries of ADB include: Austria, Belgium, Canada, Denmark, Finland, France, Germany, Italy, Japan, Korea, Netherlands, Norway, Spain, Sweden, Switzerland, the United Kingdom, and the United States.

OTHER U.S. GOVERNMENT AGENCIES

There are several U.S. government agencies providing varying amounts of assistance to American firms interested in investing in foreign businesses or projects. Some offer technical or commercial assistance. Others include financing assistance. Many federal departments (i.e., Commerce, State, Defense, and so on) have their own programs that are too specialized to examine in their entirety here. A few major ones, however, are broad enough to have universal appeal.

U.S. Department of Commerce

American companies with specific procurement needs or investment proposals for foreign countries can get assistance from the Department of Commerce. The Active Match program provides direct contacts with either foreign suppliers (for import needs) or with potential foreign joint venture partners. Though no direct funding is available, contacts with potential partners can be invaluable. There is no charge for this service.

The Department of Commerce is especially active in the Caribbean Basin Initiative (CBI). The department has even established a CBI ombudsman. This official acts as a high-level expediter and facilitator when projects get bogged down in bureaucratic red tape. The department also actively pursues investment opportunities in the Caribbean for American companies.

U.S. Department of State

Within the Department of State there is a program called the U.S. Trade and Development Program (TDP) which actually funds feasibility studies for Third World development projects. These projects must eventually lead to the export of American goods to the host country. Projects include agribusiness development, infrastructure projects (energy, communications, port development, and so on) and mining. Though this is government-to-government funding, TDP also works directly with potential U.S. investor companies in cofinancing studies leading to specific investment decisions.

U.S. Department of Agriculture

Though the Department of Agriculture isn't directly involved in funding, it does assist American businesses in identifying agribusiness investment opportunities overseas. Requests for assistance should be directed to the Private Sector Relations (PSR) division of the Office of International Cooperation (OICD) in Washington.

Office of the U.S. Trade Representative

The U.S. Trade Representative (USTR), part of the Executive Office of the President, is responsible for coordinating U.S. trade policy. Although not directly involved in financing, the USTR assists U.S. businesses investing in host countries through programs negotiated with foreign governments. Two of the most relevant programs are:

1. The Bilateral Investment Treaty (BIT) negotiated with foreign governments to serve as incentives for U.S. companies to locate in the host country.
2. Guaranteed Access Levels for Textiles and Apparel negotiated with foreign governments to provide investment incentives for U.S. firms engaged in the textile and apparel industries.

INTERNATIONAL FINANCING INSTITUTIONS

The International Bank for Reconstruction and Development (IBRD) is a hybrid international development bank. The IBRD makes project loans for roads, power plants, steel mills, and other major infrastructure or capital-intensive projects in developing countries throughout the world. Although IBRD loans directly to governments, the organization assists private enterprise to identify worthy foreign projects for investment.

The International Finance Corporation (IFC) is part of the World Bank. Among other activities, it coordinates and assists in arranging financing for U.S. and foreign joint ventures for projects located in several developing nations. It also provides equity investment and/or partial debt financing for the enhancement of productive, private enterprise in developing nations. Contacts and application should be made directly with the IFC. Currently, it is unlikely that a small or midsize company could get financing from this source. On the other hand, conditions in the global arena continually change, much faster than a book can get published. Therefore, it is entirely possible that by the time this book is read, IFC financing will filter down to smaller companies.

The International Development Association (IDA) performs the same type of financing support as the IFC. There is one major difference, however. Whereas the IFC only grants loans up to 10 years, the IDA will go as long as 50 years. Obviously, this makes IDA financing very attractive for extremely large development projects. Again, however, the probability of direct participation in the financing by smaller companies is remote—at this time.

FAR EAST CENTRAL BANK FINANCING

Once a company establishes a presence in one of the newly industrialized countries of Asia or the Pacific Basin, central bank assistance becomes available for financing imports as well as exports to the United States or other nations. These central banks operate similarly to the Eximbank in the United States. Nearly all countries have financing assistance schemes to further their own exports and imports. A foreign firm, exporting from one of these countries, can also take advantage of the programs. It may take some political maneuvering to get in the door, however. The financial assistance extended by each country is slightly different, but there are enough similarities to get a feel for how they work by examining two of the most highly developed: Japan and South Korea.

Financing from Japan

The Export-Import Bank of Japan (Japan Eximbank) offers a significant level of yen financing support for exports, imports, and direct investments overseas. This support is syndicated with major commercial banks throughout the world. Japan Eximbank, in parallel with these commercial banks, supplies yen loans of medium- to long-term duration. The commercial part of the loan must be arranged through the participating commercial bank. Japan Eximbank adjusts interest charges on its portion of the loan so that the total charge stays within the guidelines of the Organization for Economic Cooperation and Development (OECD).

Assistance from Japan Eximbank for import buyer credit and export supplier credit is available to any qualified company, foreign or domestic. Eligibility is determined based on the type of equipment, resource, service, or raw material involved. Japan Eximbank insists, however, that at least 50 percent of the contract value be made up of goods or services with Japanese content. The bank offers the following financing packages:

1. *Import credit.* Energy-related products or resources, raw materials, and manufactured products that Japan Eximbank regards as vital to the Japanese economy qualify for import credit. Applications are received directly by Japan Eximbank.

2. *Export credit.*   Major industrial equipment and ships, manufactured in Japan, and Japanese technical services sold abroad qualify for deferred payment export credit. The applicant (foreign importer) arranges the credit with the Japanese exporter who then requests Japan Eximbank to grant the credit in conjunction with a commercial bank.

3. *Overseas investment credits.*   Japan Eximbank grants overseas investment credits for the following purposes:

    a. Equity participation in foreign corporations by Japanese corporations.

    b. Long-term equity secured loans to foreign corporations, provided these companies also have equity participation by Japanese firms.

    c. Equity participation in Japanese firms whose sole purpose is to make overseas investments.

    d. Overseas projects directly operated by the borrower.

Japan Eximbank also makes direct investment loans to foreign governments for equity participation in foreign corporations that have Japanese equity participation.

Credits are in yen, but the foreign importer can usually obtain dollar-denominated credits from the exporter who in turn converts through Japan Eximbank. Down payment must be 15 percent cash; 20 percent for ships. Suppliers' credits, including commercial bank participation, cover 75 to 85 percent of the contract value of the export transaction. Japan Eximbank's portion changes periodically, but in early 1990 it was 60 to 70 percent, with the balance handled by commercial banks. Repayment begins within six months of delivery of the goods. Interest and principal are paid in equal semiannual installments.

The exporter must obtain insurance from the Japanese Ministry of International Trade and Industry. For private companies, letters of credit, government guarantees, or letters of performance guarantee from a major international bank must secure any unpaid down payment balance or deferred payment arrangement.

Financing from South Korea

The differences between South Korean financing assistance and that offered by the Japanese are slight, but indicative of the variances one can expect to find in programs from other countries as well. The South Korean Eximbank makes direct loans to foreign and domestic corporations with participation from major international commercial banks. The loans are medium- to long-term and South Korean content in the product must be 50 to 75 percent depending on the product. South Korea Eximbank loans to suppliers and buyers, as well as issues guarantees and export insurance.

1. *Export credit.*   Credit covers the export of capital goods including industrial plants, steel structures, machinery, electrical equipment, ships, and vehicles. Spare parts are also included. The installation and operating costs of plants in foreign countries are heavily subsidized.

2. *Overseas project and investment credit.*   Such credit is available for investment in any facility or equipment abroad when most of the parts or materials required for operation are imported from South Korea. Investments in foreign projects are also covered if they use South Korean materials or exports, or simply promote economic cooperation with foreign countries. South Korea Eximbank determines which projects promote economic cooperation.

3. *Major resource development credit.*   South Korea Eximbank provides funds for foreign projects which lead to the stabilization of the supply of natural resources or strengthen economic relationships with a country that supplies needed natural resources, such as oil, coal, copper, lumber, and rubber. Studies leading to the acquisition of mineral rights are also included.

4. *Direct loans.*   South Korea Eximbank loans to foreign importers who purchase South Korean goods and services, but the buyer must have an unconditional guarantee from a commercial bank, central bank, or government.

5. *Guarantees.*   South Korea Eximbank provides guarantees for 100 percent of the principal and interest to both foreign and South Korean financial institutions that cofinance loans for periods of more than five years. Foreign importers can also get 100 percent performance guarantees and advance payment guarantees.

6. *Export insurance.*   Export insurance is available through South Korea Eximbank to cover political, commercial, and *managerial* risks.

All financing is in U.S. dollars with the following terms:

- 70 percent of the contract value, less down payment, for contracts exceeding $1 million.
- 100 percent of contract value, less down payment, for contract values of $3 to $10 million.
- 70 to 90 percent of import value, less down payment, for predelivery export contracts.
- 70 percent of contract value, less down payment, for postdelivery export contracts.
- Cash down payment must be 15 to 20 percent of total contract value.
- Terms for export credits are from 180 days to 10 years: major resource development credits can extend to 20 years.
- Guarantees of 100 percent are required from all buyers.

It's fairly obvious that other countries offer significantly more attractive export and investment financing than the United States (the next chapter describes the U.S. Eximbank policies). With nearly 100 percent financial support for both exports and overseas investments, it is not surprising that Japan, South Korea, Taiwan, Hong Kong, and other Far East industrialized nations overshadow the United States in global trade sophistication. Perhaps eventually we'll catch up. But right now there are no U.S. government-supported financing programs for international trade that come close to measuring up to those offered by other countries. Chapter 18 examines the credit insurance programs available from Great Britain, France, and Germany, and here again, national assistance is far greater than that coming from the United States.

JOINT VENTURES WITH FOREIGN NATIONALS

Many sound business reasons exist for forming joint ventures with foreign nationals—either individuals or private companies. Local business practices, labor codes, tax and legal requirements, local marketing expertise, and political savvy all point to a joint venture with a foreign national for a smooth transition of direct investments. In many countries, a partnership with a national is a prerequisite to getting a license to do business in the country. Beyond licensing requirements, cooperative financing with a local company remains a very pragmatic reason for joining forces.

Several financing programs for establishing a business or project are available from nearly every country in the Western world. The United Kingdom, Germany, France, Sweden, Norway, the Netherlands, Italy, and Spain, all have government-sponsored financing schemes to assist in starting up a new business. Money is not the problem in developed countries; the lack of specific technologies is. In developing nations the lack of technology is an even more serious problem.

Hardly without exception, at least in Eastern Europe, the Soviet Union, most of South and Central America, the Middle East, Southeast Asia, and China, financing assistance will not be forthcoming unless a local company, or a government agency, retains part ownership in the new business. Foreign clearing banks and merchant banks also support business development with a local partner in preference to full off-shore ownership. And finally, many larger private companies in a host country finance the project themselves if allowed to participate in its ownership.

An example of the latter case occurred a few years ago when a client, J & L Auto Parts, wanted to open a distribution center in Spain. J & L planned to stock replacement automobile and appliance parts imported from the United States for resale in North African and Middle Eastern countries. J & L approached Citroen Hispania with a proposal that they join forces in the distribution center, each owning 50 percent and sharing the floor space. J & L wanted Citroen to provide all the financing and in return, J & L would distribute Citroen parts in the southwestern United States. In addition, the J & L sales network in East Africa and Saudi Arabia would push Citroen spare parts. The deal went through without costing my client a penny in construction cost and the partnership continues in harmony.

In another case, Queen Corporation, a midsize specialty glass manufacturer, wanted to expand its market by building a factory in Saudi Arabia. The Saudi government required that any foreign investment be 50 percent owned by a Saudi. Queen negotiated a 50/50 partnership with a Lebanese merchant who ran several retail outlets and trading businesses in Saudi and qualified as a national. In exchange for the 50 percent ownership in the glass plant, the Lebanese partner arranged with the Saudi central bank, the Saudi Arabian Monetary Authority (SAMA), to provide 100 percent funding in long-term debt for the construction of the glass plant.

Two drawbacks exist to forming joint ventures with foreign nationals: (1) sharing the ownership of a facility also means sharing its profits, and (2) the possibility exists for disagreements over operating policy. These are usually manageable, however, and a relatively small price to pay for entry into a lucrative new market.

International Executive Service Corps

The International Executive Service Corps (IESC) is a nonprofit organization funded partially by the U.S. government and partially by donations from American corporations. It was originally established as an adjunct to USAID through the Bureau for Private Enterprise. The IESC mission was to assist in the creation of joint ventures and partnerships between American companies and foreign nationals, principally in developing nations. Currently, the Corps assists American companies interested in establishing working relationships in a variety of different forms with foreign private and quasi-private businesses.

The IESC maintains a data base of over 10,000 retired American executives willing and able to volunteer their services to American companies starting up an overseas operation, either as a joint venture with another American company or with a foreign national. Volunteers also offer assistance to foreign government projects. Volunteers of IESC trained in corporate and international finance can be an enormous help in locating the right financing for the project. The IESC also provides matching grants for feasibility studies of potential overseas investments by American businesses.

JOINT VENTURES WITH U.S. COMPANIES

An increasing number of small and midsize companies are forming joint venture partnerships with other American companies either already established in a foreign country or eager to give it a try. In many respects, such a partnership carries less risk than ventures with foreign nationals. As a minimum, common language, cultural synergisms, and similar business practices make the initial breakthrough easier. At best, a U.S. cousin may have marketing or political connections in the host country and possibly financial resources.

A U.S. partnership works especially well for a smaller supplier selling patented technology or proprietary products to a large customer already established overseas. Frequently the large company finances the entire start-up operation in exchange for marketing rights of the product in designated countries. Aircraft manufacturers learned years ago that having a subcontractor risk the labor, legal, tax, and management pitfalls is less expensive than doing the whole job themselves, even if it means financing the project.

In the late 1970s, a small subcontractor to a large manufacturer of business jet aircraft discovered that such a partnership was the only way it could afford to become global.

The subcontractor wanted to penetrate the British market with its proprietary thrust reverser but didn't have the financing to open a new plant. It already sold its thrust reverser to the aircraft manufacturer in the United States. The aircraft manufacturer wanted to open up new markets in France and Italy but was not willing to incur the risk of starting up and operating a new plant overseas.

The two parties agreed that the aircraft company would provide the financing for the subcontractor to construct a new facility in Ireland for the assembly of thrust reversers. The aircraft manufacturer obtained exclusive sales rights in France and Italy while the subcontractor opened new markets for itself in the United Kingdom. The manufacturer made a $3 million equity contribution toward the Irish company (for which it received a 25 percent ownership) and loaned the new company $10 million on a 20-year note. The entire project cost the subcontractor $1.2 million of its own cash—used entirely for start-up working capital.

A different arrangement occurred with a distributor of power tools for the consumer market. A large manufacturer of one line of tools agreed to finance the purchase price and start-up expenses of the distributor's new warehouse in Spain with a long-term loan and convertible warrants for a 10 percent ownership. In return, the distributor stocked the manufacturer's tools for the entire European market. The distributor established its own markets in North and West Africa through an agreement with an Italian trading company.

Joint ventures, or partnerships, with large U.S. companies already operating overseas is probably the fastest and least expensive way for a smaller company to finance a direct investment in foreign markets. It remains one of the most widely used methods in manufacturing and distribution businesses. An established multinational company already knows how to cope with variant business practices, government restrictions, licensing and tax regulations, and marketing idiosyncrasies of the host country. Such knowledge saves a new entrant years of frustration and thousands of dollars in start-up costs. Financing provided by such a partner is really icing on the cake.

To summarize, the major advantages in arranging financing through an established U.S. partner are: (1) it eliminates the need to comply with mountains of paperwork, substantial time and effort, and reporting restrictions required when using government financing of any type, and (2) it provides the smaller company with internal assistance in mastering the host country's legal and tax requirements for starting up a foreign operation.

BANK LOAN DEBT/EQUITY SWAPS

As a by-product of the American bank and Latin-American debt fiasco, bank loan debt/equity swaps have become another way used by some companies to establish an international presence—at least in Latin America. During the 70s, American banks, as well as financial institutions from several other industrialized nations, made what may turn out to be a fatal mistake. Believing that sovereign borrowers could never follow the bankruptcy trail, these financial experts granted loans totaling billions of dollars to developing Latin-American countries. The banks should have seen that there was little or no chance of ever being repaid by these economically depressed countries, but they didn't.

As described in the previous chapter, in the mid-1980s a few American banks tried to swap their defaulted loans for equity investments in Latin-American companies and other properties. Bankers believed that a much higher price could be realized for the debt holdings through this method than by selling them in the secondary markets, even though the debt was swapped at a substantial discount. The program never really got going, however. Debtor nations were worried that issuing new currency to buy the debt would add to an already impossible inflation problem. American banks wanted only sound, business investments in exchange—and of course, there weren't very many of those around.

Eventually, some corporations began to purchase Latin debt in the secondary markets and made the exchange with the local governments. In essence, by getting in on the ground floor, they were able to get an American bank to finance their acquisition of companies and property in the host country through these swaps. The host country couldn't lose. It retired its debt at a discount from face value and received new capital investment in income-producing and foreign-exchange-creating assets.

Eventually, a few smaller manufacturers began to understand what was happening and used the secondary market to finance overseas investments at a fraction of the cost of borrowed funds. The procedure seems complex but it is really quite straightforward. A company first purchases a Latin-American loan in the secondary market at a substantial discount from its face value; for example, 50 percent. The company then offers to exchange this debt with the debtor government for local currency. The rate of exchange might be, for example, equivalent to 75 percent of the debt. This exchange currency is then used to build or purchase a plant or other facility in the host country for one half of the cost of a straight investment. Of course the investor must use its own funds to acquire the debt in the first place, but an investment at one half its normal cost is not all bad.

Swapping activity continues, though somewhat sporadically. American trade officials estimate that through 1988, debt-equity swaps reduced total Latin-American debt by about 5 percent. The figure is probably slightly higher by this time.

Debt/equity swap financing is a tricky procedure. Companies without the financial management talent to handle the deal should stay away from this method. On the other hand, for those companies with the financial sophistication to manage such a transaction, a debt/equity swap can be a viable financing alternative for direct investments in Latin America.

SECTION 936 FINANCING PROGRAM

Under Section 936 of the Internal Revenue Code, American companies that derive a significant portion of their income from Puerto Rican activities are considered *936 companies.* Chapter 3 described the tax implications of setting up a 936 company. Another feature of the 936 program relates to financing investments in Puerto Rico and in the Caribbean.

Because of the tax incentives for leaving income earned in the commonwealth in Puerto Rican banks, large deposits of 936 company funds remain available for investment options. These funds are referred to as *qualified possession source investment income* or QPSII (quipsy) funds. Under the 1986 Tax Reform Act, Puerto Rico may utilize these funds as collateral for loans on qualified projects in any country falling under the Caribbean Basin Initiative—assuming the country has signed a TIEA with the IRS. Through 1988, the countries which have signed up for participation in the 936 program were Jamaica, Barbados, Grenda, and Dominica. St Lucia is awaiting legislation from its own government to join the throng. Other countries will undoubtedly participate in the future.

The government of Puerto Rico, through private investment banks, set up a private (hopefully profitmaking) Caribbean Basin Initiative Fund to provide a vehicle to invest 936 funds in eligible countries. Underwriters sell notes and stock of the fund to investors, and hope to raise $60 million in capital. It is expected that loans from the fund will be secured, at least in part, by a combination of hard security, guarantees, and insurance coverage. OPIC and the Government Development Bank of Puerto Rico (GDB) expect to participate in providing such collateral. These loans carry very favorable interest rates resulting from the tax-exempt status of the fund.

The big catch to the entire 936 financing program is that to qualify for these funds, the project, located in an eligible country, must be complementary with Puerto Rico. In other words, the project must produce goods or services from which Puerto Rico will benefit in some direct or indirect way. Unfortunately, the vagueness of this provision probably negates some very worthwhile projects.

DEBT AND EQUITY FINANCING ON THE WORLD'S EXCHANGES

As the globalization of financial markets continues into the 90s and beyond, merchant banks and investment banks are assuming major roles in financing worldwide expansion. Stock exchanges in London, Tokyo, and New York will surely become more integrated and interactive in new issues and also for the trading of existing equity and debt instruments. Eurobonds will likely increase in importance to the American company financing direct foreign investments. Initial stock issues will assume a global flavor with the issuer no longer restricted to segmented market demand. Business owners and financial officers should have a much wider choice of banking associations with commercial lenders and investment and merchant banks. Currency and interest swaps, zero coupon bonds, and other creative financing instruments will become available to even the small and midsize global trader.

Swapping debt obligations in global financial markets is not a new creation. The classic case occurred 10 years ago between the World Bank and IBM. When the World Bank wanted to borrow low-interest rate Swiss francs to lend to developing countries, Swiss investment bankers, skeptical of the repayment ability of these nations, wanted to charge an interest rate of .2 percent above their government bond rate. On the other hand the Swiss were eager to accommodate IBM. IBM was trying to raise funds in U.S. markets but had been quoted a rate of .4 percent over the U.S. Treasury rate amounting to .05 percent higher than comparable financing offered to the World Bank from U.S. markets.

The World Bank and IBM engineered a currency swap, IBM taking the Swiss francs and the World Bank taking dollars. Both were winners and everyone was happy. Since then, both currency and interest swaps have increased in frequency. Today, with intense competition between the world's financial markets, even smaller companies can balance one market against the other to achieve the best financing terms.

Many companies worry about losing profits through currency exchange fluctuations, especially when selling through certain countertrade channels. Active trading in the U.S. foreign exchange market offers one way to hedge against currency exchange losses. During 1989, the amount of money that changed hands each day among foreign currency traders increased to $128.9 billion, an increase from $58.6 billion as recently as 1986, according to the Federal Reserve Bank of New York.

As global business increases, more companies realize that gambling on foreign exchange trading can provide far less risk than ignoring wide swings in the dollar against other currency. In many cases, it can increase the profit margin on global trading beyond the pure business transaction.

CONCLUSION

This chapter outlined several financing schemes to get companies started in global trade. Some are reserved specifically for smaller companies. Some relate more to financially sophisticated firms. Still others apply only to those companies already established in an overseas location. A few provide government-to-government financing which flows indirectly to an American start-up enterprise. Joint ventures and countertrade techniques (Chapter 15) involve little, if any, outside financing. Many of the financing sources are government agencies or government-supported organizations, both U.S. and foreign.

Unfortunately for the company just getting started in international trade, a quick lookup reference to determine which financing technique works best just isn't possible. There are too many options and combinations. The size of the company; types of products or services offered; specific foreign markets; continuing changes both in U.S. and foreign government political and economic policies; competitive market forces; the impact of economic timing on financial markets; and rapidly changing domestic and foreign tax laws, preclude businesses from having the luxury of picking and choosing from a predetermined listing of sources. Each situation is different. With the rapidly changing economic and political fortunes in Europe, Latin America, the Soviet Union, Eastern Europe, China, the Middle East, Africa, Asia, and the Pacific Basin, a financing scheme that might work today, will be obsolete tomorrow.

For these reasons, when the time seems right to enter the global marketplace, a company should begin with competent outside counsel—tax advisers, international lawyers and consultants, and global accounting firms. These are the people who have up-to-date contacts in financing circles. Following their advice and direction can usually make the difference between success or failure in international trade. The fees they charge for these services are nearly always substantially less than the cost of going global alone and paying for trial and error mistakes.

One thing managers can do on their own, however, before engaging outside advisers, is to research as carefully as possible the current status and available mechanisms for raising capital through U.S. government and other domestic agencies. Several valuable books are listed in the bibliography at the end of this book. Government publications abound. Multinational accounting firms publish periodic bulletins covering changes in tax, legal, and financing rules for international trade—usually free for the asking.

CHAPTER 14

FINANCING AN EXPORT PROGRAM

MAJOR TOPICS

KEY POINTS

1. **Trade Credit**. The use of letters of credit, banker's acceptances, and forfaiting by the exporter, working with his commercial banker, are the most common ways to convert foreign receivables into immediate cash for additional working capital.

2. **Leasing**. Either by leasing capital equipment itself or by selling the foreign receivable to an international leasing company, an exporter can effectively use leasing to finance sales of capital goods.

3. **Eximbank**. Eximbank supports several programs through bank guarantees or direct loans, either to the exporter or to the foreign buyer. This government agency provides working capital funds as well as medium- and long-term financing.

4. **The Private Export Funding Corporation.** A private organization owned by several major banks and large corporations, PEFCO bridges the gap between commercial bank short-term financing and Eximbank longer-term credit.

5. **Commodity Credit Corporation**. A Department of Agriculture agency, CCC issues buyer credits to economically depressed countries for the import of agricultural products. A special program, BICEP, subsidizes U.S. exporters to meet foreign subsidized competition.

6. The Small Business Administration (SBA). Though not active in export financing, the SBA does have a program for small exporters using bank guarantees and direct loans, but not in excess of $200,000. Recently the SBA has joined with Eximbank to participate in financing assistance of up to $1 million.

7. Eximbank's City-State Cooperation Program. Started in 1989 as a marketing tool, several cities and a few states are beginning to assist smaller exporters in arranging financing as well as providing direct bank credit lines themselves.

"Yes, I know that in 1992 the EC will open up huge new markets for American products. It sounds like a great opportunity for Heinz or Kraft, but I'm just a little guy selling salad dressing. I wouldn't know how to sell internationally if my life depended on it. Anyhow, it's too expensive to ship overseas, and my working capital line is about used up. And what if I do give it a whirl and then don't get paid? My banker would shoot me. Can't help dreaming though. A couple million dollars a year in extra sales would sure help with that excess capacity I've got in my Milwaukee plant."

Jay Olsen, owner of Northland Mixed Dressings Corp. of Fond du Lac, Wisconsin, was frustrated when he called to ask for advice about expanding his market. Obviously, my answer was to get into the global arena, preferably beginning with an export program. As a second step, I then suggested branching out in Southeast Asia where many of his herbs originated. Knowing Jay for many years I was confident he could make a go of it if we could only arrange appropriate financing. I offered my assistance to do just that. By 1988, Northern Mixed Dressings was exporting to Belgium, Norway, and Uruguay and Jay was ready to begin looking at a new plant near Jakarta. He didn't borrow a penny from his working capital line and never lost a nickel on collections.

Exporting can be an excellent first step in developing a global marketing program. It is a convenient, easy way to learn the rules of global trade. It entails the easiest and in many cases the cheapest forms of financing. And it is probably one of the least expensive ways to increase sales volume. Many smaller companies don't realize how easy exporting can be, however, and shy away from the international scene. Either they don't understand how to finance an export program with someone else's money, or they are afraid they won't get paid by the foreign customer.

Chapter 18 describes how to be sure you get paid. This chapter examines four principal ways to finance an export program:

1. By the use of trade credit, either with or without government support.
2. From government agencies specifically established to help American exporters.
3. Through a joint venture with another American exporter.
4. With countertrade agreements.

Some of these financing schemes and government programs tend to overlap. The same sources may finance exports from the United States, imports into the United States, and direct investments overseas. Chapter 13 looked at methods primarily designed to finance direct foreign investments. The following chapter describes the peculiarities of countertrade. That leaves those sources primarily used to finance exports as the subject of this chapter.

An exporter must utilize a commercial bank regardless of the specific financing agenda. As described in Chapter 12, a commercial bank is a necessary vehicle for handling letters of credit, wire transfers of funds, currency conversions, and possibly bank loans with Eximbank or SBA guarantees. To be effective, however, the bank must have an experienced, diversified international department. Without this expertise, the bank will be nothing more than an intermediary with another larger bank. This only confuses the issue, adds significant time to clearing money transfers, and makes transactions more costly.

TRADE CREDIT

Trade credit for domestic transactions refers to buying from a supplier or selling to a customer *on time*. Purchases create accounts payable and sales generate accounts receivable. Transactions are made on open account and the payee makes payment in 30, 45, 60 or some other agreed-upon time frame. However, trade credit applied to international finance has different connotations. To grasp the meaning, one has to understand some of the basic terminology unique to global trading and used by global bankers, government agencies, trading companies, and customers throughout the world.

Supplier credit refers to credit extended to the buyer from the seller (exporter). It doesn't make any difference if the exporter, in turn, obtains outside financing from government agencies, banks, or elsewhere. As long as the receivable resides on the exporter's books (even temporarily) it is referred to as supplier credit.

The term *buyer credit* refers to credit extended to the buyer by someone other than the supplier. This third party to the transaction could be an American bank, a foreign bank, a U.S. government agency, or a foreign government agency. Whether such credit carries outside guarantees or not is irrelevant to the use of the term. The exporter does not record the receivable on his books because he receives cash, or cash equivalents, at the time of shipping.

The term *recourse* in trade credit measures the degree of responsibility for paying off any indebtedness incurred by the buyer in an export transaction. *Full recourse* means the seller takes full responsibility for such obligations. A *nonrecourse* document means that he has no responsibility for payment and is completely off the hook if the buyer defaults.

A *limited recourse* obligation means that if there was fraudulent representation in any of the export documentation, the seller has full responsibility to make good to the financing agency on any default deficiency from the buyer. If there is no fraud, then there is no recourse. The use of limited recourse documents, restricting the exporter's liability to a specified percentage of shipping values, is infrequent. Except in very rare instances, an exporter should avoid such conditions when negotiating the sales contract.

LETTER OF CREDIT

Letters of credit are the heart and soul of global trade credit. In global trade, a letter of credit (L/C) is universally accepted as a normal form of payment. An L/C comes in many forms. It can have a variety of provisions attached. It can be revocable or irrevocable, confirmed or advised, a straight or negotiated letter, payable at sight or over an extended period of time. An L/C may be transferable, assignable, or restricted.

An L/C is normally payable upon presentation of bills of lading or other transport documents. These documents may read "clean on board," "about," or "approximately" (referring to quantities shipped). They can cover partial shipments, full shipments, or transshipments. The L/C can be for one shipment or it can be revolving. Proper preparation and execution of L/Cs and their supporting documentation are such a crucial part of exporting that entire books are written with complete instructions for handling the various options. A full dissertation of the interaction of L/Cs and shipping documentation is far beyond the scope of this book. It is such an important subject, however, that anyone still confused after reading this section should research the details in one or more of the exporting books listed in the bibliography.

There are four ways to use L/Cs to obtain working capital for the production of the product or performance of the service to be exported: back-to-back L/Cs, off-balance-sheet credit extension, assigned proceeds, or transferred L/Cs.

Back-to-Back L/Cs

The best way to grasp back-to-back L/Cs is by example. Assume Color Company has a contract to ship pigment solutions to a customer in Denmark. The Danish customer places an L/C for the full amount of the order on a U.S. bank, allowing partial drawdowns against four partial shipments. Prior to the first shipment, the customer issues orders to hold the pigment shipment at the dock until he requests its release. Of course the expiration date on the L/C must be extended accordingly.

Now assume that the five Color Company suppliers are unwilling to wait for the Danish company to order shipment and want their payments within 15 days. The controller of Color Company takes the Danish L/C to his banker and asks the bank to issue new L/Cs to the five suppliers to be drawn down as they deliver their material to Color Company, using the Danish L/C as collateral. These are called back-to-back L/Cs.

Some bankers frown on back-to-back L/Cs because the bank remains at risk for its customer's performance on the first L/C. This is where international experience comes into play. Any banker who thoroughly understands the complete mechanics of L/Cs should have no difficulty going along with the deal, assuming a good relationship between the customer and the bank exists. A large New York bank may be unwilling to issue back-to-back L/Cs for a small or midsize company simply because personal relationships are rare with large banks. A customer's creditworthiness is frequently unknown to those in charge. Regional banks with closer relationships usually issue back-to-back L/Cs for their regular customers. Also, some bankers like them because issuing L/Cs requires less internal approval than making a loan.

Off-Balance-Sheet Credit Extension

Off-balance-sheet credit is a variation on the back-to-back L/C theme. Off-balance-sheet credit means that the bank does not use the customer's L/C as collateral and, therefore, is not boxed into its customer's performance against it. Instead, the bank issues L/Cs directly to an exporter's suppliers using the general credit of the exporter as collateral. Another way of looking at it is that the bank agrees to an extension of its customer's open line of credit. A bank should be willing to do this because it assumes that when the foreign L/C is drawn down, the moneys will be deposited in the bank and can be used to reduce other outstanding loans.

At first glance this doesn't seem like a very important financing method. It can be very helpful, however. Normally the issuance of supplier L/Cs draws down a working capital line. By supporting specific export transactions and issuing supplier L/Cs without a corresponding reduction in the line, the bank essentially grants additional credit. As additional security, the bank has the option of making a Uniform Commercial Code (UCC) filing against the goods to be shipped. This way it is assured that its customer will, in fact, deposit the proceeds of the L/C drawdown.

Whether using back-to-back L/Cs or off-balance-sheet credit extensions and supplier L/Cs, expect to pay the bank for its efforts. A commercial bank seldom, if ever, does anything free. They charge for issuing L/Cs just like any other service. Rates vary considerably, but expect to pay between 0.5 to 2 percent of the value of the L/C. Some banks charge as much as 5 percent. There is always the possibility of a commitment fee for another 0.5 to 5 percent.

Assigned Proceeds

Assigning the proceeds from a customer's L/C is probably the easiest way to finance supplier payments. The proceeds from any L/C may be assigned without permission from anyone. Just tell the bank holding the letter of credit that it should pay either the entire proceeds or a percentage of the proceeds drawn on the L/C to a specified supplier rather than to you, the exporter. Neither notice of assignment to the buyer nor additional bank credit are required.

If a supplier insists on verification of the existence of the L/C and wants to know its terms of payment, copies of the L/C documentation can be forwarded with the name of the buyer blacked out. The only potential disadvantage to a supplier occurs if, for some reason, the shipment is help up. A supplier might also run into trouble when an imperfection in the customer's L/C prevents drawdowns. Assigning an L/C involves no additional cost. It merely requires completing a simple assignment form.

Transferred L/Cs

Transferring a letter of credit is slightly more complicated than a straight assignment. In some instances an exporter might require certain materials, assemblies, or components to be shipped directly to his customer as part of the complete order. If the exporter merely buys the goods complete from a supplier rather than manufacturing them himself, the exporter's function becomes that of a middleman, or broker, in the transaction. If the components delivered direct from his supplier are high-value items, the supplier might want the customer's L/C transferred to him to avoid reliance on the exporter's performance as a condition of getting his money.

To transfer an L/C, either partially or in its entirety, the exporter must get permission from the buyer. This automatically informs the buyer that a third party is the original supplier of these goods. It might also indicate to the foreign buyer that the exporter may not be financially viable in the eyes of his supplier. A foreign buyer, of course, has the right to refuse such a transfer. Normally, however, unless the exporter-buyer relationship is antagonistic, the buyer shouldn't object.

All terms of the L/C transfer intact (e.g., total value, shipping date, insurance requirements, and special shipping instructions). One provision, however, saves the exporter from negotiating a new L/C with the foreign buyer for merchandise not shipped by the specific supplier receiving the transferred L/C. The exporter can instruct the paying bank to limit payment on the L/C to the amounts due a supplier, and substitute the exporter's invoices for the balance of the L/C. This is common practice. Although it creates additional paperwork, most banks allow it for a small additional charge.

The name of the foreign buyer can also be hidden from the supplier receiving the transfer. In this case when invoices are presented for payment the documentation must call for the notification of the original exporter, or his freight forwarder, rather than the buyer. Again this is not an unusual request and most banks and buyers go along with it.

If a foreign buyer has his own cash problems and can't raise the capital or credit to place a confirmed, irrevocable L/C as immediate payment against the exporter's shipping invoices, there are other ways to make the sale and still fund working capital needs. One way makes use of a documentary banker's acceptance.

DOCUMENTARY BANKER'S ACCEPTANCE

A documentary banker's acceptance (BA) can be used to collect on a foreign sale to a buyer who has poor credit rating or is otherwise short of cash. In essence, by using a BA, an exporter agrees to extend his own credit to the foreign buyer. Once the sale culminates, the exporter then sells the buyer's receivable at a discount, similar to factoring domestic receivables. The mechanics of this transaction work as follows:

1. The buyer executes a time letter of credit, referred to as a *usance* L/C in some quarters, for the full amount of the sale price. The L/C carries instructions that it is payable in a specific number of days after the exporter presents shipping documentation. An exporter should insist on a fixed date not in excess of 180 days from the date of sight. This is the maximum time frame that a BA remains in effect.

2. When the exporter presents his shipping documentation, the bank issues him a BA in place of cash. The BA is nothing more than the exporter's draft with a bank mark of "accepted" stamped across its face. The draft is then presented for payment against the L/C. This marking means that the bank promises to pay the exporter, or any other holder of the BA, on the fixed date of the L/C.

3. The exporter then presents this BA to the same bank issuing it and requests the bank to discount the document, paying the face value minus the discount interest. Even though the amount received is less than the invoice price, when the exporter negotiates the deal with the foreign buyer, he compensates for this by increasing the price of his products in an amount approximating the discount rate. The buyer conserves his cash for up to six months, and the exporter gets his cash immediately. Both sides win.

Even without an increase in the sell price, the discount rate (really interest) on BAs is usually the least of any type of financing. To compensate, the bank also charges an acceptance fee for handling the transaction. This ranges between 0.5 to 2 percent per annum of the face amount of the L/C. Sometimes a buyer might be willing to pay this acceptance fee even if he won't pay the higher price for the goods.

CLEAN BANKER'S ACCEPTANCE

A clean BA differs from a documentary BA in that it is not supported by a buyer's L/C. Instead it is arranged by the exporter with his own bank for his own use. A clean BA relates to a specific transaction or shipment, however, just like a documentary BA. The exporter discounts the BA with his bank. The bank then takes this readily negotiable instrument and sells it in the secondary bond market. The BA never hits the bank's balance sheet and it is always readily negotiable. However, because the borrower's performance on the transaction supporting the BA underlies the borrower's credit with the bank, very few banks grant clean BAs to smaller companies. On the other hand, large corporations use them all the time. If you can sell a banker on the concept of a clean BA, however, it is a cheap way to finance working capital.

The normal size of a clean BA is $500,000 although some banks go as low as $100,000. Normally, only very large regional banks or money center banks work in this area. Interest rates on clean BAs are usually less than LIBOR (London Interbank Offer Rate). LIBOR is almost always less than the American prime rate. Acceptance fees range up to 2 percent per annum on the face amount of the BA.

Some companies negotiate export orders with shipments extending over several years. A typical example would be for equipment and components for the construction of an electric power plant or a large factory. The construction of the facility and the installation of equipment might take three to five years. The high cost of the equipment and its installation usually precludes such a long-term transaction from falling within the confines of typical L/C trade credit. Forfaiting, a scheme used throughout the world, but infrequently in America, offers a more ingenious financing scheme to handle this type of transaction.

Financing with Forfaiting

Forfaiting is a French term. It defines a process whereby the exporter gives away, or forfeits his rights to receive future payment in exchange for immediate cash. The process was developed years ago by large corporations exporting out of Europe. It has become a popular means of providing supplier credit for large or long-term export projects. Although most Americans have never heard of either the term or the process, forfaiting is gradually becoming acceptable to some of the more progressive U.S. international traders.

The transaction should be at least $250,000 and normally doesn't exceed $10 million. The discount rate ranges up to 2 points over LIBOR, and commitment fees go up to 0.75 percent per annum. The financing covers a period of from 1 to 10 years, although 5 or 6 years are the most common.

Forfaiting works as follows:

1. The exporter and the buyer, who for his own reasons wants long-term credit for the deal, negotiate a series of notes, drafts, bills, or other instruments. These documents are used to pay off the balance due the exporter over the term of the transaction.
2. The exporter contacts a forfaiter and the forfaiter and the buyer negotiate with a foreign bank to provide a guarantee of the buyer's credit as an endorser of the note, draft, or bill. In the parlance of international finance this endorsement, together with a promissory note or bill from the buyer, is called an *aval*. The simplicity of this transaction has great appeal to bankers and buyers alike. No contracts are involved that could require litigation in the event of default.
3. When the exporter presents the forfaiter a complete set of shipping and customs clearance documentation, the forfaiter pays him his money.

There are three broad advantages in forfaiting:

1. It provides medium- to long-term financing when short-term credit won't work.
2. Forfaiting covers the entire sale, not just 85 percent (the maximum for an Eximbank guarantee).
3. It costs less than borrowing from a bank.

The primary disadvantages are that it cannot be used for short-term credit, and many American banks just don't understand the mechanics yet. In addition, banks in some developing countries are still reticent to handle the guarantee portion of the deal for the buyer.

Any large money center bank in New York should be able to help locate an appropriate forfaiter and assist in arranging the deal. Most have their own internal forfaiting departments which eliminates the need to hire one from the outside. Chase, Citicorp, Bank of America, and Security Pacific are all experienced in this technique. Most major European banks with branches in New York also act as forfaiters.

LEASING

Leasing has become a popular means of furnishing supplier credit for the sale of capital assets. The exporter either does the leasing himself or arranges for a leasing company to buy the goods and then lease them to the buyer. International Leasing Corporation is one of the largest and best-known companies in the international leasing game. They handle most of the foreign leasing for Boeing and other aircraft companies. As popular as leasing is in this country, many smaller leasing firms have ignored the international market. They seem to fear buyer credit risks or potential foreign government expropriations of their assets.

Insurance coverage from the FCIA (examined in Chapter 18) adequately covers both of these risks. Therefore, there really isn't any reason for not entering into a long-term lease with a foreign buyer. It's not a bad idea to hold the lease yourself rather than selling it to a leasing company. With minimal risk and an opportunity to increase profits beyond the normal sales transaction, leasing can be an easy, safe way to maximize returns.

Leasing is especially attractive when financing exports to developing countries with soft currency. Payment terms can be structured over a period of time to meet the needs of both buyer and seller. Countertrade or barter arrangements frequently covert the payments into hard currency or goods. Many large corporations finance their export programs to developing nations almost entirely with leases and countertrade arrangements.

EXIMBANK

During the past 20 years, entire infrastructures of developing nations have been built with products and services furnished by American companies, with help of course from the British, Japanese, French, Italians, and Germans. Most of these long-term projects have been financed through government agencies with little or no financing provided directly by the exporter. Even though an exporter often initiates the financing scheme, it's really up to a foreign buyer (many times a foreign government) to arrange its own financing, frequently with U.S. government assistance.

The use of trade credits is certainly the least expensive and easiest way to finance export sales. In many cases, however, smaller businesses cannot compete in the world market with trade credit alone. Something else must be arranged to match the subsidies offered by many foreign governments to their own private sector. Eximbank stands ready to help.

The Export-Import Bank (Eximbank) was established by Congress originally to compensate American exporters for competitive financing schemes subsidized by foreign governments. Originally founded in 1934, the principal governing legislation is the Export-Import Bank Act of 1945, as amended through October 15, 1986. An independent, corporate agency of the U.S. government, Eximbank coordinates its policies with other government agencies to ensure consistency with overall foreign policy and objectives. Normally, it will not support exports to communist or aggressor countries nor finance the sale of military products or services. A company must export goods or services with at least 50 percent U.S. content to be eligible.

The following five questions must be answered in the application for Eximbank assistance for each transaction:

1. Is there a U.S. export involved?
2. What foreign competition exists, and is it officially subsidized?
3. Is the transaction economically feasible?
4. Is there reasonable assurance of repayment?
5. Would voiding the transaction create an adverse effect on the domestic U.S. economy?

A negative response to even one of these questions exempts a transaction from Eximbank assistance, except in the case of small businesses (as defined by Eximbank). Evidence of foreign competition is not required for exports from small businesses when Eximbank supplies less than $2.5 million in guarantees or loans.

The cost of Eximbank assistance includes initiation fees and interest charges, both based on the perceived risks in doing business in a specific country. Even though it does not receive congressional appropriations for its operations, the bank's annual financing support authorization ceiling is established by Congress. Through fees and interest charged for its guarantees and loans, and recoveries on previous claims, Eximbank has been largely self-sufficient and not financed by tax dollars (except for its initial capital provided by Congress in 1945). Because it is self-sustaining, Eximbank cannot always compete effectively with the rates and terms offered by foreign export credit agencies (see Chapter 18). By and large, however, it has remained in the running in most transactions.

Eximbank services are available to any American exporter of any size and in any industry. As with many government agencies, most of the support from Eximbank has gone to large corporations. In recent years, however, in an effort to brace against increasing foreign trade deficits, Eximbank has established several programs especially helpful to small and midsize exporters. As part of this effort, Eximbank established a "hotline" counseling service to answer questions from smaller businesses about financing and other assistance involving exporting. The toll-free number is (800) 424-5201. Four of the most popular programs offered by Eximbank to help small and midsize exporters are:

1. The commercial bank guarantee program.
2. The foreign credit insurance program.
3. A cooperative financing facility with overseas banks.
4. The discount loan program with U.S. banks.

Eximbank Preliminary Commitment

The Preliminary Commitment consists of an offer from Eximbank to finance a specific export sale in advance of the transaction. It outlines the bank's willingness to participate, and the terms and conditions for loan or guarantee support. It covers all products and services eligible for Eximbank participation. They must be nonmilitary and have at least 50 percent U.S. content. Any business may file an application for commitment. A $100 fee accompanies the application. The commitment remains valid for 180 days, although it may be extended by Eximbank.

With a preliminary commitment, an exporter, borrower, lender, or other responsible party to the transaction can then establish terms and conditions of financing for planning and marketing purposes. Obviously, a foreign buyer assured of Eximbank support will be more likely to negotiate a contract with a small exporter than he would if only trade credit were offered.

Eximbank Working Capital Guarantee

The Eximbank Working Capital Guarantee program was designed specifically to help smaller U.S. exporters obtain bank working capital financing for export products and services. These loans go to the exporter directly, not the foreign buyer. All eligible products and services are covered. An exporter should first obtain a preliminary commitment from Eximbank and then shop for the best credit line from commercial lenders.

Any commercial lender willing to extend such export-related credit to small- and medium-size businesses can get the loan guaranteed by Eximbank. The guarantee covers up to 90 percent of the principal balance, and interest up to one point over the U.S. Treasury rate. Repayment must occur within 12 months, unless previous arrangements are made with both the lender and Eximbank. The exporter pays for this guarantee. Eximbank also charges an up-front facility fee of 0.5 percent of the loan, and quarterly usage fees of 0.25 percent of the loan's average outstanding balance.

The guarantee is with recourse to the exporter. The exporter must provide the lender with adequate collateral (usually inventory used to produce the products) so that the loan balance never exceeds 90 percent of the collateral value. The Eximbank Working Capital Guarantee may be used either for a single export transaction loan or for an export revolving credit line. It can also be combined with the SBA's Export Line of Credit program. Approved lenders receive Eximbank's guarantee on loans up to $300,000 on a discretionary basis.

Eximbank Guarantee for Medium- and Long-Term Loans

A buyer purchasing capital equipment usually requires longer term financing. To compensate for these longer terms, Eximbank established a Medium- (1–7 years) and Long-Term (7–10 years) Guarantee program.

Such guarantees are also applicable to U.S. exports of products with foreign-made components. In such a case, the guarantee covers up to 100 percent of the American content of the product only. The guarantee has two restrictive provisions: (1) that the U.S. content does not exceed 85 percent of the contract price of each item, and (2) that the total U.S. content is not less than 50 percent of the total contract value.

This guarantee can only be used for loans made by either a U.S. lender or a foreign lender, directly to a foreign borrower for the purchase of American goods. It cannot be used to guarantee direct loans to American exporters. A foreign buyer must pay 15 percent of the contract value as a down payment, either in the form of cash or an irrevocable, confirmed L/C.

Guarantees cover up to 100 percent of the financed portion. For medium-term loans, the guarantee extends to balances up to $10 million. Either the exporter or the lender must counterguarantee Eximbank for 2 percent of the commercial risk. Eximbank charges interest on fixed rate loans equal to the lesser of the U.S. Treasury bill rate plus 0.5 percent, or the U.S. Treasury note rate minus 0.5 percent. On floating rate loans the interest rate is calculated as the lesser of the U.S. Treasury note rate minus 0.5 percent, or a preselected rate from the following: prime minus 2 percent, LIBOR minus 0.25 percent, or U.S. Treasury bill plus 0.5 percent.

The repayment period must comply with the following schedule:

Contract Value	Maximum Term
$50,000 or less	2 years
$50,000 to $100,000	3 years
$100,000 to $200,000	4 years
$200,000 or more	5 years

Under exceptional cases Eximbank will go seven years for larger loans. Prenegotiated long-term loans of over $10 million can be repaid over 10 years.

The costs to the exporter for medium- and long-term guarantees for foreign buyers are:

1. A $100 processing fee.
2. An up-front exposure fee based on the term of the loan, country risk, and category of borrower, paid on each disbursement.
3. A commitment fee of 0.125 percent per annum on the undisbursed balance of the guaranteed loan.

Eximbank guarantees for medium- and long-term loans are unconditional and freely transferable. The guarantee can also be combined with an intermediary loan (discussed later). A preliminary commitment is available to any responsible applicant. Claims against the guarantee must be filed between 30 and 150 days after default by a buyer.

Eximbank Direct Loans

Eximbank provides two types of direct loans: (1) loans direct to the foreign buyer of U.S. exported goods, and (2) loans to intermediaries who in turn fund the foreign buyer. These intermediaries are usually financial institutions—either American or foreign. There are similarities as well as differences between the two types of direct loans.

Intermediary loans are structured as *standby* loans. This means that the lender may draw down on the loan at any time during its term. The lender can utilize this flexibility to take advantage of lower rates than those established by OECD, if available. OECD is the acronym for Organization for Economic Cooperation and Development, an organization of 22 developed nations that sets parameters for interest rates and terms applicable to its members' export credit activities. Maximum coverages and repayment terms for both categories of loans are the same as for the Eximbank guarantee program. Foreign buyer and intermediary direct loans both require a 15 percent down payment by the buyer.

The interest charged on intermediary and direct loans to foreign buyers is based on fixed rates established by OECD, but they do vary between the two programs. Under the direct loan program, the category of the country within which the buyer is located determines the interest rate, according to the table in Figure 14–1:

FIGURE 14–1
Interest Rates by Country Category

Country Category	Up to 5 years	Over 5 years
I (Rich)	CIRR	CIRR
II (Intermediate)	9.15%	9.65%
III (Poor)	8.30%	8.30%

CIRR stands for the Commercial Interest Reference Rate and is revised monthly. The appendix defines which countries fall into each category.

The table in Figure 14–2 establishes the interest rate charged on intermediary loans, assuming that the intermediary makes the loan to a foreign borrower at the minimum OECD fixed rate:

FIGURE 14–2
Interest Rates for Intermediary Loans

Loan Commitment	Eximbank Interest Rate
Less than $1 million	OECD rate less 1.5%
$1–$5 million	OECD rate less 1.0%
$5–$10million	OECD rate less 0.5%

Additionally, if an intermediary loan is not combined with a guarantee Eximbank waives the commitment fee; otherwise the guarantee fee remains the same as for a direct loan to the buyer—0.5 percent per annum.

Engineering Multiplier Program

Surprisingly, the Engineering Multiplier Program has not received wide use by American exporters. It was designed specifically for two purposes:

1. To provide funding for engineering firms and other preconstruction service companies.
2. To fund feasibility studies by architectural and design firms.

It also serves to promote the exporting of goods used in the construction of these projects. Medium-term loans of up to $10 million are provided direct to foreign buyers.

If the engineering contract results in the export of American-made goods for the project, it can be rolled into a long-term project loan. Loan criteria call for the export contract to be the greater of $10 million, or twice the value of the engineering contract. Rates, repayment terms, and fees are similar to those of other programs previously described. Eximbank financing of costs incurred by U.S. firms for contracts covering the operation and maintenance of foreign projects is also available.

The FCIA risk coverage programs, also sponsored by Eximbank, are of special interest. They include insurance coverage for lease payments, foreign expropriation, foreign currency translation, and export-related foreign currency swaps—as well as several specialized coverages. The entire FCIA program is examined in Chapter 18.

THE PRIVATE EXPORT FUNDING CORPORATION

The Private Export Funding Corporation (PEFCO) is a private organization closely associated with Eximbank. Formed by several U.S. banks and large corporations, it supplements long-term financing for foreign buyers of American exports. Typically, PEFCO becomes involved in export programs requiring longer-term financing than a commercial bank will handle, but shorter than provided by Eximbank. PEFCO also works with exporters and foreign buyers to structure financing packages with unique interest rate and repayment stipulations. PEFCO receives its investment funds from selling Eximbank-guaranteed negotiable debt instruments on the open market.

Though not widely used by smaller exporters, the PEFCO facility is available if needed. Somewhat restrictive, PEFCO only handles projects exceeding $1 million and restricts foreign buyer loans to periods exceeding five years. PEFCO funding cannot be used for smaller projects. If the parameters fit, however, it offers another way to promote American competitiveness in the global marketplace. It gives the smaller exporter one more option in making the sale.

U.S. DEPARTMENT OF AGRICULTURE

The Department of Agriculture administers several specialized export assistance programs for companies selling agricultural products in the export market. Programs vary depending on the specific agricultural product being sold. To learn more about specific program options, contact a local Department of Agriculture office. One agency within the Department supports universally applicable programs, regardless of product: the Commodity Credit Corporation (CCC). The CCC offers financial assistance in the form of buyer credits based on government-to-government agreements. With a knowledge of how the programs work, the exporter can benefit directly.

Two of the most popular programs are the Export Credit Guarantee program and the Intermediate Credit Guarantee program. Both programs consist of a CCC guarantee against a foreign letter of credit for up to 98 percent of the value of the product. The former program issues these credit guarantees for up to 3 years: the latter extends credit to 10 years. Both programs specify unlimited amounts of credit, and are intended to assist those countries with major economic problems.

A third CCC program, the Bonus Incentive Commodity Export Program (BICEP) enters the picture when the CCC determines that an exporter must be subsidized in order to compete with foreign government subsidized companies. This subsidy takes the form of a certificate—an EEP bonus certificate—with a value equal to what the exporter needs to effectively compete. Redeemable for any surplus commodity held by the CCC, this certificate can be sold or traded in secondary markets, making it as good as cash. In many cases the sale or trade value of the certificate exceeds the certificate value by a substantial premium. This permits the exporter to make a profit on this transaction as well as on the original export sale.

SMALL BUSINESS ADMINISTRATION EXPORT FINANCING

Although not frequently used, financing assistance from the Small Business Administration (SBA) is also available to exporters meeting the definition of a *small business*. The SBA special Export Revolving Line of Credit program (ERLC) has been in effect for years. It has received little emphasis from agency offices, however, hardly any publicity, and very little use from exporters. Provisions in the Omnibus Trade Bill of 1988 theoretically changed the program to be a viable source of export financing for small businesses, but so far its use has been minimal. Congress gave the SBA a mandate to support small exporters with the hope that small and midsize companies would begin taking advantage of the program.

In August 1984, in an effort to reach more small businesses with its Working Capital Guarantee program, Eximbank reached an agreement with the SBA to extend co-guarantees under the SBA's ERLC program. Under this agreement, Eximbank participates equally with the SBA to guarantee working capital loans to small businesses for export programs. This risk sharing permitted an increase in the loan limit to $1 million. Thus, if an exporter qualifies as a small business under SBA criteria, and needs $1 million or less, the resources of both the SBA and Eximbank are available.

SBA continues to handle amounts below $200,000 solely through its ERLC program and Eximbank supports the difference. Other qualification requirements and definitions fall within the same SBA parameters as those established for domestic assistance.

Through 1989, many local SBA offices have tried to recruit staff personnel familiar with international trade. So far, most have fallen short. This lack of global expertise, coupled with stringent budget cuts from the Reagan and Bush administrations, casts a gloom over any significant active participation by the SBA in export financing in the near future. If increased allocations become available from Congress and more qualified staff are hired, the SBA could be a good place to start looking for export financing. In the meantime, other facilities are more helpful.

It can't hurt to try your local SBA office, however. They may be able to get you started. If the SBA can't help, perhaps they can direct you to one of the recently established city or state export finance programs.

EXIMBANK'S CITY-STATE AGENCY COOPERATION PROGRAM

Early in 1989, in an effort to encourage local support for the smaller exporter, Eximbank launched its City-State Cooperation program in California; Massachusetts; Maryland; Tucson, Arizona; and Columbus, Ohio. City and state agencies participated with Eximbank in its loan guarantee and its foreign credit insurance programs. The idea was to open up export financing direct to the small exporter, rather than to the foreign buyer or to large corporations. Eximbank's traditional preference for the latter two has brought public and congressional criticism and this was an attempt to rectify a badly skewed export financing system. The fact that Eximbank has operated at a loss since 1982 may have opened some eyes to the fact that to survive financially, the bank would have to get more involved with smaller exporters.

The new City-State Cooperation program started as a marketing tool for Eximbank. City and state agencies market Eximbank guarantees and FCIA credit insurance through direct mailings, calls to local banks and merchants, seminars, and a modest advertising campaign. These agencies also provide technical support to smaller companies. This makes exporting more accessible and creates less confusion and wasted time for local banks.

A few wise Washington bureaucrats finally realized that commercial banks throughout the country had drawn away from smaller businesses and concentrated their efforts and their business on larger corporations. The time finally arrived to try to change their minds about their smaller customers. And it seems to be at least partially working. Eximbank approved over $95 million for more than 100 working capital guarantees in 1988. Under this new pilot program alone, in 1989 the bank approved 36 deals worth $25 million. However, 80 percent of this volume was in credit insurance; loan guarantees amounted to only $5 million for 18 deals with an average transaction size of about $275,000. It does seem to be a step in the right direction though.

The city of Los Angeles has taken Eximbank's program one step further. It formed an agency called L.A.XPORT to handle the marketing of Eximbank guarantees. L.A.XPORT obtained a separate line of credit from a local bank for $15 million, specifically set aside for small exporters. The Los Angeles LDC, Inc., functions as the administrative arm for the program, and through April 1989 had completed four transactions worth $1.2 million. Eximbank reports that through mid-1989, 15 states and cities had applied to the bank to become part of the City-State program.

Eximbank officers state that they are confident that many of these applicants will pick up on the scheme worked out in Los Angeles. Before applying for any assistance from Eximbank directly, it wouldn't hurt to check with your state Department of Commerce, or city Chamber of Commerce, to see what similar programs might be available locally.

CONCLUSION

The variety of export financing sources can be intimidating to the uninitiated. The intent of this chapter has been to provide business managers with an overview of the major sources and types of available export financing. All sources are not applicable to all businesses. Size of the company, amount of the export transaction, type of products or services being exported, the country of destination, and even the company's state of residence have a direct bearing on where to look for export funding.

CHAPTER 15

USING COUNTERTRADE TECHNIQUES

MAJOR TOPICS

KEY POINTS

1. Countertrade for the Smaller American Business. Throughout the world, and especially in developing nations, countertrade is rapidly becoming the only way trade can be accomplished. It is also an excellent way to establish a foreign presence. To compete globally, companies of all sizes eventually have to engage in countertrade in one or more of the six acceptable forms.

2. Countertrade Strategies and Guidelines. Several crucial decisions enter a countertrade transaction. A company's global objectives, its product or service, market demand in the host country, and the identity of the customer. Countertrade can be costly, and careful planning is necessary to minimize expenditures.

3. Getting Involved in Countertrade. Countertrade is not for the neophyte. Companies inexperienced in this technique should either contract with a trading specialist to manage the activity or add a competent, experienced staff. A minimum staffing configuration is presented.

4. Pros and Cons of Countertrade. Both parties must benefit in a countertrade transaction or the deal won't work. On the plus side, countertrade offers a financing mechanism when other sources are unavailable, it allows a company to compete with Japanese and European firms, it enables a company to establish a foreign presence, and valuable management techniques can be gained through countertrade partners. On the negative side, it is a costly and time-consuming way to conduct business, the end results are not guaranteed, and exchanged goods must be disposed of.

5. Should Your Company Try Countertrade? A comprehensive questionnaire is included to assist in determining the advisability of using countertrade for exporting purposes and for direct foreign investment.

Anyone who has taken a course in high school physics remembers the basic principle of motion: for every action there is an equal and opposite reaction. In its simplest terms, countertrade is this physical law applied to international trade. For example, an action may be represented by a sale of goods from a U.S. to a foreign company. The reaction, or payment for these goods, is the sale of goods from the foreign company to a U.S. company. Currency may or may not be involved, depending on the structure of the deal. Sometimes the reaction involves a third, or even a fourth party.

In some cases a sovereign government enters the loop. In others, a U.S. competitor or a private company in a third country becomes a conterminous party to the transaction. Direct investment by an American company in a foreign business can enter into the deal. Or a direct investment by a foreign company in the United States might play a part. The most common form of countertrade involves combinations of these events.

Countertrade is probably the best guarded secret in international trade. In a sense, countertrade is similar to the use of bank accounts in tax haven countries. The privacy of a safe foreign bank account provides security to the bank customer. Convinced that the only purpose in banking privacy is to cheat on taxes, the U.S. government objects. Those who use tax haven accounts don't talk about it because they don't want the IRS to know what they are doing; and the tax haven bank or trustee respects this privacy.

This same secrecy pervades the world of countertrade. The federal government doesn't favor it because the IRS can't easily verify income transactions. Companies engaged in countertrade don't talk about it because they want to safeguard the privacy of the transaction from competitors. However, countertrade has been a popular way of conducting business since caveman days. Today, even though most American companies still don't understand how to use it, countertrade remains one of the most popular financing tools in global trade. Developed and developing countries alike use countertrade extensively to export and import products. Foreign private enterprises use countertrade to gain an investment foothold in a competitor's country.

Partly to support the IRS and partly because barter and offsets somehow seem "un-American" to congressional leaders, the federal government has taken a dim view of countertrade. The Office of Management and Budget (OMB) has stated that the U.S. government views countertrade as contrary to the best interests of the country and as diametric to the free market philosophy. Fortunately, the OMB has also stated that the government will not oppose the use of these techniques as long as they do not endanger national security.

The government may have a variety of reasons for not liking countertrade, but it seems clear that most of the strong opposition comes from the IRS. By trading goods for goods, taking part of a sell price in coproduction effort, or disposing of traded goods through third parties in foreign countries, the IRS has a very difficult, if not impossible, task auditing the tax returns of U.S. firms. And this they do not like.

The accounting profession is also at wits' end when it comes to recording countertrade transactions. No official proclamation has been issued by the American Institute of Certified Public Accountants (AICPA) yet. Apparently no one knows quite what to say. Some of the crucial questions currently being wrestled with by the AICPA, the SEC, and the IRS are: At what value does a company record a purchase or a sale? During what time period are these transactions recorded? What value do assets held over a year-end have to a company? What about contingent liabilities for contracted performance in the future? And the most important question: How can these policing bodies force a company to record a countertrade sale or purchase at all?

There is nothing un-American about countertrade that I can see. In fact, it is a widely accepted, internationally practiced method of doing global business. The global American firm must participate in countertrade at some point to wage a global battle. Later in this chapter, the mechanics of doing so are reviewed.

Currency fluctuations, the lack of hard currency, and the need to develop infrastructures and basic industries create a never ending quest for countertrade financing from the emerging former communist bloc and developing countries. Large corporations whose global survival depends on substantial export programs, such as international construction companies and transportation equipment and military hardware manufacturers, get showered with requests for countertrade. Western European, Eastern bloc, Pacific Basin, and Middle East nations, have used countertrade for years as a primary source of financing intercountry sales. Experts estimate that Eastern European countries, the Soviet Union, Singapore, China, Malaysia, Thailand, and Indonesia probably account for 75 percent of the world's countertrade transactions.

Because of their geographically advantageous locations between East and West, both Switzerland and Austria function as important sites for countertrade middlemen. One Austrian bank estimated in 1985 that 20 to 30 percent of world trade involves countertrade. Today, that percentage is probably closer to 50 percent, although because of the cloak of secrecy, no one really knows. Press releases from the International Monetary Fund (IMF) and the World Bank indicate that 40 to 50 percent is probably not a bad estimate. In any event, there is little doubt in global circles that countertrade flourishes worldwide.

American aerospace corporations could rarely sell either military or commercial aircraft to foreign governments or airlines without countertrade. The same holds true for many capital goods companies, construction companies, pharmaceuticals, and more recently, large computer mainframe manufacturers. Beginning to join the throng, African and Latin-American countries will undoubtedly demand the increased use of countertrade to finance imports and eventually exports.

Countertrade has thus far eluded most smaller American businesses. To develop a global mentality, however, and become competitive in world markets, managers must educate themselves in this relatively new-to-America form of international finance.

Countertrade applies most directly to exporting goods and services from the United States. However, once an overseas presence is

established—and especially a manufacturing or distribution facility—
the global trader will have to learn countertrade to sell products in countries other than the host country or back to the United States. In fact, as
we approach the next century, the probabilities remain high that countertrade will be used more in this arena than for financing exports from
the United States. Countertrade exists as an indirect, or backdoor approach to establishing a presence in a foreign country.

COUNTERTRADE FOR THE SMALLER AMERICAN BUSINESS

Countertrade can be applied by small and midsize businesses most effectively as a means of financing sales into a market which does not have
hard currency (such as the Eastern bloc or most of Africa and the Middle
East). It also works well in debt-poor Latin-American countries. Countertrade procedures are relatively straightforward to negotiate, although
somewhat complex to administer. Many countertrade variations exist,
but six basic types predominate:

- Barter.
- Compensation.
- Counterpurchase.
- Buy-backs.
- Coproduction.
- Offset.

Barter

Barter is the oldest form of trade, dating from the earliest history of civili-
zation. It is merely a trade of one commodity for another, without regard
for the intrinsic or market value of either commodity. For instance, I manufacture chrome chairs and you grow wheat. You want to buy a dozen
chairs but have no dollars. We negotiate a contract wherein I give you four
chairs and you give me 10 bags of wheat. Deal completed; except for one
problem. If I have no use for the wheat I have to sell it to get my cash.

This is where barter normally breaks down. It becomes too costly and
takes too much effort for me to convert wheat to dollars. Also, if the
wheat doesn't bring a price equivalent to four chrome chairs, I have lost
money on the deal. Straight barter arrangements are seldom used in international trade except when two parties each have something the
other can use; as in the case of trading between some Middle East countries and Soviet Russia in the 1970s when one had oil and the other guns.
A more common barter arrangement involves additional financing techniques as part of the overall package, such as bank letters of credit.

Compensation

A modern form of barter, compensation can be employed when the exchanged products are valued, and invoiced, in different currencies. Compensation adds a financing dimension to barter that frequently involves a
third party. Returning to my chrome chairs and your wheat: assume my

chairs are worth $1,000, and your wheat, coming from Argentina, is worth 2.5 million pesos (roughly the equivalent of $1,000). I agree to take payment in three bags of wheat now, and 2 million pesos, payable in dollars through an irrevocable, confirmed L/C which I can draw down in equal installments over the next 12 months. I then contract with a trader in Puerto Rico to sell the wheat on the open market for U.S. dollars.

Though similar to barter, this arrangement is different from other forms of countertrade because the entire transaction is covered by a single contract. It can get very unwieldy, and therefore is not frequently used.

Counterpurchase

Related to barter, yet significantly different, counterpurchase (also referred to as parallel barter) involves actual cash transfers. Both cash transfers may be in dollars, or they may be denominated differently. Again using my chrome chairs as an illustration: assume that instead of barter or compensation, we negotiate a deal for the Argentinian to pay me $1,000 cash (this could be in Argentine pesos) and I agree to buy 10 bags of wheat from him over the next 12 months for $100 each.

We execute two separate contracts, one for the chairs, and one for the wheat. Each contract is independent of the other and each enforceable separately. I make a profit on my chairs and hope to be able to sell the wheat on the open market for at least $100 per bag. To accomplish this, of course, I will have to use a third-party trader.

Counterpurchase has been for years the predominant method of financing imports to Eastern bloc nations, especially Yugoslavia. Generally, the value of the imports does not exceed the value of the goods exported. Many Latin-American countries are beginning to encourage counterpurchase arrangements as a way to balance imports and exports, stabilize their currencies, and control inflationary pressures. Though larger companies manage counterpurchase arrangements themselves, smaller businesses are usually ahead by working through a trading company.

Buy-backs

Although buy-back countertrades can be used for importing subassemblies, components, or other products which the exporting company then turns into finished products, it is most commonly used in construction projects. These projects are nearly always turnkey. The contractor guarantees that the project will work when completed, such as a telecommunications network, electric utility, or water purification plant. The exporter, or contractor, gets paid first for the project. Then he agrees either to buy back products or services from the completed facility, or to serve as a distributor for products exported from the host country.

This arrangement works well in China, for example. When American companies sell turnkey manufacturing facilities to the Chinese, they agree to export a certain percentage of the production back to the United States or other hard currency countries. This creates an export market and hard currency flow for the Chinese, and transfers valuable technology to them. It also results in additional profits to selling companies.

Buy-backs are especially useful to smaller contractors who do not have the political influence either in the United States or in the host country to negotiate a standard progress payment contract. Buy-backs can also be useful in dealing with countries having soft currency. Two separate contracts, one for the initial transaction and another for the buy-back are essential in buy-back arrangements. The contractor or exporter wants to be certain he is paid on schedule and does not have to wait for completion of the project or the beginning of production. It is also quite common to combine a buy-back agreement with other forms of countertrade financing to ensure currency translation.

Coproduction

Coproduction countertrade is used principally for the transfer of technology or management expertise. A company wishes to sell widgets in Malaysia. A Malaysian company wants to purchase widgets but also wants to learn how to produce them at home. The two companies build a plant together to manufacture widgets in Malaysia—just like a joint venture. The American company may take an equity interest in the facility. It may also furnish management support to run the facility. In either case the facility is usually co-constructed between the American company and a foreign contractor.

Operating the facility becomes known as coproduction, since both parties are responsible for the production of the facility's products. With equity interests, both parties benefit from the sale of these products. The host company gains by sales within its country's borders and by exporting. The American company profits through exports either to the United States or to other nations.

Coproduction is used throughout the developing world as a method to bring technology and management know-how into the country. Western firms, large and small, use this technique to acquire a direct investment in a foreign country without the difficulty of starting a business from scratch. It also provides a mechanism to learn the process of direct foreign investment with relatively minimum risk.

Offset

Offsets are currently used primarily by larger corporations manufacturing aircraft, military equipment, or large infrastructure equipment (turbines, boilers, smelting furnaces, and so on). The customer is normally a sovereign government, not a private sector customer. Offsets are principally used to improve a customer's foreign exchange position. The deal normally involves a package of transactions, carried out over a defined period of time and theoretically, at least, compensates the acquiring or importing country for loss of jobs, currency, and local development of technologies.

For example, if an American company (Amerco) wanted to sell 70 gas turbines to Ghana but the Ghanian government didn't have the dollars or credit to buy them, the following deal could be structured. Amerco finances the buildings of a plant in Ghana to process rubber. Amerco gets a 35 percent equity interest in the business for its investment. Rubber products are then exported from Ghana to Germany for deutsche marks. These marks are then used to pay for the gas turbines. Amerco, in turn, uses the deutsche marks to pay for the importing of German components into the United States for its gas turbine assemblies.

The Ghanian government has created jobs, foreign exchange, and a viable industry. Amerco expects to reap profits from its 35 percent equity ownership of the rubber company as the business grows. As a side issue, since Ghana falls within the list of countries eligible for USAID financing, most of the cost of building the rubber plant gets financed by the U.S. government.

COUNTERTRADE STRATEGIES AND GUIDELINES

Negotiating opportunities using countertrade seem limitless. Seldom does only one form of countertrade prevail. Deals are seldom consummated without a portion being structured with money payments. A business new to global trade that wishes to implement either an export program or a direct foreign investment strategy, or both, should seriously consider using countertrade as an effective tactical means to achieve competitive edge. Strategy and tactics depend on five factors:

- The objectives expected to be achieved.
- The products or services involved.
- The degree to which the purchaser wants or needs the goods or services.
- The level of support the purchaser gets from his local government.
- The ownership of the customer—private or sovereign.

Objectives

Two objectives stimulate companies to enter the countertrade war for the first time:

1. To finance a specific export transaction when other, more conventional means are not available.
2. As an alternative financing scheme to establish a presence on foreign soil.

The basic premises under the exporting scenario are that the export deal is a single transaction to a single customer, and that there isn't any other way to finance the sale. It makes little sense to incur the expense and complexities of countertrade if an export transaction can be financed through one of the Eximbank programs, a state-sponsored scheme, the SBA, letters of credit, or other trade finance. A first-time exporter should certainly look at these avenues first.

If they won't work and the transaction still makes sense, then by all means try countertrade. One word of caution, however: smaller firms should stay away from offsets. The big boys can get by with multinational manipulations of currencies. They can afford to wait several years for an offset to pay off. A small or midsize firm generally cannot. Any of the other forms of countertrade are manageable, but offsets can be dangerous.

A strategy to use countertrade as a means of establishing a foreign presence makes a lot more sense for the smaller company. Beginning global business with an export program is certainly faster, less expensive, and easier than buying a company or starting one from scratch in a foreign country. By negotiating a buy-back or coproduction deal, a company gets a toehold on foreign soil with very little risk.

The negotiating strategy should be aimed at establishing a long-term presence, not just a single transaction. This may require taking a lower sell price for the order than desired. Or it may necessitate a management training period in the host country at the expense of the exporter. It could involve structuring a joint venture or an equal partnership. Or it may require a minority interest in the facility, perhaps with an option to increase ownership in the future.

A negotiating strategy could also include an agreement for a getting out position after the facility is on-line. Some companies have been able to negotiate a barter arrangement to swap ownership in one facility for a stake in a different one at a later date.

Whatever strategy might make sense at the time, it's important to keep in mind that the objective is to establish a foreign presence—not merely to make an export sale.

Products or Services

As mentioned earlier, construction projects lend themselves to buy-back arrangements, and technology or skill transfers fit coproduction schemes more readily than product exporting. This doesn't mean that companies producing products can't use both techniques. They can. But more care must be exercised when structuring the deal. One of the same problems that exists under international licensing agreements—loss of product rights—occurs with buy-back or coproduction agreements. Once the product technology, management skill, or process methodology are put in place in a new facility with joint ownership, they lose their proprietary nature. It can also be dangerous to form a joint venture with a sovereign customer, especially in developing nations.

How Much Are the Products Needed?

Even though the customer may be a private company, actions that the company may take and the agreements it reaches are frequently controlled by the host government. It's only through the government that business licenses, import approvals, and foreign exchange translations can be obtained. Consequently, the ease of making a countertrade deal and the potential benefits of the transaction depend to a large extent on how much the host government needs or wants the product or project in the country. If the country really needs the specific goods or project, an exporter wins significant leverage in negotiating price, terms, delivery schedules, and a host of other matters under local government jurisdiction. In this case, the exporting firm should demand that a sizable percentage of the transaction be compensated for in cash rather than countertrade.

On the other hand, for many consumer products or so-called luxury items, the likelihood of significant negotiating leverage is remote, as Rick Swanson learned when he tried to structure a compensation/barter deal with Kiasan Roi, Ltd. in Seoul, Korea.

Swanson was the chief financial officer of Rankin Chemical Corp., a producer of fragrances for soap, cosmetics, and perfume. The marketing department landed a significant order from Kiasan Roi but Rick Swanson had been unsuccessful in arranging any type of supplier or buyer credit. The customer suggested a barter arrangement and Rankin's CEO sent Rick to Seoul to wrap up the deal, with strict instructions to get at least three fourths of the order covered with an L/C.

Never having been to Korea, and a neophyte in countertrade arrangements, Rick had no idea what to expect. Being a good soldier, Rick tried to follow his boss's direction and adamantly held fast for the L/C coverage. Seven days later, the Kiasan Roi purchasing manager called the Rankin sales manager and told him two things: get Swanson on a plane back to the States immediately, and either accept a 100 percent barter arrangement or the deal was off.

On his flight home, Rick met an executive from General Dynamics (GD). They began comparing notes on their respective negotiations. The GD exec just completed a coproduction deal with the Koreans for military hardware. He negotiated a guarantee from the Korean central bank for 35 percent of the contract payable in nine months. "If you don't sell them something they really want, these Koreans can be tough cookies," was the only advice he had to give Rick Swanson.

Ownership of the Customer

In the countertrade game, the identity of the customer makes a big difference in negotiating strategy. The same principles apply as when negotiating a domestic contract. When negotiating with the army, navy, EPA, or other government agency, terms and conditions are generally less flexible than with a private party. In international trade, although private companies are often at the mercy of their government's regulations, at least they usually have some flexibility.

Sovereign customers, on the other hand, are more intransigent. Little leverage can be expected. Prenegotiation agreements and informal discussions with appropriate government officials normally prove the only meaningful strategies. As mentioned throughout this book, bureaucratic officials expect favors. Gifts, face-saving concessions, kickbacks, all enter into countertrade negotiations as well as most other business dealings. A global mentality requires Americans to find a way around, through, or over this roadblock.

The Cost of Countertrade

Countertrade is significantly more costly than traditional export financing. If you plan to handle the sale of the exchanged goods yourself, the disposal cost could easily reach 10 percent or more of the value of the goods. When using a countertrade house or an export trading company, the cost could escalate to as much as 20 percent. Furthermore, third-party assistance for deals of less than $1 million is difficult to come by.

Time is another cost, although hard to measure. Any countertrade transaction slows up the selling process. With potentially lengthy negotiations and complex side arrangements, a countertrade transaction easily takes at least four to six months to close. And then if it doesn't close, the time spent on it was wasted. Administrative cost must also be included as an add-on.

GETTING INVOLVED IN COUNTERTRADE

Countertrade is not for amateurs. But then neither is anything in the global arena. Trade barriers, U.S. and foreign government interference in free markets, difficult languages, cultural and travel obstacles, third-party marketing, complex financing and banking structures, and currency translation restrictions all lend an air of mystery to global business. As seen in earlier chapters, however, to survive competitively now and in the future, companies must face up to mastering global techniques. One of those techniques is countertrade.

But saying one wants to do something and actually doing it are two different matters. With a basic understanding of the techniques, the next step is to get an organization in place that can function in countertrade.

By some estimates, nearly half of the Fortune 500 are either currently involved in countertrade or have been in the past. These large firms can afford to staff divisions, subsidiaries, or departments with high-priced specialists well versed in countertrade techniques. General Electric, Campbell Soup, Boeing, and General Motors are examples of corporations that have established either subsidiaries or divisions to manage countertrade transactions for the entire company.

Obviously, a small or midsize company getting started in countertrade can't afford such a luxury. Certain basic organization staffing is crucial, however. Fortunately, some reorganizing must take place to handle a standard export program as well as other global matters, so staffing for countertrade transactions won't be a large net addition. A company entering the countertrade war must have a minimum of five key people devoted to arranging and managing countertrade transactions:

1. A highly competent secretary with some foreign language background.
2. A marketing specialist who can first identify opportunities and then get the order.
3. A financial specialist experienced in international finance generally, and countertrade techniques specifically, to manage negotiations and contract administration.
4. An administrative manager to track the transaction, follow up on schedule slippages and missed milestones, and generally manage the transaction once it is in place.
5. A trading specialist to manage the disposal of exchanged goods.

In the beginning, smaller companies can do without the trading specialist. A brokerage house specializing in countertrades can handle infrequent countertrade deals. Such a specialist can also manage infrequent disposals of goods acquired in buy-back or coproduction transactions. There are about 20 to 30 of these trading houses throughout the country. Trade specialists in Department of Commerce offices maintain current listings of names, addresses, and specific qualifications.

Using an outside brokerage is expensive, however. As mentioned earlier, trading fees run up to 20 percent of the product value. For some smaller trades it can be even steeper. So in the long run, to develop a competent countertrade department, it's normally more cost-effective to hire a trade specialist full time and let him do other assignments when not busy.

On the other hand, in some cases an outside trader can be worth his weight in gold and his benefit far outweighs the 20 percent cost. A qualified trader with good product knowledge performs an array of services. He offers advice on countertrade practices in specific countries before a company gets involved in a deal. He performs market assessments to determine the advisability of entering a given market. He can be a major help in negotiations, especially in developing nations. The better houses even lend a hand in arranging financing and assisting in transportation. And of course, he acts as a broker in the deal.

A qualified secretary heads the list of in-house personnel because without competency in this position deals will almost certainly fall apart—regardless of the abilities of the other staff members. Some background in a second language can be an invaluable asset. During the bidding and negotiating process as well as in the administration of a contract, continual contact with overseas bankers, foreign and U.S. government officials, lawyers, accountants, and foreign visitors to the United States must be handled. Making overseas travel arrangements; overseas communications by telex, telephone, and computer; arrangements for passports, visas, and work permits; coordination with consulates and embassies in the United States and abroad, must also be managed efficiently and timely. Preparation and dissemination of bid packages, coordination with freight forwarders, outsider traders, and export management companies are necessary. The grasp of a second language plus extraordinary administrative skills in this position often makes the difference between a profitable project and a losing venture.

The second most important position is the marketing specialist. Experience with countertrade transaction isn't mandatory although it can certainly be helpful. A marketing specialist has primary responsibility in five areas: sourcing overseas buyers and projects, obtaining customer inquiries, closing the order, assisting in the preparation of the bid package, and following up and coordinating with other managers while the project or shipment is in process. A marketing specialist assists in resolving disputes with the customer. If required, this specialist also assists the trading specialist or outside trader in disposing of exchanged goods.

To be effective in this role, a marketing specialist must have a background in selling to foreign buyers. He should know his way around the international travel circuit and have a fair understanding of export shipping and collection procedures. This specialist will be traveling overseas most of the time so obviously his or her family and personal status must allow such freedom of movement.

The financial specialist must have experience in countertrade activities. He should also have a thorough background in other phases of international finance. A good part of his job is the negotiation of a countertrade contract. He is also responsible for collecting against the contract and revisions to it. Good rapport with global banking sources makes the job a lot easier and the position more effective.

The financial specialist is also responsible for minimizing losses (or maximizing gains) on currency exchange transactions. He must arrange short-term working capital funds, buyer financing (if needed), collections from purchasers of exchanged products, buyer financing of exports from the overseas facility, and other worldwide banking and money transfer activities. Finally, the financial specialist is responsible for adherence to compliance reporting under IRS, SEC, and other U.S. regulations, as well as foreign reporting requirements.

When the marketing specialist sources a customer inquiry, the financial specialist must handle the country survey and other administrative details necessary for accurate and timely preparation of the bid package. He should also arrange for appropriate accommodations, work papers, and customs clearance for American expatriates.

Once a countertrade project begins, the administrative manager is responsible for managing the contract. This involves continual follow-up with company personnel on the job, preparation of status reports, implementing the paperwork for change orders, and generally administering all facets of countertrade contracts. The ideal administrative manager has worked overseas for an extended period in either a marketing, production, or financial capacity. He should have a basic understanding of at least one second language. An engineering background can be very helpful. And of course, the administrative manager must be diplomatic and capable of negotiating and communicating with people from other cultures.

This group of four, or five, should be capable of handling two or three countertrade contracts simultaneously. They should also be capable of interacting with and assisting other functional managers in the preparation of products for export. Coordinating with outside professionals in shipping, banking, insurance, and marketing activities is also part of the group's responsibility.

If a company is serious about getting into countertrade transactions, this contingent of personnel dedicated to countertrade and other global trading activities becomes essential. If a company feels it cannot afford a countertrade department, it should not get involved in these complex transactions. It will be better off restricting its global activities to standard exporting arrangements financed through traditional channels.

PROS AND CONS OF COUNTERTRADE

The whole purpose behind countertrade is to create a transaction between two trading parties that benefits both sides beyond the single transaction itself. It should be accomplished with a minimum amount of currency exchange. The Soviet Union needs wheat which the United States supplies. The United States needs electronic products which Japan supplies. Japan needs oil which the Soviet Union supplies. If private companies, or government agencies, or a combination of both, negotiate countertrade agreements, each company in each country benefits.

Although buy-backs, coproduction, and offsets come into play, the essence of countertrade is exchanging one type of product or service for another. That's why the process began with straight barter deals. Today, of course, international trade has become much more sophisticated. Nevertheless, the same barter advantages have existed for generations. Competitive modern market forces merely make the process more complicated.

From the perspective of small and midsize companies, four advantages stand out in favor of entering into countertrade arrangements:

1. Countertrade is a way to finance an export deal when other means are unavailable. A buyer may be unable to arrange guarantees from his banks. The project might call for longer term financing than Eximbank will provide. The country might not fall within the acceptable definition for U.S. government support, including USAID (such as Libya and Iran). In any of these circumstances, countertrade could be the only way to close an order.

2. Countertrade gives American companies a way to be competitive with Japanese and European trading companies. These experts in countertrade recognized their role in global trading centuries ago. Their techniques for arranging deals and disposing of exchanged goods are well honed. If one of these giant global traders really wants an order, an American company will not stand a chance with traditional financing. At least with countertrade they remain in the ballgame.

3. Countertrade provides a way to obtain a foreign presence or make a direct foreign investment without starting from scratch or going through the difficult process of buying a going business. If structured properly, a coproduction arrangement puts a company directly into new foreign markets. This might be in addition to exporting or, in some cases, take the place of further exporting. A local distribution network is an obvious advantage.

4. Countertrade, especially coproduction, permits a company to acquire long-range management and technical benefits through joint venture partnerships. In most cases a host country partner brings local management techniques and protocol to the partnership that may take an American company years to develop on its own. In some cases, the foreign partner brings technical or application techniques unique to his cultural environment.

There are also some serious disadvantages to engaging in countertrade.

1. Countertrade contracts involving the exchange of unusable goods require their sale or other disposition. Even if done through an in-house trading specialist, the process is time-consuming and costly. Using an outside trader doubles or even

trebles the cost of disposing of the goods. Added profits on their resale might compensate somewhat but generally the net effect is a loss.

2. Countertrade success means the establishment of an in-house department dedicated to arranging and managing countertrade deals. This can be a costly addition for a smaller company. Unless it gets involved in several countertrade deals, these personnel can easily become nonproductive.

3. Countertrade deals require a long time to negotiate and close. Many months and dollars can be spent trying to make an arrangement only to have the deal fall through at the end.

4. Countertrades offer no surefire end results. In many cases the final result won't be realized for many years. Political and economic conditions change rapidly in world markets, and it's entirely possible that when the deal finally culminates, the results may be different than originally intended.

SHOULD YOUR COMPANY TRY COUNTERTRADE?

No one can definitively state that one company will be more successful in countertrade than another. Or that one product is more adaptable than another. Or that one country or region of the world is more amenable to countertrade than another. There are just too many variables. The best advice may be not to go looking for countertrade deals. Other financing methods available for exporting, and for direct foreign investment, are usually less costly, less complex, and more fruitful than countertrade. Let countertrade deals come to you.

On the other hand, going global mandates that a company be prepared to compete wherever and however it can. And that means using countertrade if it is the only way to make a sale. Figure 15–1 provides a questionnaire that should be helpful in determining the advisability of entering a countertrade transaction.

If the answers are predominantly affirmative, a company should be able to cope with the complexities of countertrade.

CONCLUSION

Countertrade will certainly remain a viable way to do business in the global markets of the next century. Most smaller companies are still learning how to use countertrade as a financing technique. Most who have tried it, however, are convinced that in one form or another, countertrade makes both export sales and establishing a foreign presence possible when other financing methods are cost prohibitive. In some cases, countertrade is the only feasible way to gain access to the host country's markets.

As mentioned earlier, don't look for assistance or support from the federal government in countertrade transactions. Until our leaders wake up to global realities, trade policies will probably continue to ignore countertrade as possibly the only way American firms can remain competitive over the long term.

FIGURE 15–1
When to Use Countertrade

For Exporting Purposes:
1. Is the transaction valued at more than $1 million?
2. Do competitors offer countertrade as an inducement to buy?
3. Does the customer have good credit references?
4. Does the customer have good banking relations?
5. Is the customer located in a soft currency country?
6. Is the customer privately owned or sovereign?
7. Does the customer have products I can use?
8. If so, is the value to me equivalent to that demanded in a countertrade?
9. If I can't use the product, can I arrange for resale before closing the countertrade deal?
10. Would such a resale open additional markets for further exports?
11. Can I afford to add a complement of countertrade personnel?
12. Can I recruit them?
13. Do I thoroughly understand all other financing possibilities both domestic and foreign?
14. Have I exhausted all these possibilities?
15. Do I have the global mentality to become involved in such a complex deal?
16. Do my managers have the right global mentality?
17. Is my company financially viable in case the deal falls through?
18. Will my banking relationships support a countertrade arrangement?

For Direct Foreign Investment:
1. Will importing products produced in the foreign facility add value to other products or product lines?
2. Have I done sufficient country research to know this is the best location to establish a facility?
3. Have I done sufficient market research to make the same decision?
4. Will my foreign partner have sufficient technical expertise or will additional outsiders be brought in?
5. If a private company, does my customer/partner have the right political connections?
6. If a sovereign, am I dealing with the right people to achieve political expediency?
7. Does the customer/partner have good market connections or will we have to establish a whole new sales force?
8. Will the facility be flexible enough to change product lines and emphasis as global markets demand?
9. Does my trading partner have the same global objectives as I do?
10. Does he have local banking connections?
11. Will I have to put up any additional money either for working capital or equity?
12. Does my U.S. bank know what I'm doing and are they in agreement?
13. Will they continue to support the company?
14. Is my company strong enough financially to withstand start-up expenses and lost time?
15. Are my goals truly global and not just a one shot expansion?
16. Can I use products from this facility in my U.S. production?
17. Are there any governmental or other prohibitions against exporting to other countries?
18. Will the facility produce standardized products?
19. Do I have and can I spare management talent to be transferred?
20. Is it certain that there are no local patent infringement problems?

Fortunately, trade associations are beginning to be formed to sift through reams of data about countertrade successes—and failures. They will eventually offer technical and probably even management assistance to help smaller companies participate in global countertrades. The two formed so far are the Defense Industries Offset Association (obviously sponsored and controlled by major defense contractors) and the American Countertrade Association supported by nondefense firms. Regional offices can be located through the auspices of your Chamber of Commerce.

SECTION IV

MARKETING IN THE GLOBAL ECONOMY

CHAPTER 16

DEVELOPING A GLOBAL MARKETING STRATEGY

MAJOR TOPICS

KEY POINTS

1. Sales Channels. Identifies five sales channels in global trade. Export management companies (EMCs) can be very helpful to the first-time exporter. EMCs either take title to goods and resell them in foreign markets or act as a commission sales force. American export trading companies (ETCs) have never lived up to their expectations. Only a few large corporate trading companies remain, mostly to manage counter-trade arrangements, but these are not open to the public. The disadvantages of either an EMC or an ETC tend to outweigh their benefits, except for the very small, first-time exporter.

2. Foreign Trading Companies. Both private and government-owned foreign trading companies function differently than their American counterparts. Japan, Great Britain, and the Netherlands have developed extremely effective trading companies to sell and distribute in the global market. State-owned trading companies are the principal mechanism for selling in the Soviet Union or Eastern Europe. American foreign subsidiaries frequently use foreign trading companies to sell to Cuba.

3. In-house Marketing Organization. Managing the sales function in-house seems to be the most fruitful way to tap global markets. Selling to foreign distributors is another way to avoid using low-margin trading companies. An independent distribution network still requires management supervision and monitoring from company personnel. Direct sales to the customer is the most effective method for retail consumer goods, construction projects, and service contracts.

4. Joint Ventures. Many companies find joint ventures with host country partners to be the best, and in many cases the only way to penetrate new foreign markets. A partner's marketing and distribution presence can be invaluable. Stringent trade barriers in many countries require a local marketing partner. Some industries are dominated by a few very large producers, such as telecommunications, automobiles, and supercomputers. A joint venture with one of these Goliaths yields rapid and profitable market entry.

5. Pricing. Market demand and competition influence product pricing in the same way as they do domestically. Estimating product costs for the third leg of the pricing triumvirate can be tricky. Worksheets help structure such estimates of incremental costs for exporting from the United States and for American firms exporting from foreign countries. The basic premise for global product pricing is that everything is negotiable.

6. The Sales Contract. Sales contracts may be verbal, but if the seller reduces it to writing, either in correspondence form, by telex, or a formal contract, aggravation and disputes at a later date can be mitigated. Items to include in a sales contract are specified. Provisions for arbitrating and resolving disputes are crucial.

7. Assistance in Identifying Markets. International trade shows are a good starting point to learn of potential markets. Seminars conducted by the Department of Commerce and the Export Management Association are also helpful. Eximbank, several departments of the federal government, and the U.S. Trade Representative furnish reams of statistics, trends, and agent/distributor listings. Some industry trade associations offer assistance in identifying foreign markets and distributors, as do several state and major city commerce bureaus. *Super* international development banks are helpful in pinpointing market needs in developing nations. The Agency for International Development assists American companies in AID-participating countries.

8. Intellectual Property Piracy. Problems with patent, trademark, and copyright piracy are always present with technology licensing. Several methods and sources of assistance are described for companies exposed to such theft.

The globalization of trade is a fait accompli. Domestic business has disappeared as a self-contained market. Those companies that recognize the implications of globalization and who are capable of adapting to the new realities of conducting business in the global sphere succeed. Those who do not will surely stumble. The previous chapters highlighted how globalization affects American enterprises through:

- The restructuring of national economies to global markets.
- Increasing competition from global companies, both within the United States and abroad.
- A worldwide integration of financial markets.
- The development of global networks of factories, distribution cen-

ters, sales offices, and research laboratories producing value-added products and services.

Although international trade has existed for centuries, global competition is increasing at an ever accelerating pace. Many companies that took the global plunge years ago, did so by producing goods domestically and shipping them to foreign customers. To maintain a constant supply of materials and parts, some were forced to branch out and began importing to keep their production lines running. Now, however, traditional exporting is becoming archaic in many industries. International trade is developing into a far more complex pattern. And the complexities will inevitably increase.

In growing numbers, materials, parts, components, packaging, subassemblies, finished products, and services are produced any place in the world that provides competitive advantage. Reports in newspapers, magazines, and TV news broadcasts continually identify companies that use global value-added networking to increase competitiveness and profits.

In early 1990, the example of VLS Technologies, a custom chip maker from Silicon Valley was reported. VLS designs its products in one of its design centers in North America, Asia, or Europe. Specifications are then transmitted via computer telecommunications channels to Silicon Valley, where photo masks are produced. These are then forwarded to Japan where wafers are etched. Wafers go to South Korea for dicing and mounting. Completed chips are assembled in Malaysia. The final product is then shipped to the customer, wherever he may be.

American Airlines, several banks, insurance companies, and credit card companies perform data entry and check writing activities out of Caribbean locations. Many insurance companies process claims for American policies in the Caribbean, Ireland, and Guatemala to take advantage of low labor costs. Law offices and accounting firms utilize overseas locations to keep abreast of global trade laws, tax regulations, and contract idiosyncrasies. American research labs and analytic firms station branches or divisions in Germany, England, France, and the Scandinavian countries to test drugs and techniques too expensive to develop in the restrictive U.S. market. Value-added networking is not a future phenomenon. It is already with us.

Although value-added networking may serve to reduce production costs or tap foreign technology resources, most companies discover that once engaged in globalized production, selling and distributing these products in global markets become a logical outgrowth. Selling Malaysian finished products to Indonesian customers offers more competitive advantage than shipping from the United States. Japanese import trade barriers necessitate local production facilities to tap that market.

Although no longer representing the be-all and end-all for American firms engaged in global trade, exporting from the United States remains an important adjunct to globalization. Consumers throughout the world continue to demand American-produced consumer products as well as capital goods. American contractors remain in contention for most worldwide construction projects. American technology continues to lead the industrialized world in creative innovations. Much of the world's military weaponry is still designed and manufactured in the United States.

Long a favorite of smaller global firms, technology transfers remain in full bloom. The sale of technology will inevitably increase as Eastern Europe and the Soviet Union evolve into consumer market economies. With virtually no financial commitment and eager markets, American firms must stand ready to lead the way in the sale of technology to developing nations in Africa, Latin America, and Southeast Asia as more developing nations swing into the newly industrialized classification.

A global mentality demands that a company look at global opportunities as one vast market, unfragmented by such prosaic divisions as exporting, the European Community, Japan, Latin America, and so on. While maintaining the integrity of country or regional submarkets as integral parts of the whole, a company truly globalizing its efforts must plan its marketing strategy as if these demarcations didn't exist.

Market strategy must be dedicated to the capture of long-term market share; not restricted to short-term returns. Structuring a marketing organization and developing market leverage at key points around the globe can only be accomplished with the long term in mind. As seen in earlier chapters, Avon, GE, Campbell Soup, IBM, and other successful global entrants were willing to forsake short-term gains for long-term market position. That is exactly what smaller companies must do, even if it means incurring short-term losses during the development stage.

Global market strategy for the new entrant can be viewed in four segments:

1. How to locate and sell to customers.
2. How to price the order.
3. How to structure sales contracts.
4. Where to get assistance in getting started.

SALES CHANNELS

Techniques for marketing in the global arena are no different than those applied domestically. Some of the players go by different names. Time frames may be longer. Unfamiliar language and cultural barriers cause some confusion. But as far as how the selling process works, techniques for selling overseas are the same as those used at home. There are two fundamental ways to sell goods or services: through an agent, or direct to the customer. The following variations on these themes are used in global trade:

1. Selling to or through an export management company.
2. Selling to or through an American export trading company.
3. Using a foreign trading company.
4. Contracting with a foreign distributor.
5. Selling direct to the end customer.
6. Utilizing joint ventures.

Export Management Companies

An export management company (EMC) functions similarly to a manufacturers representative. It acts as the selling arm for many manufacturers of noncompeting products. Many EMCs go one step further. They purchase goods directly from manufacturers and then resell them overseas for their own account. Others restrict their operation to straight commission sales. In both cases, an EMC acts as the export sales department for its manufacturing customers.

Nearly all of the larger EMCs have sales representative networks in various regions of the globe which they use to facilitate overseas selling and distribution. It is up to the EMC to develop market strategy, arrange for shipping and customs documentation, purchase foreign risk and ocean shipping insurance coverage, and in some cases, even arrange for supplier or buyer credit.

When transferring title to the EMC the manufacturer treats the export sale as if it were a domestic transaction, which in fact it is. No credit risks, shipping costs, overseas sales network, or customer service costs are incurred. The producer doesn't even know who the customers are. Clearly, for a manufacturer who is unwilling or unable to structure an internal global marketing function, EMCs provide a method to increase sales without incurring any risk.

A producer pays a steep price when abdicating direct marketing responsibility, however. Since the EMC must make its profit on sales to the ultimate customer, pricing from the manufacturer to the EMC is very low. It usually amounts to no more than the manufacturer's product cost plus a small markup negotiated with the EMC. The real profit in export sales flows to the EMC who incurs all the selling costs and credit risks.

When the EMC acts as a commission sales agent, similar avoidance of international marketing effort by the producer prevails. In this case, however, the manufacturer retains title to the goods until transferred to the customer. Financing and credit risks are also borne by the producer. The EMC makes its profit on sales commissions from the manufacturer and usually a base retainer. In some cases when an EMC also acts as a distributor in a foreign country, inventory must be carried. Further deterioration in the manufacturer's gross margin is caused by compensation to the EMC for added carrying and storage costs.

U.S. Export Trading Companies

In 1982, Congress passed the Export Trading Company Act permitting the formation of export trading companies (ETC) by groups of competitors without fear of antitrust action. It also allowed bank-holding companies to own and operate ETCs. The avowed purpose of the Act was to allow American companies of all sizes to band together in trading companies, similar to the Dutch, Japanese, and British.

The theory also held that by allowing banks to enter into commercial, nonbanking transactions, augmenting their support of international financing, more American companies would be encouraged to export. Within the Department of Commerce, the Office of Export Trading Company Affairs oversees the activities of ETCs.

After passage of the Act, individuals, companies, trade associations, states, cities, and banks (through 1982, 42 banks had formed ETCs), jumped on the bandwagon. Enamored by the presumed success of giant Japanese trading companies, Americans were eager to partake of the vast profits offered by global trade. Unfortunately, few took the time to understand what international trade was all about. Fewer still had a global mentality. As a result, ETCs failed as fast as they were formed. Though bank holding companies invested over $85 million in these new ventures, little impact was felt in the world marketplace. Without the knowledge of even the barest essentials of doing business in the global economy, many tried ETCs, and most failed.

> A perfect example of the stampede to obscurity by neophyte American investors occurred when Roy Stephenson, insurance salesman from Sioux Falls, South Dakota, abandoned his insurance business for the pot of gold. He incorporated himself as an ETC, packed his bag for a four-day stay, and took off for Hong Kong expecting to land several orders for whatever anyone wanted to buy. On the flight over, his seat-partner asked what product lines he represented. His response typified the naiveté of the new traders. "Any product you want. I'm going to get the order first and then source out a supplier back in the States."

> Another example comes from Orion Window Shade Corp. which formed an ETC with two of its competitors, expecting to penetrate the Mexican market for window coverings. The chief financial officer of Orion, who also headed the ETC, arrived at the office of R. Gomez, an architect in Guadalajara for his first appointment. After waiting six hours, he was finally shown in to Gomez's private office. Gomez stopped the CFO during his presentation. "I thought you wanted to engage my services, not sell me window blinds." The Orion officer returned to the States trying to figure out what went wrong.

Although similar to EMCs, export trading companies exhibit some important differences. An ETC acts as an independent sales agent on a case-by-case basis. It does not maintain a retinue of client customers as does an EMC. An ETC performs basically a sourcing, or wholesale function, between buyer and seller. It does not assume any responsibility to either party in a transaction.

Some American ETCs do not carry inventory in their own name nor do they perform after-sales customer service functions. This type of ETC operates principally on a commission basis, charging the seller, or the buyer, a percentage of the export transaction. Most export trading companies, however, do just the opposite. They buy everything from manufactured goods to raw materials at 10 to 15 percent below wholesale price and then resell them for their own account.

Very few bank ETCs have survived in an active form as trading companies. Bank of America Trading is one of the few still actively soliciting business. One reason, aside from the normal lack of business acumen in banking circles, is probably that the bank mentality stressing the avoidance of any risk does not match well with risk-oriented global trading.

Trading companies originated by major corporations have also fallen on hard times. Most of those continuing to function do so almost exclusively to set up and administer countertrade agreements. They are not active in marketing the company's products. General Motors' Motors Trading Corporation, Monsanto Trading, Caterpillar World Trading, and GE Trading Company are a few examples of corporate trading companies devoted to countertrade administration. Sears World Trade, formed to present Sears an opportunity to capture the Japanese market, failed miserably and is now practically immobile.

For those interested in exploring the possibilities of forming an ETC or utilizing one already in existence, the Office of Export Trading Company Affairs provides a current directory of who is doing what in the field. The directory is entitled *Partners in Export Trade* and is available from the government bureau at Room 122, U.S. Department of Commerce, Washington, DC 20230. Seminars and regional conferences on the Export Trading Companies Act are also sponsored by this bureau. Information and dates can be obtained from the nearest Department of Commerce office.

From a practical perspective, many third-party exporters have evolved into a combination of EMC and ETC. Others do business in both the import and export markets. Local chapters of export management or trading associations (most major cities have them) can direct you to one that specializes in your specific product line.

The principal advantage in choosing either an EMC, an ETC, or a hybrid, as a company's marketing arm is that it offers a fast, low-cost method to make an initial entry into the global marketplace. The biggest disadvantages seem to be:

1. It prevents a company from learning global trade and developing a global mentality for future international expansion.
2. A company loses control of its own marketing strategy.
3. A company has no control over after-sale customer service, or customer pricing.
4. Profit margins are meager.
5. Some foreign buyers are reluctant to deal through a third party.

Many American companies have not yet learned the difficulty of trying to conquer the world through someone else's effort. The dismal record of American trading companies and the wreckage strewn by major corporations and banks attempting this tack offer ample evidence of the fallacy. Trading companies are trading companies, that's all. Relying on an export management company or American trading company to further a company's global interest, except in countertrade arrangements, merely emphasizes the *us* versus *them* or the *home country* versus *foreign country* attitudes pervading American business.

In and of itself, such an approach is the antithesis of a global view. A company's stake in either domestic business or global trade cannot be proxied to an agent, regardless of whether he calls himself a manufacturers' rep, an export management company, or a trading company.

FOREIGN TRADING COMPANIES

Contrary to the American experience, companies in Japan, Great Britain, the Netherlands, and several other traditional trading nations learned over the years that using their versions of trading companies to market and distribute products around the globe was the most efficient way to penetrate and retain these markets. Large and small trading companies have been predominant in these countries for years and evolved in tandem with merchant banks. In fact, centuries earlier, trading companies were part of merchant banking.

As merchant banks turned more toward the financing arena, trading companies evolved on their own as the selling arm of manufacturers. Today, trading companies remain the principal form of marketing activity worldwide. In addition to the traditional trading nations, Germany, Argentina, and Brazil rely heavily on this form of global marketing.

Trading companies also assume a predominant role in selling to and between Eastern European nations, the Soviet Union, and China. Western companies entering one of these markets, even surreptitiously through the backdoor via foreign subsidiaries, find that trading companies offer the best, and many times the only, way to sell and distribute goods. An interesting example of the latter case involves the sale of goods to Cuba, long suppressed by the U.S. trade embargo.

Major trading companies, predominantly Japanese, handle the sale of American products to Cuba, and the concurrent sale of Cuban goods throughout the world. Under pressure from Canada and Argentina, since 1975 the U.S. government has permitted American companies to sell goods to Cuba through their subsidiaries in third-party countries. Ford Argentina sells the Cuban Tourism Ministry trucks. Goodyear Canada sells tires to Transimport, a Cuban firm. Currently, U.S. subsidiaries in 21 countries sell products in Cuba ranging from hydraulic hoses to gelatin capsules for medicine.

Of course licensing is required. Once they understand the process, however, American companies find that obtaining a license is child's play. A study conducted by John Hopkins University concluded that in the end, Cuba gets the products it needs and sells its goods for hard currency. American subsidiaries show a profit and foreign workers clearly benefit. The only losers are corporate America and American workers. Of course, U.S. Commerce officials dispute these findings.

Foreign trading companies continue to actively function as a vehicle to stimulate Western trade with Eastern Europe and the Soviet Union. Many are government owned. A few are private. For example, trading companies such as the state-owned Genex and Inex, are active in Yugoslavia. They provide an easier and cleaner path for Western companies selling to Yugoslav markets than dealing directly with cumbersome government bureaucracy. Torimex in Poland serves the same purpose. The Soviet center for trading with the United States is the Amtorg Trading Company in New York. This is an umbrella organization for the representative offices of some 50 foreign trade organizations that specialize in various areas of Soviet imports and exports.

Foreign trading companies are entirely different from U.S. trading companies. The only similarity is the designation *trading company*. Japanese trading companies such as Mitsui & Co., Mitsubishi, C. Itoh, and Sumitomo are huge conglomerates with marketing, financial, and distribution arms extending their domain to investments in foreign manufacturing companies.

In 1989, Mitsui was the largest exporter from the United States. Smaller trading companies, specializing in specific products, dot the British landscape. They serve as excellent export vehicles for small or midsize companies. Metallgesellschaft and Ruckhauser are two good-sized trading companies from Germany. Bunge Trading Company is predominant in Argentina and Brazil. Some American corporations formed joint venture trading companies with foreign partners. One example is Lor-West out of Bermuda. Lor-West is 20 percent owned by Westinghouse and 80 percent by the English Wraxall Group.

The fastest and easiest way to contact any of these trading companies is through the respective country's consulate office in the United States. All are located in Washington. Many have branches in New York or Los Angeles.

DEVELOPING AN IN-HOUSE MARKETING ORGANIZATION

Sooner or later, remaining competitive in the global arena mandates a full-time marketing organization. This may take either of two forms:

1. One or more key sales personnel operating out of the home office and monitoring foreign distributors.
2. A network of sales personnel stationed in key regional submarkets around the world.

Even though a company may begin with one or two sales offices, eventually competition forces expansion of coverage.

Regardless of whether a company elects the distributor route or chooses to establish its own marketing system, the first steps in developing a global marketing strategy are to target the right markets, make appropriate contacts, and adapt products to individual tastes in those markets. The experience of Beauty Products International (BPI), founded by James Yoder and Kenton Post, as reported in *World Trade,* (February/March 1990), illustrates how one midsize company developed its market strategy.

Beauty Products International manufactures high-quality cosmetics. Executives of the company began the pursuit of foreign markets by consulting with the Los Angeles office of the Department of Commerce and attending its seminars to learn about export licensing. The Department of Commerce led them to the Export Managers Association of California which furnished information about freight forwarding, export documentation, and letters of credit. BPI advertised its products in the Commerce Department's *Commercial News USA,* participated in trade shows in Mexico and Korea, and with a small trade group met retailers and distributors in Japan. These efforts led to sales contracts with retailers, distributors, and manufacturers in all three countries. What started out as a two-man operation is now selling cosmetics in 3,500 stores in Japan, 1,000 in South Korea, and through 8,000 sales reps in Mexico. In 1989, the company turned $2 million in sales.

When asked the secret of their success, Yoder answered that the education process taught them what consumers wanted in each of the markets. They then designed a different product for each individual market. Packaging, price, and distribution channels dictated by each market were weighed against quality and profit margins the company felt it could live with. The moral to the story is that market research, the right sales contacts, and appropriate product and packaging design had to be specifically geared to each market.

Distributors

Some companies find that local distributors offer the best market strategy in some global regions. Being resident in the host country, distributors know the markets, customs, pricing strategies, distribution mechanisms, and customer expectations. Just as important for many companies is the after-sale customer service managed by a local distributor. Finally U.S. government restrictions, such as complying with the Foreign Corrupt Practices Act, boycott regulations, and other legislation, preclude American companies from conducting competitive business on their own in some countries. A local distributor, not bound by these straitjacket restrictions, offers competitive parity with European and Japanese firms.

Some companies provide training programs for their foreign distributors to be certain that they know the product. Others stock parts and materials at the distributor's warehouse for repair and maintenance work. Regardless of the specific distributor relationship, it is crucial to negotiate the right contractual terms, in writing, to forestall future misunderstandings.

Just as when selling through domestic distributors, a global company must provide management personnel to monitor their performance. Wyeth Labs (pharmaceuticals) retains local distribution networks throughout the African continent. Home office operations managers regularly visit these locations to monitor performance and offer company assistance and support when required.

Valseon Corp. (computer accessories and supplies) sells to South and Central America and the Caribbean through local distributors. They also maintain company sales offices in Georgetown, Barbados; Rio de Janiero; Quito, Ecuador; and Panama City. Regional marketing managers from these offices regularly travel to distributor's offices to provide technical, sales, customer service, and, when necessary, financing assistance. As the vice president of marketing for Valseon often repeats, "Face-to-face meetings are the only way to supervise distributors and sales reps. If a company is not willing to spend the resources to do this it might as well forget about selling globally."

One of the most comprehensive sources of names, addresses, and specialties of foreign agents and distributors is a report generated by the Agent Distributor Service, an agency of the Department of Commerce. A report costs $90 per country or Canadian province and can be obtained within 60 days. The ADS report contains information on up to six qualified representatives with interest in your company's sales proposal. It also comments briefly on the suitability of each representative as a trade contact.

Direct Sales

Some companies use in-house sales personnel to sell direct to the customer, bypassing both trading companies and distributors. Some smaller firms try to cut costs by staffing an international sales department at the home office. This involves an enormous amount of international travel, which in itself tends to diminish the effectiveness of sales personnel. At worst, sales contacts with customers thousands of miles away make it virtually impossible for the customer to get quick answers to pricing, contractual, or technical product performance questions. It also creates a poor image in the global arena when competitors have sales personnel stationed in the host country and your company doesn't.

Direct sales can be especially effective when selling consumer goods to retail establishments, certain types of construction projects, and service contracts. Many European and Japanese large retail chains maintain buying groups throughout the world, including the United States. Selling to these chains doesn't even require traveling overseas. Sales calls are made in your own backyard.

Smaller construction contractors also employ the direct sales approach effectively. Company sales personnel, either stationed overseas or in the home office make productive sales calls, explore alternative bidding options, and negotiate sales contracts far more effectively than a representative, especially for subcontract work.

Service contracts can also best be handled by direct sales efforts. Each sale is different: it has its own time parameters, technical requirements, guarantees, financing scheme, and contract terms. Only company sales personnel are qualified to deal with all these matters. Even if a trading company or other sales agent solicits customer inquiries, company personnel must close the order and negotiate its terms. L & C Contractors of Philadelphia tried to pass this responsibility to their international consultant in the Dominican Republic and booked an order they could not fill.

Paul Horsky, an international management consultant, was hired by L & C to solicit bid opportunities through his contacts in several Caribbean government offices. When he submitted an inquiry to L & C for the erection of five small electric substations along the north coast of the Dominican Republic, his client was jubilant. So enthralled was the president of L & C with the prospect of opening up this new market, that he quickly prepared the bid package, forwarded it to Paul Horsky in Santo Domingo, and instructed the consultant to negotiate the contract. Paul tried to convince his client that this was the wrong way to close a deal, but the president insisted. Paul negotiated the best contract he could, wired his client for a performance bond, and went on to another job in Trinidad for a different client.

Six months later, Horsky received a telex from L & C stating that the company could not comply with the terms of the Dominican Republic contract at the price negotiated and were stopping work immediately before their losses became unmanageable. The telex ended by notifying Horsky his services would no longer be required.

JOINT VENTURES

The popularity of cooperative business structures has escalated in the global economy. High risks, unfamiliar business practices, language dissimilarities, and political clout all contribute to the desirability of teaming up with another company to enter a new market or increase a share of an existing market. These cooperative structures attract various labels. Cooperative alliances, cooperative ventures, partnerships, and joint ventures are a few of the more common. In addition to sharing research, production, financing, and facilities costs and obligations, joint ventures serve a very real purpose in marketing strategy.

Marketing/Distribution Channels

A manufacturer of rattan furniture may have a significant market presence in the United States, complete with an established distribution network. When entering the Caribbean market, however, he is the new kid on the block. Rather than incurring the enormous costs, risks, and time of competing from the ground up, it could be beneficial to join with an importer of chrome furniture in Puerto Rico who already has marketing and distribution networks throughout the islands.

A classic case of shared marketing know-how occurred when Glaxo, the British firm, wanted to distribute its FDA newly approved Zantac product in America. Without a marketing presence, Glaxo teamed up with Hoffman La Roche who already had a commanding marketing and distribution network throughout the United States. The result has been a rapid market gain by Zantac in a highly competitive field.

Breaking Protective Trade Barriers

In most South American, Middle East, and North and Central African countries, governments exert stringent protective barriers against foreign entrance to local markets. Strict laws prohibit foreigners from having a controlling interest in a company. Joining forces with a host country partner is the only feasible way to enter these markets. But the advantages of a joint venture go beyond pure legal compliance.

In controlled economies, political domination of pricing, distribution, customer service, and contractual arrangements make it nearly impossible for an outsider to penetrate either consumer or capital goods markets. Established local companies and favored joint ventures encourage government officials to keep new competition from entering the market. A local partner, on the other hand, who knows the ropes and has contacts in high circles, can normally penetrate these formal and informal protective barriers.

Entering a Dominated Market

In some markets, a few large corporations dominate the pricing, quality, and distribution channels to such an extent that new, smaller competitors are automatically locked out. High capital investment industries or those with significant ongoing research efforts epitomize heavy concentration in a few large companies. Telecommunications, supercomputers, automobiles and trucks, and large gas turbines are examples of dominated markets. Joining forces with a company already established in the country is about the only way to enter such a market.

PRICING

Pricing a product or service in any market is based on three factors: market demand, competition, and cost. Market demand and competition influence pricing globally the same as in domestic markets. High demand and low competition obviously yield higher prices. The reverse is also true. Promotional sales, loss leaders, volume discounts, and new product or market entrants weigh qualitatively in the pricing spectrum for any market and any product or service. Balancing these factors in the global economy is no different from recognizing their respective influence on domestic pricing.

On the other hand, the cost element is significantly different in global markets. Products exported from the United States might be produced in the same type of facility and with the same labor content as their domestic counterparts. By adding the incremental costs of getting these products to a foreign market, however, total cost of sales becomes significantly higher. The same products produced in different facilities in foreign locations exhibit different product cost structures. Using materials imported to a foreign plant from a third country, also changes the product cost structure from that in the United States. Selling, distribution, and administrative costs may be higher or lower than those in the United States, but they will certainly be different. Taxes are generally higher; insurance lower.

The intent here is not to elaborate on the textbook theory of product pricing nor is it to detail the accounting aberrations used to build product costs. The only reason to mention pricing at all, is to draw attention to those costs associated with both exporting and foreign production that may be unfamiliar when just getting started in global trade.

Export Pricing

Several incremental costs incurred when exporting a product are not present for domestic sales. Although all export sales will not incur all of the costs listed in the worksheet in Figure 16–1, most generally apply.

In order to cover all incremental costs and still yield the same profit as a domestic sale, it is not unusual to find an export price equal to twice that charged domestically. This, in and of itself, frightens many would-be exporters off the global trail. Others decide that because such a price appears to be noncompetitive with foreign companies selling into the same market, establishing a production facility within the host country is a far more prudent way to capture the market.

FIGURE 16–1
Worksheet for Estimating Incremental Export Costs

Customer:
   1. Name   _____
   2. Address   _____
   3. Cable/telex address   _____
   4. Telephone   _____
Product:
   5. Product description   _____
   6. Quantity   _____
   7. Gross and net weight of order _____
   8. Dimensions   _____
   9. Cubic measure   _____
Product cost:
  10. Manufacturing cost per unit   _____
  11. Number of units   _____
  12. Total manufacturing cost of order _____
  13. Allocated selling, general, and administrative
       costs for order   _____
  14. Allocated interest expense   _____
  15. Other allocated costs   _____
  16. Total cost of order before export _____
Export costs:
Selling and administrative:
  17. New product packaging   _____
  18. Promotional and sales literature _____
  19. Foreign trade exhibitions   _____
  20. International travel expenses   _____
  21. Credit search   _____
  22. Risk insurance   _____
  23. Financing costs   _____
  24. Commissions and retainers   _____
  25. Export license   _____
  26. Certificate of origin licenses   _____
Shipping:
  27. Export packaging   _____
  28. Freight forwarding charges   _____
  29. Export documentation fees   _____
  30. Cargo insurance   _____
  31. Labeling and packing   _____
  32. Inland freight   _____
  33. Loading and unloading charges _____
  34. Customs duties   _____
  35. Total export costs   _____
  36. Total cost of order   _____
  37. Mark-on percent   _____
  38. Estimated selling price   _____

Foreign Pricing

Developing a cost estimate for products to be produced overseas, perhaps with several third-country sources of materials and subassemblies, is a far more complex procedure; especially if the estimate is used for comparative purposes with a comparable American manufactured product. For value-added materials, components, or subassemblies, care must be exercised in adding all the costs of transport to the product cost as goods move from one finishing location to another. In the VLS Technologies case related earlier, the costs of moving chips from Japan to South Korea to Malaysia became as much a product cost as the material, labor, and overhead incurred in the basic design and production efforts. Only the costs of distributing the final product to customers are considered selling expenses.

Every manufacturing facility whether located in the United States or in a foreign land must have a product cost accumulation system, even if it is very rudimentary. To the final, accumulated product cost must be added the expenses of getting the product to market. These incremental costs obviously vary by country. The worksheet in Figure 16–2 serves as a guide to establish cost estimates for use in pricing a bid or for comparative purposes.

Standard product price sheets are seldom used outside of the United States. Even if printed and distributed to sales personnel, they are seldom followed. Prices for the same products sold to separate customers vary substantially, even without volume discounts. The basic principle in global product pricing is that everything is negotiable. Whether a construction project bid, a piece of capital equipment, computer chips, or ladies' gloves, expect to negotiate a mutually agreeable price with every customer. Also expect these prices to be different, regardless of what appears on the cost estimate worksheet. The worksheet yields only the starting point, not the final price.

THE SALES CONTRACT

A sales contract of some form must be executed between buyer and seller, whether exporting from or importing to the United States, doing the same from a facility in a foreign country, or winning a bid for a construction project. If and when a conflict between the two parties arises in the future, the sales contract forms the basis of resolution. It is vitally important that the contract be negotiated with care. Both parties must agree that they can, and will, perform within its confines.

Obviously, both buyer and seller must have a clear understanding of all the terms and clauses incorporated in the contract. Many sales contracts are written under the laws of foreign countries where the U.S. Uniform Commercial Code (UCC) does not prevail. In this case, competent legal counsel in the host country must be retained to ensure equitable clauses commensurate with local law.

Sales contracts may take a variety of forms. They may be verbal or written. When written, they may be in the form of a letter, a telex, a cable, or a formally drawn contract. These form the legal basis under which agreement has been reached to sell and buy. Frequent modifications to the original contract common in international construction projects, nearly always appear as telexes or facsimile transferred correspondence.

In addition to the name and address of both buyer and seller, minimum inclusions in an international sales contract should encompass:

- Description of goods or services, price, weight, quantity, and reference to any special customer-defined specifications.
- Shipping and delivery instructions including required documentation such as export/import licenses and permits.
- Payment terms, conditions, and currency, including which party

FIGURE 16–2
Worksheet for Estimating Incremental Export Costs from a Non-U.S. Location

Customer:
   1. Name   _____
   2. Address   _____
   3. Cable/telex address   _____
   4. Telephone   _____
Product:
   5. Product description   _____
   6. Quantity   _____
   7. Gross and net weight of order   _____
   8. Dimensions   _____
   9. Cubic measure   _____
Product cost:
  10. Final assembly cost per unit   _____
  11. Interfacility price per unit   _____
  12. Total product cost per unit   _____
  13. Number of units   _____
  14. Total manufacturing cost of order   _____
  15. Allocated selling, general, and administrative
       costs for order   _____
  16. Allocated interest expense   _____
  17. Other allocated costs   _____
  18. Total cost of order before export   _____
Export costs:
Selling and administrative:
  19. Promotional and sales literature   _____
  20. Foreign trade exhibitions   _____
  21. International travel expenses   _____
  22. Home office personnel travel expense   _____
  23. Credit search   _____
  24. Risk insurance   _____
  25. Buyer credit costs   _____
  26. Commissions and retainers   _____
  27. Export license   _____
  28. Certificate of origin licenses   _____
  29. Warranty and after-sale service   _____
  30. Value-added tax (VAT)   _____
  31. Favors, gifts, and other promotion allowances   _____
  32. Field service training   _____
  33. Customer training   _____
  34. Legal and audit   _____
  35. Special in-country taxes   _____
Shipping:
  36. Export packaging   _____
  37. Freight forwarding charges   _____
  38. Export documentation fees   _____
  39. Cargo insurance   _____
  40. Labeling and packing   _____
  41. Inland freight   _____
  42. Loading and unloading charges   _____
  43. Customs duties, export country, and import
       country   _____
  44. Total export costs   _____
  45. Total cost of order   _____
  46. Mark-on percent   _____
  47. Estimated selling price   _____

is responsible for paying customs duties, taxes, and other special fees.
- Insurance coverage for goods-in-transit and the party responsible for the respective costs.

Although more difficult and time consuming to negotiate, a sales contract that includes the following provisions will save untold hours in resolving future disputes over long distances:

- Method of packaging and marking.
- Inspections and tests by the buyer before goods are accepted.
- Seller warranties.
- Provisions for bid and performance bonds or guarantees.
- Special financing provisions.
- Provisions for patent and trademark protection.
- Remedies allowed either party in the event of default.
- Location and mediation service designated for arbitration.
- Jurisdiction under which disputes will be resolved.

No contract can be foolproof. Each sales transaction in each country is different. The above merely indicates the type of common matters to include. Specifics can only be determined between the two parties and competent legal counsel. Domestically, sales transactions occur daily without any reference to a sales contract and disputes are usually readily settled. In global trade, however, semantics often confuse the parties. Taking the time to negotiate a formal sales contract prevents a profitable shipment or project from turning into a disaster.

ASSISTANCE IN IDENTIFYING MARKETS

With instantaneous media coverage, profuse government pronouncements, and foreign trade names becoming household brands, global trade has certainly invaded the American public consciousness. Any company wishing to avail itself of global opportunities has little difficulty obtaining information about any specific global market for its products or services. Many U.S. government sources have already been revealed. Some of the other sources of specific marketing information are:

1. International Trade Shows. Trade shows of every type and size are frequently held throughout the United States and in many other regions of the world. A company just starting in global trade can probably glean enough information by attending one of two of these trade shows to determine what approach will work best with its specific personnel and financial resources.

2. Department of Commerce Seminars. These seminars are presented throughout the country in every major city and many smaller ones. Subjects include everything from how to contact reputable agents and distributors to arranging financing and identifying potential market areas.

3. Export Management Association (EMA) Seminars. These seminars are also presented in major cities across the country. The EMA is primarily interested in attracting exporting companies, however, so don't look for much help here in identifying direct investment markets.

4. Other U.S. Government Agencies. Eximbank, the Foreign Credit Insurance Association, the Departments of Agriculture and Transportation, U.S. trade representatives, Department of State country desks, and many other agencies have reports, statistics, and informational brochures by the truckload covering everything imaginable about international markets. These are available free or for a small fee. The Agency Distributor Service assists in locating qualified foreign agents and distributors. The *Foreign Trader Index* customizes lists of key foreign trade contacts, major potential customers, and sources of additional information for overseas sales.

5. Industry Trade Associations.   Many trade associations are eager to get on the global bandwagon. Seminars, brochures, trade statistics, marketing data, surveys, tax advice and a myriad of other assistance can be gleaned. The fastest way to learn if a specific trade association is active in supporting members in international trade is to ask.

6. Cities and States.   Nearly every state and major city is actively pursuing foreign trade. Commerce bureaus and international departments have been set up to assist the American producer establish contacts overseas. Los Angeles, Chicago, Miami, Houston, and New York are especially active. The same holds true for Illinois, California, Pennsylvania, New York, Massachusetts, Texas, and Hawaii among the states.

7. International Development Banks (IDBs).   The super IDBs for Asia, Latin America, Africa, and the recently formed reconstruction bank for Eastern Europe, offer assistance in identifying countries and regions where specific products and services are needed. They also arrange contacts with distributors, international consultants, and even potential customers.

8. U.S. Agency for International Development.   USAID is actively pushing the economic development of Third World nations. Any host country office of the agency is normally most willing to put an American company in touch with appropriate government officials who can identify products needed and potential customers. Call the Washington office of AID for a continually changing listing of its foreign offices and projects.

9. Journal of Commerce.   This daily paper publishes timely sales leads from overseas firms seeking to buy American products or to represent U.S. firms.

10. Commercial News USA.   This is a monthly magazine sent to all U.S. embassies and consulates, U.S. chambers of commerce, and Department of Commerce agency offices. It accepts advertising and publicity announcements from companies wishing to promote their products or services overseas.

INTELLECTUAL PROPERTY PIRACY

Firms and individuals reliant on intellectual property (IP) as the foundation of their business, such as biotechnology, computer software, music and film companies, and authors and publishers, know that the effective protection of these rights is crucial to the prosperity and even survival of the business. The U.S. patent, trademark, and copyright laws do not apply overseas, however. Therefore, other means must be used to at least try to protect IP. There are principally two ways to reduce piracy infringement:

1. Register your IP in the host country if it has applicable laws and where piracy may be a problem. This normally requires retention of local counsel to be certain of complying with local laws.
2. File your patent under the Patent Cooperation Treaty, to which 40 countries are parties. This can be difficult and expensive, however. The fees are substantial and all claims and documents must be translated into other languages.

Unfortunately, even with IP laws in effect, many countries do not enforce them. If piracy is suspected, two choices are available: retain local counsel and bring suit in the appropriate foreign court, or, try to pressure the pirates to stop. The best way to accomplish the latter is to get both local government officials and the American government on your side. This sounds like a reasonable expectation, but it frequently isn't. Without political pressure, it's doubtful whether the pirates will cease and desist.

A third possibility exists under Special Section 301 of the Omnibus Trade and Competitiveness Act of 1988. Section 301 requires the U.S. Trade Representative to annually list "priority watch list" and "watch list" countries known or suspected of IP piracy. In 1989, Carla A. Hills named 25 countries deemed to be particularly lax in their enforcement of laws to protect IP. Such identification may dissuade a U.S. company from transferring technology or otherwise trading with a listed country.

The United States also insisted during the Geneva-based Uruguay Round multilateral trade negotiations that GATT be amended to establish adequate rules protecting IP. So far this has not happened. In the meantime, IP piracy remains a very real threat to technology transfer and other global trade in susceptible products. American government assistance or information about protecting IP can be obtained from any of the following:

1. Office of the Trade Representative (202) 395–7320.
2. Patent and Trademark Office (703) 557–3065.
3. U.S. and Foreign Commercial Service (202) 377–8300.
4. Department of State Bureau of Economic and Business Affairs (202) 647–7971.

CONCLUSION

This chapter dealt with the topics to be considered when developing a marketing strategy for selling globally. Although exporting remains a favorite method for many companies experimenting with global trade, the web of value-added networking grows daily. To remain competitive, a company cannot avoid direct foreign investment as a serious consideration for its next step in global expansion. Not all topics covered in this chapter apply to all companies, but portions of each prove helpful in structuring a strategy that fits the specific objectives and product lines of any company.

CHAPTER 17

SHIPPING AND TRANSPORTATION

MAJOR TOPICS

KEY POINTS

1. Freight Forwarder. Hire a freight forwarder to coordinate preparation of shipping and collection documents. He knows what carriers to use, when they leave, what loading and unloading requirements exist, how to ship at the least cost, and what peculiar host country licenses apply. Freight forwarders exist in virtually every country.

2. Getting the Product Ready. Products must be packed properly before leaving the shipper's dock. Either unitizing or palletizing should be considered. Shipboard containerization specifications need to be determined.

3. Shipping Documents. A variety of licenses is required. The United States requires validated licenses for the export of many products. Most foreign countries have their own licensing regulations. Some require consulate validation. Special project, distribution, or service supply licenses may be necessary. Customs declarations are always required.

4. Collection Documents. To get paid, collection documents must be properly prepared. Various types of collection documents are described with the emphasis on bills of lading. Some countries require consular invoices.

5. Ocean Marine Cargo Insurance. All financing institutions and most customers require cargo insurance. Loss or damage during ocean shipping is not uncommon. *All risk* and *warehouse-to-warehouse* policies are preferable. Cost varies with coverage and destination. Limitations of cargo insurance are explained.

6. Intermodal Shipping. Integrated transport with one carrier provides the best door-to-door service. Commonly used in the Far East and Asia, intermodal shipping is just coming into its own in the United States.

7. Air Freight. Some products can be economically shipped by air. The Federal Express's acquisition of Flying Tiger opened the door to air freight, intermodal transport. Rates remain high, but delivery time is far superior to ocean shipping. Losses are substantially lower.

Joe Caraborski was assigned the task of determining how to transport his company's export products from the main manufacturing facility in Reading, Pennsylvania, and from two satellite plants in Manchester, England, and Utrecht, Holland. Joe was vice president of operations with Northeastern Furnace Accessories, Inc., (NFAI). The company made replacement parts, components, and a line of accessories for large industrial furnaces.

NFAI exported from the three locations for several years but always relied on an export management company in the United States and trading companies in Europe. These agents handled all shipping documentation and transportation of the goods. They also obtained license and permit applications, customs clearances, and other shipping documentation. The CEO of NFAI decided to improve export margins by managing these matters in-house. Since Joe was responsible for domestic shipping activity, he was nominated for the export portion as well.

The first shipment going from the Port of New York to Brazil was a disaster. Joe used his own personnel to pack and mark the containers and to arrange details with the ocean shipping company. Joe personally contracted with a trucking company in Brazil to move the goods from the port of Santos, near São Paulo, to the customer's warehouse near Brasilia.

The cartons finally arrived, three months late. Out of a total of 19 cartons, 8 were missing and 10 of those arriving were ripped open or otherwise damaged. For the next order, Joe contracted with a New York freight forwarder and purchased cargo insurance—both marine and inland. He also consulted with the EMC that NFAI had used in the past to learn what shipping documentation should be prepared and by whom. By the time export orders flowed from Manchester and Utrecht, Joe had learned his lesson well.

Transporting goods overseas follows the same principles as shipping in the United States, but the mechanics and complexities are entirely different. Packing, labeling, documentation, and insurance must be managed regardless of the port of embarkation. Each country has special regulations for moving goods. In principle, however, the following descriptions, with minor modifications, are applicable worldwide. Adhering to these principles, a person should be able to manage the shipping activity from any country with only slight variations for local regulations and practices.

There are basically four aspects of moving product overseas: packing and labeling, shipping documentation, collection documents, and cargo insurance. If the shipper is responsible for transporting the goods from the port of debarkation inland to a customer's destination, arrangements must be made with local carriers. The shipper should also monitor the shipment's progress to be certain that the transport company fulfills its obligation. Assuming that acceptable formats of invoices, bills of lading, packing lists, and so on, are already known from experience in domestic shipping, elementary document samples are omitted from the following review. For those unfamiliar with these documents, any of the export books listed in the bibliography illustrate common formats.

THE FREIGHT FORWARDER

Although an experienced export shipping staff could handle everything in-house, nearly all companies find that a freight forwarder performs the tasks cheaper and more efficiently. A freight forwarder acting as the liaison between the company, transporters, bankers, and a variety of other parties, is well worth the minimal fees charged. All freight forwarders are licensed: ocean forwarders by the Nonvessel Operating Common Carriers, air forwarders by the International Air Transportation Association. Most competent forwarders handle both ocean and air freight.

A freight forwarder acts as a shipping and transport agent. He prepares all documentation necessary for shipping goods, insuring cargo, and collecting from a customer. He also provides information for bid packages. All licensed international freight forwarders know how letters of credit work. As soon as the L/C is written, a copy of it and any special shipping instructions should go directly to the forwarder. He then advises what special packing, labeling, and licensing may be required. A listing of the services performed by a freight forwarder is voluminous. The following is merely a sampling of some of the ways he can be of assistance. A freight forwarder can:

1. Research tariff rates and determine the most economical method of transport.
2. Offer advice about current conditions in the buyer's country relative to dockage and airport facilities.
3. Arrange to obtain licenses, permits, certificates, consular invoices, legalizations, and other regulatory documents—both to satisfy U.S. laws and to comply with the laws of the country of destination.
4. Make appropriate contacts for arranging inland transport in the United States to the port of embarkation and in the destination country to the customer's location.
5. Consolidate shipments, including containerization, and transport goods to the appropriate carrier.
6. Arrange for special crating, packing, loading, and unloading equipment.
7. Receive a clean bill of lading or waybill consistent with L/C or shipping instructions.
8. Prepare export declaration, customs clearance documentation, bank documents for L/C drawdowns, and claims against airlines or ocean carriers.

FIGURE 17-1
Guidelines for Choosing a Freight Forwarder

1. Large enough to have clout with major shipping lines, but small enough to give personal service. Those that handle the major corporations are often too busy to care about small accounts.
2. Located near the United States port you plan to ship from.
3. Willing and able to prepare all license applications, declarations, collection documentation, and customs forms.
4. Maintain listings of import restrictions from foreign countries worldwide.
5. Good reputation with your international bank.
6. Offer consolidation services.
7. Willing to come to your office rather than meeting at his location.
8. Furnish references from other customers.
9. Allow you to check with these references.
10. Permit bank references to be checked.

 9. Arrange for cargo insurance.
 10. Track the shipment to its destination.
 11. Provide communications and courier service during the entire transportation period.

Such services are not only valuable but absolutely essential for those companies without a full staff of export, shipping, and transportation experts. If a company wants to remain in control of its own collections, the forwarder sends all documents to the company's office for verification before presentation to a bank. The *Pacific Shipper,* the *Journal of Commerce,* and, for the east coast, the *Shipper's Digest,* keep shippers informed of vessels leaving and arriving in various ports around the world and enable a company to track its own shipments.

The best way to locate the right freight forwarder is to ask other companies in your area or industry who have been in the export business for a while. Incompetent forwarders are easily weeded out.

Figure 17-1 offers a set of criteria to help choose the right freight forwarder.

GETTING THE PRODUCT READY

There are three conditions to prepare for when getting products ready to ship overseas:

1. Moisture, breakage, pilferage, and minimum weight.
2. Unit shipment, palletizing, containerization.
3. Exterior identification of product.

Proper packing ensures the first; the size of the product and the quantity of parcels determines the second; and the degree of product hazard stipulates the third.

PACKING

A variety of packing forms and materials are available to protect goods against moisture and breakage. Their suitability in any given situation depends on the nature of the product. Fiberboard boxes remain one of the most popular exterior containers for hard goods. They are relatively inexpensive, strong, and lightweight. Proper support by tension straps, water-resistant glue and tape, and staples, normally prevents breakage in cartons of at least a test strength of 275 pounds per square inch. Impregnated, multiwall fiberboard boxes are usually impervious to moisture — except when submerged for extended periods. Fiberboard remains one of the lightest weight materials available.

The insertion of fiberboard cartons into a nailed wooden box provides added security and strength. The box won't keep out the moisture but will protect against breakage. Weight is an important factor in overseas shipping, however, and wooden boxes add substantially to this dimension.

Wirebound boxes and crates, cleated plywood boxes, drums and kegs, either steel, fiber, or wooden, are good packing materials for heavy loads or granular, liquid, or gelatinous products. These containers all add significantly to shipping weight, however. Multiwall shipping sacks and bales are used primarily for agricultural, powdered, or granular products — especially dry chemicals. Both bales and sacks are subject to moisture damage, pilferage, and breakage by lift hooks and should be containerized.

Fragile or brittle goods must be cushioned against shock and vibration. The type of material chosen depends on size, weight, surface finish and built-in shock resistance of the goods. Any freight forwarder can advise the best form and material for a specific shipment.

Unitizing, Palletizing, Containerization

Whenever possible it's a good idea to use either unitizing, palletizing, or containerization to facilitate moving the goods and to afford stowage and cargo protection. In shipping parlance, unitizing means the assembly of one or more items into a tightly compacted load, secured together with cleating or skids for ease of handling. Palletizing refers to the assembly of one or more containers on a pallet base and securely fastened to the pallet. Most overseas shipments of hard goods are either unitized or palletized. Both systems offer several advantages:

1. Manual handling damage is eliminated. Forklifts, cranes, and other mechanical devices must be used to move the load.
2. Since the load is handled as a unit, individual packages are further protected from handling damage.
3. Theft is reduced.
4. Loading and unloading from the vessel is faster.
5. Physical inventory counts are facilitated.
6. Waterproof coverings are more easily attached.

To further protect against moisture, breakage, and pilferage use shipboard containerization. Shipboard containers are large, metal, free-standing enclosures that contain several unit loads or pallets. They can be stacked, thus saving space aboard ship. They are easily loaded and unloaded by cranes. They may reside for long periods dockside waiting for a ship or inland transport without damage to the enclosed goods.

Nearly all ocean freight vessels accumulate loads for containerization. Ideally, one exporter fills one or more containers with his own merchandise. But this isn't necessary. Partial loads can be combined, at the option of the vessel's captain, to save space and secure the loads. When more than one shipper's goods are consolidated in a container, the loading and unloading costs are shared. Freight forwarders normally arrange for shared containers.

Exterior Identification - Labeling

Usually a buyer specifies what type of labeling should be affixed to the exterior of the cartons, crates, or other shipping containers. These markings may be in pictorial form, stenciled, or marked with any other indelible ink process. Labels should be at least two inches high and appear on the top of the package and at least one side. Sacks should be marked on both sides: drums marked on both top and side. The reasons for accurate labeling are probably obvious, but it can't hurt to review the major ones. Markings and labels identify the following:

1. Shipper, consignee, reference number, and contract or purchase order number.
2. Country of origin.
3. Weight in both pounds and kilograms.
4. The number of packages, if there are more than one in the shipment.
5. Handling instructions: "fragile," "this side up", "store in heated place", and so on.
6. Final destination and the port of entry (Guatemala City via Livingston).
7. Whether the package contains hazardous material.

All labels and markings should be in both English and the language of the country of destination. It's extremely important to label shipments according to the laws of the host country. Freight forwarders keep track of these changing laws for every port in the world.

SHIPPING DOCUMENTS

In international trade, shipping documents serve a far broader purpose than merely authorizing shipment and providing a record of the transaction. All kinds of bad conditions occur when a seller doesn't pay close enough attention to shipping documents. Without proper documentation a seller may not get paid on time, or at all. The shipment may not clear customs at the destination port. This results in charges, fines, and penalties. The goods may be returned to the exporter, thereby incurring additional freight charges and customs fees. In some ports, goods without proper documentation will certainly be seized by customs officials.

There are three broad types of shipping documents: general export licenses, validated licenses, and export declarations. Some licensing activities are controlled by the federal Bureau of Export Administration (BXA) in close association with the Departments of Defense and State.

Others are controlled by a 16 nation committee — the Coordinating Committee for Multilateral Export Controls (COCOM) — that coordinates restrictions on shipments to communist nations. Current members of CO-COM are Belgium, Denmark, Germany, France, Greece, Italy, the Netherlands, Japan, the United States, the United Kingdom, Luxembourg, Norway, Portugal, Spain, and Canada.

The primary purpose in granting export permission through the licensing process is to enforce export trade barriers. Other than Eastern Europe, the Soviet Union, and other remaining communist countries, the United States maintains the most restrictive and rigid barriers to export trade. This seems contradictory to the government's publicly avowed attempts to reduce the trade deficit. Certainly, there are few faster ways of doing this than to increase American exports. Yet, influential lobbying from corporate, congressional, and activist power groups continue to insist on the imposition of rigid, often unreasonable, export restrictions through the licensing process.

General License

The general license acts as a blanket permit to allow exports of different types of goods to a variety of countries. It is obtained from the BXA. Any freight forwarder can file the application for you. It's a good idea to do it before finalizing a sales contract however. That way a shipper can be certain the goods to be shipped are not defined as strategic commodities. It is also helpful to know that the buyer's country is not included in a *sensitive* area. A general license takes about two weeks to wind its way through the approval cycle. Information about its status can be obtained from the Office of Export Licensing (202) 377-4811 or (714) 660-0144.

Validated License

A validated license gives a company permission to sell specific goods to specific countries. It must be obtained for the export of strategic goods that the government wants to control, for any reason. It also permits export to a country on the government's restrictive list. This license requires a lengthy and costly application and review process. The Departments of Defense and State get in the approval loop. It's very possible COCOM will want to approve the transaction also.

If an application goes through the entire approval process, 120 days seems to be the norm. Partial approval steps require correspondingly less time. Rapid changes in world political institutions and U.S. trade policies cause both the strategic product list and restrictive country classifications to vacillate continually. When you are ready to make an application, call the Export Licensing office for current definitions.

Special Licenses

There are also a few special licenses. A project license covers the export of all goods requiring validated licenses for certain large-scale operations, such as construction or development projects. One-year distribution licenses are granted for exports to consignees in countries sporting good relations with the United States. A service supply license is required to provide service on equipment exported from the United States or produced abroad with parts imported from the United States.

Foreign Export Licensing

Each country has its own export trade barriers and definitions of strategic goods and restricted countries vary accordingly. However, few developed nations are as paranoid as the U.S. government about what can and can't be done. Traditional trading nations such as Great Britain and Japan realize that the well-being of the country depends on an active domestic export program. Exporting from these nations, or even from developing nations, usually involves substantially less paperwork than exporting from the United States. Caribbean nations, falling under the Caribbean Basin Initiative program, have relatively open export policies, especially for shipments to the United States.

Wherever your export facility may be located, however, some type of licensing will probably be required. Contact the local trade or commerce office for details.

Shipper's Export Declaration

A shipper's export declaration must be completed for all shipments valued in excess of $1,000 and for which a validated license is required. An export declaration identifies the license under which the export is being shipped. This verifies that the shipment complies with authorization regulations. The declaration also shows appropriate U.S. government product codes, quantities shipped, value of the shipment, and destination. The Census Department requires this data for statistical reports published monthly.

COLLECTION DOCUMENTS

Collection documents must be submitted to the importer, the importer's bank, or the shipper's bank before payment can be made. These documents vary from country to country, from importer to importer, and from bank to bank. A specific transaction will probably never require all of the following documents. For any company engaging in global trade, however, a knowledge of at least the general types of collection documents should be helpful.

1. *Commercial invoice.* As with domestic sales, a commercial invoice follows every export shipment. Some countries require special certification incorporated in the invoice, often in the language of the host country. The Department of Commerce keeps a list of requirements from each country.
2. *Consular invoice.* In addition to a commercial invoice, most Latin-American countries, and other developing nations, require a consular invoice prepared on forms supplied by their respective

consulates. These invoices are prepared in the language of the host country. They are visaed by the resident consul, certifying the authenticity and correctness of the documents.

3. *Bill of lading.* Of the two types of bills of lading — "straight" or nonnegotiable, and "shipper's order" or negotiable — the latter is used for sight draft or L/C shipments. According to the rules of international trade as specified in the *Guide to Incoterms,* 1980 edition, issued by the International Chamber of Commerce, a bill of lading acceptable for credit purposes must be marked "clean on board". This means that the carrier has not taken any exception to the condition of the cargo or packing, and that the goods have actually been loaded aboard the carrying vessel. A bill of lading is the most important document accompanying a foreign shipment. It serves three functions:

   a. It is a contract between the carrier and the shipper.

   b. It verifies the receipt of goods.

   c. It identifies the right of title to the goods.

   A signed copy of a negotiable bill of lading is sufficient evidence of ownership to take possession of the goods.

4. *Packing list* A packing list is even more important overseas than for domestic shipments. Very often customs officials at both the port of embarkation and the port of debarkation use the packing list to verify the goods in the shipment. The list should include a complete description of the goods being shipped.

5. *Certificate of origin.* Some countries require a separate certificate stating the origin of the goods. This certificate is normally countersigned by a chamber of commerce member and usually visaed by the country's resident consul at the port of embarkation.

6. *Inspection certificate.* Many buyers request an affidavit, called an *inspection certificate*, from the shipper or an independent agent, certifying to the quality, quantity, and conformity of the goods as specified in the original order.

7. *Dock receipts, warehouse receipts, etc.* If a shipper's responsibility is limited to moving the goods to a warehouse or dock at the port of embarkation, a buyer often requests receipts from the storage company that the goods have been received and await further disposition.

8. *Certificate of manufacture.* The manufacturing cycle for goods can be quite long. If the buyer intends to pay for the goods before shipment with a down payment or an advance payment, a certificate of manufacture is prepared by the manufacturer. It states that the goods have been completed in accordance with the order and have been set aside awaiting orders for shipment. As soon as payment and shipping orders are received, the goods ship.

9. *Insurance certificate.* In cases where the seller provides cargo insurance, an insurance certificate must be furnished, indicating the type and amount of coverage.

For a small charge, a freight forwarder prepares all documents required by the order. Even large exporters look to the forwarder to take care of all this paperwork. Smaller exporters should do the same. Although the form of these documents varies between countries, the content remains approximately constant. Foreign freight forwarders know a lot more about what paperwork is required and how to fill in the various forms than an American producer. It only makes good sense to let them set the pace when exporting from a foreign country.

OCEAN MARINE CARGO INSURANCE

Coordinating financing through banks, following the proper shipping procedures, and reducing the amount of risk in a transaction are all essential ingredients of global trade. Regardless of which country a company may ship from, all three elements must be managed efficiently to remain competitive. The shipping procedures enumerated in this chapter, and the rules of financing examined in Chapters 12 through 15, should provide fundamental knowledge in these two activities. The reduction of credit and political risk through the Foreign Credit Insurance Association (FCIA) and corresponding foreign agencies is reviewed in the next chapter. That leaves the matter of insuring the safe delivery of goods to be reviewed here.

Although an increasing amount of merchandise is shipped overseas by air, the high cost, weight, and size restrictions imposed by air carriers, makes ocean shipping the predominant mode of transport for most products. Ocean shipments are exposed to several unique hazards. Damage or loss of cargo is a real possibility from such causes as fire, stranding, moisture, collision, rolling of the ship, and theft.

Because of the dangerous nature of ocean shipping, the liability of carriers is severely limited by the Carriage of Goods by Sea Act of 1936. The Act limits carrier liability to $500 per package. Therefore, practically all ocean shipments are independently insured against damage or loss.

All financing agencies, (banks, joint ventures, private financing sources, or government agencies) require export shipments to be fully insured. Either the importer or the exporter may arrange for marine cargo insurance, depending on terms in the sales contract.

Types of Policies

Marine cargo insurance comes in two types: specific or special policies written for each individual shipment, and open policies covering all shipments by the insured as long as the policy is in effect. The first is used mainly by infrequent exporters; the latter by everyone else. With an open policy, the shipper must inform the underwriter of each shipment made, including all the particulars. Premiums are billed each month depending on the number of shipments reported. An insurance certificate issued by the underwriter evidences effective coverage for a specific shipment.

It is difficult to get an open policy directly from an underwriter until a company has an established record of continuous and fairly substantial shipments. Therefore, most smaller companies use an insurance broker. A broker knows what underwriters currently handle the size of shipment to the specified export location. The underwriter, not the shipper, pays the broker's fees.

Cost

The cost of marine cargo insurance varies all over the lot. A few of the determinants are the type of coverage desired, shipping routes, types of conveyances, nature of goods shipped, and the duration of the voyage. The best type of coverage for most smaller exporters is the all risk policy. This covers loss or damage to cargo for any reason. It's also a good idea to be sure the insurance covers losses warehouse to warehouse. This type of coverage begins when the goods leave the company's shipping dock, and remains in effect until the goods arrive at the customer's receiving dock. It covers both marine and inland transport.

Shipments made by aircraft and connecting conveyances are also included. Generally, premiums for air freight coverage alone are substantially less than charges for ocean shipments because the risks of loss are lower, the time duration is shorter, and fewer losses from pilferage are realized.

Limitations

All risk policies generally exclude war risks, but do include losses due to strikes, riots, and civil commotion. The exception, of course, would be for those countries or parts of the world where the chances of such losses occurring are high. Then the corresponding premium becomes exorbitant. Additional limitations to cargo insurance include:

1. Losses due to the inherent nature of the goods being shipped. For example, losses incurred because the goods deteriorated on the journey (perishable goods), improper packaging, or normal wear and tear.
2. Loss of market due to delays en route.
3. If the shipment itself is illegal and the shipper fails to provide this information to the underwriter. By definition, a shipment is legal if it complies with the laws of the export country and any international agreements in effect at time of shipment.

One advantage to the beginning global trader in using an export management company is that an EMC can handle the complete coordination of shipping a company's products. If the shipper wishes, an EMC arranges for a freight forwarder to manage the preparation of all licenses and shipping documentation, all collection documentation, and will itself arrange for appropriate cargo insurance. Of course, by engaging an EMC, a company loses control over the entire shipping transaction. It may also end up paying more for freight forwarding and insurance services than necessary.

Cost, inconvenience, and complexities notwithstanding, a company entering the unfamiliar world of global trade would be "penny wise and

FIGURE 17–2
Guidelines for Choosing a Cargo Insurance Carrier

The marine insurance underwriter should:
 1. Have an office in close proximity to a shipper's location.
 2. Be willing to meet in your office.
 3. Offer a comprehensive package of marine, air, and land cargo insurance, including all risk.
 4. Encourage the all risk option.
 5. Not push for third-party joint beneficiary.
 6. Offer competitive rate comparisons.
 7. Provide a claim procedure you can understand.
 8. Have representatives and adjusters stationed throughout the world.
 9. Provide financial statements and bank references.
10. Encourage reference checking with other customers.

pound foolish" to ignore, or underestimate the importance of door-to-door cargo insurance.

A small international contractor client was installing a replacement turbine for a power station in the hills of Guatemala. I warned him to be sure to take out an all risk insurance policy covering door-to-door transport. Trying to cut a few corners, my client decided to insure only the ocean transport part of the voyage. The equipment reached Puerto Barrio all right. it was then unloaded onto several trucks for the long overland haul to northwestern Guatemala. When the trucks finally arrived at the job site two weeks later and the equipment was off-loaded, substantial damage had occurred to several pieces.

A claim was first filed with the ocean carrier. The carrier turned it down flat claiming the damage occurred during inland transport. Efforts to obtain reimbursements from the Guatemalan trucking company were laughable. They claimed the damage occurred on-board ship. In the end, no amounts were recovered and my client had to stand the cost of replacing the damaged equipment—for $162,000!

There are many reputable marine insurance companies to choose from. CIGNA, for example, offers as complete a package as most companies. There are many others, however. Your freight forwarder can make helpful recommendations, an insurance broker can find one, or you can select one yourself. Regardless of who does the selection, the guidelines in Figure 17–2 can be of assistance in getting a qualified carrier.

INTERMODAL SHIPPING

One of the most interesting developments in the international freight handling business is the concept of intermodal shipping. Although not yet in vogue in this country, the 1990s promise rapid innovations in contracting with one carrier to be responsible for moving merchandise door to door.

Currently used extensively in the Far East and Asia, intermodal shipping is gradually coming to America. Large international carriers such as American President Companies and CSX Corp. are actively marketing this concept to American exporters and importers. From a shipper's perspective, door-to-door transport solves a huge problem in determining where the loss occurred when filing an insurance claim, as my contractor client learned in Guatemala. An intermodal carrier assumes responsibility for the cargo regardless of what actual carrier does the transporting.

Unfortunately, such an integrated transportation concept is undergoing a difficult sales acceptance in the United States. The obstruction arises partly because of the structured transportation departments within large shipping organizations. The lack of cooperation between American ocean, rail, air, and truck carriers also contributes. Nevertheless, the favorable economics of integrated transportation, including a shortened shipping time, single insurance coverage, and simplified rate tariff charges, makes the concept viable.

Several organizations are pushing forward trying to sell the idea. At the same time they are attempting to encourage carriers to restructure internally to handle intermodal shipping. The Intermodal Marketing Association, the National Railroad Intermodal Association, and the Intermodal Transportation Association are all working diligently to find the right answers.

Third parties who don't own any transport assets are also entering the intermodal fray. Bay State Shippers, Inc., for example, has no carrier assets. As a transport packager, Bay State puts together the best freight package available for door-to-door shipments. They utilize ocean shipping, air freight, rail, and truck lines in any combination that gives their customers the best service and lowest cost. In reference to these third-party freight packagers Leo Donovan, of Booz, Allen & Hamilton, Inc., has been quoted by *World Trade*, as saying that "Owning assets will not be the way of the 1990s."

Although not yet popular in the United States, intermodal transport companies are accepted overseas. Any American company exporting from a foreign country, especially from the Far East and Asia, should seriously consider sourcing either a broker-packager such as Bay State, or an intermodal steamship line to carry their products to foreign markets.

AIR FREIGHT

Although ocean shipping remains the predominant method for moving large cargo, it has some definite drawbacks. High cargo insurance and risk of damaged goods are two of the worst. The length of time it takes to move merchandise across the high seas often means disgruntled customers or a changed market by the time the merchandise arrives at its destination. Multiple handling at the loading and unloading stages and lengthy dock storage increase the likelihood of damage or pilferage. For smaller exporters, it may not be possible to fill an entire shipboard container. Sharing with another shipper can mix up the merchandise and delay receipt at the buyer's destination. To overcome these hazards, many companies increasingly turn to air freight.

As more developing countries improve airport facilities and encourage multiple airline service, the old problem of finding a carrier willing to carry to a remote location has all but vanished. Mergers and combinations of worldwide delivery services further enchance air freight as a viable alternative. The recent purchase of Flying Tigers by Federal Express is seen by some as the most significant development in the industry in years.

Air carriers such as Federal Express are encouraging shippers to consider intermodal shipping. With the vast worldwide stable of inland transport contacts acquired with Flying Tigers, the company offers door-to-door service to most areas of the globe. Some analysts believe that air cargo companies offering intermodal service could heat up the entire industry by jeopardizing the role of freight forwarders. It's entirely possible that Federal Express has the potential to shape the international shipping market as it did the domestic.

Even with the rapid, reliable service offered by many air freight carriers, this mode of transport continues to be applicable to a limited number of shippers. Shipping containers must be small enough to fit into a 747 plane — the largest commercial air carrier in use today. The goods must be relatively insensitive to low pressures and wide variations in temperature. The value of the products must be high enough to justify the significantly greater freight cost. Because of a lack of capacity, air freight continues to be a seller's market. This causes continually escalating rates.

Regardless of the drawbacks, however, for certain types of goods, air freight can't be beaten, especially when time of delivery is crucial. For an example of how popular air freight has become, one need only look at the shipping statistics from the three New York airports in 1988. During that year, over 1 million tons were shipped internationally, an increase of nearly 11 percent over the previous year.

Most reliable freight forwarders can handle air freight as well as ocean shipments. The same types of shipping and collection documentation is required. The smaller company would be well advised to use a forwarder regardless of the mode of transport chosen. In choosing an air carrier, the same reliability looked for in ocean lines should be applied. A real plus for using air freight from different countries of embarkation is that nearly every country has its own airline, and most of them carry freight — at least for smaller parcels.

CHAPTER 18

GETTING PAID

MAJOR TOPICS

KEY POINTS

1. **Terms of Payment.** An analysis covers the advantages, risks and availability of advance payments, progress payments, and sales on open account. Letters of credit and documentary drafts remain the principal payment methods in most global transactions. Consignment sales could be useful in certain circumstances.

2. **Creditworthiness.** Accounting and business practices at variance with American custom make analyzing the financial viability of foreign customers extremely difficult. Credit references from the U.S. government, American credit bureaus, and foreign credit bureaus are frequently used. Credit reports are required by Eximbank and Foreign Credit Insurance Association (FCIA) for financial assistance. Banks and suppliers often produce better credit references than credit bureaus.

3. **Credit Insurance.** The FCIA offers credit insurance to American exporters covering commercial or political risk, or both. A private insurer, AIG, also sells commercial risk coverage. Neither FCIA nor AIG cover risks of foreign direct investment. ECGD in England, COFACE in France, and Hermes in West Germany offer variations of commercial and political risk coverage. ECGD has the broadest coverage. COFACE even insures risks of not realizing sales in new marketing ventures.

Since 1980, RhoGee Corporation, a closely held manufacturer of replacement parts for several major brands of farm implements and equipment, exported to the Caribbean, West Africa, and Mexico. Some export sales went direct to sovereign customers; others went to private distributors. Even a few American-German joint ventures were customers. For five years, RhoGee purchased FCIA insurance to cover potential commercial losses but never had occasion to file a claim.

In 1986 the company opened a new machining and assembly plant in Egypt with a British firm as a 50 percent partner. RhoGee Egypt took over the West African customers and opened new markets in Saudi Arabia and Kenya. Rho-Gee's British partner encouraged the managing director of RhoGee Egypt to apply for credit insurance from the Exports Credit Guarantee Department (ECGD), the export credit insurance arm of the British government. Since many of the semifinished parts flowed through the British partner's plant west of London, the company would qualify for ECGD coverage. But the managing director of the Egyptian company procrastinated.

Eighteen months later a private customer in Kenya went out of business. The company owed RhoGee Egypt 1.2 million Egyptian pounds, equivalent to about $1.8 million at the current exchange rate. Two days after the CEO of the American parent company heard of the fiasco, he fired the RhoGee Egypt managing director and agreed with his British partner to begin to utilize ECGD coverage immediately.

Collecting receivables from a customer in another country can be one of the biggest nightmares of global trade. Threats of court action are ludicrous. In which court will you sue? Reclaiming goods is next to impossible. National protection against foreign expropriation prohibits anyone from moving goods out of a country without an export license. And how can you reclaim grain that is already turned into flour, or a structure that has already been completed? Refusing to do further business with a customer only brings chuckles in the highly competitive global marketplace. And what if the host country government expropriates the goods? The answers lie within the normal preparatory credit checks and procedures typically employed for domestic business and supplemented by credit insurance.

TERMS OF PAYMENT

Terms of payment for goods or services sold domestically typically involve either one or a combination of:

- Cash in advance for the entire purchase.
- A down payment with the balance on open account.
- Progress payments as each stage of the project is completed.
- Open account trade credit.

Terms for international sales are structured similarly, but with little or no recourse to the buyer in the event of default. Therefore, basic safeguards must be guilt in. Ideally, instruments are executed to transfer the responsibility for collecting the credit portion of the sale from the seller to an agency of the buyer. Such an agency may be a clearing or merchant bank, a central bank, a foreign government agency, a U.S. government agency, or other intermediary. Usually, however, a seller and a buyer's intermediary share the collection responsibility. Five methods constitute the most widely used terms of payment:

1. Advance payments.
2. Progress payments.
3. Open account.
4. Letters of credit.
5. Documentary drafts.
6. Consignment.

Advance Payments

Advance payment in one form or another is normally required for special orders of products manufactured to a customer's specifications. For long lead-time products or for orders requiring costly or special materials, the customer might be expected to pay for the entire order before it enters the production cycle. If a full advance payment cannot be negotiated, a company should at least get a substantial down payment. Full advance payments are very unusual in global trade. However down payments are customary for special orders or large projects from either a private or sovereign customer.

Progress Payments

Progress payments are customary for construction projects lasting several months, or years. Calculations of payment milestones normally reflect the percentage of completion of the project in the same manner as domestic construction projects. If the customer is a private company, escrow amounts of 10 or 15 percent of the contract value might be required, subject to completion and acceptance of the project. More often, and especially with a sovereign customer, escrows cannot be negotiated.

Open Account

Open account is exactly what the term implies: a customer has 30 days, 60 days, or some other time period after receiving the goods to make payment. Obviously, such terms imply a high level of confidence in the ability and willingness of the buyer to pay. Open account sales are seldom used in international trade except between very large corporate sellers and buyers. Several developing nations forbid open account terms because their balance of payments cannot be controlled with a free flow of currency in and out of the country.

Occasionally sales are made to sovereign powers on open accounts. Grain sales to the Soviet Union are a good example. But as banks learned in Latin America and grain merchants learned when selling to the Soviets, just because the customer is a foreign government doesn't mean that payment will be made on time. Regardless of the identity of the customer, a smaller company cannot afford to finance a whole nation. Selling on open account is dangerous, and seldom worth the risk of not getting paid on time, or at all.

Letters of Credit

Letters of credit (L/Cs) are the customary terms of sale in developing nations. They are also very popular throughout the world, especially when selling to a customer of questionable pay practices or one new to the seller. Chapter 14 examined various forms of L/Cs and the advantages and risks of each. Since an L/C is issued by a buyer's bank, presumably the buyer must be considered creditworthy in his own country. This certainly eases the burden when negotiating sale conditions not covered by the L/C.

Terms and conditions of sale included in an L/C vary enormously. Normally, however, an L/C contains at least the following:

- Purchase price.
- Quantity to be shipped.
- Shipping date.
- Complete or partial shipments.
- Cargo insurance.
- Documentation required for drawdown.
- Conditions precedent to drawdown.

The beneficiary of the L/C must also be included, although there may be more than one. In that case, the division of L/C drawdowns between beneficiaries must be stipulated. All L/Cs have expiration dates. The seller must be sure that the date stipulated allows enough time to make the shipment.

Prudent sellers always insist that the L/C be irrevocable, confirmed through a U.S. bank, and payable by the seller's bank. Confirmation is extremely important. A confirmed L/C means that the U.S. bank making the confirmation promises to pay the amount of the L/C when the seller meets the stipulated conditions.

Documentary Drafts

Documentary drafts, or bills of exchange as they are known in some quarters, have taken the place of L/Cs in many regions where competition forces a more flexible credit instrument. Documentary drafts are either payable on delivery (*sight drafts*) or payable in 60 days, 90 days, or some other time frame (*acceptance drafts*). These are the most common forms, although *time drafts* and *date drafts* are also used on occasion. Under a time draft the buyer takes possession of the goods and the seller draws his payment at a later date. A date draft allows the seller to retain title to the goods until a specified date when drawdown occurs. The problem with both time and date drafts is that the buyer may become insolvent before payment comes due.

A sight draft, as the name implies, is payable when the seller presents the specified documentation to the proper authority. It usually works in the following manner. The seller ships his goods and then takes his own draft and the shipping documents to his bank. This bank then forwards the documents to the buyer's bank, which notifies the buyer when they arrive. The buyer then must institute payment, either on his own or through credit with his bank, before he can obtain the shipping documents and hence his goods.

The same procedure is followed with an acceptance draft except that the buyer takes possession of the shipping documents and the goods, while delaying payment to a future agreed-upon date. Before the buyer's bank releases the documents, however, the buyer must make arrangements to have the bank make the payment against the draft when the date comes due.

When using documentary drafts it is important to negotiate payment either in U.S. dollars or another hard currency. Zambian kwachas won't do much good when trying to pay American employees or suppliers!

Consignment

Consignment sales, in which the seller doesn't get paid until the buyer resells the goods, are not common in international trade. On occasion, when a seller wants to test a market with new products or in a new country, an arrangement might be made with an international distributor to take the goods on consignment. In this case, L/Cs are the preferable form of payment with drawdown provisions tied to the resale of the products.

CREDITWORTHINESS

Up-to-date, accurate credit information can be even more important in doing business in global markets than domestically. Sovereign and private customers, sales and distribution representatives, even banks, should be checked out thoroughly before agreeing to any business transaction. Just because the customer is a government agency doesn't mean an obligation will be paid; as pointed out earlier regarding Latin-American debt and Soviet agricultural purchases. Global marketing representatives that are not creditworthy at best might engage in fraudulent transactions in the name of the company. At worst, they could actually steal company property, merchandise, or money.

Without adequate credit, even when using a letter of credit a customer could be forced to delay confirmation of the instrument until it is too late to open the L/C. Banks, considered by the uninitiated to be the safest custodian of drafts and deposits, fail in other countries as well as in the United States. When a bank is owned or controlled by a government and fails, the depositor seldom has any recourse.

Without question, the creditworthiness of any foreign individual or company with whom a company plans a joint venture should be verified completely. Too many times, even when forming a domestic joint venture, an unscrupulous partner, or one not financially viable, has not only destroyed the partnership but caused irreparable damage to the other partner. At least domestically, if financial problems arise between two partners that cannot be resolved amicably, the court system stands ready to adjudicate. With a foreign partner, no such "court of last resort" exists, as Novation Curling Company found out when it ran into trouble with its Indonesian partner.

Novation formed a joint venture with a private Indonesian company to assemble and distribute proprietary hair curling appliances in Southeast Asia. The controller of Novation did not bother to check the credit references of the partner, Mertant Asia, S.A., principally because he didn't know how to do it. The joint venture ran smoothly for the first year. Mertant management ran the Jakarta plant. Novation furnished subassemblies from the United States.

During the second year, the president of Novation began to question why Mertant management continued to request increasing amounts of operating cash from Novation. The president hired an international consultant and assigned him the task of ferreting out what was happening in Jakarta. The report stunned the CEO and led to the firing of his controller.

While digging into the financial background of Mertant, the consultant learned that other investments the company made in two Chinese trading companies turned sour prior to the Novation partnership. Mertant management was siphoning off cash from the joint venture to pacify a nefarious creditor of one of the Chinese companies. He also learned that the unreliable financial reputation of Mertant was well known in Indonesian and Chinese circles. A rudimentary credit check in the beginning could have prevented Novation from entering the venture. As it turned out, Novation lost nearly $400,000. A court in Jakarta refused to consider Novation's suit because of close family ties between court officials and Mertant.

Evidence of a buyer's creditworthiness is also a prerequisite to utilizing buyer credit financing backed by the U.S. government. Eximbank always insists that credit references be provided before entering into either a guarantee or direct loan transaction. The FCIA also demands credit data before granting insurance coverage.

Financial Statements

Logically, the first step in assessing the creditworthiness of a buyer is to analyze its financial statements. Domestic credit managers always insist on financial statements from a new customer when the sales transaction involves a sizable amount. However, obtaining and analyzing financial statements from overseas buyers is not a straightforward process.

Accounting procedures and compliance reporting, well established in the United States, vary with each country. A financial statement for a company in England, France, or Japan looks entirely different from one prepared by American accountants. Middle Eastern nations rarely require any type of financial reporting other than an annual tax return. Few companies bother with financial statements. Caribbean, Central American, and many South American companies operate large portions of their businesses on the cash basis. Many do not keep a set of accounting records. In Saudi Arabia, companies are permitted to write off most of the fixed assets they purchase rather than record them on a balance sheet as depreciable assets.

It's always a good idea to try to get a buyer's financial statements, but don't be surprised if they aren't available. Even if they are available, they probably won't provide much of a measure of a company's financial position. Obviously, selling to a sovereign customer precludes any financial statements.

Business Practices

Vast variances in business practices between the world's cultures create serious problems for a company trying to determine financial viability of a foreign customer. Doing business on a cash basis has already been mentioned. Variations in business contracts also stymie many American firms. The Dutch, for example, as well as the Germans, thrive on detailed, lengthy, fully documented contracts for nearly every major transaction. The Japanese like to write their own contracts with phrases and meanings obscure to Westerners. In the Middle East, written contracts are practically nonexistent. There, a handshake seals a deal. Breaking a contract sealed with a verbal commitment often brings more severe consequences than any court in the United States could mete out.

Asian and Southeast Asian nations transact business the Chinese way. In these countries, verbal contracts are also the norm. Written documents are rarely used, except to pacify an American company. Business negotiators rely strongly on family connections and support. When a verbal contract is broken or modified, private compromises are reached. Once two parties verbally agree that a debt should be written off, custom dictates that the two parties continue doing business as usual.

The mixing of personal and business assets in smaller, family-dominated businesses, also makes financial statements meaningless as a measure of a company's pecuniary standing. A company's creditworthiness is evaluated not on financial statements but on personal references, connections, and on widely acknowledged reputations in the region.

Because of variant accounting and reporting rules and dissimilar business practices, the best way to verify creditworthiness of a foreign buyer is through credit agency reports augmented by several bank and supplier references.

Credit Reports

Anyone who has relied exclusively on Dun & Bradstreet credit reports to assess the financial viability of closely held domestic customers should be well aware of the fallacy in this approach. Nearly all of the information appearing on D&B reports is provided to the credit agency directly by the company, and often in cursory form. The agency relies on phone contacts with company personnel to obtain verbal descriptions of the current and projected outlook for the business, data about officers and directors of the company, and historical financial performance.

Privately held companies are asked to transmit financial statements to the agency but many do not comply. In fact, many refuse to even speak with D&B representatives. Statements that are submitted are often unaudited and prepared internally by company personnel. Names and addresses of supplier references are furnished by company personnel who of course use only those with whom a company has good relations. Credit reports from D

& B and other credit agencies may serve some purpose for larger, publicly traded companies, although even here their validity is questionable. For closely held firms, such reports remain practically worthless.

Even though credit reports on foreign buyers lack the same accuracy as those issued domestically, FCIA, Eximbank, U.S. banks, and others demand that they be furnished. One really doesn't have much choice. From a practical perspective, there are two far better sources, however: references from other American companies that have done business with the customer and bank references.

Three primary sources furnish credit reports on foreign customers:

- U.S. government agencies.
- U.S. credit agencies.
- Foreign credit agencies.

Credit reports from any of these sources fulfill FCIA and Eximbank requirements.

U.S. Government Credit Sources

Simply by filling out a request form and paying a small fee, a company can get a World Traders Data Report (WTDR) on foreign buyers that other American companies have done business with, or for whom credit information has been requested. The Department of Commerce's newly installed computer data base, Commercial Information Management System (explained in Chapter 8), can easily retrieve a WTDR report for any company in the data base. A company may request a report in either hard copy or by telex.

American commercial attachés stationed around the globe prepare WTDR reports in response to requests for information on a given company in a specific country. If the company you are interested in is not already in the CIMS data base, you can request the preparation of a new report directly from the Department of Commerce. These reports do not contain financial information. However, they do include information about the company's business activities, its business reputation, numbers of employees, ownership, products, and general operations. These reports also express the attachés' opinion as to the company's general creditworthiness and its reliability as a trade contact. No specific trade or credit references are included.

Eximbank and the FCIA also furnish credit data. Both agencies maintain computer-based listings of the credit records of foreign companies they have done business with, or whose credit they have checked on request from other American companies. Credit information from Eximbank can be quickly obtained by calling the Eximbank Credit Information Service at (202) 566-4690. The FCIA office is reached in New York at (212) 306-5077.

American Credit Agencies

Unquestionably the largest and best-known American credit and collection agency, Dun & Bradstreet, also provides credit reports on foreign companies through its international division. To utilize this service a company must subscribe to an expensive annual contract for a minimum number of reports. D&B's response time is fairly quick and a report comes in hard copy or by computer. Many firms subscribing to this service complain that the information rendered, especially on smaller foreign firms, is at best sketchy, and at worst totally worthless. Recognizing D&B's process for gathering credit data in the United States, as described earlier, the complaints of international ineffectiveness are not surprising.

A few of the lesser known American credit and collection agencies maintain credit data about specific companies overseas, mostly larger ones. None offer a comprehensive data base of companies or an efficient service for special account investigations.

The FCIB-NACM Corporation is a trade association for financial and credit managers. Although not a credit bureau, it provides assistance in obtaining credit information on foreign companies. It can be contacted at 520 Eighth Avenue, New York, NY 10018. FCIB-NACM retains a credit-reporting service compiled by independent correspondents worldwide. The organization charges an annual membership fee and a nominal fee for each credit report requested. In addition, regular meetings enable members to discuss their experiences with customers and exchange credit information.

Foreign Credit Agencies

Foreign credit reporting firms do a better job than D&B, and they always seem to be less expensive. They are more familiar with local companies, respond quicker to individual requests, and most produce credit reports far more comprehensive than D&B's. Inaccuracies persist, however. Appendix F lists several of the more reputable firms. The FCIA publication *Guide to Agencies Providing Foreign Credit Information* provides as complete a listing as available anywhere.

Two British credit agencies can be very helpful: Amalgamated Trades Protection, Ltd. (A.T.P. International) Sutherland House, 70/78 Edgware Road, Staples Corner, London NW9 7BT, and Graydon America, Inc., a subsidiary of the Graydon firm formed through the merger of three European bureaus. Graydon can be contacted at 71 West 23rd Street, Suite 1629, New York, NY 10010. Graydon does an especially good job on individualized credit searches of European firms. Its reports are generally far superior to D&B's. Both of these firms perform credit evaluations of individual companies without requiring subscription to an expensive annual contract.

Although all credit bureaus suffer the same malady (i.e., inaccurate and incomplete information about closely held companies), the following seem to do a fairly good job in their respective jurisdictions:

1. *Southeast Asia, the Pacific Basin, and China.* Asia Mercantile Agency (H.K.) Ltd., 1301-3 Chiao Shang Bldg., 92-104 Queen's Road, Central, Hong Kong.
2. *Middle East.* Argus Information Services, 15 Archbishop Makarios Ave., Nicosia, Cyprus.

3. *Australia, New Zealand, and the South Pacific.* Australian Mercantile Bureaux & Agency Ltd.-Amba, 363 Kingsway, 1st Floor, P.O. Box 291, Caringbah N.S.W. 2229, Australia.
4. *Japan.* Credit Exchange Agency, Ltd. (Shingo Kokansho Co., Ltd.), 22-1 Chome, Azuchi-Machi, Higashi-Ku, Osaka, Japan.

Credit bureaus in Caribbean, Central, and South American countries tend to be small and to concentrate only on one or two countries. The listing in Appendix F gives the names and address of those acceptable to the FCIA.

Banks

All major international banks retain their own credit departments. Chances are good that if a customer has purchased goods from a U.S. exporter in the past, a major American bank either has credit information about the customer or can get it from another bank. Some may refuse to go to the trouble of doing this. Most banks familiar with international transactions should be willing to do it, for a fee. A customer's foreign bank also provides credit references. Your bank can request this information from one of its overseas correspondents.

USAID

As pointed out in Chapter 13, the U.S. Agency for International Development (USAID) provides financial and technical support on a government-to-government level to specific developing countries for building infrastructures and economic bases. One of the indirect benefits of USAID to American companies doing business in these same countries comes through assistance in collecting receivables.

A public customer in a USAID country buying from an American contractor, exporter, or investor pays for the goods and services with USAID money. Since USAID must have a hand in approving the purchase in the first place, when a recalcitrant sovereign reneges on paying an American supplier, officials of USAID nearly always intervene on behalf of the supplier. Political pressure on the public agency results in faster, more certain payment than most other means. Don't hesitate to contact the host country office of USAID, or its Washington office, if you are having difficulty getting paid.

REDUCING GLOBAL RISK WITH CREDIT INSURANCE

Seldom, if ever, can a company purchase insurance against credit risk for domestic sales. In the global marketplace, however, credit insurance has become a normal cost of doing business. Small and midsize companies, especially, need to be certain that they will get paid regardless of the payment instrument or political changes. Credit insurance fills the bill. There are government-supported credit insurance bureaus throughout the world. Every major trading nation offers some type of credit insurance to reduce the risks of doing business overseas and thereby encourages export trade and foreign investment. In America, this agency is the Foreign Credit Insurance Association.

The FCIA

The Foreign Credit Insurance Association (FCIA) is an agent of Eximbank. Its purpose is to provide insurance coverage for foreign risks not normally available through private carriers. FCIA only covers export transactions from the United States, however. Insurance for direct investments in, or exports from, other countries must be obtained from insurance carriers located in the host country.

Policies available from FCIA cover a wide range of foreign risks, including expropriation, bad debts, and currency fluctuations. Eximbank lists the major objectives of FCIA as follows:

1. To protect the exporter against failure of foreign buyers to pay their credit obligations for commercial or political reasons.
2. To encourage exporters to offer foreign buyers competitive terms of payment.
3. To support an exporter's prudent penetration of higher risk foreign markets.
4. To give exporters and their banks greater financial flexibility in handling overseas accounts receivable.

To meet these objectives the FCIA offers eight different insurance policies: new-to-export; umbrella; multibuyer; short-term; single-buyer; medium-term single-buyer; lease coverage: bank letter of credit; and financial institution buyer credit.

New-to-Export Insurance Coverage

New-to-export coverage is available to companies just beginning to export, or which have had average annual export credit sales of less than $750,000 for the past two years. A company qualifies in this program for a maximum of five years. One-year blanket policies insure the collectibility of short-term credit sales. Such policies protect against 100 percent of political risk and 95 percent of commercial risk (this drops to 90 percent after two years). Interest payments due on debt obligations of up to prime rate minus ½ point are also covered. Credit terms must be 180 days or less for most products; extended to 360 days for agricultural commodities and consumer durables.

Although the fees and insurance premiums vary with each transaction according to repayment terms and type of buyer, the FCIA has a rate schedule available for the asking. A minimum annual premium of $500 is mandatory, however. Policy proceeds are assignable. No annual commercial risks first loss deductible applies for the first two years. If commercial risk coverage is not needed, political risk alone may be covered.

Umbrella Coverage

Umbrella coverage is provided to an export agent who has the capability of administering the policy on behalf of multiple exporters, such as an export management firm. The policy provides one-year coverage for short-term export sales from exporters with average annual export credit sales of less than $2 million for the past two years. An exporter must not have used FCIA during this period. Covered risks include 100 percent of political risk and 90 percent of commercial risk. Interest coverage, maximum payment terms, and assignability are the same as the new-to-export policy. A minimum annual premium of $500 is payable by the policy administrator.

The advantage in this type of policy is that it can be carried by the export management company, or other export representative responsible for the entire administration of the policy. The export administrator files reports and loss claims with the FCIA and pays all premiums. Obviously, this relieves the small exporter of a sizable administrative chore.

Both the umbrella and the new-to-export coverages insure sales of consumables, raw materials, spare parts, agricultural commodities, capital goods, consumer durables, and services.

Multibuyer Coverage

The multibuyer policy insures all exporters of goods and services shipping to more than one foreign buyer. The advantage in this policy is that it forms a blanket coverage so that each new buyer does not have to be qualified by the FCIA. It's a one-year blanket policy for either short- or medium-term credit sales, or a combination of both. There are two coverage options: (1) split (100 percent political and 90 percent commercial) after an annual commercial risks' first loss deductible, and (2) equalized (95 percent short-term and 90 percent long-term) for political and commercial after all risks' first loss deductible.

Criteria for interest coverage, repayment periods, minimum annual fee, and assignability follow other coverages. No cash down payment from the buyer is required under short-term coverage, but 15 percent must be made for medium-term.

Short-Term Single-Buyer Coverage

Short-term single-buyer coverage insures short-term credit sales from all U.S. exporters shipping to a single buyer. Political and commercial coverage are equalized based on the following schedule:

- Sovereign buyers — 100 percent
- Private sector and nonsovereign public sector buyers — 90 percent
- Letter of credit transactions — 95 percent
- Bulk agricultural sale — 98 percent

The type of buyer, repayment terms, and country of destination determine premiums. Current minimum rates are:

- Sovereign buyers and political risks only — $2,500
- Letters of credit, transaction with bank guarantors, and nonsovereign public sector buyers — $5,000
- Private sector buyers — $10,000

Medium-Term Single-Buyer Coverage

Medium-term single-buyer coverage includes 100 percent of the political risk and 90 percent for commercial risk. Repayment terms follow standard criteria. Premiums are based on the type of buyer and the country of destination. A foreign buyer must pay a 15 percent down payment before shipment.

Lease Coverage

Insurance coverage provided by the FCIA for foreign leases often determines whether or not a lease transaction makes sense. Coverage is available for both operating leases and financial leases. Operating lease coverage insures both the stream of lease payments and the fair market value of leased products. Financial coverage insures only the total payment under the lease.

Product coverage extends to new and used capital equipment and services, including automobiles, agricultural, processing, and communications equipment. Any leasing company, manufacturer, or financial institution qualifies as an eligible applicant. Coverage is equalized between political and commercial risk, with 100 percent protection for sovereign lessees, 90 percent for all other lessees, and 100 percent protection against government repossession. Buyer down payment requirements are 15 percent for finance leases and none for operating leases. Proceeds may be assigned, and no first loss deductible is required.

Bank Letter of Credit Coverage

Bank letter of credit coverage is available only to lending institutions. The exporter does not have to worry about this policy except to know of its availability to his lender. All banks handling L/Cs should know about this coverage and use it.

Financial Institution Buyer Credit Coverage

Buyer credit coverage is another policy available only to financial institutions extending direct credit loans or reimbursement loans to foreign buyers of American exports.

PRIVATE INSURANCE COMPANIES

Very few private insurance companies are willing to place coverage against export risks. AIG Political Risks, Inc., 70 Pine Street, New York, NY 10027, (212) 770-7000, is one of the few major private carriers willing to participate. AIG has been in the export insurance business for years and offers coverages priced competitively with FCIA. The carrier offers policies covering political risk for export transactions, expropriation, money transfer, contract repudiation by foreign governments, and performance bonds required in bidding arrangements. AIG also insures products that are under government restrictions (economic and foreign consideration). Policy terms range up to five years. The minimum premium is $50,000.

FOREIGN EXPORT CREDIT AGENCIES

In addition to government trade supports and financial assistance to local firms making foreign investments or engaged in exporting from the host country, over 30 countries have established their own export credit agencies. Some of these agencies interact with other government bureaus to offer financial and guarantee assistance in addition to credit insurance. Some offer only insurance coverage. There are far too many to cover here, but a representative sampling of the major, and most successful, programs should be indicative of what is available worldwide. Appendix K presents a comprehensive listing of government and private organizations offering export credit insurance.

United Kingdom

The granddaddy of government-sponsored export credit programs is the Exports Credit Guarantee Department (ECGD) of the British government. Though ECGD is expected to be commercially profitable, in the event circumstances force losses or insolvency, the British government provides full financial backing. Originally established in 1919, ECGD is one of the most successful national export insurers in the world. Many others are patterned after it. As government agencies go, it is efficient, timely, and charges reasonable fees for its services. ECGD covers approximately one third of all British exports.

Unlike American coverage from the FCIA, political and commercial risk are lumped into one package. Types of risk coverage and percentage participation by ECGD are as follows:

1. Commercial Risk:
   a. Insolvency of the buyer. ECGD covers a full 90 percent of the loss.
   b. Buyer's failure to pay within six months of due date for goods already accepted. ECGD covers a full 90 percent of the loss.
   c. Buyer's failure to accept goods which have been shipped, provided the exporter complied with all the terms of the contract. Exporter bears first 20 percent of loss, ECGD covers 90 percent of the balance. Under certain types of capital goods, this cap is completely eliminated.
2. Political Risk: ECGD covers 95 percent of any loss after shipment, and 90 percent of losses incurred prior to shipment.
   a. Government action which blocks or delays payment of sterling to the exporter.
   b. Cancellation of a valid import license or imposition of new import licensing restrictions in the buyer's country.
   c. Cancellation or nonrenewal of a U.K. export license or imposition of new export licensing restrictions.
   d. War between the buyer's country and the United Kingdom.

e. War, revolution, or similar disturbances in the buyer's country.

f. Additional handling, transportation, and/or insurance charges resulting from an interruption or diversion of the ocean shipping vessel if these charges cannot be recovered from the buyer.

g. Any other cause of loss occurring outside the United Kingdom and not within the control of the exporter or the buyer.

h. Repudiation of the contract in cases where ECGD agrees that the buyer has government status.

Premiums vary depending on whether a seller insures all export business or only specific transactions. Exporters wishing full coverage must agree to insure all export shipments for one or three years with the latter resulting in substantially reduced premiums.

The ECGD extends a much broader coverage than that granted by FCIA or other U.S. insurers. In addition to coverage for the export of all goods from the United Kingdom, including all types of consumer products, raw materials, semifinished products and capital goods, special features include:

1. Political risks of shipments to overseas subsidiaries and affiliates.
2. Exports to intermediaries.
3. Reexport of imported goods after packaging or value-added processes.
4. Nonsterling invoices.
5. Overseas stocking of a United Kingdom company's inventory.
6. Erection costs of exported capital equipment.
7. Construction goods and services.
8. Services, including technical or professional assistance, repair work, technology transfers, and so on.
9. Arbitration award where the buyer refuses to comply. ECGD also covers that portion of a contract involving a U.K. exporter and a foreign subcontractor jointly contracting with a customer.

In addition to insuring exports, ECGD offers a guarantee to banks making loans to the exporter. This important feature is available only to those exporters who have held comprehensive coverage with ECGD for at least 12 months. The department also offers a buyer credit guarantee for transactions in excess of £ 250,000. The importer must make a 20 percent down payment and pay the balance direct to the exporter or to a local bank handling the financing. It can extend to five years. Finally, ECGD guarantees lines of credit from British banks to overseas buyers.

There are also three private companies in Great Britain which insure against commercial but not political risks. They are Trade Indemnity Company, Credit Guarantee Insurance Company, and Credit Indemnity Company.

France

The French export credit agency is called the Compagnie Française d'Assurance pour le Commerce Exterieur (COFACE). COFACE provides credit insurance, but unlike the ECGD, no financing guarantees. CO-FACE works closely with the French banks, Credit National, Banque Française de Commerce Exterieur, and Banque de France. COFACE splits its commercial and political coverage. It covers 85 percent commercial risk to the United States and 80 percent to other countries. It covers either 80 or 90 percent of political risk depending upon how much the exporter is willing to pay in premiums.

Under its definition of consumer goods, COFACE covers the export of raw materials, semifinished products, metals, foods, chemicals, pharmaceuticals, electrical appliances, and small tools. It also covers the export of light machinery and other capital goods sold under contracts with credit up to three years. For large projects, COFACE extends coverage up to 10 years.

Exchange risk guarantees are also available when an exporter or contractor is required to put up a *good faith* or performance deposit. Such guarantees extend directly to the bank financing the deposit. Exchange coverage also applies when invoicing is required to be in a foreign currency and the exporter has no other way to cover the fluctuation risk.

The French go one step further than ECGD or the FCIA. As a means of supporting French companies entering new markets in foreign countries, COFACE insures the coverage of all fixed costs of marketing studies, office administration, publicity and advertising, and so on, incurred by that a company in a foreign country while trying to develop new sales. If these sales do not materialize, COFACE pays between 50 and 70 percent of these covered expenses, depending on the duration of the marketing effort and other risk classifications. It also covers 50 percent of the expenses of participating in an international trade fair if additional sales do not materialize.

Germany

German export credit insurance may be obtained either through private- or government-sponsored sources. Two of the largest private sources are Gerling-Konzern Speziale Kreditversicherungs AG (GKS) and Allgemeine Kreditversicherungs AG. Beginning in 1962, the West German government was authorized to extend credit and political risk insurance.

Two private companies administer the government program, Hermes Kreditversicherungs AG and Deutsche Revisions und Trehand AG. Exporter applications are submitted to Hermes, which performs an examination and a review. Hermes then forwards the documents to the International Committee for Export Guarantees for approval or rejection. For approved applications, Hermes issues the actual guarantee with the full backing of the German government. Hermes offers only credit guarantees, no financing.

One policy includes both political and commercial risks. Political risks are defined as:

1. Nonpayment due to general moratorium on repayment debts and other government payment prohibitions.
2. Currency convertibility and transfers restrictions or the freezing

of balances deposited in the local currency of the importer's country.

3. Losses from seizure, damage, or destruction of goods that result from political causes and not otherwise covered by private insurance.

Commercial risk coverage for sales to private buyers includes the buyer's insolvency or proven inability to pay the exporter. Sales to government customers may be insured against a flat nonpayment. Nonpayment means that the amounts due are not paid within six months. Preshipment risks are also covered when equipment cannot be delivered due to the deteriorated financial condition of the foreign buyer. Hermes covers 80 percent for commercial, 85 to 90 percent for political, and 85 percent for preshipment risks.

Special coverages may also be arranged with Hermes for:

1. Currency convertibility and transfer.
2. Inventory kept abroad.
3. Guarantees for bank loans to carry this inventory abroad.
4. Foreign exchange risk if the invoice is in U.S. dollars, British sterling, or Swiss francs, but only for two years. Losses beyond two years in excess of 3 percent are covered. If gains in excess of 3 percent are realized, they must be turned over to Hermes.

CONCLUSION

The same prudent credit and collection procedures used when selling to American firms should be applied to foreign customers. Credit insurance compensates for the general lack of financial statements and peculiar private business practices. Nevertheless, to ensure collections, special care must be exercised to be certain everything has been done that can be done *before shipment is made*. Once title passes, little incentive exists for the global customer to pay currently or completely — other than unusual honesty.

CHAPTER 19

IMPORTING TO THE UNITED STATES

MAJOR TOPICS

KEY POINTS

1. Monitoring the Movement of Goods. Includes a review of the five private and governmental parties required to move goods into the United States and the role each plays in monitoring import shipments.

2. U.S. Customs Service. Identifies the entry documents to be prepared for imports and the types of duties charged. This section also lists products admitted to the United States duty free.

3. Drawbacks. Describes the conditions under which drawbacks (refunds) of customs duties already paid can be obtained. The services a drawback specialist performs for the importer are also listed.

4. U.S. Government Restrictions. Examines examples of the types of products and countries affected by federal import restrictions and quotas.

5. Preferential Trade Partners. Trade agreements already in place with Canada, Israel, Caribbean nations, and Mexico are described. These agreements permit the duty-free movement of goods into the United States from these countries. Current Mexican negotiations attempt to go even further than the current in-bond program.

6. Foreign Trade Zones. FTZs provide a convenient method for transshipment of goods into and out of the United States duty free. This section describes how best to utilize these zones.

7. Miscellaneous Import Topics. Covers the current status of special import techniques and problems. Countertrade as a way to import goods without spending cash, using the Dominican Republic as an entry to the EC, customs audits, and quality control of foreign suppliers are described.

> Bally & Schnell, Inc. (B & S), manufactured armatures, distributor caps, alternators, and other electrical components used in small engines and motors. Recognizing the need to go global, the company started up and acquired nine assembly shops and distributors in the Pacific Basin, South America, and England. Each facility possessed unique characteristics; that is, some paid lower wages, others had ready access to materials, two countries offered free financing, and one provided a 10-year tax holiday. Since going global, annual sales at B & S have increased 20 percent, to $18 million.
>
> New markets for their electric components opened in Costa Rica and Jamaica. B & S wanted to ship direct from England. Because of peculiar British electrical standards, however, the products needed modifications prior to sale in the Caribbean and Central America. The answer was to ship the products to a foreign trade zone in Miami, make appropriate modifications, and then transship to Jamaica and Costa Rica. Using this circuitous route, U.S. customs duties, extra insurance, and taxes were all avoided. Furthermore, B & S utilized American skilled labor to make the modifications.

Importing materials and products to the United States for direct resale, for use in a manufacturing process, or for transshipment to foreign destinations has been a way of life in many industries for decades. Hardly any consumer or industrial product does not contain some foreign material or component. Cars, building materials, clothing, foodstuffs, athletic equipment, farm implements, airplanes, machine tools, electronics, and military hardware are only a few examples.

As described in Chapter 16, global value-added products have become a way of life, not only for U.S. companies, but for foreign competitors as well. Materials, components, and subassemblies moving from one country to another for assembly stages provide the global company an ever expanding panorama of combinations to gain competitive advantage. Foreign trade zones provide a cost-effective means to move goods throughout the world. A true global mentality necessitates utilizing foreign sourcing whenever and wherever it yields competitive gains. Air freight and competitive ocean shipping lines enable shippers to quickly adjust productive capabilities and raw material sourcing to the most expedient location.

Each country has its own import trade restrictions and quotas. It also has its own unique conditions for moving and storing goods. No single source of information provides sufficient guidance for importing to every country. The remainder of this chapter covers specific importing circumstances unique to the United States. These conditions provide a base from which to judge the situation in other countries. A company with foreign branches desiring to import into Europe, Latin America, the Pacific Basin, or other areas should obviously investigate importing regulations applicable to each country.

An American importer must be concerned with a variety of commercial, government, and legal matters regardless of the use made of imported goods. These matters are unique to importing. They are of no concern to a company not involved in some type of import activity. The exception involves financing. Letters of credit, banker's acceptances, and other banking instruments used in financing imports are identical to those used in exporting. Chapter 14 offers a complete description of these financing tools.

The first set of circumstances affecting an importer are those necessary to monitor incoming shipments.

MONITORING THE MOVEMENT OF GOODS

Whether importing goods to be transshipped, products to be resold domestically, or materials and components to be used in processing or final assembly, an importer must monitor their movement from embarkation to delivery. This means designating someone in the receiving organization to be responsible for the process from start to finish. It is not uncommon, especially for smaller companies, to arrange for goods to be imported and then expect delivery to their door on schedule. This never works. The complexity of the process precludes relying on outsiders to complete the transaction. Monitoring and controlling the movement of products is solely the responsibility of management within the importing organization.

Ocean or air freight companies, brokers, terminal operators, U.S. customs officials, and domestic freight carriers, all get involved in moving foreign shipments into the United States. The following outlines the responsibilities of each party to the transaction:

1. *Ocean or air freight company.*   Notifies consignee two days before arrival of goods at the port of entry. Provides freight release to terminal operator.

2. *Customs broker.*   Responsible for obtaining customs releases and necessary clearances at port of entry. Checks bills of lading and delivery orders for completeness. Forwards originals of these documents to motor carrier for pickup.

3. *U.S. customs officials.*   Verifies compliance with customs regulations and collects duty.

4. *Terminal operator.*   Arranges with domestic carrier for pickup. Makes arrangements for payment of demurrage, if any. Verifies accuracy of delivery order and loads merchandise onto domestic carrier.

5. *Domestic freight carrier.*   Receives merchandise at port of entry. Verifies clearance documents and delivery order. Delivers to importer's receiving dock.

With this many companies and people involved, Murphy's Law inevitably applies. Therefore, it's always a good idea to station a company representative at the port of entry when notified by the shipping company of the arrival date. This person then coordinates the activities of each party and is available to break bottlenecks as they occur. He should also be prepared to arrange payment of customs duties, demurrage, and any other clearance fees required.

> The president of ZE-RITE Corp., a $7 million chemical processor near Philadelphia, admits to literally missing the boat the first time around. Taking on a new line of industrial filtering compounds, ZE-RITE located three global sources for one of the compounds used in the mixture. Arranging to purchase a full container of the compound from a plant in Egypt, the company waited patiently for its delivery. Sixty days passed and nothing arrived. The president of ZE-RITE became concerned and assigned his controller the task of tracing the shipment. Three weeks later the controller was successful. The steamship company forgot to unload the container in Philadelphia. Since no one from ZE-RITE coordinated at the port, the container remained on board for the next port of call, Buenos Aires.

Maintaining close surveillance of ocean shipping may seem inconsequential, but in the long run it's safer to spend the money and take the time to be sure. Don't rely solely on customs brokers, the exporter, or ocean, air, or domestic carriers. Do it yourself. No one wants to chase a shipment to Argentina!

THE U.S. CUSTOMS SERVICE

Once a shipment reaches a port of entry in the United States, U.S. customs officials take over. All goods valued at over $1,000 arriving at American ports must go through a formal entry process. This process consists of four steps:

1. The filing of appropriate entry documents.
2. Inspection and classification of the goods.
3. Preliminary declaration of value.
4. Final determination of duty and payment.

Usually processing the entry of foreign goods requires about five days. Once the amount of duty has been established and the importer notified, the broker receives instructions to make payment and obtain release of the goods. If merchandise is not moved out within five days, customs officials transfer the goods to a warehouse and the importer gets charged for storage. If the goods remain in custody for one year, the government has the right to auction them for storage fees.

Entry Documents

Of the 22 different types of customs entries, six predominate:

1. The Consumption Entry is the most common type. It is used for goods intended for resale domestically and brought directly into the importers stock.
2. An Immediate Transportation Entry allows merchandise to be

forwarded directly from the port of entry to an inland destination for customs clearance.

3. A Warehouse Entry is used to store goods in a customs-bonded warehouse for up to five years.
4. When goods are ultimately withdrawn from a bonded warehouse, a Warehouse Withdrawal for Consumption Entry applies.
5. An Immediate Exportation Entry occurs when goods are to be transshipped to a foreign country.
6. American citizens returning from a trip abroad file a Baggage Declaration and Entry form.

Before goods are allowed out of customs certain documents must be made available to customs agents: a commercial invoice from the exporter, a bill of lading from the exporter or freight forwarder, and one of the above entry forms completed by the importer or its broker.

Each of these entry forms must contain a valuation of the shipment, its description, and the amount of duty to be paid. Goods may be removed from customs by paying this duty immediately or by posting a bond guaranteeing payment at a later date. The bond may be in the form of a single transaction bond applying to entry through one port, or a continuous bond covering all U.S. ports of entry. Either a broker or the importer arranges for this surety bond.

Types of Duty

Whether an item is dutiable or free from duty frequently influences a business decision to import or not. Import duties are classified into three types:

1. Specific duties assessed against a unit of the goods, such as 5 percent per pound.
2. Ad valorem duties assessed as a flat percent for the total value of the import transaction, such as 10 percent of the total value imputed to the goods.
3. A compound duty combining specific duties and ad valorum duties, such as $5 per pound of a commodity *plus* a percentage of the value of the transaction. Certain types of agricultural commodities are assessed in this manner.

All duties assessed by U.S. Customs are included in a voluminous document called the *Tariff Schedules of the United States.* It resembles freight tariff schedules for rail and trucking lines. An official ruling from the head office of the port of entry determines the type and rates of duties applicable to specific goods.

In addition to types and rates of duties assessed by commodity, the U.S. government enforces statutory duties. These apply to imports of any goods, either directly or indirectly, from countries the government deems unfriendly. Obviously this list keeps changing as foreign policy vacillates. In 1989, imports from the following countries were assessed statutory duty rates: Afghanistan, Bulgaria, Cuba, Czechoslovakia, Estonia, East Germany, Vietnam, Laos, North Korea, Kurile Islands, Lat-

FIGURE 19-1
Items Imported Duty Free as of 1990

1. Materials or goods imported specifically to be repaired, modified, or processed in the United States with the intent of shipping the final product offshore. The product may also be totally destroyed while in bond rather than exported. The end product cannot contain perfume, alcohol, or wheat. A complete accounting of the articles must be made and any scrap or waste turned over to customs.
2. Women's clothing to be used strictly for modeling in a U.S. garment-maker's establishment.
3. Samples used solely to attract sales.
4. Motion picture advertising films.
5. Items intended solely for review, testing, or experimentation, such as drawings, plans, or photos.
6. Containers for handling or transporting items.
7. Items used solely in the preparation of illustrations for catalogs, pamphlets, or advertising.
8. Professional equipment, trade tools, repair components for these tools and equipment, and articles of special design for temporary use in the manufacture or design of items for export.
9. Props, scenery, and apparel for temporary use in theatrical performances.

via, Lithuania, Outer Mongolia, Southern Sakhalin, Tanna Tuva, and the Soviet Union.

For purposes of valuation, currency exchange rates from the exporting country are determined by the daily buying rate for foreign currency established by the Federal Reserve Bank of New York.

Duty-Free Items

The U.S. Customs Service defines certain types of imported items as duty free. A bond must be posted with U.S. Customs upon importing these items to guarantee that they will either be exported or destroyed. Though slight variations occur periodically, Figure 19–1 lists current duty-free items.

Foreign residents may also import personal items (cars, films, boats, and so on) for use while temporarily in the United States.

In all of the above cases, if the articles imported or modified while in the United States are not exported or destroyed within a year, the bond will be forfeited and the goods seized.

DRAWBACKS

The term *drawback* as used in reference to U.S. customs regulations refers to refunds of duties previously paid on imported goods. Normally drawbacks on imported goods are not allowed if the goods are subsequently exported after they are released from customs. However, as with everything else involving government regulations, there are exceptions:

1. A total of 99 percent of duties paid is refundable if the goods are used in the manufacture or production of final products in the United States and these final products are exported.
2. If goods are rejected by the importer as not meeting order specifications, they may be returned to customs for supervised shipment back to the exporter. A 99 percent drawback is allowed.
3. The same 99 percent drawback is allowed if the imported goods

are returned to the exporter within three years, in the same condition as they were received.

4. Goods found to be banned from import by U.S. government decree. They must be returned to the exporter or destroyed by customs officials. All duties paid are included in a drawback.

5. Total refunds are also granted if goods are exported from a customs-bonded warehouse or if the goods are withdrawn from the warehouse for repair, supplies or maintenance of vessels and aircraft (under certain conditions).

As described later in this chapter, the use of a foreign trade zone serves as a popular method for exporting previously imported goods from customs warehouse. These duty-free areas, sanctioned by the U.S. Customs Service, are increasingly used for transshipment of goods requiring modification or repackaging.

Preparing the paperwork for a drawback can be extremely involved. Most companies engaged in importing and then exporting, utilize the services of a specialist to handle drawbacks. These experts are customs brokers specializing in drawback management. A summary of the qualifications for receiving drawbacks, as defined by these specialist brokers, seems clearer than the legalese descriptions from the U.S. Customs Service. One such drawback specialist, Comstock & Theakston, Inc., of Oradell, New Jersey, defines qualifying drawback applicants as importers who export their products or exporters of articles manufactured with imports. If your company falls into one of these slots, contact a drawback specialist to be certain of receiving full refunds.

A drawback specialist handles the entire drawback process. It prepares all paperwork and processes all claims. A competent drawback broker can design applicable in-house procedures to assist in identifying drawback items. It can also structure a coordination program with in-house financial personnel. Most import/export companies find that drawback specialists more than pay for themselves in cost savings and actual cash recoveries.

U.S. GOVERNMENT IMPORT RESTRICTIONS AND QUOTAS

Nearly every country enforces import restrictions and quotas of one type or another, just as they control the export of goods. Chapter 6 described how Japan is currently under indictment by the U.S. Trade Representative to loosen up its import barriers and allow the free flow of more American goods into its home markets. The United States is not free from import restrictions either. In fact, in some instances, U.S. barriers are more severe than those practiced by the Japanese.

American import trade barriers fall under four headings:

1. Goods that the government deems detrimental to the well-being of its citizens as a whole or to special interest groups of citizens.
2. Quantities or quotas of specific goods.
3. Antidumping regulations to protect certain U.S. industries from foreign competition.
4. "Preference" regulations applying to favored nations.

FIGURE 19–2
Imported Goods Considered Detrimental to U.S. Citizens

1. Alcoholic beverages.
2. Arms, explosives, ammunition, and implements of war.
3. Automobiles and accessories.
4. Coins, stamps, currencies, and other monetary instruments.
5. Eggs and egg products.
6. Fruits, vegetables, plants, and insects.
7. Milk and cream.
8. Electronic products.
9. Food, drugs, and cosmetics.
10. Animals.
11. Wild animals and endangered species.
12. Wool, fur, textile and fabric products.
13. Livestock and meat.
14. Pesticides and toxic substances.
15. Viruses and serums.
16. Rags and brushes.
17. Narcotics.
18. All products from *communist countries* (the definition keeps changing).

Goods Detrimental to U.S. Citizens

For a variety of reasons, including but not limited to pressure from special interest groups, perceived moral standards, and congressional favoritism, the federal government has declared specific products harmful to American citizens. Consequently, trade barriers either prohibit or severely restrict importing these goods. The most severe restrictions call for the seizure of such goods by U.S. customs authorities. Less severe barriers include limiting entry to certain ports; restricting the routing, storage or use of the goods; or requiring special labeling or processing before goods can be released to the market.

These restrictions apply to all imported goods, whether or not foreign trade zones are utilized. The list of items falling under these restrictions is voluminous and constantly changing. U.S. Customs offices retain complete up-to-date listings, but Figure 19–2 lists some of the better known items.

Quotas of Specific Goods

Most import quotas are administered by the district director of customs. Other government agencies handle special products. For example, quotas for dairy products are established by the Import Branch, Foreign Agricultural Service (a section of the Department of Agriculture); fuel and oil products quotas by the director of Oil Imports at the Federal Energy Administration; watches and watch movements by the Special Import Programs Division of the Department of Commerce.

There are two types of import quotas: tariff-rate and absolute. The federal government uses tariff-rate quotas to manipulate the pricing of domestic products and thus inhibit free market movement. If consumer prices are higher than the government wants, it sets tariff-rates quotas allowing the importing of specific products at very favorable duty rates for a specific period of time. Tariff-rate quotas are frequently used to keep the price of agricultural products down when free market prices escalate from bad weather conditions. Some current products susceptible to tariff-rate quotas are milk, fish, tuna, and potatoes. They also apply to whisk brooms and large motorcycles!

Absolute quotas have nothing to do with favorable duty rate adjustments. They are established solely to control the quantity of specific goods that may be imported during any given period of time. Some examples of imports restricted by absolute quotas include: peanuts, ice cream, steel bars and rods, cotton, sugar, and condensed milk. Because all quotas are for specific periods of time, it is impossible to predict with any certainty in advance of shipment whether or not a given import transaction will be restricted by quotas at the time of arrival in port. If your shipment hits when quotas have already been filled, an over-quota duty applies, which easily makes the imported products noncompetitive.

Antidumping Regulations

In another effort to buoy up inefficient producers by restricting free market trade, the federal government administers antidumping laws. These laws restrict the importing of goods that, according to the federal government, present unfair competition to domestic U.S. producers. The determination is made solely on a comparison of the price an importer pays for the merchandise against what he would pay if purchasing the goods domestically. Inefficiencies or other barriers to lower prices from American producers are not taken into consideration.

The test of whether a product is *dumped* or not is very straightforward. For the products similar to those produced in the United States, a straight price comparison holds. For goods not sufficiently similar to American-made goods, a constructed value test ensues. Constructed value is the total of: costs of materials and labor; factory and administrative overhead; reasonable profit; and the cost of packing and shipping the products to the United States. If a product falls within the antidumping provisions, additional duties apply. Theoretically, at least, these additional duties make the domestic sell price of imported items competitive with domestic products.

PREFERENTIAL TRADE PARTNERS

Two categories of preferential trade partners exist:

1. Designated developing nations or territories.
2. Canada, Israel, the Caribbean, and Mexico.

The list of designated developing nations or territories currently consists of over 140 entries, but the list keeps changing every month. Preferential items fall under what the government calls the General System of Preferences (GSP). Over 2,700 products in the *Tariff Schedules of the United States* are classified as being produced in these countries. Contact the Trade Policy Staff Committee, Office of the Special Representative for Trade Negotiations, 1800 G Street, Washington, DC, 20506, for a current listing.

Canada

Chapter 6 described the recently enacted U.S.–Canada Free Trade Agreement (FTA) that essentially removes all trade barriers between the two countries in gradual steps over the next few years. The timing of the removal of tariffs and quotas depends on the specific products involved. Some have already been removed. Others fall in 5-year increments: still others in 10-year steps.

The FTA impacts American importers in a major way. As duties fall, prices of Canadian-produced goods become directly competitive with those manufactured in the United States. For many global firms, this common market with Canada should take some of the sting out of trade barriers inevitably coming from the European Community.

Israel

In 1985, the United States enacted a similar trade agreement with Israel. The idea behind this agreement was to create a free trade market between the two countries. The agreement calls for all customs duties and most nontariff barriers to be abolished on both sides. The changes by product classifications become effective in increments through 1995, closely resembling the step process enacted with Canada. When the agreement went into effect, such products as metalworking equipment, machine tools, and many electronic components became immediately duty free. The Israeli Government Investment and Export Authority publishes a booklet entitled *Guide to the Israel-U.S. Free Trade Area Agreement* which should be must reading for any company planning to import products from or export products to Israel.

Caribbean Basin Initiative

Chapter 7 examined the major provisions of the Caribbean Basin Initiative (CBI) program enacted by Congress in 1983. During the past seven years, additional provisions and agencies have been established to assist in the development of Caribbean countries. The initial purpose of the CBI however, was to encourage exports from CBI nations to the United States. Nearly all import restrictions were lifted for CBI-produced goods.

Special financing schemes were enacted to assist the American importer pay for the goods in U.S. dollars. Technical assistance teams flooded the Caribbean, offering assistance in everything from growing sugar cane to assembling watches. With low-labor costs and ready access to certain raw materials, CBI nations offer the American importer an excellent opportunity to acquire parts, materials, subassemblies, and a variety of other goods and services at prices substantially below U.S. standards. The Department of Commerce publishes an excellent recap of the CBI program entitled *Guidebook to the Caribbean Basin Initiative*. This should be must reading for every global American company.

Mexican in-Bond Program

This program has been in effect since 1965. It offers American manufacturers the opportunity to utilize low-cost Mexican labor. It also affords the Mexican government additional revenues and Mexican laborers a chance to earn a livelihood. The program works as follows: an American company ships raw materials to its 100 percent owned manufacturing plant located in special Mexican free zones, referred to as *in-bond* zones. There, the goods are processed into finished or semifinished products. The products are then shipped back to the United States. Duty is paid only on the value-added labor.

The Mexican government allows U.S. firms three incentives, in addition to permitting 100 percent American ownership of the facility:

1. Duty-free entry of machinery and equipment to be used in the production of these goods.
2. No restrictions on the type of goods produced for export.
3. Authorization to lease land and facilities within these coastal and border zones under a 30-year, beneficial trust arrangement.

Currently, over 1,000 American plants dot the landscape along these border and coastal free zones. Any company wishing further information should contact the Mexican Desk Officer at the Department of Commerce.

During 1990, negotiations began between U.S. and Mexican officials to attempt to reach an agreement to eliminate most trade barriers between the two countries. Expectations that such an agreement will be structured after the U.S.–Canada Trade Agreement seem optimistic. Nevertheless, indications received to date point to some type of arrangement removing or significantly reducing trade, currency, and travel restrictions between the two nations. Government officials in the United States also indicate, however, that negotiations will probably be protracted. It could be several years before the parties reach final agreement.

FOREIGN TRADE ZONES

Foreign trade zones, or FTZs, provide a convenient way to import products, repack, modify, or otherwise finish them, and then ship them offshore to the ultimate customer without being subject to customs duties and other import restrictions. FTZs exist in nearly every trading country, including the United states. They have been used for years throughout the world as a means of transshipping goods between countries without the imposition of local customs duties.

A foreign trade zone is defined by regulations as an isolated, enclosed, policed area, operating as a public utility. Although FTZs are located within the boundaries of the United States, they are treated as if they were outside U.S. customs territory. Currently, 141 FTZs exist in the United States. Only South Dakota, West Virginia, and Idaho do not have at least one; Texas has 16 FTZs.

FTZs may be used for a variety of purposes including storage, distribution, assembly, light manufacturing, modifications of products, or transshipping. Goods in an FTZ may also be sold, exhibited, broken up, repacked, repackaged, graded, cleaned, and mixed with other foreign or domestic merchandise. One of the most interesting applications of FTZs, in the context of savings costs for a company producing goods overseas, is as an intermediate stop for adding value to the product on its way from the overseas manufacturing location to the ultimate offshore customer.

For example, assume you have a plant in Italy assembling washing machines. You want to ship the machines to a customer in Trinidad. The most direct route would be to ship direct from Italy to Trinidad. However, the ocean freight might be substantially less by shipping only the components, and perhaps some subassemblies part way, say to the Jacksonville or Miami FTZ. There they could be assembled, tested, and packed, and the final product shipped to Trinidad.

Ordinarily, customs duties would have to be paid coming into the United States. Insurance, taxes, and additional paperwork would be required to ship the products to Trinidad. No duties are paid on products entering an FTZ, however. There is no tax liability and no additional insurance coverage required. The FTZ is treated as a foreign port. The U.S. government keeps its hands off. This can amount to substantial cost savings. Using an FTZ also permits a parent company to utilize American labor and management for the final assembly and testing of the goods.

One unusual, and at times very helpful, feature of FTZs is that an importer has the ability to exhibit his wares. This means a company maintains its own showroom in the zone and displays its merchandise for an indefinite period of time. Since goods may also be stored and processed in the zone, a company can stock merchandise in its display room and sell wholesale quantities directly from the zone without incurring any duty.

IMPORTING THROUGH COUNTERTRADE

Countertrade procedures as a way of financing exports to, or investment in, a soft currency country were described in Chapter 15. Countertrade arrangements also conserve cash for the American importer. The most ideal arrangement combines exports to a country in the CBI, for example, in exchange for imports from that country to be used directly in producing a company's product line. An arrangement nearly as favorable was engineered by UltraSafe Toys in 1988.

UltraSafe produced dolls, stuffed animals, and other "soft" products for handicapped preschool children. Several product lines required hand sewing. Other lines used a stuffing material treated with nonflammable chemicals. As sales tapered off and competition from foreign producers intensified, it became apparent that UltraSafe must find ways to cut costs to survive in their niche markets. Concurrently, the company saw new markets opening in

Argentina and Brazil. Management found the answers in offshore material sourcing at a lesser cost and higher quality than available domestically, and in foreign sewn assemblies of several lines.

UltraSafe wanted to set up sewing shops in Guatemala to take advantage of lower wage rates. The company decided Malaysia offered the best prices for stuffing material. The final safety testing had to be performed in the United States with certified inspectors. The final products would be sold domestically as well as in Argentina and Brazil. The countertrade deals were structured as follows:

1. A major producer-distributor in Buenos Aires agreed to a three-year contract to purchase and distribute three lines of dolls and animals. In exchange, UltraSafe agreed to purchase processed beef from Buenos Aires.
2. The Argentinian beef was shipped directly to a producer in Kuala Lumpur. In exchange, UltraSafe imported Malaysian stuffing direct to its foreign trade zone plant in Los Angeles.
3. UltraSafe formed a joint venture with a Guatemalan company to perform the in-process sewing operations. These subassemblies were then imported to the Los Angeles plant.
4. The stuffing was added in Los Angeles and final assembly sewing completed. The products were then safety tested. Some lines were shipped to the distributor in Buenos Aires and the balance sold domestically.

In 1989, UltraSafe resumed its commanding position in its niche markets. Its president attributed the company's recovery to the extra profitability provided by the unusual countertrade deals.

THE DOMINICAN REPUBLIC—A NEW TWIST FOR IMPORTS/EXPORTS

Consistent with a global mentality, a producer could seriously view the Dominican Republic, or even Haiti, as a new opportunity. The former has long been a favorite location for American investment in production facilities. Low-labor costs (currently 77 cents per hour including fringes), a favorable political climate toward Americans, close proximity, and beneficial subsidies from the CBI have caused the Dominican Republic to be a principal exporter to the United States. Now an added incentive has occurred to take advantage of duty-free access to the post-1992 European Community.

Recently, the Dominican Republic and Haiti entered into the LOME IV agreement with the EC to allow duty-free exports of many products to Europe. The LOME trade agreement is an accord between the 68-member African, Caribbean, and Pacific group of nations called *ACP* and the European Commission. LOME IV, a successor to three previous 5-year agreements, is a 10-year trade agreement beginning in 1990. For the first time the Dominican Republic and Haiti have been included.

Locating a facility in the Dominican Republic now has a double-barreled advantage for the American producer. Not only can it take advantage of duty-free imports to the United States, it can also ship duty free to the EC. Conceivably, locating in the Dominican Republic provides advantages over both foreign and domestic competitors. In addition to an abundance of skilled and semiskilled labor and low wages, industrial free zones in the Dominican Republic offer companies substantial tax, tariff, and regulatory incentives. Such incentives include freedom from foreign currency holding and exchange restrictions and unrestricted repatriation of profits.

Furthermore, the pro-business climate in the Dominican Republic appears to be nearly perfect for business growth opportunities. Exports from free zones in 1989 exceeded $600 million and the number of firms using the zones has grown from 160 to 280 in just three years.

THE CUSTOMS AUDIT

Most companies have been through at least one IRS audit. Many have experienced audits from worker's compensation insurance carriers, state regulatory agencies, and a variety of other bureaucratic agencies. Now importers can add U.S. Customs auditors to the list of federal bureaucrats invading their privacy.

By importing, a company automatically consents to keep and make available certain records for examination by the U.S. Customs Service. No one is exempt. All companies, regardless of size, classification of products, or the value or frequency of imports, are subject to customs audits. And, as with the IRS, the chances of discrepancies are high.

In the past, the U.S. Customs Service has limited its investigations to large corporations engaged in importing fairly large quantities of product. But times have changed. The age of the computer has hit the U.S. Customs Service. As the federal government increases its computerized data banks, the U.S. Customs Service leads the way to automate the entire paper flow of import documentation.

National Entry Processing, also known as DABA, Paired Ports, and Triangular Processing, already utilizes a totally electronic environment for automated importers, including paperless entry and summary, electronic invoices, electronic payment of duties, preclassification of merchandise, and binding rulings attached to a company's specific style or part number. This information appears on an electronic invoice, which is then used to obtain an electronic release and entry summary to calculate the duty charges. Finally, an importer's bank account is debited automatically by the U.S. Customs Service!

The U.S. Customs Service is quick to point out that electronic processing allows an importer more rapid access to his merchandise. That is true! What they don't reveal, however, is the price to be paid for this more timely access. The biggest cost of any government audit, exclusive of discrepancy findings, is the substantial amount of nonproductive time spent by company personnel in arranging records for audit and answering auditor's questions. In addition, record-keeping which in the past could be somewhat haphazard, now must be formalized—and that costs money.

Record-keeping for import transactions must be maintained in a manner that allows rapid access to transactions in an orderly and systematic fashion. Managers of importing companies must have more than a passing knowledge of transactions.

Customs regulations (19 CFR Part 162) are quite specific about which records must be made available for examination. Regulations also specify what records must be maintained by third parties, such as customs brokers, and how they will be accessed by customs auditors separately from the broker's internal records. Invoicing requirements are also clearly delineated (19 CFR Part 141).

The U.S. Customs Service holds the importer totally responsible for all aspects of invoices relating to import transactions. To be certain that the invoice properly reflects required information, the importer should become involved in the detailed preparation of the purchase order. He then must insist that the exporter copy this data verbatim. Information about terms, inclusions or exclusions from the price, shipping instructions, dangerous markings, insurance, and so forth, must be spelled out in detail.

In addition to verifying hard data, customs auditors want to know that the importer has taken reasonable and prudent actions in the transactions. This necessitates maintaining qualified personnel in import management roles. One way to assure compliance with customs regulations is to hire an international consultant to conduct an in-house audit of a company's international transactions prior to any customs audit. Corrective measures resulting from an internal audit will go a long way toward satisfying customs auditors that reasonable and prudent management actions have been taken.

The importance of maintaining good internal controls, adequate accounting records, and qualified management personnel cannot be overemphasized. It's too late to try to put things together once notified of an audit. In addition, those companies most successful in the global marketplace recognize early in the game that good record-keeping and sound management practices are essential to remaining competitive.

IMPORT QUALITY CONTROL

American companies in general have long been criticized in the global arena for producing poor-quality merchandise. In recent years the tide has begun to turn. An increasing number of large and small companies now realize the global competitiveness of quality products. Companies spend billions of dollars annually establishing domestic quality assurance programs, testing procedures, and finite inspection criteria. Quality assurance auditors remain stationed at major supplier plants to be sure that purchased materials, parts, and components used in final production meet quality specifications.

The same cannot be said of imported materials, parts, and components, however. Assurance that imported foreign products meet the same high-quality standards as those purchased domestically is much harder to come by. It is difficult and costly to ascertain that suppliers in Jakarta, Guayaquil, Port-of-Spain, or Tel Aviv, maintain the same rigid quality standards as their American counterparts. Yet, to become an effective force in global trade, a company must implement appropriate pro-

FIGURE 19–3
Guidelines for Quality Assurance of Imported Goods

1. Know your foreign supplier. Check references from other American firms he supplies. Verify his litigation record.
2. Understand the quality control standards in place in your supplier's plant. Visit the location. Talk to quality assurance managers. Obtain a copy of his testing and inspection procedure manual, if possible.
3. Make sure your supplier understands how important high-quality standards are to you. The more dogmatic and obsessive you are about quality, the better. If possible, use a second or third source occasionally to impress on a supplier your insistence on quality products. Competition often does what mere words or contracts will not.
4. Be sure your product specifications include quality testing and inspection procedures. Clarify that the supplier understands the specifications thoroughly.
5. For large orders of critical parts, spend the money to station your own quality inspector at the supplier's location. Aerospace and military hardware manufacturers do this continually. Many times it's the only way to be sure of what you are getting.
6. When quality problems arise, communicate with the supplier immediately. Get on a plane and meet with him. Find out what caused the glitch. Be sure it is corrected before more products are shipped.
7. Make certain the purchase order/contract spells out litigation and arbitration procedures, including what laws apply in the event of dispute.
8. Use letters of credit for payment. Include receiving inspection procedures in the documentation that must be satisfied prior to payment.
9. Maintain close personal contact with your supplier. Meet at his location, invite him to yours. Stay in constant contact by telephone, telex, and fax.

cedures to verify compliance with quality standards by suppliers around the world.

Specific quality standards apply to each and every type of material and product. Clearly, successful global companies must establish detailed testing procedures to be certain imports meet these requirements. There are also some general rules to be followed. The best way to avoid lengthy negotiations and perhaps litigation of import quality problems is to avoid, or at least mitigate, them in the first place. This can be achieved by following the few simple guidelines shown in Figure 19–3.

Following these guidelines won't ensure the quality of imported products, but it's a good start. Companies that ignore these basic rules frequently learn too late that the materials or products they import don't work, last, or otherwise meet their own specifications. And recouping from a foreign supplier is significantly more difficult than recovering from a domestic vendor.

CONCLUSION

The proper use of importing to achieve global competitiveness is as important as exporting or direct foreign investment. As a company's global network of value-added products grows, importing and exporting go hand in hand. One can't be done effectively without the other. Increased shipping costs and customs duties can be mitigated by properly structuring both the company and the transaction. Countertrade can often be used to reduce cash outlays for imports.

As long as a company treats a foreign supplier with the same care as it does domestic vendors, difficulties in resolving differences across the seas will be no greater than in the United States. Although federal restrictions inhibit free trade with foreign suppliers, careful structuring and financing of the transaction coupled with a clear understanding of customs regulations reduce most importing problems to a manageable level.

SECTION V

LOOKING TO THE FUTURE

CHAPTER 20

GLOBAL TRADE IN THE 21ST CENTURY

MAJOR TOPICS

KEY POINTS

1. The Power of Economics. Political and social upheaval in Eastern Europe, the Soviet Union, Pakistan, Burma, South Africa, and many other nations points to the enormous power of economics in defining social order. Private enterprise must grasp the opportunity presented by these and other new markets developing in the 1990s and into the 21st century.

2. National Borders and Political Sovereignty. Trade in the 21st century will require companies to learn how to go over, around, or through national trade barriers. New economic coalitions crossing national boundaries will be formed. Joint ventures with national partners offer the smaller company a way to participate.

3. Environmental Safety. Economic coalitions in the 21st century will demand that products be environmentally safe. By redesigning its products now, a company will be ready to enter new markets.

4. Global Poverty. Efforts to obliterate world hunger and disease will assume major proportions in the 21st century. Forced redistribution of resources and assets will occur if the private sector doesn't find solutions.

5. Religious and Cultural Freedom. As religious and cultural persecution comes to an end, capitalist individualism must give ground to community values. Skills and talents long hidden by perverse, oppressive governments will emerge as a new management and labor pool. Matching global community assistance with the need for qualified people, smaller companies will find new resources and markets in nations currently closed to trade.

6. Action Steps to Prepare for the 21st Century. These radical changes will force companies to view material and labor sourcing, cross-border production sites, markets, and financing as global resources. Management talent with international acumen must be developed quickly.

Dateline: April 15, 2010

While getting ready for his retirement dinner, Maconnel Shushai mused over the past 20 years. "It sure has been interesting", he thought, "who would have imagined in 1990 that our little company doing $5 million in sales would end up 20 years later as the global leader in graphics arts equipment. My staff put up a lot of opposition to that first acquisition in Caracas, though. No one believed Acoro Graphics could buy a company in Latin America and make it go. We proved them all wrong. Caracas was the first, then Quito, Mexico City, Kyoto, and Edinburgh. We could never have made it through the great recession of 2002, however, without the merger with Sushimoto.

"And what a change in global markets over the past 20 years! Europe finally got their act together in 1998. Only missed the mark by six years. After losing the Baltics and their southern republics, the Soviet decision to concentrate on developing Russia rather than a whole empire has made a lot of sense. Moscow is now rapidly becoming a world economic power. It's a shame that Poland, Hungary, and the rest of Eastern Europe is dragging down the EC, but that's power politics.

"Washington's move to bring Canada, Mexico, Central America, and the Caribbean nations into the United States of North America was a real coup. It's beginning to look as if the USNA is heading toward world trade domination. The Union of European Nations seems to be faltering; the United Republics of South America are still trying to resolve credit issues; and the Pacific nations seem to be finally recovering from the massive 2001 Japanese depression."

Mac's recollections were interrupted by his vice president of African operations. "It's almost time, chief. Do you want a lift or are you planning to drive yourself?"

"I think I'll go alone. I want to get my thoughts together before giving my address. You go ahead. I'll catch up later."

Maconnel Shushai wanted to swing by his corporate office in Joburg one more time. He still relished the success of Maconnel-Sushi Enterprises, Ltd. Now with sales over $3 billion and firmly entrenched as the world power in graphic arts equipment design and manufacture, M-S E saw 15 years ago that the old South Africa would be the next boom area. Oil, lumber, rubber, magnesium, and a variety of other natural resources, plus its ideal location midway between East and West made Lobomba (née South Africa) the logical choice for the M-S E corporate headquarters.

As Mac saw it, his successor had his work cut out for him. The first step would be to get in on the reconstruction of the Middle East after their devastating and near-annihilating war. After that, the Indian subcontinent, still languishing in poverty, corruption, and religious turmoil, would be ripe for exploitation. Those two projects should take care of the next 10 years, at least. Beyond that Mac couldn't visualize, although new advances in space technology might open up whole new planets before the century ended. His decision 20 years ago to hop on the global bandwagon had certainly proved beneficial to himself, his company, and he liked to believe, the world in general.

No crystal ball can possibly conjure up the unlimited global trade possibilities in the 21st century. Perhaps some or all of the political and economic consolidations depicted above will happen. Perhaps, as democratic and socialistic capitalism flourish, nations that are destitute today will rise above their misbegotten nationalistic philosophies and become global powers. Maybe scientific discoveries and technologies resulting from space programs will obsolete current visions of optimum trade practices. As the decade of the 1990s blossoms, the dreamers and the visionaries have already discounted the economic aberrations that consume our nation's leaders. They are already preparing for the new wave of global trade waiting at the door for those individuals and companies with the foresight to move.

Several facets of future global trade have become evident already. Some are still hidden from all but the most visionary iconoclast. Radical political, social, and economic changes of the past few years do seem to point to a number of features that will influence private enterprise in the next century. It appears that the most pressing issues from the perspective of global survival can be viewed as:

1. The acceptance of the power of social and economic needs over ideological and political isms.
2. The need to find ways to deal with economic national constraints and still encourage the political sovereignty of independent states.
3. The overpowering realization that serious environmental destruction must stop worldwide for trade to continue to function.
4. The recognition that private enterprise must lead the way in the redistribution of global wealth to eradicate severe poverty pockets.
5. The comprehension that people of all races and religions must be allowed to practice individual beliefs without fear of economic deprivation or political suppression.

THE POWER OF ECONOMICS

The political outcomes of recent social struggles in Eastern Europe, the Soviet Union, Namibia, South Africa, Chile, Nicaragua, Iran, and, to a lesser extent, Ethiopia are murky. Political analysts, religious leaders, and military strategists each attribute the forces stimulating these *people revolts* to different origins. All are probably accurate to some extent in their assessments. But the common thread underlying all current popular revolutions, as well as those occurring throughout recorded history, is the economic needs of the populace.

Without bread on the table, it really doesn't matter what ism a government preaches. Capitalism, socialism, communism, racism, all falter over the long haul when people are deprived of the basic necessities of life. Tribes in the mountains of Ethiopia, peasants tilling the soil in Colombia, soldiers treading the mountain trails of Afghanistan, and even homeless people in the sewers of New York must have food, water, and clothing to subsist. When enough people are deprived of these basic necessities, political upheaval follows as sure as day follows night.

During the past five years, numerous examples of economically oppressive bureaucrats being overthrown by impoverished citizens should be positive proof that economics promoting social well-being always wins out over political dogma. The relevance of this truism to American companies entering the next century is self-evident. Regardless of power politics or inequitable restrictive trade barriers, a company must view its survival as dependent on global economics rather than on Washington, Moscow, London, Tokyo, or other bureaucratic strongholds.

A global mentality must be nurtured by owners and managers of companies of every size and in every industry. They must evaluate trade opportunities in Vietnam as well as Germany. They must consider trade with Cuba as well as cross-border trade with Canada. They must look at potential investment openings in South Africa as well as the Caribbean. Just because an existing government may violate American moral or ideological beliefs today, doesn't mean that trade isn't possible tomorrow.

When citizens are hungry for nourishment, they will inevitably throw out the perpetrators of economic misery. And history has proven, time and again, that those businesses anticipating such moves and taking appropriate strategic actions to be ready to enter markets when they open are the winners. Cuba, Vietnam, South Africa, and the People's Republic of China (PRC), for example, could easily become major markets for free enterprise in the next century.

NATIONAL BORDERS AND POLITICAL SOVEREIGNTY

Those who fervently believe that the American way is the best and only way to live, mistakenly ignore the power of national pride and cultural norms. West Indians of St. Lucia and Grenada may not have a new car every third year but they are no less happy and satisfied with their lives than Americans with a three-car garage. Japanese consumers may not be as clothes conscious as American designer fashion consumers, but centuries of island living and religious teachings provoke a satisfaction with close family ties unkown in present-day America. Micronesians may not value college degrees as Americans do, but then what would they do with a business degree when stone money adequately serves their needs?

Current battles over national trade barriers prohibiting Americans and other foreigners from investing in or selling goods to a country seem onerous. They apparently restrict the flow of goods and services we deem necessary for the well-being of the local populace. But these barriers are usually erected specifically to protect a country's citizens from outside exploitation. Smart businesspeople realize this. Intelligent global traders learn quickly that completely free trade is not a prerequisite to successful market penetration. They learn to live within the confines and barriers established by a country rather than striving to tear them down.

As pointed out several times in earlier chapters, multinationals that have successfully mastered the intricacies of global trade have done so in countries irrespective of trade barriers. Coca-Cola is not afraid of investing in Burma. Campbell's and Du Pont are firmly entrenched in Japanese markets. Bechtel and Fluor find ways to build projects in Libya, Iran, and the Soviet Union regardless of trade or political barriers.

Trade in the 21st century will undoubtedly require companies to learn how to go through, around, or over tariffs, quotas, or incestuous distribution systems rather than pushing our government to influence their removal. National pride and customs will probably never disappear.

Learning to live with restrictive regulations means a company must utilize national partners. Joint ventures both in foreign countries and in the United States are the logical answer to dealing with national trade barriers. The sooner smaller companies begin to utilize this technique the faster they will be ready for the turn of the century.

The formation of new economic and political coalitions will eliminate the need for many of the protective barriers we see today. Free trade agreements with Canada, and soon Mexico, will conceivably be added to a united Caribbean to form the United States of North America. The rest of Central America will likely be added. Sovereign boundaries will be maintained for religious, cultural, or other reasons, but trade between these nations will be open.

The unification of the two Germanys and the implementation of the European Community could very likely progress to a United States of Europe in the next century, eventually incorporating Eastern European nations. The Association of Southest Asian Nations (ASEAN) could easily incorporate Indochina, Taiwan, and even China and North and South Korea into a Union of Asian States.

ENVIRONMENTAL SAFETY

A hallmark of the 21st century will be the overt recognition by global economic powers that products, services, and methods of production must be environmentally safe. Private enterprise will inevitably find that protecting the environment is not only crucial to the survival of nations, but fundamental to continued profitability.

The days of disregarding ocean, air, and ground pollution are over. The time when the world community can ignore the destruction of whole species of wild life or the desecration of millions of square miles of forests has long past. Those developing nations dependent upon such destructive practices for their economic sustenance must be shown nonharmful ways to improve the lot of their citizens.

Environmental safety has passed the point of something that sounds good but just isn't practical. While scientists argue about the minute daily effect of destroying the ozone layer and politicians debate how many more restrictive laws they can get by with, private industry the world over has already begun to recognize the potential profitability of introducing new, environmentally safe products and processes. Biodegradable packaging, toxic-free chemical processing, and environmentally safe waste disposal are leading the way toward a contaminant-free 21st century.

As new political and economic unions are formed between sovereign countries, the effect one country has on its environment will surely impact all members, such as the spread of acid rain or unsafe nuclear plants. Pressure from member nations on violators to eliminate contaminating processes will force compliance through economic sanctions.

As developing nations begin to feel the economic pressure from these powerful new coalitions, the drive to find environmentally safe ways to bolster their economies should open significant new markets in a variety of industries, from automobiles to cosmetics. While there is still time to develop such products and processes, smaller global companies should pull out all stops to ensure a competitive position in the next century. Researching methods to transform harmful products and processes to those that will compete in an environmentally conscious world is a small price to pay for survival in the decades ahead.

GLOBAL POVERTY

Pictures of starving children in Ethiopia or disease-ravished beggars in Calcutta and Bangladesh raise sympathy in all of us. For a brief moment our compassion overwhelms us. Then, with a turn of the dial or the flip of a page, we go on to plan our own survival and forget about the world's miseries. Occasionally some of us become involved with charitable organizations trying to alleviate some of this misery. Donations to emergency funds from religious bodies and international relief organizations, or contributions of our time and skills, seem to placate our moral obligations.

Most of us feel helpless to make a dent in global poverty. If we can't even manage our own welfare programs, how can we possibly make an impact in a foreign land? The easiest way out is to look to the federal government as the end-all and cure-all of social deprivation. But there is another way, far more effective, and profitable at the same time.

With the dawn of the 21st century, obliteration of world hunger and disease will exact global concern. Impotent, financially strapped government bureaucracies will be helpless to lift a finger. The task will inevitably fall to the private sector as it always has in the past. With global markets and profits comes global responsibility. As new economic unions are formed, businesses can no longer ignore the social condition of their customers. Western companies will take a page from the Japanese book and begin to view global opportunities in terms of long-term market position and strategic leverage. Short-term gains to pacify Wall Street will become a concern of the past.

In order to maximize long-term competitive advantage, American companies must take an active role in developing technology, products, and services that further the social cause of potential consumers in far-removed markets. These consumers will become the backbone of customers as the century progresses. To ignore millions of potential buyers of products and services makes poor business strategy.

Larger corporations are already being pressured by consumer advocates to pay attention to social needs. But the political maneuvering of large bureaucracies prevent many of these giants from stepping up to consumer demands. Smaller companies can step into the vacuum created by this abdication of social responsibility. Smart managements, those with a true global mentality, will find unusual strategic opportunities by leading the advance in these new submarkets.

RELIGIOUS AND CULTURAL FREEDOM

The 1980s witnessed a breakthrough in human rights in several sectors of the globe. The 1990s will experience even more: Jews emigrating from the Soviet Union; religious and class persecution diminishing in Central America; white supremacy crumbling in South Africa; Christian and Moslem factions reconciling differences in Lebanon; and students in Nepal, Burma, and China, fighting and dying for the right to practice their own religious beliefs.

The 21st century will bring additional upheaval in nations continuing to persecute diverse religious and cultural groups: the appreciation in black African of unique variations in tribal customs; Indian and Pakistani religious differences reconciled; Northern Ireland finally settling antagonisms between Protestants and Catholics; and acceptance of minority cultural and religious groups in Albania, Cuba, Cambodia, and North Korea.

During the next century, peoples of the world coming from diverse dogma and customs will finally learn that living in peace with each other is their only chance for survival on an ever more crowded Earth. Parity in destructive nuclear capability will inevitably drive home the realization that like it or not, only two choices exist: either people must live together in harmony or blow up the world and let someone else start over again.

Commercial opportunities in a peaceful world loom bright on the horizon. Without restrictive immigration quotas, work prohibitions, and political antagonisms between culturally dissimilar societies, companies can take advantage of the enormous capabilities of a global manpower pool. Skills, technical expertise, and creative talents hidden in regions long repressed will become available to the highest bidder. The highest bidder, not necessarily in wages, but in work and living conditions, will give permission for laborers to participate in the products of their efforts, and freedom for people to choose their own livelihoods.

Such global competition for talent and skills should have a profound effect on the structure of private enterprise. Shared company ownership and partnerships between employer and employees should become pronounced. Many social welfare programs, long cast as a responsibility of central government, will be transferred to private businesses. As companies compete in the global arena for qualified personnel, employee assistance programs will eventually overshadow wages as the primary attraction. Womb to tomb programs, long advocated but seldom practiced in corporate America will determine which companies attract the brightest and most qualified employees.

The days of dictatorial rule and employee unsurpation are over. The companies that survive are those that recognize employees as their most important asset and structure their businesses to enchance the wellbeing of employees rather than short-term financial returns to investors.

As the dawn of the 21st century pushes away the haze of religious and cultural persecution, companies must be prepared to compete for the artisans, technicians, creative geniuses, and workers of the world. To do this, capitalist individualism must give ground to community values. Financial rewards must bow to assurances for bread on the table, universal education, health and welfare programs, and sufficient guaranteed retirement income as the carrots to attract the best people. Companies will realize that the development of scientific and technological innovations are the cornerstone of long-term success in global markets. They will also recognize that to achieve predominance in new product introductions, qualified people must come first.

As religious and cultural oppression subsides, the demographics of the global labor, managerial, and technical pool changes. A company can no longer enjoy the luxury of picking and choosing sites for manufacturing, distribution, or retail facilities based on short-term market advantage or material sources. It must locate where the people are, whether in Central Africa, Indonesia, Brazil, or China. Companies must go to the available talent source rather than expect qualified employees to move. Complacency and lumbering bureaucratic obstinacy in large corporations opens the door to smaller companies able to move quickly to take advantage of these new people resources as they become available.

ACTION STEPS TO PREPARE FOR THE 21ST CENTURY

In addition to these macroglobal changes in the 21st century, there are five specific actions private enterprise must focus on to prosper in this new economic environment. Size or nationality notwithstanding, every company that plans to be in existence 20 years from now must:

1. Learn how to source material and labor requirements from a global reservoir.
2. Recognize the necessity of establishing global networks for value-added production.
3. View markets as global, not as domestic, export, or international.
4. Structure growth-oriented financing plans to utilize global financial systems.
5. Recruit and train top- and middle-management personnel with a global mentality.

To develop a global mentality, a company must begin taking these actions immediately. They cannot be put off waiting to see what happens in domestic markets or world politics. The decade of the 1990s is the training period during which a company must fine-tune its global characteristics to be ready for the next century. As global competition increases over the next 20 years, smaller companies should have the mechanisms already in place to hone their postures to meet rivals head-on. Only by beginning now, can they enjoy a few years of learning experience before the onslaught of European, Pacific Basin, Latin, and Soviet competition.

Sourcing Material and Labor from the Global Reservoir

The draining of domestic natural resources, political, and environmental opposition to expanding basic industries, the development of new alloys based on scarce natural elements, and cost competitiveness, will force global materials sourcing far beyond current practice. Rather than striving to become self-sustaining, developing nations will learn to exploit their own natural resources and labor pools in the global economy. They will concentrate efforts and financial resources on developing their strengths for export to the world.

Any company with global foresight should position itself to get in on the ground floor of these industries. Rather than limiting its actions to importing materials, parts, and subassemblies, a global mentality dictates that a company establish a presence directly in the country best equipped to supply its material needs. The same holds true for companies producing labor-intensive products. It only makes sense to establish a facility in a low-cost, labor-intensive country rather than importing subassemblies.

Political and social stability throughout the world makes such moves viable. As nations begin to specialize in their own natural strengths, dependence on global trade to sustain their economic development will mitigate local government trade interference. Without fear of government expropriation or armed revolution, a smaller company can easily establish a secure presence.

Global Networks for Value-Added Products

Along with global sourcing of materials and labor, a company should stand poised to take advantage of broadening 21st-century opportunities for the global design, engineering, and production of its products. Value-added networking is already upon us. Successful multinational corporations have broken ground in Europe, the Pacific Basin, Central and South America, and parts of Africa.

From the design stage to final assembly, products are currently being produced throughout the world, regardless of the country of origin of the parent company. Automobile subassemblies produced in North Carolina are shipped to Japan for final assembly in Toyota and Mitsubishi cars. Oil-based chemicals ship from Texas to the Pacific Basin for conversion to polyethylene compounds which, in turn, get processed into plastic in Kansas and New Jersey plants. Meat from New Zealand combined with vegetables from South America and other ingredients from the United States go into soups canned in American plants. Tuna from South Africa, Japan, and Mexico are mixed with American ingredients to make pet food for sale in the United States and Canada. And on and on it goes.

Value-added production must become the predominant means of manufacture in the 21st century. No other way can utilize competitive global production resources. As new entrants to global economic warfare, American companies should begin immediately to reassess the design, engineering, processing, and assembly components of their products. Should any activity be transferred to a foreign location to take advantage of lower cost or resource availability? Will technicians and engineers needed in the next century come from Europe, Japan, Australia, or South Africa? Can markets for end products in South America and the Caribbean be served more competitively from local facilities? These questions, and more, must be analyzed and answered to compete in the next century.

Global Markets

As material and labor sourcing and value-added networking become the predominant way to produce global products in the 21st century, customer markets for goods and services of every variety will expand throughout the world, even more than now. A global mentality dictates that companies look at markets for their products and services through global glasses. Artificial demarcations currently used to define markets will be abandoned. However, opportunities in submarkets, such as exporting, Europe, the Middle East, and Japan, will continue.

To meet global competition, a company must visualize shifting demand and supply curves for worldwide markets. This means developing a market strategy to highlight opening trade opportunities wherever and whenever competitive advantage dictates. It means planning to leverage cracks in a competitor's armor by superior pricing, delivery, quality, and customer service. Such an offensive strategy requires production, labor force and technical resources stationed in key regions around the world.

With economic deprivation in massive world markets beginning to lighten, the next century will bring hordes of new consumers for every type of goods and service imaginable: from autos to stereos, from shoes to hats, from tomato paste to breakfast cereal, and from aluminum beams to graphite epoxy structures. Smaller companies, untainted by past mistakes and unfettered by bureaucratic ineptitude, stand the best chance of usurping submarkets from foreign competitors.

However, they must be ready. They must prepare during this decade by developing a global market strategy and lining up appropriate resources. They must structure a global marketing organization adept at selling to and servicing diverse cultural demands. Finally they must view marketing strategy from the perspective of establishing secure market shares over the long term rather than maximizing short-term sales gains.

Global Financing

To support worldwide sourcing, value-added networking, and global market penetration, companies must utilize global financing sources. As world financial markets in Tokyo, Frankfort, Moscow, Rio, Kuala Lumpur, and others open to the global community, smaller companies must be prepared to use these financial resources to their advantage. Blinders to public ownership must be thrown off. Fears of ownership sharing must be abated. Joint ventures, partnerships, and other forms of combining structures must be viewed as a logical extension of global trade. These new combines can be used to provoke interest from the financial community. Combined asset bases, management talent, and creditworthiness will encourage global financial sources to participate in funding new ventures and expanded markets.

Multinational corporations already have a head start in global financing. Well-known, firmly established throughout the world, these Goliaths already evoke substantial interest from the financial community. This means that the smaller company, regardless of the form it chooses to enter global trade, must develop a financing strategy along with its global marketing plans. It must begin now.

Europe is about to open its borders to global trade. The Eastern bloc and the Soviet Union stand ready to participate in global trade as soon as internal social and political conflicts are resolved. Latin America beckons foreign entrance into its economic development. Africa remains poised to erupt into substantial markets. The Pacific Basin, already bursting at the seams with economic advancements, offers unimagined opportunities for participation by smaller companies.

To enter these burgeoning markets, a company must have money. Although federal funds can help in the beginning, the financial impunity practiced in Washington forebodes even greater deficits and credit shortfalls in the future. To expect significant, long-term financing help from this source seems overly optimistic. Regulations restricting creative financing by American commercial banks will undoubtedly give way to a more open, competitive banking policy. But this could take many years. In the meantime, American companies with the foresight to plan for global financing will get a head start on those relying solely on government or bank financing.

To take advantage of opening public financial markets, during the next decade a company should learn how to cope with public ownership. It should adopt a policy now of exploring the likelihood of small public debt and equity issues on American exchanges to get a flavor for the future. This means staffing a competent financial organization to handle a domestic issue. It also means this organization will be in place and ready to function efficiently when the opportunity arises to float worldwide public issues. Once again, a global mentality dictates a company take a long-term view of the financial function. It cannot be harnessed to traditional short-term cost savings.

Global Management

No company, large or small, can reasonably expect to survive in the competitive arena without knowledgeable, well-trained management personnel. In the global community, this translates to dedicated interest and hard-core experience in international circles. From the top down, a $5 million company or a $200 million company must recruit and train management personnel in the art of global trade.

Waiting for global market opportunities to become visible will be too late. By that time, others, with greater foresight and daring, will already be established. Recognizing the need for qualified management, companies on the cutting edge of global trade will already have recruited managers with appropriate experience. Even today several companies large and small, have begun filling new presidencies and top executive openings with experienced global traders.

Reorganizing a management team is never easy. Past loyalties, human caring, federal wage and hour regulations, domestic competitive pressures, and an array of other forces act to restrict a smaller company from restaffing. The smaller the company, the more relevant it becomes to keep the few good people you have. Obviously, there is no easy way out of this dilemma. Nevertheless, to compete in the 21st century, a company must be run by a management well versed in global trade.

Even if restaffing isn't practical, everyone has the capacity to learn. Starting right now, there is still time to get an education in at least the rudiments of global trade. Several excellent books are now coming out that deal with various aspects of the subject. Earlier in this book, a number of magazines were listed as excellent background sources for learning international trade. Seminars, conferences, and special programs covering global trade from a variety of dimensions are available in any medium or large city.

An increasing number of colleges and universities offer courses and symposiums on international trade. A conglomeration of federal and state agencies provides literature, conferences, and a variety of other information on the subject. There is certainly not a lack of information available to educate management personnel. All it takes is the desire to learn.

The 1990s will still tolerate beginners in global trade. The next century will surely not.

CONCLUSION

Though no crystal ball projects the future with certainty, recent political, social, and economic changes throughout the world point to a radically different scenario in the 21st century from that which we see today. The past 20 years have only given us a taste of the marvels to come. With the EC opening in the 90s, Japan's economy maturing, markets in Latin America and the Pacific Basin bursting at the seams, open trade treaties with Canada and Mexico, and the rapid inclusion of Caribbean nations into the American economic fold, this is an exciting time to be involved in the business community.

Companies of any size, with virtually any product, or service, stand on the threshold of enormous opportunity. Those with isolationist blinders will surely falter: those with a global mentality stand to reap vast profits. The time to prepare for this stirring advance in global trade is right now. Waiting only allows others to gain competitive advantage. The Japanese, British, and Germans may have a head start, or they may not. American companies have led the way in creative business acumen for two centuries. Continuing leadership into the 21st century is there for the taking. Those with courage and foresight will survive and prosper. Those without, won't.

Nothing comes easy in this life. No panacea of methods, policies, or strategies exists to bring a company into the global limelight. It takes hard work. It takes stamina. And it takes a willingness to forego short-term gains for long-term prosperity. This book has attempted to open the doors of global trade for those who have been afraid to try, for a variety of reasons. It has shown how many small and midsize companies have made the effort to learn global trade and have been enormously successful. And it has tried to point the way for managers of smaller companies, perhaps as yet uninitiated in global trade, toward the many aids, supports, and tools available to make an entrance into global markets as smooth as possible.

Going global now is the right move regardless of a company's size or past history. Going global is the way of the future. Going global is the only way to survive in the 21st century. Give it a try. The odds are high you'll make it. Godspeed!

APPENDIX A

FOREIGN OFFICES OF AMERICAN CHAMBERS OF COMMERCE

REGIONAL OFFICES

Latin America

**Regional AMCHAM Organizations
AACCLA**
David A. Wicker, *President*
Association of American Chambers of
Commerce in Latin America and
National Distillers do Brazil
Av. Brig. Faria Lima, 4 e 5 andar
01451 São Paolo, SP-Brazil
Phone   55-11-813-4133

Argentina
Federico Dodds, *President*
Union Carbide Argentina
S.A.I.C.S.
Virrey Loreto 2477/81
1426 Buenos Aires, Argentina
Phone   54-1-782-6016

Bolivia
Charles Bruce, *President*
The Anschutz Corp.
P. O. Box 160
La Paz, Bolivia
Phone   591-2-35-55-74

Brazil—Rio de Janeiro
John P. Polychron, *Director President*
R. J. Reynolds Tobacos do Brazil, Ltda.
Rraia de Botafogo, 440/25
P. O. Box 3588
22.250 Rio de Janeiro, RJ-Brazil
Phone   55-21-286-6162

Brazil—São Paulo
Enrique Sosa, *Director President*

Empresas Dow
Caixa Postal 30037
01051, São Paolo, SP-Brazil
Phone   55-11-212-1122

Chile
M. Wayne Sandvig, *Director*
Fundación Chile
Casilla 773
Santiago, Chile
Phone   56-2-28-16-46

Colombia
William Wide, *Chairman of the Board*
Fiberglass Colombia S.A.
Apartado Aereo 9192
Bogotá, Colombia
Phone   57-1-255-7900

Branch Office
Richard Lee, *General Manager*
Goodyear de Colombia
Apartado Aereo 142
Cali, Valle, Colombia
Phone   57-3-686-141, 57-3-689-868

Costa Rica
Federico A. Golcher, *Managing Partner*
Peat Marwick Mitchell & Co.
Apartado 10208
1000 San José, Costa Rica
Phone   506-21-52-22

Dominican Republic
Jaak R. Rannik, *President*
Baez & Rannik, S. A.
P.O. Box 1221
Santo Domingo, Dominican Republic
Phone   809-565-6661

Ecuador—Quito
Robert L. Rice, *General Manager*
Xerox del Ecuador, S.A.
P.O. Box 174-A
Quito, Ecuador
Phone   593-2-245-229, 593-2-451-614

Ecuador—Guayaquil
Carson Watson, *Managing Director*
Johnson & Johnson del Ecuador
Casilla 7206
Guayaquil, Ecuador
Phone   593-39-96-00

El Salvador
Ramsey L. Moore, *President*
Moore Commercial S.A. de C.V.
29 Avenida Sur 817
P.O. Box 480
San Salvador, El Salvador
Phone   503-71-1200

Guatemala
Spencer Manners, *Vice President, Latin American Operations*
Foodpro International, Inc.
12 Calle 1-25, No. 1114
P.O. Box 89-A, Zona 10
Guatemala City, Guatemala
Phone   502-2-320-490

Haiti
Robert L. Burgess, *General Manager*
Sylvania Overseas Trading Corporation
P.O. Box 1005
Port-au-Prince, Haiti
Phone   509-1-6-0037, 509-1-6-3859

Honduras
J. Mark Werner, *Attorney-at-Law*
21 Ave. S.O. 9 y 10
C. #88 Coloia Trejo
P.O. Box 500
San Pedro Sula, Honduras
Phone   504-54-27-43, 504-54-42-58

Mexico
Purdy C. Jordan, *Director*
Embotelladora Tarahumara S.A. de C.V.
Río Amazonas No. 43
06500 Mexico City, Mexico
Phone   52-5-591-0066
Branches also in Monterrey and Guadalajara

Nicaragua
Julio Vigil, *President*
Vigil y Caligaris
Apartado 202
Managua, Nicaragua
Phone   505-2-262-491

Panama
Robert M. Cooney, *Vice President*
Citibank, N.A.
Apartado 555
Panama 9A, República de Panamá
Phone   57-64-4044, 57-64-1255

Paraguay
Desiderio Enciso, *Director*
Petroleos Paraguayos
Chile y Olivia, Piso 4
Asunción, Paraguay

Peru
Miguel J. Godoy, *President*
M. J. Godoy & Co., S.A.
P.O. Box 5661
Lima 100, Peru
Phone   51-14-28-7006, 51-14-28-7515

Uruguay
John Dale, *Financial Director*
General Motors Uruguay, S.A.
Sayago 1385
Casilla de Correo 234
Montevideo, Uruguay
Phone   598-2-38-16-21/28

Venezuela
Donald H. Veach, *Executive Director* and *General Manager*
Cartón de Venezuela, S.A.
Apartado 609
Caracas 1010, Venezuela

Pacific Rim
APCAC Asian-Pacific Council of American Chamber of Commerce
Warren W. Williams, *Chairman*
APCAC
c/o Burston Marsteller
KS Building, 5 Kojimachi, 4-chome
Chiyoda-ku

Tokyo 102, Japan
Phone   81-03-264-6701

Australia
Joseph D. Berrier, Jr.
American Chamber of Commerce in Australia
3rd Floor, 50 Pitt Street
Sydney, N.S.W. 2000, Australia
Phone   61-2-241-1907

China
Sally A. Harpole
Graham & James
Jian Guo Hotel, Room 140
Jian Guo Men Wai
Beijing, People's Republic of China
Telex: 22439 JGHBJ Cn

Hong Kong
Gage McAfee
Coudert Brothers
32/F Alexandra House
3105 Alexandra House
16 Charter Road, Central
Hong Kong
Phone   852-5-26595

Indonesia
Harvey Goldstein, *Executive Vice President*
P. T. Resources Management Indonesia
J1. Melawai VI/8
Kebayoran Baru
Jakarta Selatan, Indonesia

Japan—Tokyo
Herbert F. Hayde, *Chairman*
Burroughs Company, Ltd.
13-1 Shimomiyabicho
Shinjuku-ku
Tokyo 162, Japan
Phone   81-03-235-3337

Japan—Okinawa
Murray V. Harlan, *President*
The American Chamber of Commerce in
Okinawa
P.O. Box 235, Koza
Okinawa City, 904, Japan
Phone   81-098945-4558

Korea
James H. Riddle, *Vice President*
Teledyne
Room 3203, Namsong Mansion

260-199, Itaewon-dong
Yongan-gu, Seoul, Korea

Malaysia
Russell A. Klingler, *Vice President*
American International Assurance Ltd.
AIA Building
P.O. Box 759
Kuala Lumpur, Malaysia

New Zealand
Maurice P. Boland, *Director*
3M New Zealand Ltd.
P.O. Box 33-246, Takapuna
Auckland 9, New Zealand
Phone   64-9-444-4760

Pakistan
Hasan I. Kazmi, *President*
American Business Council of Pakistan
3rd Floor, Shaheen Commercial Complex
M. R. Kayani Road, GPO Box 1322
Karachi, Pakistan
Phone   92-526436

Philippines
A. Lewis Burridge, *President*
Sterling Asia
8th Floor, Teza Towers
Herrera Village, Makati, Metro Manila
Philippines
Phone   63-2-815-9526

Singapore
Dorsey Dunn, *Chairman*
Mobil Oil Singapore
18 Pioneer Road
Jurong Town, Singapore 2262

Taiwan
Robert Hoffman, *General Manager*
General Electric Technical Service Company
7F, 201, Tin Hwa North Road
Taipei, Taiwan
Phone   886-2-713-1065, 886-2-713-6518

Thailand
Thomas J. White, *President*
Phelps-Dodge (Thailand) Ltd.
6th Floor, Panunee Building
518/3 Ploenchit Road
Bangkok 10500, Thailand
Phone   66-2-251-2251

Europe, Africa and the Middle East
European Council
Frederic G. Drake, *Chairman*
European Council of American Chambers of
Commerce
President
General Electric-Deutschland
Praunheimer Landstr. 50
6000 Frankfort 90, Germany
Phone   49-69-030-34071

Austria
Dr. Elemer T. Balogh, *President*
The American Chamber of Commerce in Austria
Turkenstrasse 9
A-1090 Vienna, Austria
Phone   43-222-31-57-51

Belgium
John E. Egbers, *Managing Director*
Du Pont de Nemours (Belgium)
rue de la Fusée 100
110 Brussels, Belgium
Phone   32-02-722-06-11

Egypt
Sam Zavatti, *President*
American Chamber of Commerce in Egypt
Cairo Marriott Hotel, Suite 1537
P.O. Box 33 Zamalek
Cairo, Egypt
Phone   650840-1

France
John Crawford, *Partner*
Surrey & Morse
53, avenue Montaigne
75008 Paris, France
Phone   33-1-359-2349

Germany
Frederick G. Drake, *President*
General Electric—Deutschland
Praunheimer Landstr. 50
6000 Frankfort 90 Germany
Phone   49-069-7607-325-6

Greece
Charles J. Politis, *President*
APCO Industries S.A.
Group Corporate Offices
18 Academias Street
Athens 134, Greece
Phone   30-1-3618-008

Ireland
A. J. Fox, Jr., *Managing Director*
Union Camp Ireland
Ashbourne
County Meath, Ireland
Phone   353-350411

Israel
Arik Makleff, *President*
Israel-American Chamber of Commerce
Dexter Chemical (International) Ltd.
P.O. Box 300
Yavne 70652, Israel
Phone   972-08-437011

Italy
Michael N. Bitas, *Senior Partner*
Peat Marwick Mitchell & Co.
Piazza Meda 3
20121 Milano, Italy
Phone   39-02-77-351

Morocco
Jean-Pierre Bernex, *General Manager*
Colgate Palmolive Maroc
11 Avenue des Forces Armées Royales
Casablanca, Morocco

The Netherlands
Sig E. Von Kutzleben, *Managing Director*
Fluor Nederland B.V.
c/o The American Chamber of Commerce in the
Netherlands
2517 KJ The Hague, The Netherlands
Phone   31-70-023-339020

Portugal
Robert R. Langelier, *Director Gerente General*
General Motors de Portugal
As Marcechal Gomes de Costa 33
1800 Lisbon, Portugal
Phone   351-1-853996

Saudi Arabia—Dhahran
Charles M. Thompson, *President*
American Businessmen's Association, Eastern
Province
P.O. Box 4, Dhahran Airport 31932
Dhahran, Saudi Arabia

Saudi Arabia—Jeddah
Bob F. Reece, *President*
The American Businessmen of Jeddah
P.O. Box 5019

Jeddah, Saudi Arabia
Phone   966-651-7968

Saudi Arabia—Riyadh
Keith Poulin, *Chairman*
American Businessmen's Group of Riyadh
P.O. Box 8273
Riyadh 11482, Saudi Arabia 07045
Phone   966-1-476-5578

South Africa
W. J. DeGenring, *Managing Director*
S. A. Cyanamid (pty) Ltd.
Elmer Park Center, 1st Floor
Corner 1st Avenue & Adjutant Street
Edenvale, Transvaal, South Africa

Spain
Max H. Klein

Max H. Klein y Cia
Paseo de Gracia, 95
Barcelona-8, Spain

Switzerland
J. Quincy Hunsicker, *Managing Director*
McKinsey & Company
Zollikerstrasse 225
8008 Zurich, Switzerland
Phone   41-01-53-44-44

United Kingdom
John D. Philipsborn
The Chase Manhattan Bank, NA
Woolgate HSE
Coleman Street
London EC2P 2HD
Phone   44-01-726-5000

APPENDIX B

COUNTRY DESK OFFICERS

(All in area code 202)
(All in exchange 377)   *Phone Number*

Headquarters: 3022

GATT Division   3681

International organizations   3227

U.S. Trade by Region:

Africa   2175

Canada   3101

Caribbean Basin and Mexico   5327

China and Hong Kong   3583

Eastern Europe   2645

European Community   5276

Israel Information Center   4652

Japan   4527

Near East   4441

Pacific Basin   4008

South America   2436

South Asia   2954

USSR   4655

Western Europe   5341

APPENDIX C

TRADE DEVELOPMENT OFFICERS BY INDUSTRY ORGANIZATION

(All in area code 202)
(All in exchange 377)
This is a partial listing only. For more information call the headquarters office.

Phone Number

Headquarters	1461
Aerospace	8228
Automotive	0823
Chemicals and allied products	0128
Computer and business equipment	0572
Consumer goods	0337
Energy	1466
Export statistics and trade data (domestic)	4211
Export statistics and trade data (foreign)	4211
Export trading companies	5131
Forest products and domestic construction	0384
General industrial machinery	5455
Instrumentation	5466
Major projects and international construction	5225
Medical services	0550
Metals, minerals, and commodities	0575
Microelectronics and instrumentation	2587
Service industries	3575
Special industrial machinery	0302
Telecommunications	4466
Textiles	5078
Trade information analysis	1316

APPENDIX D

INTER-AMERICAN DEVELOPMENT BANK OFFICES

Argentina
Calle Esmeralda 130, Pisos 19y20
(Casilla de Correo No. 181, Sucursal 1)
Buenos Aires

Bahamas
IBM Building, 4th Floor
P.O. Box N 3743
Nassau

Barbados
Maple Manor, Hastings
P.O. Box 402
Christ Church

Bolivia
Edificio "BISA," 5 Piso
Avenida 16 de julio No. 1628
La Paz

Brazil
Praia do Flamengo N 200, 21 andar
Caixa Postal 16209, Z0-01
22210 Rio de Janeiro

Chile
Avenida Pedro de Valdivia 0193, 11 Piso
Casilla No. 16611, Correo 9 Providencia
Santiago

Colombia
Avenida 40 A No. 13-09, 8 Piso
Apartado Aereo 12037
Bogotá

Costa Rica
Edificio Centro Colón, Piso 12
Paseo Colón entre Calles 38y40
San José

Dominican Republic
Avenida Winston Churchill Esquina
Calle Luis F. Thomen, Torre BHD
Apartado Postal No. 1386
Santo Domingo

Ecuador
Avenida Amazonas 477 y Roca
Edificio Banco de los Andes, 90, Piso
Apartado Postal 9041-Sucursal 7
Quito

El Salvador
Condominio Torres del Bosque
Colonia La Moascota-10 Piso
Apartado Postal No. (01) 199
San Salvador

Guatemala
Edificio Geminis 10
12 Calle 1-25, Zona 10, Nivel 19
Apartado Postal 935
Guatemala City

Guyana
47 High Street, Kingston
P.O. Box 10867
Georgetown

Haiti
Batiment de la Banque Nationale de Paris
Angle de la Rue Lemarre et Calve
Boite Postale 1321
Port-au-Prince

Honduras
Edificio Los Castaños, Pisos 5y6
Colonia Los Castaños

Apartado Postal No. C-73
Tegucigalpa

Jamaica

40-46 Knutsford Blvd., 6th Floor
P.O. Box 429
Kingston 10

Mexico

Paseo de la Reforma 379, 7 Piso
Col. Cuauhtemoc
Delgación Cuauhtemoc
06500 Mexico, D.F.

Nicaragua

Edificio BID
Kilometro 4½ Carretera a Masaya
Apartado Postal 2512
Managua

Panama

Avenida Samuel Lewis
Edificio Banco Union, Piso 14
Apartado Postal 7297
Panama 5

Paraguay

Edificio Aurora I
Calle Caballero Esquina

Eligio Ayala, Pisos 2y3
Calle 1209, Asunción

Peru

Paseo de la República, 3245, 14 Piso
Apartado Postal No. 3778
San Isidro,
Lima 27

Suriname

Zwartenhovewn Brugstraat
32 Boven
Paramaribo

Trinidad and Tobago

Tatil Building, 11 Maravel Road
P.O. Box 68
Port-of-Spain

Uruguay

Andes 1365, 13 Piso
Casilla de Correo 5029, Sucursal 1
Montevideo

Venezuela

Nucleo A, Piso 16
Conjunto Miranda
Multicentro Empresarial del Este
Avenida Liberador, Chacao
Caracas 1060

APPENDIX E

LISTING OF ASSOCIATIONS, BUREAUS, AND AGENCIES FOR INTERNATIONAL TRADE

Council for Export Trading Companies
1200 19th Street NW, Suite 605
Washington, DC 20036

Overseas Private Investment Corporation
1615 M Street NW
Washington, DC 20527

U.S. Agency of International Development
Office of Small and Disadvantaged Business
Utilization/Minority Resource Center
1100 Wilson Blvd., Room 1400-A
Rosslyn, VA 22209

U.S. Department of Commerce
International Trade Administration
14th and Constitution Ave. NW, Room 1128
Washington, DC 20230

U.S. Department of Commerce
Office of Trade Finance

14th and Constitution Ave. NW, Room 4420
Washington, DC 20230

U.S. Department of Commerce
United States and Foreign Commercial
Service
14th and Constitution Ave. NW, Room 3012
Washington, DC 20230

U.S. Small Business Administration
Office of International Trade
1441 L Street NW, Room 501-A
Washington, DC 20416

World Bank
1818 H Street NW
Washington, DC 20433

FCIA
40 Rector Street
New York, NY 10006

APPENDIX F

CREDIT AGENCIES PROVIDING CREDIT REPORTS ON ENTITIES IN FOREIGN COUNTRIES

Brazil

Assessoria Empresarial e Informacoes Comerciales
Rua Brigaderio Tobia-577
6th Floor, Suite 605
São Paulo, Brazil CEP 01032

Morocco

Afric Gestion
95 Rue d'Azilal
Casablanca, Morocco

Gabon, Ivory Coast
Senegal, Togo

Afrique Service—AFSER
08-P. B. 18
Abidjan, Ivory Coast

Saudi Arabia
United Arab Emirates

Afro-Asian Trading Office
Sulieman Al Hamad Bldg.
4th Floor Flat #27
King Abdul A 212 St.
P.O. Box 587
Jeddah, Saudi Arabia

Greece

Alpha M. I.
3 Aghiou Constantinou St.
Athens 101 Greece

Most Countries

Amalgamated Trades Protection Ltd. (A.T.P. International)

Sutherland House
70/78 Edgware Road
Staples Corner
London NW9 7BT, United Kingdom

Panama

Andres F. Archibold S.A.
Apartado 6369
Estafeta Balboa
Panama 5

Andorra

Antony Forne Jou
Carrer Les Canbals 13,
Zalet Forne
Andorra La Vella

Afghanistan, Cyprus, Egypt,
Iraq, Israel, Jordan, Kuwait,
Malta, Oman, Qatar, Saudi Arabia,
Sudan, U.A.E., Yemen Arab Republic

Argus Information Services
15 Archbishop Makarios Ave.
Nicosia, Cyprus

Burma, China (PRC), Hong Kong,
India, Indonesia, Korea, Morocco,
Malaysia, Philippines, Singapore,
Sri Lanka, Taiwan, Thailand

Asia Mercantile Agency (H.K.) Ltd.
1301-3 Chiao Shang Bldg.
92-104 Queen's Road
Central, Hong Kong

Dominican Republic

Asociación De Cedito C Por A—Acca

Apartado Postal #988
Zona Postal 1
Santo Domingo, Dominican Republic

Philippines

Associated Credit Bureau
Room 306 Pilar Bldg. #2
507 Gastambide Street
Sampaloc Manila 2906
Philippines

**Bahrain, Cyprus, Jordan,
Yemen Arab Republic**

Atlas Credit Marketing Services
117 Athalassa Avenue
P.O. Box 2136
Nicosia, Cyprus

Colombia

"Audirriesgos" Auditores de Riesco Asociados
Carrera 9, No. 17-47 OF. 404
Apartado Aereo 8182
Bogotá, Colombia

Costa Rica

Augusto J. Amador
Apartado Postal 2-810
San José, Costa Rica

**Australia, British Pacific Islands,
Fiji, French Pacific Islands, Nauru,
New Zealand, Papua New Guinea,
Solomon Islands, Tahiti**

*Australian Mercantile Bureaux Agency Ltd—
Amba*
363 Kingsway 1st Floor
P.O. Box 291
Caringbah N.S.W. 2229, Australia

Bermuda

B.C.A.—Bermuda Credit
P.O. Box 280
Hamilton 5, Bermuda

Brazil

Brasinform, Ltd.
Rua 24 de Maio, 188
3 Andar 5/304
01041 São Paulo
Brazil

**Austria, Belgium, Canada, Denmark,
Finland, France, Germany, Iran,**

**Ireland, Italy, Liechtenstein,
Luxembourg, Morocco, Netherlands,
Netherlands Antilles, Norway,
Portugal, Saudi Arabia, Spain,
Sweden, Switzerland, Turkey,
United Kingdom, Yugoslavia**

Burgel GMBH—Centrale Der
Veringten Auskunftei
Elisabethstrasse 14
Postfach 310
D-5100 Aachen, West Germany

Colombia

Irving C. Byington
Ave. Jimenez 7-25
Ofic. 1025
Apartado Aereo 45-62
Bogotá, Colombia

Algeria

Cabinet Zemouchi
5 Rue Mahmond Bendali
Algiers, Algeria

Canada

Canadian Credit Reporting, Ltd.
2175 Sheppard Ave. E.
Suite 305
Willowdale, Ontario M2J 1W8
Canada

Nicaragua

Centro Informativo de Crédito—C.I.C.
Apartado Postal 2391
Managua, Nicaragua

Taiwan

Chinese United Credit Center
7th Floor, KUO Hwa Bldg.
#154 Po Ai Road
Taipai, Taiwan

Lebanon

Clement H. Dana
Commercial & Financial Service
136 Robeiz Street
P.O. Box 11.436
Beirut, Lebanon

Ethiopia

Commercial Bank of Ethiopia
P.O. Box 255
Addis Ababa, Ethiopia

Fiji, Papua New Guinea, Samoa

C.C.C.—Commercial Credit Centre
89 Robertson Road
G.P.O. Box 926
Suva, Fiji

Argentina

Compañia Argentina de Seguros de Crédito a la Exportación S.S. (C.A.S.C.)
Sarmiento 440, 4o Piso
1247 Buenos Aires, Argentina

Guatemala

Continental Credit Co.
12-Calle 6-27
Zona 1-2o Piso
P.O. Box 579
Guatemala City, Guatemala

Trinidad and Tobago

Credit Bureau Port-of-Spain
P.O. Box 31
23 Chacon Street
Port-of-Spain, Trinidad W.I.

Jamaica

Credit Consultant, (JA) Ltd.
P.O. Box 131
Kingston 10, Jamaica

Japan

Credit Exchange Agency, Ltd.
(Shingo Kokansho Co., Ltd.)
22-1 Chome, Azuchi-Machi
Higashi-Ku
Osaka, Japan

Iceland

Credit Information (Upplysningar Um Lanstraust)
Laufasvegur 36
P.O. Box 515
Reykjavik, Iceland

Peru

Credit Report S.A.
Jiron Zepita No. 423 Of. 303
Edificio Ferrand
Casilla 208
Lima, Peru

Most Countries

Dun & Bradstreet
Dun & Bradstreet International
One World Trade Center, Suite 9069
New York, NY 10048

Bahamas, Trinidad

General Credit
Columbus House
East & Shirley Street
P.O. Box N 7343
Nassau, N.P., Bahamas

Guyana

Charles Gonsalves
4 D'Urban & George Street
P.O. Box 663
Georgetown, Guyana

El Salvador, Guatemala, Honduras

Robert Gregg
Apartado Postal CC-208
San Salvador, El Salvador

Brunei, Malaysia

The Guardian Mercantile Agency
G.P.O. 2669
116-B Jalan Tuanku
Abdul Rahman
Kuala Lumpur 01-07, Malaysia

Suriname

J. Ch. Heave
P.O. Box 1015
Paramaribo, Suriname

Ecuador

Infae
Informes Agencias Estudios
Edif. "Benalcazar Mil" Apto. 1101
Apartado 1321
Quito, Ecuador

United Kingdom

Info Check
Shaibern House
28 Scrutton Street
London EC2A 4RQ, U.K.

Paraguay

Informconf
Fulgencio R. Moreno 536
Asunción, Paraguay

Mexico

Inform Credit S.A.
Lopez 15-309 y 310
Apartado Postal 572
Mexico City, Mexico

Singapore

International Credit and Trade
Information Agency Pte. Ltd.
Suite 507, 5th Floor
Katong Shopping Center, Singapore 1543

Denmark

Kobmandstandens Oplysningsbureau A/S
Gammel Mont 4
Post Box 2187
1117 Copenhagen K, Denmark

Korea

Korea Credit Guarantee Fund
Credit Informations Dept. I
Dae Woo Bldg.
C.P.O. Box 1029
Seoul 100, Korea

South Africa

C. Loynes Commercial Reports
P.O. Box 3488
Capetown, South Africa

India

Mida Inform Private Ltd.
P.O. Box 7690
Shankar Lane
Kandivi,
Bombay 400 067, India

Portugal, Cape Verde

Mope Ltda.
Agencia Informadora Commercial
Rue Rodrigue Sampaio 52-h
Lisbon, Portugal

Chile

Oikos
Estudios Económicos e Informes Crediticios
Miraflores 686-DPT 901
Casilla 359-V
Santiago, Chile

Burkina Faso, Cameroon, Congo, France, Gabon, Ivory Coast, Monaco, Togo

Piguet Afrique Centrale
B.P. 1470
Doula, Cameroon

Belize

G.A. Roe & Sons Ltd
6 Fort Street
Belize City, Belize

Mauritius

S.A.M. Import and Export
Commercial Reporting Service
P.O. Box 37
Quatre Bornes, Mauritius

Zimbabwe

Socrat (PVT) Ltd.
P.O. Box A 60
Avondale
Harare, Zimbabwe

APPENDIX G

COUNTRY CATEGORIES FOR OECD ARRANGEMENT ON OFFICIALLY SUPPORTED EXPORT CREDITS

The interest rates on Eximbank's loans are determined by the classifications of the country to which the export will be shipped. Eximbank uses the following country classification adopted in the OECD Arrangement on Officially Supported Export Credits:

Rich Countries

Andorra	Greece	Norway
Australia	Iceland	Qatar
Austria	Ireland	San Marino
Bahrain	Israel	Saudi Arabia
Belgium	Italy	Spain
Bermuda	Japan	Sweden
Brunei	Kuwait	Switzerland
Canada	Libya	United Arab Emirates
Czechoslovakia	Liechtenstein	United Kingdom
Denmark	Luxembourg	United States
Finland	Monaco	Union of Soviet Socialist
France	Netherlands, The	Republics
Germany	New Zealand	Vatican City

Intermediate Countries

Albania	Ecuador	Macao
Algeria	Fiji	Malaysia
Argentina	Gabon	Malta
Bahamas	Guatemala	Mauritius
Barbados	Hong Kong	Mexico
Belize	Hungary	Montserrat
Botswana	Iran	Morocco
Brazil	Iraq	Namibia
Bulgaria	Ivory Coast	Nauru
Chile	Jamaica	Netherlands Antilles
Colombia	Jordan	Nigeria
Costa Rica	Kiribati	Oman
Cuba	Korea, North	Panama
Cyprus	Korea, South	Papua New Guinea
Dominican Republic	Lebanon	Paraguay

Peru	Seychelles	Trinidad and Tobago
Poland	Singapore	Tunisia
Portugal	South Africa	Turkey
Romania	Suriname	Uruguay
St. Kitts—Nevis	Syria	Venezuela
St. Lucia	Taiwan	Yugoslavia

Poor Countries

Angola	Guinea	Niger
Bangladesh	Guinea-Bissau	Pakistan
Benin	Guyana	Philippines
Biliva	Haiti	Rwanda
Burkina	Honduras	Senegal
Burma	India	Sierra Leone
Burundi	Indonesia	Somalia
Cameroon	Kenya	Sri Lanka
Central African Republic	Lesotho	Sudan
Chad	Liberia	Tanzania
China, Peoples Republic of	Madagascar	Thailand
Congo, People's Republic of	Malawi	Togo
Egypt	Mali	Uganda
El Salvador	Mauritania	Yemen
Ethiopia	Mozambique	Zaire
Gambia	Nepal	Zambia
Ghana	Nicaragua	Zimbabwe

Note: Not all of the countries listed are eligible for Eximbank financing.
Source: U.S. Export-Import Bank.

APPENDIX H

SELECTED SOURCES OF FINANCING FOR CARIBBEAN BASIN INITIATIVE PROJECTS

Financing Source	Type of Assistance
Overseas Private Investment Corp. 1615 M St. NW—Fourth Floor Washington, DC 20527	Loans and loan guarantees, political risk insurance.
U.S. Trade and Development Program Room 301—SA—16	Reimbursable grant for feasibility studies.
U.S. Department of State Washington, DC 20520	
U.S. Export-Import Bank 811 Vermont Ave. NW Room 1229 Washington, DC 20571	Trade finance, loans for feasibility studies.
Private Enterprise Bureau U.S. Agency for International Development Washington, DC 20523	Trade finance, loans for joint ventures with foreign firms.
Caribbean Project Development Facility *International Finance Corp.* *The World Bank* Washington, DC 20433	Arranges financing from multiple sources.
Latin American Agribusiness Development Corp. 225 Alhambra Circle—Suite 905 Coral Gables, FL 33134	Loans for agribusiness projects.
International Executive Service Corps *Joint Venture Feasibility* *Fund Planning Office* 440 Middlesex Road Darien, CT 06820	Matching grants for feasibility studies.
Government Development Bank San Juan, Puerto Rico	Loans

Financing Source	**Type of Assistance**
Caribbean Financial Services Corp. (CFSC) Chapel Street Bridgetown, Barbados	Equity participation.
BANEX Apartado 798-3 1000 San José, Costa Rica	Trade finance, long-term loans.
Banco Central de Costa Rica P.O. Box 10058 1000 San José, Costa Rica	Trade finance, long-term loans through commercial banks.
Corporación Costarricense de Financiamento Industrial Internacional (COFISA) Apartado 10067 1000 San José Costa Rica	Trade finance, long-term loans.
Private Sector Corporation (PIC) P.O. Box 8609 1000 San José Costa Rica	Equity participation, long-term loans.
Development Finance Corporation (SOFIHDES) 11 Harry Truman Blvd. Port-au-Prince, Haiti	Loans.
Financiera Industrial Agropecuaria S. A. (FIASA) Avenida la Reforma 10-00 01009 Guatemala	Loans.
Banco de Exportación Avenida la Reforma 11-49, Zona 10 Guatemale City, Guatemala	Trade finance.
Financiera Guatemalteca Avenida la Reforma 11-49, Zona 10 Guatemala City Guatemala	Trade finance.
Financiera Guatemalteca 1A. Avenida 11-50, Zona 4 01010, Guatemala	Equity participation, loans, grants for feasibility studies.

Financing Source	Type of Assistance
Financiera Industrial, S.A. 7A. Avenida 5-10, Zona 4 Torre II Centro Financiero 01004 Guatemala	Loans.
Financiera de Inversión 10A. Calle 3-17, Zona 10 01010 Guatemala	Loans.
FIDE P.O. Box 2029 Tegucigalpa, Honduras	Equity participation, loans.
FEPROEXAAH P.O. Box 1442 San Pedro Sula, Honduras	Equity participation, loans.
FIA Centro Comercial Centroamerica Blvd. Miraflores Tegucigalpa, Honduras	Equity participation, loans.
FIDE *Banco Central De La República Dominicana* Ave. Pedro Henriques Urena Santo Domingo, Dominican Republic	Loans.
Trafalgar Development Bank The Towers, 2nd Floor 25 Dominia Drive Kingston 5, Jamaica	Equity participation, loans.
Development Bank of the Netherlands Antilles Salinga 206 Willemstad, Curaçao	Trade finance, equity participation, loans.
Korpodeko Breedstraat 39-C(p) Willemstad, Curaçao	Equity participation, loans.
Guyana Development Bank 126 Parade and Barrack Streets Kingston, Georgetown Guyana	Loans for agribusiness.
Credit Discount Fund Central Bank of Belize Public Building Belize City, Belize	Trade finance.

Source: *1989 Guidebook,* U.S. Department of Commerce, International Trade Administration, U.S. and Foreign Commercial Service, The CBI Center, Room H-3203, Washington, DC 20230, October 1988.

APPENDIX I

MAJOR FOREIGN BANKS WITH OFFICES IN THE UNITED STATES

Banca Serfin, S.N.C.
88 Pine Street
Wall Street Plaza, 24th Floor
New York, NY 10005

Banco di Napoli
277 Park Avenue
New York, NY 10172

Banco Popular de Puerto Rico
7 W. 51st Street
New York, NY 10019

Banco Santander
375 Park Avenue, 29th Fl.
New York, NY 10152

Bancomer, S.N.C.
15 E. 54th Street
New York, NY 10022

Bank Bumi Daya
350 Park Avenue, 7th Fl.
New York, NY 10022

Bank of East Asia, Ltd.
450 Park Avenue
New York, NY 10022

Bank Leumi Trust Co. of New York
579 Fifth Avenue
New York, NY 10017

Banque Nationale de Paris

499 Park Avenue
New York, NY 10022

The Fuji Bank and Trust Co.
1 World Trade Center, Suite 8023
New York, NY 10048

Israel Discount Bank of New York
511 Fifth Avenue
New York, NY 10017

Kansallis-Osake-Pankki
575 Fifth Avenue
New York, NY 10017

Krung Thai Bank
452 Fifth Avenue
New York, NY 10018

Lloyds Bank of California
612 S. Flower Street
Los Angeles, CA 90017

Mitsui Manufacturers Bank
515 S. Figueroa Street, 4th Fl.
Los Angeles, CA 90071

Barclays Bank of California
111 Pine Street
San Francisco, CA 94104

Chicago-Tokyo Bank
40 N. Dearborn Street
Chicago, IL 60602

APPENDIX J

COORDINATING INTERNATIONAL DEVELOPMENT BANKS

African Development Bank and Fund
B.P. No. 1387
Abidjan,
Ivory Coast

Asian Development Bank
2330 Roxas Boulevard
P.O. Box 789
Manila, Philippines 2800

Inter-American Development Bank
808-17th Street NW
Washington, DC 20577

APPENDIX K

EXPORT CREDIT INSURERS OF MAJOR COUNTRIES

Argentina
Compañía Argentina de Seguros de Crédito, S.A. (CASC)
Calle San Martín No. 440
Capital Federal, Buenos Aires

Australia
Export Payments Insurance Corporation (Epic)
P.O. Box 2595
2 Castlereagh Street
Sidney, New South Wales

Austria
"Garant" Versicherungs (Garant)
A/G Wohllebengasse 4
Vienna 4

Öesterreichische Kontrollbank (OKB)
A/G Am Hof 4,
1010 Vienna

Belgium
Cie. Belge d'Assurance-Crédit SA (CBAC)
15 Rue Montoyer
Bruxelles 4

Les Assurances du Crédit SA (AC)
Avenue Prince de Liège
Jambes-Namur

Office National de Ducroire (OND)
40 Square de Meeus
Bruxelles 4

Brazil
Instituto de Resseguros do Brazil (IRB)
Avenida Marechal Camara, 171
Rio de Janiero, GB Brazil

Canada
Export Credits Insurance Corporation (ECIC)
P.O. Box 655
Ottawa 4, Ontario

Czechoslovakia
Statni Pojistovna (Statni)
Insurance and Reinsurance Corporation
Prague 1, Spalena 16

Denmark
Eksportkreditradet (Export Credit Council)
Codanhus (EKR)
G1. Kongevej 60
Copenhagen V

Finland
Vientitakuulaitos (Export Guarantee Board)
Etearanta (VTL)
6, Helsinki 13

France
Compagnie Française d'Assurance pour le
Commerce (COFACE)
Extérieur, 32 Rue Marbeuf
75-Paris 8émé

Germany
Hermes Kreditversicherungs AG (Hermes)
2000 Hamburg 13, Hallerstr.1
Gerling-Konzern Speziale
Kreditversicherungs AG (GKS)
5000 Köln, Gerling-Hochhaus

Hong Kong
Hong Kong Export Credit Insurance
Corporation (HKECIC)
International Building
141 Des Voeux Road, Central
Hong Kong

Hungary
Allami Biztosito (Insurance Enterprise of the State) (ALLAMI)
Budapest IX, Ulloi ut. 1

India
Export Credit & Guarantee Corporation, Ltd. (ECGC)
4 Ramtart Row
P.O. Box 1932, Fort
Bombay 1

Ireland
The Insurance Corporation of Ireland, Ltd.
3336 Dame Street
Dublin 2

The Hibernian Insurance Co., Ltd.
Hawkins House
Hawkins Street
Dublin 2

Israel
The Israel Foreign Trade Risks Insurance Corporation, Ltd. (IFTRIC)
74 Petah Tikva Road
Tel Aviv

Italy
Instituto Nazionale delle Assicurazioni (INA)
Via Sallustiana 51
00100 Roma

Comitato Assicurazioni Creiti all'Esportazione (SIAC)
c/o The Italian Institute for Foreign Trade
Via Lisazt 21
00144 Roma

Societa-Italiana Cauzioni (SIC)
Via Crescenzio 12
00193 Roma

Japan
Export Insurance Section (MITI)
International Trade Bureau
Ministry of International Trade and Industry
1, 3-Chome Kasumigaseki
Chiyodu-ku
Tokyo

Luxembourg
Office du Decroire Luxembourgeois (ODL)
8 Avenue de l'Arsenal
Luxembourg

Mexico
Banco de Mexico SA
Fondo de las Exportaciones de Productors Manufacturados (Fondo)
Av. 5 de Mayo No. 2
Mexico DF

The Netherlands
Nederlandsche Credietverzekering Maatschappij NV (NCM)
Keisergracht 271
P.O. Box 473
Amsterdam-C

New Zealand
Export Guarantee Office (Exgo)
P.O. Box 5037
Lambton Quay
Wellington

Norway
Garanti-Instituttet for Eksportkreditt (GIEK)
Fr. Nansens Plass 2
Oslo

Pakistan
Pakistan Insurance Corporation (ECGS)
Export Credit Guarantee Scheme
Pakistan Insurance Building
Bunder Road
P.O. Box 4777
Karchi 2

Poland
"Warta" Insurance and Reinsurance Company, Ltd. (Warta)

Portugal
Comissão de Creditos e de Seguro de Creditos a Exportacao Nacional
Fundo de Fomento de Exportacao (CCSCEN)
Rua Camilo Castelo Branco 2
Lisbon

South Africa
Credit Guarantee Insurance Corporation of Africa, Ltd. (CGIC)
Avril Malen Building
57-59 Commissioner Street
Johannesburg, P.O. Box 9244

Spain
Cia. Española de Seguros de Crédito y Caución SA (CESCC)

R. F. Villaverde, 61,
Madrid-1

Sweden
Exportkreditnamnden (EKN)
Box 16015
S-103, 21 Stockholm 16

Switzerland
The Federal Insurance Co., Ltd. (The Federal)
Eidegenossische Versicherungs AG
Flossergasse 3
Bern

Taiwan
Central Trust of China (Central Trust)

Purchasing Department
49 Wu Chang Street
Sec. 1, Taipei

United Kingdom
Exports Credit Guarantee Department (ECGD)
Aldermanbury House
Aldermanbury
London EC2P 2EL

Yugoslavia
*"Yugoslavia" Insurance & Reinsurance
Company (Yugoslavia)*
Knez Milahilova 6
P.O. Box 250
Belgrade

APPENDIX L

U.S. HEADQUARTERS OFFICES OF MAJOR JAPANESE TRADING COMPANIES

C. Itoh
335 Madison Avenue
New York, NY 10017

Kanematsu Gosho (USA) Inc.
1133 Avenue of the Americas
New York, NY 10036

Marubeni America Corp.
200 Park Ave.—42nd Floor
New York, NY 10166

Mitsubishi International Corporation
520 Madison Ave.
New York, NY 10022

Mitsui & Co., (USA) Inc.
200 Park Ave.
New York, NY 10166

Nichimen America, Inc.
1185 Avenue of the Americas

Nissho-Iwai America Corp.
1211 Avenue of the Americas
New York, NY 10036

Sumitomo Corp. of America
355 Park Ave.
New York, NY 10054

Toyo Menka (America) Inc.
1286 Avenue of the Americas
New York, NY 10019

APPENDIX M

DOCUMENTATION CHECKLIST FOR LETTERS OF CREDIT

General Document Review

1. Are all documents accounted for?
2. Do all documents show appropriate identification numbers—import license, letter of credit, invoice, bill of lading?
3. Will the L/C be presented within the expiration date?
4. Are there clear and complete instructions in the cover letter?

Letter of Credit

1. Do credit terms agree with contract?
2. Are there any limitations stated for merchandise shipped—stowage, weight limits, partial shipments, and so on?

Commercial Invoices

1. Does invoice conform with *all* terms of the L/C—amount, unit price, description of goods, description of packing, declaration of clauses, foreign language?
2. Is the name on the invoice the same as on the L/C?
3. Is invoice signed?
4. Are any countersignatures required?
5. Are shipping marks the same on invoice and bill of lading?
6. Are freight charges the same on invoice and bill of lading?
7. Does invoice comply with partial shipment provisions if permitted in L/C?
8. Are partial shipments properly noted on invoice?

Consular Invoice

1. Does this invoice have the same information on it as the commercial invoice and the bill of lading?
2. Is description of goods in foreign language, if required?
3. Is official form completely filled out?
4. Is it free of alterations?
5. Have sufficient copies been legalized, if required?

Bank Drafts

1. Are amount, currency, date, and interest rate consistent with L/C terms?
2. Does it show the proper drawee?
3. Is it properly signed?
4. Are endorsements correct?
5. Is it drawn at proper tenor indicated by L/C?

Insurance Documents

1. Is the amount sufficient?
2. Is there an insurance certificate attached?
3. Is coverage consistent with L/C requirements?
4. Is certificate countersigned?
5. Are endorsements proper?
6. Do all shipping marks coincide with invoice and bill of lading?
7. Are all corrections or changes signed or initialed properly?

Bills of Lading

1. Are they in negotiable form?
2. Are all copies properly endorsed?
3. Are they clean, and so noted?
4. Is there a notation that goods were loaded within terms of the contract?
5. Are the names, addresses, descriptions, and so on in conformity with L/C?
6. Is prepaid freight clearly stamped as "prepaid"?
7. Are quantities shipped correct?
8. Are all markings properly included, if required by L/C?
9. Does it show any transshipment?
10. Are all corrections or changes duly initialed or signed?

Certificates

1. Are names, addresses, and country of origin consistent with invoice and L/C?
2. Are they dated properly?
3. Are they signed and notarized properly?
4. Do they meet all the requirements of the L/C?
5. Are all certificates required by the L/C accounted for?

Packing List

1. Do quantities and descriptions agree with invoice?
2. Are quantities contained in packages detailed?
3. Is the packing the same as stipulated in the L/C?

Summary

1. Have at least two company representatives reviewed and compared all documentation prior to forwarding to the bank?

BIBLIOGRAPHY

Axtell, Roger E. *The Do's and Taboos of International Trade.* New York: John Wiley & Sons, 1989.

Davison, Ann. *Grants from Europe: How to Get Money and Influence Policy,* Bedford, England: Brookfield Publishing Co., 1986.

Fatemi, Khosrow. *International Trade and Finance.* New York: Praeger Publishing, 1988.

Goldsmith, Howard R. *Import/Export: A Guide to Growth, Profits, and Market Share.* Englewood Cliffs, N.J.: Prentice Hall, 1989.

Graham, John, et al. *Macmillan Directory of Global Financial Markets,* New York: Macmillan, 1989.

Guttman, H. Peter. *The International Consultant.* New York: John Wiley & Sons, 1987.

King, Philip. *International Economics and International Economic Policy.* New York: McGraw-Hill, 1990.

Lindsey, Jennifer, ed. *Offshore Financing: The Opportunities and Issues in Obtaining Foreign Business Capital,* Chicago: Probus Publishing, 1987.

Manring, A. B. *Exporting from the U.S.A.* Vancouver, Canada: International Self-Counsel Press, Ltd., 1986.

Morris, Charles R. *The Coming Global Boom.* New York: Bantam Books, 1990.

Oxelheim, L., and C. Wihlborg. *Macroeconomic Uncertainty,* New York: John Wiley & Sons, 1987.

Pattison, Joseph E. *Acquiring the Future.* Homewood, Ill.: Dow Jones-Irwin, 1990.

Reed, Stanley Foster, and Lane and Edson, P. C. *The Art of M & A,* Homewood, Ill.: Dow Jones-Irwin, 1989.

Rodriguez, Rita M. *The Export-Import Bank at Fifty: The International Environment and the Institution's Role.* Lexington, Mass.: Lexington Books, 1986.

Rossman, Marlene L. *The International Businesswoman.* New York: Praeger Publishers, 1986.

Schaffer, Matt. *Winning the Countertrade War.* New York: John Wiley & Sons, 1989.

Smith, Roy C. *The Global Bankers.* New York: E. P. Dutton, 1989.

Venedikian, Harry M., and Gerald A. Warfield. *Export-Import Financing.* New York: John Wiley & Sons, 1986.

Wells, L. Fargo, and Karin B. Dulat. *Exporting from Start to Finance.* Blue Ridge Summit, Pa.: TAB Books, Inc., 1989.

Wood, Christopher. *Boom & Bust: The Rise and Fall of the World's Financial Markets.* New York: Macmillan, 1989.

Wood, Geoffrey E. *Financial Crisis and the World Banking System.* New York: St. Martin, 1986.

Zimmerman, Mark. *How to Do Business with the Japanese.* New York: Random House, 1985.

INDEX